PROBLEMS OF PHILOSOPHY

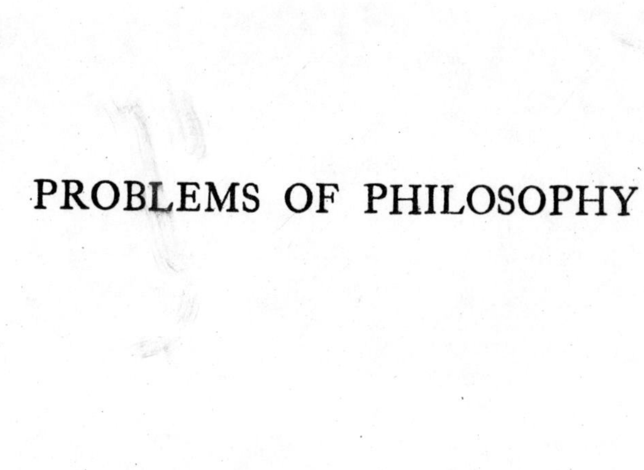

PROBLEMS OF PHILOSOPHY

G. WATTS CUNNINGHAM

DISCOVERY PUBLISHING HOUSE
NEW DELHI - 110 002

Published by:

DISCOVERY PUBLISHING HOUSE PVT. LTD.

4383/4B, Ansari Road, Darya Ganj
New Delhi-110 002 (India)
Phone : +91-11-23279245; 23253475; 43596065
E-mail : discoverybooksindia@gmail.com
discoverypublishinghouse@gmail.com
namitwasan9@gmail.com
web : www.discoverypublishinggroup.com

Reprinted: **2022**

ISBN: 978-81-7141-202-0

Problems of Philosophy

Printed at:
Infinity Imaging Systems
Delhi

FOREWORD

By Viscount Haldane

A book such as is this one has been needed for some time. No introduction to the study of philosophy covering so much ground uncontroversially has appeared so far in these islands. We have admirable histories of philosophy, as well as special expositions of particular points of view, but we have not produced simply constructed and dispassionate expositions of the competing first principles which belong to our time.

Professor Watts Cunningham is admirably qualified to produce such an exposition. Those who know the great esteem in which his writings are held on the other side of the Atlantic are aware of the width of his outlook. But they may not have been prepared for such impartiality in exposition of views other than his own as he has here shown. The book has many references to American as well as to English philosophy. I do not think that this is any disadvantage. We are learning to study American writers on philosophy, and we are coming to realize how good a thing it is for us to be guided by their fresh outlook on common problems. Professor Cunningham is familiar with what has been accomplished on both sides of the ocean, and he has employed the results of his studies fully in the pages which follow.

The author aims at something different from a history of opinions. He states the problems of thought in simple language, and then shows how these problems, with their solutions, have presented themselves in different schools. The student can read the book without a preliminary study of philosophy. He is shown what the real problems are, and how they are related to corresponding questions in science. The exposition is so detached that unless he reads Professor Cunningham's other works he will find it difficult to discover any tendency of the author in the answers given to the questions raised.

There was great need of such a book. It is not always easy to interpret the question "What is Philosophy?" merely by reading its history. That which many beginners have asked for was a book which would tell them what philosophy was about, and the bearing of its principles on other departments of knowledge. Such students will learn from what is written here the meaning of a proposition that is being increasingly insisted on, the principle that knowledge is a whole and must be so regarded.

As I have said, there was much demand for such a book in this country. The want was much felt in connection with the growing system of adult education. This volume may well find a place in the local and central libraries which are playing to-day a great part in the new endeavour after higher education. But the value of the book is not confined to education. It is a work which will help the general reader who is so often struggling to get his mind clear about an outlook on life wider than he can find in any one creed.

HALDANE

PREFACE

The aim of this book is two-fold: to give a preliminary survey of some of the problems of philosophy in as direct and simple a manner as possible, and to encourage on the part of the beginner a reasoned consideration of them. To this end the effort has been made to emphasize some of the main features of the method of reflective thinking, to indicate broadly how the problems arise out of experience, to give some of the high points in the historical background of the several problems presented, to suggest the main drift of thought upon the problems, and to direct attention to some of the factual data relevant to the debate. The choice of problems has been partly determined by considerations of the purposes of the book and the interests of those for whom it is primarily written. It is hoped, however, that all of the more basal problems have at least been touched upon. In any event, the book does not presume to compass philosophical problems in their entirety or to treat those discussed in any very thorough-going fashion; above all, though the discussion is necessarily colored by the writer's point of view, the book does not undertake to outline or defend any system of philosophy. If the problems presented have been formulated in such a manner as to enable the beginner to feel their push, and if their discussion has been so oriented as to encourage and assist him to pursue them beyond the letter of the text out into their broader reaches, the book may be said to have accomplished its primary purpose.

Instead of giving a separate summary survey of the main historical systems of philosophy, as is sometimes done in introductory texts, I have undertaken the more difficult (but I think more fruitful) task of weaving the relevant historical material into the consideration of the problems as they severally arise. This promises more for the student, even if it makes greater demands upon the author; I can only hope that I have escaped from at least the more dangerous pitfalls that beset such an undertaking. The questions and exercises at the end of each chapter are designed partly to test the student's comprehension of the text but primarily to open doors for his further studies. No general reading lists are set down in connection with the various chapters; it seemed more profitable to make the references as direct as possible, and this has been undertaken in the footnotes and the questions and exercises. The appended bibliographical note gives in alphabetical order the books to which reference is made in the exercises; other books referred to in the footnotes scattered throughout the text are not here listed. Since the headings of the various sections give in itemized manner the material of the book, I have not thought it worth while to burden it with an index of its subject-matter; the index is, consequently, limited to names.

In the course of the preparation of the book many helpful suggestions and criticisms have been received from my colleagues, Professors A. P. Brogan, F. A. C. Perrin, and E. T. Mitchell, of the Department of Philosophy and Psychology in the University of Texas. Professor Brogan read the larger portion of the first draft of the manuscript and gave me the advantage of many pointed criticisms; Professor Perrin enabled me to view through the psychologist's eyes the earlier chapters on the problem of mind;

and Professor Mitchell rendered invaluable service in the tedious task of proof-reading, while his numerous suggestions, always helpful, not infrequently resulted in the decided improvement of both the form and the content of the book. Mr. C. M. Perry and Mr. S. G. Slavens, student assistants in philosophy, gave generously of their time to verify the numerous references. To all of these I gratefully acknowledge my indebtedness, as also to my wife, whose sympathetic interest in the progress of the work and many suggestions concerning puzzling questions of exposition have been of the greatest assistance to me.

G. W. C.

BIBLIOGRAPHICAL NOTE

The following list includes only the books referred to in the questions and exercises appended to the various chapters. It is given as a summary statement of the main bibliography to be used by the student.

ARISTOTLE, *Politics* (transl. by J. E. C. Welldon; Macmillan, 1888).

BABBITT, I., *The New Laokoon* (Constable, 1910).
BAKEWELL, C. M., *Sourcebook in Ancient Philosophy* (T. Fisher Unwin, 1907).
BARRETT, W. F., *Psychical Research* ("Home Univ. Library," Williams and Norgate, 1911).
BERGSON, H., *Introduction to Metaphysics* (transl. by T. E. Hulme; Macmillan, 1913).
BERGSON, H., *Mind-Energy* (transl. by H. W. Carr; Macmillan, 1920).
BERKELEY, *Principles of Human Knowledge* (Open Court Publishing Company, 1901).
BURY, J. B., *History of Freedom of Human Thought* ("Home Univ. Library," Williams and Norgate, 1914).

CALKINS, M. W., *The Good Man and the Good* (Macmillan, 1918).
CARR, H. W., *The Philosophy of Benedetto Croce* (Macmillan, 1917).
COE, G. A., *The Psychology of Religion* (University of Chicago Press, 1916).
COLUMBIA ASSOCIATES IN PHILOSOPHY, *Introduction to Reflective Thinking* (Houghton Mifflin Company, 1923).
COOLEY, W. F., *The Principles of Science* (Henry Holt and Company).
CREIGHTON, J. E., *An Introductory Logic* (Macmillan, fourth edition).

DARWIN, F., *Life and Letters of Charles Darwin* (2 vols., Murray, 1891).

DE LAGUNA, T., *Introduction to the Science of Ethics* (Macmillan, 1914).

DESCARTES, *Discourse on Method* (Open Court Publishing Company, 1899).

DESCARTES, *Works* (transl. by Haldane and Ross; 2 vols., Cambridge University Press, 1911–1912).

DEWEY, J., *How We Think* (D. C. Heath and Company, 1910).

DEWEY, J., *Essays in Experimental Logic* (University of Chicago Press, 1916).

DEWEY AND TUFTS, *Ethics* (G. Bell and Sons, Ltd., 1908).

DUNCAN, R. K., *The New Knowledge* (Hodder and Stoughton, 1905).

DUNLAP, K., *A System of Psychology* (Kimpton, 1912).

EINSTEIN, A., *Special and General Theory of Relativity* (Methuen, 1920).

EVERETT, W. G., *Moral Values* (Heinemann, 1918).

GALLOWAY, G., *The Idea of Immortality* (T. and T. Clark, 1919).

HAINES AND HAINES, *Principles and Problems of Government* (Harper and Brothers, 1921).

HALDANE, J. S., *Organism and Environment* (Oxford University Press, 1917).

HENDERSON, L. J., *The Fitness of the Environment* (Macmillan, 1913).

HOBBES, *The Leviathan* (Routledge).

HOERNLÉ, R. F. A., *Matter, Life, Mind, and God* (Methuen, 1922).

HOERNLÉ, R. F. A., *Studies in Contemporary Metaphysics* (Kegan Paul, 1920).

HOLT, E. B., *The Concept of Consciousness* (Allen and Unwin, 1914).

HOLT, E. B., *The Freudian Wish* (T. Fisher Unwin, 1915).

HUDSON, J. W., *The Truths We Live By* (D. Appleton and Company, 1921).

HUME, *Treatise of Human Nature* (second edition, by Selby-Bigge; Oxford University Press, 1896).

JAMES, W., *Pragmatism* (Longmans, 1907).
JAMES, W., *The Will to Believe* (Longmans, 1897).
JAMES, W., *Human Immortality* (Constable, 1898).
JUDD, C. H., *Psychology* (Ginn, 1907; second edition, completely revised, 1917).

KANT, *Perpetual Peace* (transl. by M. C. Smith; Allen and Unwin, 1915).
King's College Lectures on Immortality (edited by W. R. Matthews; University of London Press, 1920).

LAIRD, J., *Problems of the Self* (Macmillan, 1917).
LANGFELD, H. S., *The Aesthetic Attitude* (Harcourt, Brace and Howe, 1920).
LEIGHTON, J. A., *The Field of Philosophy* (D. Appleton and Company, 1923).
LOCKE, *Essay Concerning Human Understanding* (edited by Fraser; 2 vols., Oxford University Press, 1914).
LOCKE, *Two Treatises on Government* (edited by H. Morley; Routledge, 1884).
LOEB, J., *The Organism as a Whole* (G. P. Putnam's Sons, 1916).
LOEB, J., *The Mechanistic Conception of Life* (University of Chicago Press, 1912).
LORENTZ, H. A., *The Einstein Theory of Relativity* (Brentano's, New York, 1920).

MACHIAVELLI, *The Prince* (edited by H. Morley; Routledge, 1883).
MACKENZIE, J. S., *Outlines of Social Philosophy* (Allen and Unwin, 1918).
MARVIN, W. T., *A First Book in Metaphysics* (Macmillan, 1912).
MCDOUGALL, W., *Body and Mind* (Methuen, 1911).
MILL, J. S., *On Liberty* (Routledge).
MILLS, J., *The Realities of Modern Science* (Macmillan, 1919).
MOORE, G. F., *History of Religions* (2 vols., T. and T. Clark, 1913).

PAULSEN, F., *Introduction to Philosophy* (transl. by F. Thilly; Kegan Paul, 1907).
PAULSEN, F., *A System of Ethics* (transl. by F. Thilly; Kegan Paul, 1903).

PEARSON, K., *Grammar of Science* (A. and C. Black, third edition, 1911).

PERRY, R. B., *The Approach to Philosophy* (Longmans, 1905).

PERRY, R. B., *The Moral Economy* (Charles Scribner's Sons, 1909).

PERRY, R. B., *Present Philosophical Tendencies* (Longmans, third impression, 1916).

PILLSBURY, W. B., *Essentials cf Psychology* (Macmillan, 1911).

PLATO, *The Republic* (transl. by Davies and Vaughan; Macmillan, 1904).

PRATT, J. B., *Matter and Spirit* (Allen and Unwin, 1922).

ROGERS, A. K., *The Theory of Ethics* (Macmillan, 1922).

ROUSSEAU, *Social Contract* (Allen and Unwin).

ROYCE, J., *Conception of Immortality* (Constable, 1900).

RUSSELL, B., *Problems of Philosophy* ("Home Univ. Library," Williams and Norgate, 1912).

RUSSELL, B., *Political Ideals* (The Century Company, 1917).

RUSSELL, B., *The ABC of Atoms* (Kegan Paul, 1923).

SETH, J., *Ethical Principles* (Blackwood, ninth edition, 1907).

SPAULDING, E. G., *The New Rationalism* (Henry Holt and Company, 1918).

STEINMETZ, C. P., *Space and Relativity* (McGraw-Hill Book Company, 1923).

STRATTON, G. M., *Experimental Psychology and Culture* (Macmillan, 1903).

TANSLEY, A. G., *The New Psychology and its Relation to Life* (Allen and Unwin, 1920).

THOMSON, J. A., *The Bible of Nature* (T. and T. Clark, 1908).

THOMSON, J. A., *Introduction to Science* ("Home Univ. Library," Williams and Norgate, 1911).

THOMSON AND GEDDES, *Evolution* ("Home Univ. Library," Williams and Norgate, 1911).

TYNDALL, J., *Fragments of Science*, vol. ii (D. Appleton and Company, 1896).

WOODWORTH, R. S., *Dynamic Psychology* (Oxford University Press, 1918).

WRIGHT, H. W., *Self-Realization* (Henry Holt and Company, 1913).

WRIGHT, W. K., *A Student's Philosophy of Religion* (Hodder and Stoughton, 1922).

YOUNG, J. S., *The State and Government* (A. C. McClurg and Company, 1917).

TABLE OF CONTENTS

PART VI

PROBLEMS OF PHILOSOPHY

PART I

COMMON SENSE, SCIENCE, AND PHILOSOPHY

PROBLEMS OF PHILOSOPHY

CHAPTER I

INTRODUCTION: PHILOSOPHY AND LIFE

The discipline called "philosophy," though one of the oldest, suffers more than any other perhaps from general misapprehension as to its subject-matter and aim. Where there is not total ignorance of the subject, there is only too likely to be a false notion both of its field and of its method of procedure. The popular conception of philosophy seems to be that it is a tumble-ground for fancy; to philosophize, it seems to be commonly supposed, is to dream hazily about things in general. For the scientists, philosophy is frequently little more than vain speculation about problems which, if not of only secondary importance, at least are insoluble mysteries and so should be permitted to rest in peace or turned over to the delectation of our more mystical and less scientific moods. These misapprehensions are not without their reasons for being, but into these reasons it is useless for us here to enter. Let it suffice that such conceptions of philosophy are misapprehensions, and do a serious injustice to the study which has always had and, so long as man struggles to expand his intellectual horizon, will always continue to have a place of great importance among the disciplines of the human mind. This book aims to disclose the injustice of such misconceptions of philoso phy, and may be taken as an answer to the criticism of philosophy implied in them. But a few introductory remarks designed to show the continuity of philosophy with life may prove helpful.

§ 1. *The aim of philosophy*

Human life is a fact, whatever may be its significance. To us individuals it is a gift; we did not will it. It is also an obligation which we cannot escape. Whatever may have been its origin and whatever may be its destiny, it at least is a reality to those of us who are living, and we must make some sort of use of it. Furthermore, we live in the midst of a situation that places imperious demands upon us. The inescapable urge of life brings us face to face with an environment that calls from us certain types of activity: to live is to be compelled to do something under definite circumstances.

One important aspect of the activity which we call living is that, in the case of human beings at least, it is self-conscious. We not only live; we know that we live, and we sometimes consider how best to live. Not only do we act, but we are prone to believe that certain ways of acting are necessary or expedient or right. In other words, human life is partly reflective. And, be it noted, this reflective side of life is at once the chief inconvenience and the chief glory of it. Reflection is an inconvenience, because it is so halting and, frequently, so apparently futile; it is a glory, because from it spring the magnificent achievements in culture and civilization that mark the course of human history. But whether regarded as an impediment which we should long to be rid of or as a power to be prized, reflection is a basal characteristic of human life.

What is reflection? In its most obvious features, it is the power to ask and answer questions, to set and solve problems, to look ahead and plan conduct. It is the capacity to be curious about ourselves and our environment; "to look before and after, and pine for what is not." Two aspects of it are, for our purposes, of great importance, and should be distinguished. On the one side, reflection seeks consistent answers to the questions it raises; it cannot be content with answers that contradict each other, or that are inconsistent with each other. On the other side, reflection strives, so far as possible, to see how the various answers to its questions are related to each other; it is not satisfied to leave different solutions of different problems lying loosely side by side, but it persists in inquiring what these several solutions have to do with each other logically. In short, reflection demands, at least as an ideal, consistent answers to all possible questions and a logical interconnection of all possible answers — an exhaustive, harmonious and systematic view of the world.

As we shall see more in detail in our study, it is out of this reflective capacity of the human mind that philosophy, like the sciences, comes. In fact, philosophy is precisely the discipline that undertakes to realize most completely this ideal of reflection. Herein lies its difficulty, but herein also is to be sought its true nature. Philosophy is not idle dreaming about superficialities; on the contrary, it is reflection at work trying to accomplish its task. It is, or aims to be, a thoroughly reasoned view of the problems that have to do with man's world and his place in it. As Professor James picturesquely phrases it, philosophy is an unusually strenuous effort to think consistently.

Philosophy, thus, grows directly out of life and its needs. Everyone who lives, if he lives at all reflectively, is in some degree a philosopher. "He is not only a potential philosopher, but a partial philosopher. He has already begun to be a philosopher. Between the fitful or prudential thinking of some little man of affairs, and the sustained thought of the devoted lover of truth, there is indeed a long journey, but it is a straight journey along the same road. Philosophy is neither accidental nor supernatural, but inevitable and normal. . . . In the hands of its devotees it grows technical and complex, as do all efforts of thought, and to pursue philosophy bravely and faithfully is to encounter obstacles and labyrinths innumerable. The general problem of philosophy is mother of a whole brood of problems, little and great. But whether we be numbered among its devotees, or their beneficiaries, an equal significance attaches to the truth that philosophy is continuous with life."[1] Let us undertake to see in some greater detail how this is so.

§ 2. *The individual*

When we human beings first awaken to that degree of self-consciousness at which we are capable of reflecting upon our own nature, we discover that our life consists in numerous desires and interests which we are continuously struggling to gratify. We desire food, shelter, and property; we want association with our fellows; we struggle to attain honors; we hunger for the esteem of those whose opinions we value; we are curious about ourselves and our world. And we are constantly trying to satisfy these longings of our nature by scheming and planning and devising methods of procedure. In other words, each one of us is a centre of activity struggling to attain the satisfaction of wants and interests; and this activity and these wants are the manifestations of that within us which we call the urge of life. As living, therefore, the individual is "dynamic," active, on the go. To live is to be active, and to be

[1] Perry, *The Approach to Philosophy* (1905), p. 22.

active for the accomplishment of certain ends, the gratification of certain desires, the fulfillment of wants and interests. Such is life as it expresses itself in human beings — a struggle to attain "ends."

Two points are involved in this analysis. They should be noted by the reader and taken along into his further study of these pages. The first is that the individual, as *living*, is active and not passive, "dynamic" and not "static." And the second is that each one of us, as dynamic, has his behavior or conduct focussed in "ends" — desires, interests, wants.

§ 3. *The environment*

Throughout our lives we find ourselves in the midst of an environment which places sundry limitations upon us and demands of us specific types of response. Into this environment we are born, and its presence is continuous and compelling until death removes us from the scene. In attaining our "ends" it is just this environment that we have to take into account. It helps, it hinders, it puzzles, it gratifies; it is, in short, the object of our activity. And our reaction to the environment is precisely what we mean by living. Let us glance at some of the chief features which this environment presents; these will be very important for our future considerations, and they should therefore be noted carefully.

(1) THE ENVIRONMENT AS PHYSICAL. In the first place and most obviously, the individual's environment is physical. By the physical environment is meant that order of objects and events with which we are in bodily contact. It is omnipresent and inescapable, whether for weal or woe. We feed upon it, we make use of it for the accomplishment of many of our purposes, not infrequently are we injured by

it, always must we take it into account, and at the last we are apparently destroyed by it. This environment presents three fairly obvious aspects which, for the sake of clearness, it will be well for us to distinguish before passing on. These are matter, space, and time.

(a) *Matter.* In our physical environment there are many particular things or objects which have different qualities or characteristics. We classify these objects in various ways and to the different groups we give different names, such as, tree, mountain, apple, the earth, the solar system, and the like. But we also lump all such objects together indifferently into one group or class without reference to their individual differences. And to this general group we give the name "matter." Matter, thus, is our most general term for the content, or data, of the physical environment.

(b) *Space.* The various objects or things of the physical environment bear to each other certain relations of size, of configuration, of nearness or remoteness, and of direction either of rest or of motion. These relations we designate by the term "space." Space thus is a name for different sorts of relations which the various constituents of matter bear to each other in so far as they have quantitative features.

(c) *Time.* The objects of the physical environment are related in another way. They co-exist or they follow each other in the sense of existing before or after each other. These relations of simultaneity or succession are what we denote by the term "time." Time, therefore, is the name which we use to designate the relations existing among objects in so far as they are changing.

It should be noted that matter, space, and time are not ultimately separable from each other. They cannot readily be conceived as existing independently. They are rather three distinguishable aspects of the environment in so far as it is to be called physical, and are in some sense interdependent. It should be noted, furthermore, that time is not confined exclusively to the material order. Ideas also change, organisms grow old, and social institutions have their history. Time seems to belong to our entire environment, whether physical or otherwise.

(2) THE ENVIRONMENT AS VITAL. Some objects of our environment are characterized by another peculiar and basic quality which we call life. Objects, as living, we speak of as "organisms." Their distinguishing marks are certain activities, such as, nutrition, reproduction, maturation, and decay; and there is a peculiar relation connecting one generation with another to which we give the name of heredity. These organic forms constitute the content, or data, of our environment as vital. And the two great classes here are plants and animals, with the latter subdivided into vertebrates and invertebrates. For the distinguishing marks of these two general classes of organisms the student should consult the biological text-books.

(3) THE ENVIRONMENT AS SOCIAL. In addition to our physical and vital environment we find ourselves confronted by an environment of another sort which we call social. We are born into a group of beings like ourselves, and this group has certain customs, traditions, beliefs, and laws which define the relations obtaining among the individuals who compose the group. The group we call society; and the embodiments of the customs, traditions, beliefs, and laws defining the relations which obtain among the different individuals of the group are social institutions. The environment as social presents six distinguishable aspects which we shall here briefly note. These are: the traditional

or customary, the civil and economic, the moral, the aesthetic, the religious, and the scientific.

(a) *The traditional or customary.* The environment as social is, in the first place, a complex of customs and traditions which have grown up more or less unreflectively in the long and arduous development of the human race and which vary from generation to generation and from nation to nation. Many of them are survivals from primitive conditions, while others are outgrowths of later stages in the historical process. All of them are natural products of man's group-organization. They might be called social habits, since they arise in society very much as habits are developed in the individual and they function as a tendency towards group-conduct. As examples of them may be mentioned: manners of dress and speech, fashions of recreations and amusements, racial prejudices, views on marriage and on sex-relations generally, and the like. Such beliefs and tendencies to believe hang over from age to age in the development of society and send their roots deep within the social group. They constitute the traditional environment into which each new member of the group is born and from the imperious demands of which no one can wholly escape. "It becomes a part of each person's nature, a standing habit of mind, or fixed set of mental tendencies, according to which particular experience is interpreted and particular persons appreciated."[1]

(b) *Civil and economic.* In the second place, the social environment acts as an organization functioning under certain rules — laws — consciously made by the group for the accomplishment of common ends. In the interest of the group the rights and privileges of the individual are defined and his responsibilities towards his fellows set down in

[1] Grote: *Plato and the Other Companions of Sokrates*, Vol. I, p. 249.

precise terms. He is told what he may call his own and what not, what proportion of that which is his own may be used for the gratification of his individual desires, and what general types of behavior he may not practice. To a very marked degree these regulations shape the individual's destiny by delimiting the opportunities for initiative and self-expression that fall to his lot. Though largely negative, they are none the less potent.

(c) *Moral.* In the third place, the social environment is moral. The social group passes verdicts upon certain types of conduct, calling some right and others wrong. It places its approval upon right conduct and its disapproval upon the wrong. Some of the wrong types of conduct the group prohibits by explicit laws and regulations, while other types it discourages only by means of public opinion. But the behavior that is held to be wrong is always in some manner frowned upon and its practice condemned; that which is regarded as right is praised and its practice encouraged. Such estimates of behavior constitute the content of the social environment as moral.

(d) *Aesthetic.* The social environment presents yet another aspect which we may designate as aesthetic. Society expresses estimates of objects in terms of beauty and ugliness. Just as some types of behavior are esteemed to be good and others bad, so certain objects are appraised as beautiful and others as ugly; and just as the good conduct is approved and encouraged while the bad is disapproved and forbidden, so beautiful objects are desired while the ugly are shunned. Estimates of beauty and ugliness form a very important aspect of the social environment — the aspect called aesthetic.

(e) *Religious.* Again, the social environment is religious in its nature. It is not easy to say what precisely we mean by religion, and at this stage of our study no accurate definition is necessary. For our present purpose it is sufficient to note that society lays emphasis upon certain beliefs concerning a power, or powers, regarded as in some sense divine and inculcates an attitude of worship or reverence as springing from these beliefs. These beliefs and this attitude constitute perhaps the basic elements of the religious aspect of the individual's environment.

(f) *Scientific*. Over against the customary and traditional beliefs, largely unreflective as they are, there stands a system of reasoned convictions which have resulted from prolonged and careful reflection. These reasoned convictions we call scientific to distinguish them from the unreflective beliefs of custom and tradition, and the different systems in which they are formulated are the several sciences. Such convictions and the systems in which they find expression constitute the scientific aspect of the social environment, and they have played a rôle of ever-increasing importance in the life of man.

§ 4. *The individual and his environment*

The individual human being, we have seen, is immersed in an environment which makes demands of him that he must meet if he is to live. Its matter and distances, its growth and decay, are hard brute facts whose claims are unyielding; while its customs and traditions, its moral and religious insights, and its reasoned convictions must perforce be reckoned with. But, on his side, the individual has interests of his own. He is not wholly passive with reference to his environment. He is active, a dynamic centre of needs and desires with a will to satisfy them. He possesses the capacity to make use of his environment and to shape it in some measure for the accomplishment of his own ends.

He is not a plaything of physical and social forces, but he reacts to them in ways determined partly at least by his own nature. The types of response which the individual makes to his environment are quite numerous and no effort will here be made to enumerate them in detail. There are three of special importance.

(1) SENSITIVE REACTION. The first type of response is what we may call sensitive reaction, or response in terms of the sensibilities of pleasure and pain. The human individual is so constituted that he feels pleasure or pain and endeavors to avoid the one and secure the other. So he reacts to his environment by seeking those things that give pleasure and by fleeing those things that bring pain. Apparently he shares this type of response with all forms of animal life; it seems to be characteristic of the simply organized living beings as well as of the more complex forms. Obviously it is an exceedingly important type of response.

(2) EMOTIONAL REACTION. The second type of response we may call the emotional type. Any attempt to analyse adequately this type of response would involve us in an extended consideration of different sorts of emotions and so would carry us far beyond the limits of this preliminary statement. It must here suffice to note that the emotional type of reaction is a very complex type, involving the sensibilities above referred to plus numerous organic reverberations and a considerable degree of intellectual activity. Illustrations of it are numerous, their very frequency and variety being indicative of the commonness of this type of response. Fear, anger, love, hatred, sorrow, pity, enjoyment, worship — these are examples of it. In general, this type of reaction would by virtue of its complexity seem to be characteristic only of those organisms with a rather

complex nervous system. How far down the scale of living beings it is to be found would here be an idle question —however, it is fairly obvious that to speak of an amoeba or an earthworm as being in love is a meaningless metaphor.

(3) INTELLECTUAL REACTION. The third type of reaction characteristic of human beings is the intellectual type. This response consists essentially in formulating and undertaking to solve problems presented to the individual by his environment. By means of it he reads the meaning of various objects, gives them names and so creates language, appraises their value or lack of it, and makes inferences from one object to another or from one situation to another. Where in the scale of life this type of response first makes its appearance is, once again, a question that need not here be discussed. It seems to shade off by imperceptible stages into what generally we, vaguely enough, call instinct, which may be either a form of it or yet another distinct type of reaction. However that may be, intellectual reaction obviously belongs to the human individual and that fact is for our present purpose sufficient.

§ 5. *The intellectual enterprise*

Of the three types of reaction mentioned in the preceding section the third is from the standpoint of our present study the most important. For it is from this type of reaction to his environment that man's science and philosophy spring. This response is thinking; and thinking gives rise to that knowledge which science and philosophy are. The intellectual enterprise, thus, is what we shall be dealing with in a general way throughout the course of this study. Just now let us recall that it is an inevitable undertaking of human beings and note some of its main features.

(1) THINKING A NECESSITY. As has already been in-

dicated, the individual is a creature of needs and his environment makes manifold demands upon him as he undertakes to secure the satisfaction of these needs. He needs food and shelter; and to secure these intelligent reaction to his environment is demanded of him. To get from the soil the food he requires, when the soil will not yield it without his interference, and to protect himself against the inclemencies of climatic conditions intelligent behavior is absolutely essential. Again, he has social needs, he desires companionship and intercourse with his fellows; but the satisfaction of these needs requires of him foresight and sympathetic conduct. He must at least get the point of view of his fellows and sufficiently adapt his behavior to avoid conflicts of interests and to secure the benefits of coöperation, otherwise his needs as a social individual could never be met. Finally, he is a creature constantly confronted by novel situations to which he must adapt his life; and such adaptation is the very essence of intellectualized conduct. His environment is shot through and through with problems; every object is in some sense a question-mark, every individual is something of a mystery. The problems of the youthful Shelley are, in some measure, the problems of every human being:

> Whence are we and why are we? Of what scene
> The actors or spectators?

And the answers to such problems are impossible apart from intellectual activity.

Thus it is that out of man's needs and interests as a living being arise the impelling motives of the intellectual enterprise, the voyage of discovery, that issues in his science and philosophy. He thinks because he must, and he must because his nature is as it is and because his environment forces upon him certain demands which he cannot ignore and continue to exist. Thinking is a necessity of human existence; it is man's most efficient means of prolonging and expanding the life that is his.

(2) TWO ASPECTS OF THE INTELLECTUAL ENTERPRISE. There are two main aspects of the intellectual enterprise into which humanity is thus thrust. These we may here briefly refer to, reserving a fuller discussion for later chapters.

The first of these is the discovery of new facts. In order that man may pursue his intellectual way through his environment he must gain ever more information about it. He must observe what before was unobserved; he must make problems grow where none existed before; he must propound solutions for these problems, and ever press onwards to conquer new fields. This expansion of the field of knowledge is, as we shall see shortly, the primary aim of the sciences; the business of science is to make discoveries concerning the world in which we live.

But progress in the intellectual enterprise means not merely the acquisition of new knowledge, the making of discoveries. It means, on the other side, removal of contradictions and inconsistencies in the knowledge already at hand. Not only does intelligence demand that new facts be progressively revealed, it demands further that the results obtained be made consistent each with all. What is won by conquest must be ordered and systematized. And this systematization in its broader reaches is the primary aim of philosophy, as will be manifest in the course of our further survey. It thus appears that philosophy follows upon the heels of the sciences. As Hegel[1] poetically states

[1] Hegel was a German philosopher who during the last years of his life was professor of philosophy at the University of Berlin. His dates are 1770–1831.

it: "The owl of Minerva takes its flight only when the twilight shades begin to fall."

§ 6. *Summary of chapter*

In this chapter we have touched upon the fundamental nature of the individual, the main features of the environment that envelops him, and the chief types of his reaction to that environment. The individual, we have seen, is dynamic, a centre of desires and interests which express themselves in behavior. We have found the environment to be of a three-fold nature: it is physical-vital-social. As physical, it is an indefinite number of particular objects which we lump together and call by the name of matter, these objects bearing certain relations to each other some of which relations we call spatial and some temporal. As vital, the environment is a complex of organic forms characterized by a type of activity known as *living*. As social, it is the multitude of interpenetrating persons living under the compulsion of their traditional, economic, moral, aesthetic, scientific, and religious interests. This physical-vital-social environment circumscribes the individual in various ways by placing sundry limitations upon him. But these limitations invite, yea, even compel, that reaction on the part of the individual which is the essence of his being. Of this reaction there are three main types: sensitive, emotional, and intellectual. The last of these is of special importance for us, since it issues in what we call knowledge of our environment and gives us both our science and philosophy. On the one side, it expresses itself in progressive discovery; on the other, in progressive organization of, the removal of inconsistencies from, the discoveries made.

Chapter I. Questions and Exercises

1. Explain fully your understanding of the following statements:

   (*a*) Philosophy grows directly out of life and its interests.

   (*b*) Philosophy is an unusually strenuous effort to think consistently.

2. What is meant by the physical environment? the social environment? Distinguish the six aspects of the social environment mentioned in the text, and illustrate each by an example of your own.

3. What do you understand by the individual's "reaction" or "response" to the environment? Show how this reaction is necessary. Give examples illustrating the three types of response mentioned in the text.

4. Show in general how the development of science exemplifies the two aspects of the intellectual enterprise.

5. Summarise the main points in Perry, *The Approach to Philosophy*, Chapter I.

6. Summarize the main points in:

   (*a*) Tansley, *The New Psychology*, Chapter III.

   (*b*) Woodworth, *Dynamic Psychology*, Lectures III, IV.

CHAPTER II

COMMON SENSE AND SCIENCE

The discoveries which man from time to time makes about his environment constitute the content of his knowledge. His investigations disclose certain aspects of his world which, when disclosed, are said to be known by him: his intellectual inquiry thus leads him to knowledge. But while they answer some of his questions, his investigations at the same time give rise to numerous other problems for which a solution must be sought. When it is known, for example, that the flowing of a stream is due to the fact that water always seeks the lowest level, this knowledge is the solution of certain problems raised by the environment; but, at the same time, it creates other problems connected with this newly discovered fact that water does seek lower levels. Why should this be? So it happens that the intellectual enterprise results, on the one hand, in a fund of information definitely formulated in general statements or accurate description of newly discovered facts; and on the other, it gives rise to new problems which for the time remain unsolved and stand on the frontier of knowledge demanding investigation. For these new problems, however, solutions are sooner or later arrived at and the sum-total of the content of knowledge is thereby increased; but still other problems emerge out of the solution of the old, and the frontier of knowledge is pushed farther on. And this process goes on indefinitely. The intellectual adventure, thus, is an unending one. This feature of it, however, constitutes its chief fascination, since an intellect with nothing to do would be at best but a sort of useless ornament — if indeed it could be anything at all.

This unending adventure presents certain well-defined stages, two of which it is our purpose briefly to describe in the present chapter. These are the stages of common sense and of science.

§ 1. *Common-sense knowledge*

By common-sense knowledge, broadly defined, is meant the view of the world which by any generation is generally accepted as true without question. It is knowledge of the first look, self-evident knowledge. 'Such and such is a matter of common sense,' we say — meaning thereby that it is so obviously true that no one ought to doubt it. There are certain characteristics of common-sense knowledge needing emphasis, three of which we shall here set down.

(1) IT IS A THEORY. In the first place, the student should carefully note that so-called common-sense knowledge is a rather elaborate theory concerning our environment. This may sound odd at first, but little reflection is needed to disclose its accuracy. Objects do not appear in perception, for example, as common sense says they really are. The sun appears to rise in the east and set in the west; but common sense — of our age, at any rate — says that the sun is stationary while the earth turns on its axis. Moving objects appear to change their shapes and sizes with the changing of their spatial relations to the eyes of the observer; but common sense says that their shapes and sizes remain constant. A cavity in a tooth is small when seen in the dentist's mirror and large when felt by the tongue; but common sense insists that it is always and under all circumstances of the same dimensions. In short, objects appear in direct perception as presenting certain

features; but common sense very often maintains that they are quite other than they appear. And this means that common sense is a theory, or, better, a complex of theories, about the environment. It is not *given* knowledge, it is knowledge that is created by the activity of the mind. It results from interpretation.

(2) IT IS LARGELY INHERITED. What was said in the preceding paragraph must not be understood to mean that the common-sense view of things results from the individual's own theorizing. Quite the contrary is the case. The common-sense view accepted by any individual is largely inherited by him and his generation from preceding generations. And the media through which it is transmitted are chiefly traditions and language. As we have seen in the preceding chapter, the individual is born into a group of his fellows with many customs and traditions established. These customs and traditions bring to bear upon him the common-sense views of his group on various and sundry problems, and these he accepts as a matter of course; but these customs and traditions are society's memory. Through language, also, the individual inherits a whole set of views about his world from his forefathers; and these he accepts and adopts without reflection either concerning their accuracy or their source. Thus it happens that the common-sense knowledge of any generation has grown up gradually through long ages of mental toil in which the individual who accepts the gift did not share. It is the legacy of the past to the present and is transmitted through the conservative forces of group life.

(3) IT IS VAGUE. Finally, it is obvious that, while there is an element of truth in the common-sense view of our environment, many of its interpretations are extremely unsatisfactory. They are vague — so vague, indeed, that

they often cannot even be defined with any precision. They vary from age to age, and not infrequently from community to community; and among these variations undetected contradictions often occur. They are very superficially founded, resulting as they generally do from inaccurate observations and from careless descriptions of what is observed. Many of them rest upon uncriticized prejudices and assumptions which themselves are false or open to serious question. Nor does common sense offer any satisfactory criterion by means of which error may be distinguished from truth; the 'self-evidence' which it suggests is too vaguely conceived to be of service in any serious process of reflection. It is not surprising, therefore, that common sense does not carry us very far in our intellectual voyage of discovery; it is too leaky a vessel to sail treacherous waters. To pursue this voyage with any hope of success mankind has been compelled to construct a more seaworthy craft. Common sense has been abandoned for science.

§ 2. *From common sense to science*

When we pass from common sense to science we are only pushing on towards an understanding of our world. It must not be supposed that science deals with a set of problems wholly different from those in which common sense is interested. On the contrary, scientific knowledge turns toward the same puzzling environment with which common-sense knowledge is concerned. The goal which science aims at is precisely the goal towards which common sense vaguely and ineffectually struggles, namely, the solving of the riddles of the world. Thomas Huxley [1] was so

[1] Huxley (1825–1895) was one of the greatest of English scientists of the last century.

impressed by this fact that he insisted: " Science is nothing but trained and organized common sense."

There is, however, a marked difference between science and common sense, as is suggested in Huxley's statement. Science is " trained and organized " common sense. That means that it is transformed common sense. Common sense is without any definite plan of procedure, while science makes use of a carefully defined method. The essence of science is a certain critical quality, the lack of which in common sense renders common sense vague and forces the mind of man beyond its points of view in the search for knowledge of the hidden secrets of the world. As we shall see in some detail in the following section, scientific knowledge is more vigorously controlled than is common-sense knowledge, more penetrating in its analyses, more comprehensive in its reaches, and so more gratifying to man's intellectual interests. It is not knowledge of a different world, then, that science gives us; it is rather a *critical* and *ordered* knowledge of precisely that world in which common sense is keenly interested but which it comprehends only vaguely and in a haphazard manner. Science demands more systematic theorizing than common sense is capable of; it criticises common sense, not for constructing theories, but for doing so without testing their claims.

§ 3. *Main characteristics of scientific knowledge*

The chief features of scientific knowledge, in which it differs markedly from that of common sense, are three: accuracy, universality, and organization.

(1) ACCURACY. In the first place, scientific knowledge is characterized by an accuracy that is unknown to common sense. Science is not satisfied with vague guesses; she demands definiteness and precision. The true scientist

is possessed of what Huxley calls "the fanaticism of veracity"; he continues to search until the exact truth is revealed.

(a) *Accuracy of observation.* The first demand of science is that the facts be adequately, precisely, and unprejudicedly observed. Upon this foundation modern science is built. During the Middle Ages it was pretty generally assumed that science could dispense with the observation of facts; then the aim was to build science largely upon tradition. Francis Bacon,[1] however, opposed this view as erroneous and insisted that truly scientific knowledge can be attained only through accurate observation of nature; this, he urged, is the indispensable first step. And all modern scientists agree with Bacon in this regard. So nowadays the first requisite of a scientist is that he shall be a careful observer. To be sure, accurate observation is not easy. It is far easier to mingle, as common sense does, imagination with observation and to report for a fact what one imagines ought to be a fact or what is only an approximation to the true nature of the fact. But science requires the more difficult task; she accepts no short-cuts, nor will she be put off with mere guesses and approximations. "Man, unscientific man, is often content with 'the nearly' and 'the almost.' Nature never is. It is not her way to call the same, two things which differ, though the difference may be measured by less than the thousandth of a milligramme or of a millimetre, or by any other like standard of minuteness. And the man who, carrying the ways of the world into the domain of science, thinks he may treat Nature's differences in any other way than she

[1] Francis Bacon (1561–1626), at one time Lord Chancellor of England, did much to emphasize the importance of a method of science different from that which it had followed during the Middle Ages. His most important treatise on the subject is the *Novum Organum* (1620).

treats them herself, will find that she resents his conduct."[1] Science can never be satisfied with 'the nearly' and 'the almost.' In her domain approximations do not succeed; only accurate observation is here acceptable.

(b) *Accuracy of description.* Not only does science require that facts be observed with precision, she also demands that what has been thus observed be faithfully reported In the description nothing must be arbitrarily added, nor must anything be subtracted. "The assertion that outstrips the evidence is not only a blunder but a crime," Huxley urges. Here Huxley primarily intends, doubtless, to condemn the common practice of basing a conclusion upon insufficient evidence. But his phrase is apt as a condemnation of the tendency, no less common and perhaps even more difficult to curb, to report faithlessly the results of observation. Accuracy in description is as fundamental to science as is accuracy of observation. For accurate observation falsely, or even vaguely, reported is of no scientific value. Apart from either accurate observation or accurate description scientific knowledge is impossible.

(2) Universality. In the second place, scientific knowledge is concerned with general principles or laws rather than with particular facts in their isolation. The scientist does not limit himself to the observation and description of this or that particular fact, he is not interested in the isolated fact for its own sake alone. To be sure, he must know precisely what the facts are; and to this end he must accurately observe and describe them. But his chief concern is to read out of them what they have in com-

[1] Sir Michael Foster in the presidential address delivered before the British Association in 1899 . . . quoted by Thomson, *Introduction to Science*, pp. 18–19.

mon with other similar facts—in short, to see them in their relations. The physicist, for example, is not content merely to observe and accurately record the peculiarities of a given ball rolling down a particular inclined plane; he is more interested in knowing why any ball should move as this one actually does move and what this particular ball, *as moving*, has in common with other similar moving objects. In other words, what he wants to discover are the laws of motion exemplified in this special object of observation. And the same is true of all scientists. They are primarily interested, not in the individual facts which they observe, but in the general relating principles that shine through their observations and experiments. In this sense scientific knowledge is universal, its goal is generalization. And in this respect it is in marked contrast to common-sense knowledge which is satisfied to move among particular things and events without penetrating below the surface where lie their connecting bonds.

(3) Organization. The third fundamental characteristic of scientific knowledge is that it is systematic. Common-sense knowledge is haphazard and chaotic; one bit of it is not logically related to other bits, and so it not infrequently involves contradictions. Scientific knowledge, on the contrary, is organized knowledge. It is a system in which various bits of information find their respective places and interlock in such a way that contradiction is reduced to a minimum. If apparent contradictions arise, a problem for the scientist is immediately created; and he does not rest content until the contradiction is removed. This aspect of scientific knowledge is closely connected with the one discussed in the preceding paragraph. Science searches for generalizations in terms of which numerous individual facts may be brought together into a

coherent group; and, obviously, the more successful it is in discovering these generalizations or laws — laws of motion, of gravitation, and the like — the more coherent and systematic does the knowledge it gives us become. The goal of science is the construction within limits of an organized body of knowledge, and this is accomplished through generalizations.

§ 4. *Superiority of scientific knowledge*

The knowledge which science gives us of our environment is nowadays generally accepted as superior in value to common-sense knowledge. Time was when such was not the case; not so many centuries ago science was looked upon with suspicion, and the scientist was pretty generally regarded as a sort of mischievous delver into matters with which it was supposed man had no business to meddle. And the undercurrent of this distrust has continued well into the modern era. Even to-day a survival of it is evident in the more or less common sneer at the 'expert' and the fear of 'too much science.' But at present, broadly speaking, scientific knowledge is accepted as superior to the view of the world which unsupported common sense is able to give us.

This confidence in science is wholly justified. Scientific knowledge is based upon a more exhaustive investigation of the facts and a more systematic inference from the facts investigated than is the knowledge of common sense. And for this reason we may justly place more confidence in the results of science and insist that, where science and common sense are at variance, the verdict of science must be accepted. If science tells us that what we call material objects are really complexes of elements so small that they cannot be seen through the most powerful microscope, that light actually travels through space with an unimaginable velocity, that the planets swing about the sun in enormous ellipses, that the solar system is only a tiny speck in the stellar world, that the centuries of human history are but a moment in the evolution of our little earth — we accept such statements as truer than any deliverances of common sense, even though they reach far beyond the horizon of common-sense knowledge. And we feel that we are justified in doing this, primarily because of the confidence we have in the method which science employs in making its discoveries. So when humanity passes from common sense to science it takes a second very important step in its intellectual journey through the world.

§ 5. *Summary of chapter*

In the present chapter we have glimpsed the main characteristics of common-sense and scientific knowledge, and we have drawn a general contrast between them. We have noted that common sense is really a theory about the world and is, thus, man's first step in his intellectual journey through his environment. We have noted, further, that common sense is an unsatisfactory theory; because of its superficiality and inconsistencies it cannot be looked upon as a final answer to the problems raised by the environment. So the mind of man is driven on into the realm of science in its quest for truth. This realm is not a realm of new facts; it is rather a new way of dealing with the same old facts. The chief characteristics of scientific knowledge which mark it off from the knowledge of common sense are its accuracy, universality, and organization. In attaining its knowledge of things science employs a special method which we shall study in the following chapter.

CHAPTER II. QUESTIONS AND EXERCISES

1. In our knowledge of the rotundity of the earth is theorizing involved? Explain. Can you think of any bit of common-sense knowledge that is wholly free from theory?

2. Give examples illustrating the vagueness and inconsistency of common-sense knowledge.

3. Show in general how scientific knowledge is more organized and systematic than is the knowledge of common sense.

4. Explain the meaning of Huxley's statement: "Science is trained and organized common sense."

5. In those instances where science seems to contradict common sense which is to be accepted? Why?

6. Compare and contrast the scientific and common-sense conceptions of:

   Water
   Ocean tides
   Fire
   The flowing of a stream
   The growth of a plant or an animal

7. In each of the cases mentioned in the preceding question indicate the element of universality involved in scientific knowledge, and show how it is lacking in common-sense knowledge.

8. Outline the main points developed in the first five sections of Pearson's *Grammar of Science*, 3rd edition, Part I, Chapter I.

CHAPTER III

THE METHOD OF SCIENCE

The purpose of the present chapter is to note the chief features of the method made use of by science in the acquisition of its knowledge about the world. No attempt can be made here to enter upon a consideration of the numerous details that arise in connection with variations in applications of the method in different fields of investigation; that is a subject on which investigators in the several fields can alone speak with authority. Here we are concerned exclusively with this question: What are the main characteristics of the general method of science? And to a discussion of this question we now turn.

§ 1. *Essentials of the scientific method*

"The student of science takes more pains than the man in the street does to get at the facts; he is not content with sporadic knowledge, but will have as large a body of facts as he can get; he systematizes these data and his inferences from them, and sums up in a generalization or formula. In all this he observes certain logical processes, certain orders of inference, and we call this *scientific method*."[1] In this description of the scientific method Professor Thomson suggests what may be regarded as the essentials of it. These are: getting the data or facts, making logical inferences from these data, and summarizing these inferences in the form of generalizations or laws. Or,

[1] Thomson, *Introduction to Science*, pp. 57–58.

to state the matter more shortly and perhaps in terms more familiar, the aim of science is accurate *observation* and logical *explanation* and the method by which this is accomplished is the method of science. So our study of the scientific method reduces itself to a consideration of observation and explanation — the two main steps in the procedure of the scientist. As we proceed with this inquiry the student must not permit the familiarity of the words used to name these processes to blind him either to the importance or to the complexity of the processes named.

§ 2. *Observation — its nature*

As we have already seen in the preceding chapter, the first demand of the scientist is for an accurate observation of facts. He wants to know what the facts are, and he wants to know *precisely* what they are. This is essential to his whole enterprise. Apart from an accurate and thorough grasp of the facts he finds himself unable to take a single step forward. Precise observation is his indispensable first step.

(1) Observation as involving effort. It might be, and by the thoughtless frequently is, supposed that no special effort is demanded by observing, and that anyone in his senses is capable of it. Very little reflection is needed, however, to disclose the error involved in such an assumption. Observation, scientific observation, is not aimless gazing at things in general, a blank and passive staring at the world. On the contrary, it is genuine intellectual work; its difficulty varies with the complexity and intricacy of the facts, but it is always in some degree difficult. Precise and trustworthy observation of even the simplest and most obvious facts, such, for example, as a house or the

face of a friend, demands a concentration which few of us ordinarily exercise; while more complex facts, like a delicately adjusted piece of machinery or a social phenomenon, defy the power of observation of the majority of people. Genuine scientific observation is impossible apart from special and rather prolonged training; in science one must consciously learn to observe. Observation, then, as distinguished from meaningless and fruitless gazing abroad, is not easy. Even in its simpler forms it demands an effort that most people seldom exert, while in its more complex forms it is possible only for those who have been specially trained through protracted work in the field of inquiry in which the facts to be observed fall. True observation — observation, that is, which is accurate and reliable — results only from persistent and concentrated attention. Why this should be so is evident when one considers the two basal aspects of the process, namely, analysis and synthesis.

(2) OBSERVATION AS ANALYSIS. By observation is meant, in the first place, breaking facts up — mentally, of course, not physically — and noting their constituent features. This is called *analyzing* the facts. To observe a building, for example, one must note its several qualities such as color, shape, architectural design, and so forth; that is, one must take cognizance of the various aspects of the building as distinct features of it. And until this is done observation of the building cannot in any meaningful sense be said to have taken place. Observation means here mentally breaking the building into its significant elements — taking mental note, so to speak, of its different characteristics. And this is always an essential feature of observation, whatever may be the object observed — whether it be a building or a chemical process in a test-tube, a unit of human society or an amoeba. Dissecting an animal, mak-

ing microscopic slides of a plant or rock, gathering samples of earth from different levels penetrated by an oil well, noting instances of a disease or of a social movement — these all illustrate the same truth: Observation is analysis.

From this truth emerges one reason why observation involves effort and why its difficulty increases with the complexity of the facts to be observed. Observation is analysis; analysis is intelligence at work; the work expended is necessarily proportionate to the intricacy of the facts to be analyzed.

(3) OBSERVATION AS SYNTHESIS. By observation is meant, in the second place, viewing the various constituent elements in their natural context. This is what is known as *synthesis*. Observation of a watch, for instance, means not only analysis of the mechanism into its component parts of spring, wheels, and so forth; it means, in addition, comprehending or seeing — mentally, of course — the relations existing among these different parts when each is performing its proper function in the structure of the watch as a whole. Until this synthesis has been accomplished the watch cannot be said to have been adequately observed. The small boy is 'observing' the watch in a very questionable manner when he tears it to pieces and scatters broadcast its parts; only the individual who can put the parts together again and knows why they go where he puts them can be said really to have observed the mechanism. Synthesis, thus, is essential to the observation of the watch *as a watch* — that is, as an actually existent object made of parts. And this is true generally. Whatever the object of observation may be — from the amoeba to man, from the molecule to society — genuine observation of it involves some sort of comprehension of the interrelations existing among its constituent aspects.

And just here is an added reason for the difficulty of observation. To the difficulty of analysis is added the difficulty of synthesis, which in some respects is perhaps even greater. Like analysis, synthesis is intelligence at work; and the difficulty of its task grows with the complexity of the facts under observation.

(4) ANALYSIS AND SYNTHESIS. To prevent misapprehension of the true nature of the process of observing, it is necessary for the student to bear in mind that analysis and synthesis are not isolated and independent activities. Discussion of them is clearer if they are dealt with separately as above. But this pedagogical necessity must not blind the student to the fact that in any actual process of observing analysis and synthesis are inextricably bound up with each other. One does not first analyze and then later, after the work of analysis is finished, proceed to synthesize the parts or elements disclosed by analysis; on the contrary, analysis and synthesis run along together, intermingling. The truth is, analysis and synthesis are two sides of one and the same identical process of thinking; we analyze through synthesis, and we synthesize through analysis. To illustrate: the very act of analyzing the watch has for its other side, as essential and necessary to it, the synthesis of the several parts of the watch; the spring, as an element within the watch, is observed (analysis) only in so far as its function in relation to the escapement wheel is noted, that is to say, only in so far as its position within the mechanical whole is discerned (synthesis). This interrelation of analysis and synthesis in the act of observing is important. Observation is not two acts; it is one act presenting two distinguishable sides.

§ 3. *Observation — its technique*

In the course of its development science has worked out certain general methods of procedure in the observation of facts. These we may call the technique of scientific observation.

(1) EXPERIMENTATION. Chief among these is experimentation. By experimentation is meant observation of facts under conditions which are definitely known to, and partially at least controlled by, the observer. How to experiment must of course be learned through practice, and the manner in which experiments are made varies with the nature of the facts to be observed. But in all cases experimentation means observing under known conditions which may be reinstated by any other observer with sufficient scientific training. The aim of scientific observation is best accomplished by means of experimentation, and consequently the scientist makes use of experimentation wherever it is possible for him to do so. The other methods of observation strive to approximate experiment, and their value is proportionate to the degree in which this approximation is attained. Perhaps the most significant feature of experimentation is that it enables many different observers to study exactly the same situations and so to check, correct, and supplement each other's results.

(2) STATISTICS. Statistics may also be regarded as a method of observation. Some facts are so complex and the conditions under which they happen are so vaguely known, if known at all, that experimental observation of them is wholly impossible. Social phenomena are illustrations of such facts. Where this is the case statistics may frequently lead to valuable analyses. It is sometimes said that the statistical method gives us only an approximate

description of the facts observed, being limited as it is to averages and consequently applicable only to groups. But not infrequently it is the most satisfactory method of observation that can be employed, and it has shown itself to be sufficiently accurate for many practical purposes.

(3) GENERAL OBSERVATION. There are some facts to which neither of the above methods of observation is applicable. In such cases the scientist has to fall back upon what we may, for lack of a better term, call general observation — observation, that is, of facts in their natural contexts without full acquaintance with, or control over, their conditions, and without attempting to arrive at statistical averages concerning the facts observed. The observation of the flora and fauna of any given locality, of the growth of a plant in one's garden, or of the motions and relative positions of the heavenly bodies would be instances of such general observation. The aim of this type of observation is to approximate as closely as possible to the experimental type, and in any event the conditions of the observation must be sufficiently described to enable other interested and competent investigators to observe similar facts in essentially the same setting.

§ 4. *Explanation — its nature*

Observation of facts is only the first step in the scientific method, though an indispensable one. However carefully and thoroughly it be done, taken by itself it does not satisfy our intellectual curiosity about our environment. It tells us what the facts are, but it leaves unanswered the important question as to why they should be as they are observed to be. By observation we may learn, for example, that water will rise in a pump a certain distance; but observation alone does not answer the question as to why this should be, or even why water should rise at all. So the mind is forced to go beyond mere direct observation to what we call explanation. Explanation, thus, is a necessary second step in scientific knowledge. The chemist can have no knowledge of what takes place in his test-tube unless he observes precisely what is going on there; this is obvious. But it is equally obvious that, unless he can explain what happens after he has observed it, his knowledge is incomplete; the situation confronting him is still primarily a problem demanding solution. By explanation is meant giving reasons why the facts observed are as they are, that is, discovering the conditioning circumstances surrounding them. Observation shows us that water rises in a pump; explanation reveals the conditions that are responsible for this event, the circumstances essential to its happening, and the maximum height (approximately thirty-four feet). By observation the chemist learns that hydrogen and oxygen combine in a certain fixed ratio to form water; when he discovers the secret of this peculiar combination he is said to have explained it. Through observation we learn *what* exists; through explanation we discover *how* it exists.

It is important, however, for the student to note carefully that there is no sharp break between observation and explanation. In point of fact, explanation is identical with completed observation, or, rather, with observation carried farther into the surrounding conditions of the fact or event observed. For when one explains a fact one merely observes the fact in its relations to environing and conditioning facts. The motion of a billiard ball on a table, for example, is explained by carefully observing the total situation relevant to the motion of the ball in question — the surface of the table, whether level or smooth; the resiliency of the cushion; the force of the impact between cue and ball, the point of the surface of the ball struck by the cue, the 'English' applied to the ball; and so forth. When one has carefully noted these aspects of the situation one has explained the ball in so far as its motion is concerned. The explanation of the motion of the ball, thus, consists in describing its determining conditions; the answer to the question as to why and how it moves lies in the discovery of the conditions under which it is observed to move. Of course this more extended observation of the conditions surrounding the fact whose explanation we are seeking gives rise in turn to other problems; every explanation results in a demand for further explanation. But this is only another proof of what has been pointed out above, namely, that the intellectual enterprise itself is an endless one. The important point here is simply that what we call observation and what we call explanation are only two different stages in that enterprise, and that they merge into each other. In so far as it solves problems, observation is identical with explanation; in so far as it raises problems, it is bare observation calling for explanation. So the distinction, after all, is largely arbitrary; though it is helpful to distinguish these two stages in reasoning whose distinguishing marks are, on the one hand, the raising of problems and, on the other, the solution of problems.

From the preceding paragraph it follows that analysis and synthesis, the two fundamental characteristics of observation, are present in explanation. When one has analyzed the watch into its parts and has comprehended the parts in their relation to each other, one has explained the watch so far as its mechanical structure is concerned — though, of course, many other questions may remain unanswered. Thus we are led to the important conclusion that the whole intellectual enterprise is analytical-synthetical. This two-fold movement is a basal feature of reason itself.

§ 5. *Explanation — its steps*

Let us now look briefly at the main stages in the process of explaining. An example will help us, so we shall analyze the procedure of Benjamin Franklin in his famous explanation of lighting.

(1) FRANKLIN'S EXPERIMENT AND INFERENCE. From time immemorial human beings have cringed in terror before lightning and have wondered concerning the secret of its power. Franklin became interested in this problem and devoted considerable attention to it. In 1747 he received from an English friend a Leyden jar — an early type of condenser for statical electricity. In experimenting with the jar and observing its peculiarities Franklin noted that the spark it gave off when it was discharged had many similarities to a flash of lightning. As a result of this observation it occurred to him that perhaps lightning is nothing but an electric spark on a gigantic scale. To test the significance of this supposition he performed his famous kite experiment. He sent a kite into a storm-cloud, and by means of a key attached to the ground end of the string that flew the kite he succeeded in getting a spark from the cloud. He therefore concluded that his guess was right, and scientists generally accepted his conclusion. Lightning was thus at last explained: it was shown to be electricity passing from cloud to cloud, or from cloud to the earth. On the basis of this conclusion Franklin proceeded to make other inferences. If lightning is electricity, he reasoned, then lightning should act as electricity acts under essentially the same conditions. And one result of

his reasoning was the invention of the lightning-rod, which to this day is frequently used to protect buildings from the effects of lightning.

In this concrete case of explanation three steps are distinguishable. In the first place, observation of aspects of the fact to be explained gives rise to a guess as to its possible explanation. In the second place, this guess is tested by further observation. In the third place, since there is reason on the basis of this observation to suppose that the guess is correct, further inferences are founded upon it. The guess is called in science an hypothesis; testing the guess is the proof of the hypothesis; and reasoning from the validity of the hypothesis when shown to be true is called deduction. And what is true of this case is true generally of scientific explanation. Let us notice briefly each of these steps.

(2) FORMATION OF THE HYPOTHESIS. The hypothesis springs from observation of the facts in the case under consideration. Through analysis of the facts there arises a guess, or several guesses, as to possible explanatory conditions. This is inference. In the example mentioned above, the points of similarity noted between the electric spark and the lightning flash suggested a relation of identity. Had the points of similarity not been noted the hypothesis would not have arisen. Inference — the formation of an hypothesis — grows out of direct observation.

(3) PROOF OF THE HYPOTHESIS. After the hypothesis is formed comes the testing of it. And this process involves three distinguishable steps — though it must be borne in mind that these are only three aspects of one unbroken process. (*a*) The first step consists in figuring out what ought to follow from the hypothesis, assuming it to be true. In Franklin's experiment he reasoned that if his

hypothesis were true then a lightning flash ought, under certain definite conditions, to end in a spark identical in every essential respect with that which the Leyden jar emits when a contact is made. (*b*) The second step lies in discovering whether what ought to follow from the hypothesis does as a matter of observation take place. If it does, then the hypothesis is so far regarded as true; if not, the hypothesis is discarded as erroneous. In the experiment devised by Franklin to test his hypothesis he found that the consequence which he reasoned would follow from his hypothesis did as a matter of fact happen. (*c*) The last step in the testing of an hypothesis consists in showing that the hypothesis under test is the only supposition, or, at least, the simplest supposition, that is, the one involving the fewest assumptions, on the basis of which the observed facts can be accounted for or understood. Sometimes, as in Franklin's experiment, this last step is obvious. At other times, however, it is not so obvious and has to be worked out with difficulty. It is conceivable that several hypotheses might explain the facts equally satisfactorily. Where such is the case the simpler hypothesis, if it can be determined, is chosen; if the several hypotheses are equally simple, neither involving more assumptions than the others, then all are tentatively accepted. In this latter case knowledge is incomplete and final explanation is lacking; the only recourse is to further and more exhaustive observation.

(4) Deduction from hypothesis. When once an hypothesis has been shown to be true it becomes the starting-point of further inference. Franklin's faith in his lightning-rod was a legitimate conclusion from the hypothesis established by him. This deductive type of inference is an important stage in explanation, and it is frequently made

use of. It is an inevitable extension of the proof of hypotheses; for an hypothesis is a general principle of explanation which always reaches beyond the special fact or set of facts on which its discovery and proof were based.

(5) SUMMARY OF SECTION. Explanation proceeds through the formation and proof of hypotheses and through the deductive inferences hanging on them. The formation of an hypothesis rests directly upon the facts observed; it is not an unsupported guess, a guess about things in general, but a guess converging upon a specific situation out of which it emerges. The proof, or testing, of an hypothesis may be said to progress through three steps, though these steps are only three aspects of one continuous process of reasoning. Deductions are also drawn from hypotheses. They are indicative of the fact that the hypothesis touches other situations, other facts, than those from which it first emerged.

§ 6. *Scientific use of imagination*

It is commonly said that imagination has no part to play in the cold logic of science, that the scientist must persistently hold his imagination in check. In a very important sense this is true. The aim of the scientist is to let the facts speak for themselves, and to the extent that he permits his own preconceptions to lead to a distortion or neglect of facts to that extent he falls short of his ideal as a scientist. He cannot afford to indulge himself in idle speculations. Imagination in the sense of prejudices and pet theories has no place in the scientific enterprise. Indeed, it is worse than useless; it vitiates observation and lures the mind off into false and fruitless by-paths. Its harmful nature is copiously illustrated by 'popular' science. Against imagination in this sense the true scientist must be eternally on his guard.

There is another sense of the term, however, in which imagination may be said to be an essential aspect of the scientific method. As the capacity to formulate hypotheses, imagination — in this meaning it is sometimes called 'constructive' imagination — is an indispensable quality of scientific ability. One may perhaps lack this sort of imagination and still be a fairly good observer; but without it one could hardly be a great scientist. At any rate, all of the greatest scientists are possessed of constructive imagination in a marked degree; they are without exception active and vigorous theorizers. In his famous lecture on "The Scientific Use of the Imagination" Tyndall,[1] himself a scientist of no mean ability, maintains that the power of imagination 'brooding over facts' is the mightiest instrument of the scientific investigator. And in this he is undoubtedly right. Constructive imagination is the power of the mind to build a bridge from the known to the unknown; and without it no explanations, certainly no explanations of far-reaching significance, can be arrived at.

But there is no justification for supposing that this power of imagination is in any sense mysterious. We are all in possession of it to some degree. Every inference that we make as to the possible cause of even the most commonplace event is an expression of it. To be sure, the greater thinkers possess this power in a degree which lies so far beyond anything the average individual is capable of that we are at times inclined to regard it as in their case a different sort of power from that which the average individual manifests in his prosaic and common-sense inferences. But there is no justification for such a supposition. The

[1] John Tyndall (1820–1893) was an English scientist and lecturer on physical science.

real difference between the intellectual discoverer and the average plodding individual lies, not in the possession by the great thinker of a unique sort of power that the average individual lacks, but in breadth of vision and grasp of realities. Each possesses powers of analysis and synthesis, but the powers of the discoverer far outrun those of the plodder. To put the whole matter in a word, constructive imagination is an aspect of what we have called the intellectual type of reaction on the part of the individual to his environment; it is his capacity to formulate hypotheses; it is his power of analysis-synthesis. And the obvious fact that some individuals possess this power in greater degree than do others does not prove that in their case the power is something mysterious and inexplicable; it only proves what we all know, that there are important differences among human beings in respect of intellectual capacity.[1]

§ 7. *Summary of chapter*

Observation and explanation are the two main stages in the process of reasoning whereby human beings obtain knowledge. Scientific observation and explanation differ from the common type only in that they are more accurate and clear-sighted. Observation shows what the facts really are, and involves the twofold process of analysis-synthesis. Explanation seeks to know the conditions under which the facts exist or happen; here synthesis and analysis are again involved, synthesis expressing itself in the form of hypotheses and analysis in the form of testing the hypotheses. In each particular case the hypothesis emerges from a definite set of facts, through constructive imagination 'brooding over the facts.' Having been tested and found true,

[1] Note the saying: "Genius is one-tenth inspiration and nine-tenths perspiration."

it serves as the point of departure for other inferences called deductions from it. Constructive imagination is not a mysterious faculty possessed only by a favored few; it is the mind's power of analysis-synthesis, and is characteristic of all normal minds. The greater thinkers possess it in a marked degree.

Chapter III. Questions and Exercises

1. Show by illustration how observation involves intellectual effort.
2. Name the three methods of observation mentioned in the text, and indicate their uses.
3. In what sense may explanation be said to be only more complete and exhaustive observation? Illustrate.
4. Indicate the main steps in the process of explanation.
5. Study Chapter III of the *Introduction to Reflective Thinking* by Columbia Associates in Philosophy, and show how the solution of the scientific problem there considered illustrates the main stages in the process of explanation as outlined in the text.
6. In what sense may imagination be called an essential aspect of scientific reasoning? In what sense is it a hindrance to scientific reasoning?
7. Make a concise summary of the main points in Tyndall's essay on "The Scientific Use of the Imagination" (the essay may be found in *Fragments of Science,* Vol. II, Chapter VIII).
8. In *The Life and Letters of Charles Darwin,* by F. Darwin, find one illustration of Darwin's great powers of imaginative insight.
9. Outline the main points bearing on the nature of the scientific method as presented in Thomson's *An Introduction to Science,* Chapters I–III.

CHAPTER IV

CLASSIFICATION OF THE SCIENCES

Thus far in our study we have been speaking of science rather than of the sciences. This is because our interest hitherto has converged upon the general characteristics of scientific knowledge and the method by which that knowledge is attained. But, as the reader is of course aware, there are many sciences and these sciences are in important respects different from each other. The purpose of the present chapter is to note some of these differences by studying certain general groups into which the several sciences more or less obviously fall. Our classification, while not in any sense exhaustive, will at least call attention to the complexity of our scientific knowledge and pave the way for our further consideration of the relation between philosophy and the sciences.[1]

§ 1. *Groups of the sciences on the basis of their subject-matter*

There are in the main four groups of the sciences when divided or classified on the basis of their content or subject-matter. These are: the physical sciences, the biological sciences, the social sciences, and the formal sciences.

1 Several attempts have at times been made to outline an exhaustive map of human knowledge by giving a detailed and complete classification of all of the sciences. If the student is interested in learning what some of these more elaborate classifications are, he should consult the fourth chapter of Professor Thomson's *Introduction to Science* and the writings of the authors there referred to. A detailed study of the question will be found in R. Flint's *History of the Classification of the Sciences.*

(1) The physical sciences. Many of the sciences are devoted to a consideration of the problems that arise in connection with our physical environment. Their aim is to discover the structure of inert matter and the transformations of energy that manifest themselves in the changes in process within the material order; in other words, to observe and explain the phenomena of the physical environment. These are the physical sciences. Among them are physics, chemistry, geology, and astronomy. Physics and chemistry are perhaps fundamental within the group in the sense that they supply certain basal principles upon which the others are more or less directly built.

Some of the oldest sciences of our civilization are found within this group. One reason for this, probably, is the fact that the first and most pressing needs of life have to do with the physical environment. Man's attention was thus necessarily early turned towards the problems arising from this part of his world. The primitive needs of food, shelter, and fire for the very existence of life; the later necessities of water and grass for flocks and herds upon which the existence of the pastoral group depended; the fundamental importance of soil, climate, and seed at the agricultural stage of civilization; and the still later demands of commercial undertakings and the travel incident thereto — all of these forced man very early to study with some care the nature of his physical environment. The religious interest of humanity, too, is doubtless a potent factor in the early emergence of the physical sciences, since many of the objects of nature — such as the sun, moon, the stars, the earth, air, fire, and water — were among the earlier objects of worship.

The recent rapid progress of the physical sciences has greatly impressed the popular imagination, especially because of the numerous inventions that have resulted from their magnificent discoveries. So true is this, indeed, that the term *science* in its popular usage denotes the physical sciences almost, if not quite, exclusively. While it appears that this usage lacks justification, no one can question the tremendous significance, theoretical as well as practical, of the results achieved by this group of sciences. They have revealed many of the secrets of the physical order, from the tiniest particle of matter to the unimaginable depths of space, and their sweeping generalizations are progressively reducing the phenomena of this order to fewer and more comprehensive laws. They seem ever to be converging upon conceptions relatively few in number and of far-reaching application; among these *matter* and *energy* are of basal importance.[1]

(2) THE BIOLOGICAL SCIENCES. A second group of the sciences undertakes to discover the nature of organic matter, to reveal its structure and functions, and to formulate the laws of its activity and reproduction. This is the group of the biological sciences. In this group the sciences of botany and zoology are fundamental.

In a general way the biological sciences can be traced back to the ancient Greeks, particularly to Aristotle.[2]

[1] See *The Realities of Modern Science* (1919), by John Mills, for an interesting and fairly comprehensive account of some of the more important details in the recent development of the physical sciences. It is suggestive to notice, by the way, that in this book the term 'science' is used as synonymous with physical science, indeed, practically as synonymous with physics.

The first two chapters of the second volume of Merz's *History of European Thought in the Nineteenth Century* contain much valuable information concerning the more theoretical side of the recent development in the physical sciences.

[2] Aristotle (385–322 B.C.), son of Nichomachus, who was court physician to the King of Macedonia, was one of the greatest of Greek thinkers. He ranks high among the half dozen leading philosophers of the world; and he independently initiated the study of many sciences, making many important contributions to them. His philosophy became the dominating

Nevertheless, they have only comparatively recently come into prominence. During the last century they have made great progress in discovering the fundamental characteristics of life as it rides to its expression in generations of organisms. Three conceptions of fundamental significance in connection with the problem of life have been emphasized by them. These are: the conception of the *cell* as the morphological unit of all life, the conception of *inheritance* as the nexus between generations of living forms, and the conception of *variation* as the means whereby living forms are continuously altered. These sciences have also succeeded in formulating a general law of universal significance in the field of vital phenomena, namely, the law of evolution, which we shall consider in some detail later on in our study.

(3) THE SOCIAL SCIENCES. This group of sciences is concerned with the sundry problems that arise in connection with the social environment. Their task is to study the nature of the human individual, both as an individual and as a member of society, and to set forth the general principles that are operative within the social order. As typical of the group and at the same time of fundamental importance may be mentioned psychology both individual and social, history both political-institutional and intellectual, ethics, and economics.

The main lines of the development of the social sciences are not as clearly marked as in the case of the physical and the biological sciences. This is due largely to the

---

influence in the thought of the last centuries of mediaeval Europe. During those centuries he was known as 'the Philosopher' . . . the 'master of those that know.' He died in voluntary exile from Athens one year after the death of Alexander the Great, his most famous pupil. He left Athens to save the Athenians a second crime against philosophy, as he expressed it, the execution of Socrates being in his mind their first crime.

complexity of the phenomena with which the social sciences deal, a complexity that makes difficult the employment of a special technique of inquiry. But it can at least be said that these sciences have accomplished much by way of analysis of both individual and social consciousness, that they have disclosed many important features of present-day social organization and of the social life of various races in ages long gone by, and that they have brought into the open some of the basal characteristics of institutional development. Furthermore, their generalizations are tending to place more and more emphasis upon the fundamental importance of the individual within the social order as well as upon the essentially social nature of the individual.

(4) THE FORMAL SCIENCES. There are two sciences which do not properly fall within any of the groups so far mentioned. These are the sciences of logic and mathematics. These two sciences are peculiar in that they have for their subject-matter certain generalized forms of inference through which the human mind acquires and applies its knowledge of the environment, rather than some specific aspect of the environment itself. They study, not objects, but rather the way in which objects are known, the general forms under which the objects of knowledge fall. Hence they are sometimes called the formal sciences.

The attempt to state the discoveries of these two sciences would be useless apart from a somewhat detailed history of them. A word concerning each must here suffice. In mathematics the ancient Greeks had already made considerable advances. Their great mathematical minds — Pythagoras, Plato, Euclid, and Archimedes [1] — gave precise

1 Pythagoras (6th century B.C.) is supposed to have studied mathematics in Egypt and probably in Babylonia. If the traditions concerning

definitions of point, line, surface, and volume; developed the simpler elements of arithmetic and geometry; and proved many theorems of plane geometry and of the relations between the circle and the sphere. The modern era has witnessed such magnificent achievements as the discovery of logarithms, of analytical geometry, of the calculus, of descriptive geometry, of projective geometry, and of non-Euclidian geometries. The development of logic since Aristotle, with whom it had its origin, has been along three main lines. The first emphasizes induction and scientific method; the second conceives of judgment as the element of thinking, which finds expression in various types

---

him may be trusted, he was much interested in pure geometry and in the mathematics of physics. The school he founded, called the Pythagorean school, carried on researches in the application of mathematical formulae to physical phenomena, particularly sound. Many extravagances of theory crept into the later school and ended in idle speculations.

Plato (427–347 B.C.) came of an aristocratic family, his father claiming descent from the line of the Athenian kings. When a young man Plato came under the influence of Socrates with whom he enjoyed an intellectual companionship for eight years. At forty years of age he founded a school at Athens, known as the Academy, of which he was the directing head and the chief inspiration until his death. His writings are very numerous. They are in form of dialogues, Socrates generally being the chief speaker. They are famous for their artistic value as well as their profundity of thought. Plato's views have entered into the very warp and woof of our own civilization.

Euclid (4th century B.C.) was professor of mathematics — arithmetic and geometry — in the famous school at Alexandria, Egypt. While there he prepared for the use of his students a treatise on geometry called *The Elements,* which even to-day constitutes an important part of elementary texts. When the King of Egypt inquired whether one could not learn geometry by some easier method than the study of the difficult *Elements,* Euclid is said to have replied: "There is no royal road to geometry."

Archimedes (3rd century B.C.), interested in pure mathematics and mechanics, is generally regarded as the greatest mathematician of antiquity. His most important work is entitled *Concerning the Sphere and the Cylinder,* which probably indicates the main line of his studies. He did work at problems of mechanics, however, and many inventions are attributed to him. He devised war-engines to aid in the defense of his native city, Syracuse, against the Romans in 212 B.C. When the city fell one of the Roman soldiers brutally killed the aged scientist while he was absorbed in the prosecution of his investigations.

of knowing, such as perception, inference, and the like; while the third looks in the direction of a combination of mathematics and logic, the development of a mathematical logic. For details here the student must consult the histories of logic and mathematics.

§ 2. *Normative and descriptive sciences*

The four groups of sciences mentioned above have been distinguished from each other primarily on the basis of subject-matter or content. The physical sciences are concerned with the physical environment, with inert matter and its characteristics; the biological sciences, with the structure and evolution of living forms; the social sciences, with minds and the social order in which they exist; and the formal sciences, with quantitative relations and relations of implication and inference. But there is possible another division of the sciences based upon their aim rather than upon their content. Some of the sciences are interested mainly in describing objects as they exist in the world, while others are concerned to evaluate or appreciate the worth, or lack of it, which objects have. The former sciences are called *descriptive,* while the latter are known as *normative*. Let us consider a little further this division.

A rainbow, for example, exists as a definite entity arched across the heavens and characterized by certain qualities such as colors, shape, location, etc. But it also exists as an entity that is appreciated by the observer; it is a *beautiful* object, and as such it causes the heart of the poet, as of most men, to 'leap up' when it is observed. As a mere combination of colors spanning the heavens in the form of a semi-circle it is one sort of entity; as beautiful it is another sort of entity. Let us agree to call it in its first aspect an object-fact, and in its second aspect a value-fact.

We may then generalize by saying that all facts are either object-facts or value-facts or both. Now, some sciences are interested primarily in object-facts, while others are interested primarily in value-facts; the first are the descriptive sciences, and the second are the normative sciences.

Thus the name ' descriptive sciences ' is applied to those sciences whose primary aim is to state with all the precision possible the characteristic qualities and relations of the entities falling within their several fields of inquiry. It is the business of the physicist, for example, to describe the rainbow in so far as it is a formation of light-waves within a refracting medium; it is the business of the mathematician to describe accurately the conditions of its peculiar shape; it is the business of the physiologist and the psychologist to describe the conditions of its multiform colors in so far as these are related to the eye of the observer. In short, the aim of the purely descriptive sciences is to describe what actually exists as it exists. The ' normative sciences,' on the other hand, are concerned with evaluating objects or entities and determining the conditions under which they exist as value-facts. The arching rainbow, the surging sea, the star-filled expanse of the moonlit heavens, the misshapen face, the act of homicide, the benevolent and self-sacrificing deed, the process of reasoning — these are entities with peculiar qualities, to be sure, and as such they are entities within the fields of the descriptive sciences. But they are more. Humanity insists upon evaluating them by calling them beautiful or ugly, good or bad, true or erroneous. They are not merely object-facts, they are also value-facts; and as values they fall within the scope of the normative sciences.

Now it is obvious that this new division of the sciences cuts across the groups above described. The sciences of ethics, logic, aesthetics, and economics certainly, and in one interpretation of it history probably, would fall within the group of the normative sciences; all the others would belong to the group of the descriptive sciences. This division thus adds a new arrangement of the sciences, and it is of considerable importance as we shall have occasion to see in the course of our later discussion.

§ 3. *Interrelation of the sciences*

While it is possible to separate the sciences into various groups, as we have suggested above, it must not be supposed by the student that there is a sharp and impassable line of cleavage among them. They not infrequently overlap, the problems of one science being logically bound up with inquiries in the fields of others.

Within any given group of sciences this overlapping is obvious. Physics and chemistry, for example, often find their problems merging into each other, each science in turn being compelled to call upon the other for information necessary to the prosecution of its own inquiries. That the same is true within the group of the biological sciences is exemplified by the fact that botany and zoology have many principles in common, the cellular theory, for instance, being equally important in both. Within the group of the social sciences the interrelation is so close that frequently there is difficulty of distinguishing the province of one from those of the others; while logic and mathematics are in their fundamentals closely akin as recent developments in those sciences have clearly indicated. But the overlapping between group and group is also evident, and is becoming more and more pronounced with the progress of scientific achievement. Biology, for example, borrows more and more from chemistry; a complete study of the structure of living forms inevitably involves reference to chemical and even physical data. The social sciences, likewise, are dependent upon both the physical and biological for indispensable aid in the solution of many of their problems; psychological processes are indissolubly linked with neurological, and the institutions of the social order are thus grounded in psycho-biological principles. And mathematics and logic are inextricably bound up with the whole enterprise of scientific achievement. So there is an intricate network of relations criss-crossing throughout the various groups of the sciences.

The reason for this overlapping of the sciences is to be found in the fact that they are all dealing with the same world of reality. The different sciences are only different sides or paths of mankind's rational journey through one world of fact. "The same phenomenon may be considered without irrelevance under several sciences. Thus when we enjoy looking at a rose, there are chemical, physical, physiological, and psychological problems involved. At least four sciences have something to say, and what must be realized is that while these sciences are separated off for purposes of human convenience, because they pursue different methods, use different tools, sum up in different kinds of formulae, they are simply different modes of one rational inquiry."[1] After all, the different sciences are only different angles of vision from which humanity views the same concrete world of fact, and it is consequently inevitable that they overlap. We separate them off from each other in order that we may more easily cope with the tremendous complexity that confronts us in our inquiry about the environment.

[1] Thomson, *Introduction to Science*, pp. 121–122.

§ 4. *Summary*

There are many sciences which the human mind has discovered in its efforts to pursue the intellectual journey forced upon it both by its own nature and by the nature of its environment. Viewed from the standpoint of content or subject-matter, these sciences fall more or less obviously into four groups; viewed from the standpoint of aim, they fall into two general groups. The second arrangement cuts across the first, and is of importance primarily because it calls attention to another side of the factual order which the first arrangement leaves out of account. But whatever grouping of the sciences may be made, they are not and cannot be sharply sundered from each other; the different sciences all deal with the same world of fact, and it is inevitable that the results of one should affect the results of others. There is a criss-crossing among them which no arrangement of them into groups can fail to take account of. In last analysis, the reason why the sciences are differentiated from each other is because such a division of labor is necessary to enable the human mind to cope with the very great complexity which its environment presents.

APPENDIX TO CHAPTER IV

A brief historical note on the development of the sciences may suggest to the student something of the richness of results achieved by man's scientific inquiry into the nature of his environment. This survey is, of course, in no sense exhaustive and pretends only to call attention to some of the great achievements of the sciences and the names associated with them.

A. *The physical sciences*

The date of the beginning of these sciences cannot of course be fixed with precision. Centuries before the Christian era the Babylonians and Egyptians had started inquiries in this field that apparently yielded some important results. But, since the Greeks are the ancient people most directly connected historically with our own civilization, we may say that it is with the Greeks that these sciences have their origin. The sixth century B.C. sees the first scientific efforts of the Greeks. Thales and his companions [1] of this century began their speculations concerning the nature of the physical world, and with these speculations the physical sciences of European civilization were potentially inaugurated. Many discoveries of value were made by the Greeks during the three or four centuries they were creatively active. Perhaps their most significant contributions to the physical sciences were their general suggestions concerning the atomic or granular structure of matter and the nature of the solar system. Democritus developed a somewhat detailed theory of the granular nature of matter, arguing that matter in all of its forms, both living and non-living, is ultimately analyzable into little particles or bits of material substance which themselves are incapable of further analysis. In astronomy the Pythagoreans held with Aristotle that the earth is round; in opposition to Aristotle, who conceived of the earth as stationary at the centre of the astronomical universe, the Pythagoreans were convinced that the earth swings free in space and with the other planets revolves around some common object which for peculiar reasons they vaguely called the 'central fire.' All of

[1] Thales (flourished about 600 B.C.) was a native of the little town of Miletus and one of the reputed Wise Men of ancient Greece. His thesis is that water is the ultimate substance out of which all things have developed. He is said to have predicted the eclipse of May 28, 585 B.C. and to have known something of magnetism. His fellow-townsmen, Anaximander and Anaximenes, joined him in his speculations and succeeded in working out a simple physics and astronomy — though these sciences did not exist as separate and distinct discipline until much later. These three thinkers are usually called the Milesian school. They represent the very beginning of Greek scientific speculation and first mark a definite break with the mythological view of their age.

these early Greek views about the physical world were naturally vague guesses and never definitely proved. But as foregleams of later discoveries they are significant, and as the first expression of the scientific attitude towards the problems of the physical order of many of them are profound.[1]

Some of the magnificent results achieved by the physical sciences during the modern period, which may be said to begin with the late sixteenth and the early seventeenth centuries, are the following. Copernicus proved beyond question that the guess of the old Pythagoreans was in principle correct by showing that the earth swings with the other planets around the sun. Kepler advanced the Copernican theory by observing that the planets move around the sun in elliptical orbits, not in circles, and by demonstrating that an imaginary line drawn from the centre of a planet to the centre of the sun — called the 'radius vector' of the planet — sweeps over equal areas in equal times. The revolution wrought in physics by Galileo was no less important than that wrought in astronomy by Copernicus. By observing balls rolled down an incline plane and objects of different weights dropped from the Leaning Tower of Pisa, Galileo founded the modern science of dynamics. In this way he learned a great deal about the laws of moving bodies and, what is even more important, he gave a concrete illustration of the fact that the experimental method of observation is of indispensable importance to the sciences. The formulation by Sir Isaac Newton of the universal law of gravitation is perhaps the greatest single achievement of the physical sciences. This law is that every material body attracts every other material body with a force which varies directly with the product of the masses of the two bodies in question and inversely with the square of the distance between them. By this law Newton was able to formulate with great precision the laws of motion, to account for the elliptical

[1] Democritus (born about 469 B.C.) is one of the greatest of early Greek thinkers. He was interested not only in the physical sciences, but in the social sciences as well. The Pythagoreans were followers of Pythagoras (born about 570 B.C.), who is famous chiefly as a mathematician. Any history of philosophy such as that by Thilly, or Rogers, or Weber, will give the student an elementary survey of these early Greek thinkers. Fuller's *History of Early Greek Philosophy* gives an interesting account of their views. Burnet's *Early Greek Philosophy* contains translations of most of the fragments left from their writings, with discussions of them.

orbits of the planets and for the fact that the radius vector of a given planet cuts equal areas in equal times, and to open many doors of discovery which hitherto had been sealed.[1] Some of the more important discoveries in more recent years are: the undulatory or wave theory of light as opposed to the older emission or corpuscular theory; the kinetic theory of gases; the interrelation of magnetism and electricity; the atomic and electronic theories of the structure of matter. Among the great names here are those of Huygens, Young, Fresnel, Joule, Dalton, Faraday, Clerk Maxwell, Lord Kelvin, Sir William Crookes, and J. J. Thomson.[2]

[1] From his law of gravitation Newton was able to show "that the earth must be flattened at the poles; he explained the precession of the equinoxes, the semi-diurnal tides, the ratio of the mass of the moon and the earth, of the sun and the earth, etc." (Libby, *History of Science,* p. 112).

[2] Copernicus (1473–1543) refused for thirty-six years to publish his theory of the solar system because it was so contrary to current beliefs. On his death-bed a copy of his great work, *Celestial Revolutions,* was placed in his hands but he did not open it. His theory was at first favorably received by the Church but later was pronounced "pernicious to Catholic truth" and placed on the Index in 1616.

Galileo Galilei (1564–1642) was among the first to invent and make use of the telescope. By means of it he made four important discoveries: the satellites of the planet Jupiter, the phases of the planet Venus, the irregularities of the surface of the moon, and the existence of spots on the sun. He accepted the Copernican theory, and when sixty-nine years of age was forced by the Inquisition to recant his views with reference to the motion of the earth around the sun. The story goes that the aged scientist, as he rose from his knees after his recantation, murmured: "It moves nevertheless." Galileo's views on dynamics are expressed in his work *Mathematical Discourses and Demonstrations concerning Two New Sciences relating to Mechanics and Local Movements* (1638).

Johann Kepler (1571–1630) was for a time assistant to the famous astronomer, Tycho Brahe, and fell heir to the data which he had gathered. His views on the elliptical orbits of the planets are set forth in his *Astronomia Nova* (1609). A later work, *Harmonica Mundi* (1619), gives evidence of his inclination towards Pythagorean views. Like Galileo, he was persecuted by the Inquisition.

Sir Isaac Newton (1642–1727) is one of the greatest figures in the history of science. His *Principia Mathematica* (1687) was regarded by another eminent scientist, Laplace, as being preëminent above all other productions of the human mind.

Young (1773–1829) established, both by calculation and experiment, the undulatory theory of light. His *Principles of Interferences* was first published in 1801.

B. *The biological sciences*

As is true in the case of the physical sciences, the beginnings of the biological sciences can in a general way be found in the speculations of the early Greek thinkers. Some of Aristotle's predecessors held fairly definite views with reference to organic forms, but Aristotle seems to have been the first investigator to carry out systematic inquiry in this field. He came of a family of physicians and was himself trained for the medical profession. He was greatly interested in biological problems and accumulated what was for his day a vast amount of information relevant to them. "His works display a knowledge of over five hundred living forms. He dissected specimens of fifty different species of animals. One might mention especially his minute knowledge of the sea-urchin, of the murex, of the chameleon, of the habits of the torpedo, the so-called fishing frog, and nest-making fishes, as well as of the manner of reproduction of whales and certain species of shark. One of his chief contributions to anatomy is the description of the heart and of the arrangement of the blood-vessels. . . . Aristotle traced with some care the embryological development of the chick from the fourth day of incubation. His knowledge of the propagation of animals was, however, not

Fresnel (1788–1827) was a famous French physicist whose studies in polarization and diffraction of light did much to gain general acceptance of the undulatory theory. His *Memoire sur la Diffraction* won the grand mathematical prize of the Paris Academy of Sciences in 1819.

Joule (1818–1889) was the first to determine with precision the mechanical equivalent of heat and thus to show that heat is without question a form of energy. The law of the conservation of energy was first clearly enunciated by him in 1843.

John Dalton (1766–1844) has been called the founder of modern chemistry. He is especially noteworthy for his researches in connection with the atomic theory of matter.

Michael Faraday (1791–1867), an eminent English chemist and physicist, made important discoveries in magnetism and electricity. In this field Clerk Maxwell (1831–1879) also made discoveries of profound importance. His great work, *Electricity and Magnetism,* was published in 1873.

Lord Kelvin (1824–1907) was one of the most profound students of last century of the problems connected with the structure of matter.

Sir William Crookes (1832–1919) and Sir J. J. Thomson (b. 1856) are prominently associated with recent researches in connection with the phenomena of electrical and radiant energy.

sufficient to make him reject the belief in spontaneous generation from mud, sand, foam, and dew. His errors are readily comprehensible, as, for example, in attributing spontaneous generation to eels, the habits and mode of reproduction of which only recent studies have made fully known. In regard to generation, as in other scientific fields, the philosophic mind of Aristotle anticipated modern theories, and also raised general questions only to be solved by later investigation of facts."[1] From this quotation it is evident that, considering the fact that Aristotle was the first systematic student in the field of the biological sciences, his discoveries were truly remarkable.

But Aristotle lacked the microscope and the general technique of observation which in the modern period have made possible the systematic progress of the biological sciences and have enabled investigators to raise and solve problems which the old Greek did not glimpse at all or glimpsed only dimly. Detailed and systematic analysis of the structure of organisms and of the nature of organic processes have solved many of the mysteries of living matter; while general inferences have, as in the case of the physical sciences, brought under common laws many phenomena apparently diverse. The ground was once for all cut from under the ancient theory of the spontaneous generation of life by the discoveries of Pasteur who showed that the supposed instances of spontaneous generation can all be accounted for by the presence of micro-organisms in the surrounding air. Pasteur also disclosed the tremendously significant part played by these micro-organisms in processes of fermentation and in the spreading of infectious diseases both in plants and animals. To Charles Darwin, however, goes the honor of performing for the biological sciences the service performed by Newton for the physical sciences, the service, namely, of formulating a general law of universal significance. This he did in his theory of evolution which, though now regarded as erroneous in many of the details of his formulation, threw floods of light upon the vexed question of the connection between generation and generation of living forms and greatly influenced the drift of later thinking both within and without the biological field of phenomena. Before

[1] Libby, *History of Science*, pp. 24–25.

the days of Pasteur and Darwin there were, of course, many workers in the biological sciences who added contributions of greater or less significance. Among these two are deserving of mention even in an elementary survey. They are Cuvier, the chief founder of comparative anatomy and paleontology, and Lamarck, who labored strenuously to establish the evolutionary view of life. Among the more recent investigators should be mentioned Ernst Haeckel, who has been largely instrumental in introducing the Darwinian view into Germany. At present activity within the biological sciences is very great, and marked advances are being made.[1]

C. *The social sciences*

In one form or another many of the basal problems lying in the field of inquiry which we to-day assign to the social sciences were discussed in considerable detail by that great trio of ancient Greek thinkers: Socrates, Plato, and Aristotle. To be sure, Socrates aimed to raise problems rather than to solve them; in-

[1] Georges Cuvier (1769–1832) vigorously opposed the evolutionary hypothesis, insisting upon the fixity both of species and of varieties. In this the historical development of his science has shown him to be wrong. But his work in comparative anatomy and paleontology amounted practically to the inauguration of these sciences.

Lamarck (1744–1829) was a strenuous advocate of the evolutionary view of life, and despite the fact that he was not very influential during his life he has nevertheless been referred to as "the founder of the complete modern theory of Descent" and so "the most prominent figure between Aristotle and Darwin" (H. F. Osborn, *From the Greeks to Darwin*, 1894, p. 156). His important works are: *Studies in the Organization of Living Bodies*, 1802; *Philosophie zoölogique*, 1809; and *Natural History of Animals*, 1835–1845.

Louis Pasteur (1822–1895), the founder of the science of bacteriology, is one of the greatest of French scientists. The ambition of his life was to apply the results of his biological studies to the treatment of disease. This ambition he realised in a marked degree. His name is most widely associated with the Institute founded at Paris by popular and world-wide subscriptions for the purpose of making use of his discoveries to prevent hydrophobia.

Charles Darwin (1809–1882) began his scientific career as a naturalist on H.M.S. *Beagle* which voyaged around the world on a scientific expedition (1831–1836). The publication by Darwin in 1859 of his famous book on evolution, *Origin of Species*, was an epoch-making event, not only in the biological sciences, but in the history of modern thought generally. A sixth edition of this book was published at London in 1880.

deed, he claimed not to have any solutions to offer. His wisdom lay, as he was fond of saying, precisely in his knowledge of his own ignorance. Nevertheless, he discussed the great problems of life and social relations in such a suggestive manner that he became the fountainhead of the main currents of Greek thought after his day. Plato's dialogues, particularly his *Republic*, which is the first discussion of the ideal state, and Aristotle's *Ethics* and *Politics* compass in a very thorough manner the problems of justice, forms of government, the place of the individual in the state, the nature of education and its function in society, and in general most of the social questions which still are pressing. And their discussions are by no means out of date; on the contrary, no contemporary consideration of fundamentals in these fields can afford to leave the views of these Greeks wholly out of account.

During the modern period the various problems connected with the social order have been more sharply differentiated from each other than they were in the minds of the Greek thinkers above referred to, and so there have grown up a number of fairly distinct social sciences, such as ethics, economics, political science, psychology, history, anthropology, and sociology. Developments within these sciences have gone steadily forward and are at present advancing with increasing acceleration. These developments, however, are very complex and can hardly even be indicated in a brief survey. Among the views of importance in the general field may be mentioned: the social contract theory of the state, the opposed organic view of the state, the democratic as opposed to the autocratic conception of government, the utilitarian theory of moral conduct, the self-realization theory of moral conduct, the conflicting views of altruism and egoism in the field of ethics and of socialism and individualism in economics. Some of the more important names representative of these various views are the following: Hobbes, Locke, Rousseau, Bentham, J. S. Mill, Kant, Adam Smith, Comte, Karl Marx, and Nietzsche. Besides these there are, of course, numerous others; but for their names and views the reader must consult the detailed histories.[1]

[1] Thomas Hobbes (1588–1679) was a royalist, and he attempts to justify the monarchical theory of government in his work on political

D. *The formal sciences*

Mathematics has had a long and proud history. The most exact of the sciences, it has always appealed to minds of the first class; and, being fundamental, it has long been cultivated. Its beginnings are lost in the distant past. Long before the Greek thinkers began its study, the early Egyptians and Babylonians were familiar with many of its principles. What these peoples of the Tigris-Euphrates and the Nile valleys knew of mathematics, however, has been transmitted to us through the Greeks who, not content to be transmitters merely, added important contributions of their own. Here as elsewhere they were

---

philosophy entitled *Leviathan*. He emigrated to the continent with other English royalists at the time of the revolution in 1640 and returned to England in 1651.

John Locke (1632–1704) was one of the most influential writers of the seventeenth century. His *Two Treatises on Government* and his *Letters concerning Toleration* exerted a wide influence on political and social thought, an influence evidenced directly by the Constitution of the United States.

Jean Jacques Rousseau (1712–1778) was greatly influenced by Locke and in his turn, through his *Social Contract*, exerted a profound influence upon his age. He is a thorough-going democrat in his theory of government, substituting direct government by the people for representative government. His views are incorporated in the famous Declaration of the Rights of Man (1789). His educational novel, *Emile* advocates a natural education, free development of the child's impulses. Pestalozzi and Froebel were both influenced by his educational views.

Jeremy Bentham (1748–1832) may be regarded as the founder of the modern Utilitarian school of political and ethical philosophy. His basal principle, as stated in the opening paragraph of his *Introduction to the Principles of Morals and Legislation*, is: "Nature has placed mankind under the governance of two sovereign masters, *pain* and *pleasure*. It is for them alone to point out what we ought to do, as well as to determine what we shall do." This principal he seeks to apply both in the field of ethics and in that of government.

John Stuart Mill (1806–1873) was greatly influenced by Bentham and became an ardent and a brilliant advocate of the utilitarian doctrines. He is perhaps the leading writer in the field of the social sciences of 19th century England. Among his most important works on social problems are: *Principles of Political Economy, On Liberty, Considerations on Representative Government, On the Subjection of Women, Utilitarianism, Three Essays on Religion,* and *Auguste Comte and Positivism.*

Immanuel Kant (1724–1804), one of the greatest figures in modern philosophy, vigorously opposed the utilitarian theory in his ethical writ-

creators. So once again we find ourselves debtor to this wonderful little nation of the half-decade immediately preceding the Christian era. Their great mathematical thinkers — Pythagoras, Plato, Euclid, and Archimedes — made important discoveries which greatly enriched the science and indelibly associated their names with its early history. The modern period has witnessed many magnificent discoveries in mathematics and its centuries are dotted with famous names. What the more important of these discoveries are has been indicated in the text of this chapter. The names associated with them are: Viete, Napier, Descartes, Leibnitz, Newton, Monge, Pascal, Lagrange, Gauss, Riemann, Cantor, Dedekind, and Einstein. François Viete (1540–

---

ings and developed another doctrine — the doctrine of the 'good will' and of the moral law or 'categorical imperative' — which has been of great influence in later thought. His works on social problems are: *Metaphysics of Morals, Critique of Practical Reason,* and *Perpetual Peace.*

Adam Smith (1723–1790) is sometimes spoken of as the founder of political economy. By this is meant that he was the first to isolate economic facts and treat them scientifically. He was also interested in ethical problems. *The Theory of Moral Sentiments* and *An Inquiry into the Nature and Causes of the Wealth of Nations* are his two most important works.

Auguste Comte (1798–1857) claims for himself the honor of being the founder of the science of sociology. He urged the application of the scientific method to the solution of social problems. His most important work is the *Positive Philosophy* in six volumes.

Karl Marx (1818–1883) attempts to found a doctrine of socialism upon the view of social evolution advocated by Hegel. He emphasized the growing importance of capitalism in the economic organization of society, and pointed to the dangers inherent in it. Private property is the root of all economic evil, he thought.

G. W. F. Hegel (1770–1831) taught a general view of society which places the idea of humanity in the foreground as the principle lying at the foundation of all cultures and civilizations. This Hegelian view marks one of the main lines of development of later social philosophy. The books in which he sets forth his view are: *Philosophy of Mind, Philosophy of Right,* and *Philosophy of History.*

Friedrich Nietzsche (1844–1900) opposes all of the traditional ethical and social theories. He insists upon a thorough-going individualism, both in individual and social life, and denies the old belief in the equality of men. The democratic ideal, he holds, is an illusion; only the aristocratic ideal is justifiable in the light of facts. His works are numerous and have been translated into English under the editorship of A. Tille. Among them may be mentioned: *Thus Spake Zarathustra, Beyond Good and Evil,* and *Genealogy of Morals.*

1603) is the inventor of modern algebra; John Napier (1550–1617), Laird of Marchistown, Scotland, discovered the logarithms — one of the most important discoveries of the seventeenth century from the standpoint of applied mathematics; René Descartes (1596–1650), the reputed founder of modern philosophy, created the analytical geometry; Leibnitz (1646–1716), a universal genius, being a lawyer, statesman, mathematician, and philosopher, formulated the calculus several years after Newton's discovery of the same subject though in ignorance on his part of Newton's work; Gaspard Monge (1746–1818), Count of Peluse, created the descriptive geometry; Blaise Pascal (1623–1662) made contributions of importance to arithmetic, geometry, algebra, and mechanics, and is particularly noted for his formulation of the calculus of probabilities; Joseph Louis Lagrange (1736–1813) established the principle of virtual velocities and made mathematical studies of vibrations which had important bearings upon the vibratory theory of light; Karl Friedrich Gauss (1777–1855) was the first to use the method of least Squares and is a pioneer of the more recent developments in mathematics; Pierre Simon Laplace (1749–1827), famous as an astronomer and physicist as well as a mathematician, is noteworthy, among other reasons, because of his researches in statistics and particularly his studies of the application of the statistical method to the investigation of social questions; George Friedrich Riemann (1826–1866) developed the theory of functions; while Cantor, Dedekind, and Einstein are prominent figures in the more recent developments of mathematics especially in regard to the theories of point sets and relativity.

Logic, it seems, first began as a systematic study with Aristotle whose formulation in *The Organon* of the syllogism and the fallacies of deductive reasoning remained the final statement of the essentials of the science until the beginning of the modern era — though, as Aristotle himself recognized, the principles formulated by him had been more or less consciously in the minds of his predecessors, Socrates and Plato. In opposition to the emphasis placed by Aristotle on the syllogism, a type of deductive reasoning which starts with certain assumed truths called 'premises' and from these derives conclusions in accordance with the laws outlined by Aristotle, Francis Bacon (1561–1626) emphasized the importance of inductive reason which starts with the observation of facts and from such observation derives general principles or laws. In his *Novum Organum* — so named to indicate its opposition to Aristotle's *Organon* — Bacon points out in some detail the main steps in this method of inductive inference as he conceives it. This point of view was further elaborated by later English thinkers, particularly by John Stuart Mill, who gave important hints concerning various methods employed by the inductive sciences in the determination of causal relations — the methods of agreement, difference, concomitant variations, and residues. This tradition in logical theory is closely connected with the recent theories of Pragmatism sponsored by William James (1842–1910) and of Instrumentalism advocated and expounded by Professor John Dewey (born 1859). A second line of development of modern logical theory was inaugurated by Kant and elaborated by Hegel. In his *Science of Logic,* published (1812–1816) in three volumes and later abridged in one volume known as the *Shorter Logic,* Hegel undertakes to establish the thesis that reason progresses from relatively simple beginnings to more and more complex forms, and that there is a certain definite order in the process of its development. This point of view in logical theory is continued in the so-called Hegelian school of logicians. This school has been, and still is, very influential both in this country and in England. Prominent among its representatives are: Francis Herbert Bradley (born 1846) whose *Principles of Logic* exerted a wide influence; Bernard Bosanquet (1848–1923) whose *Logic, or the Morphology of Knowledge* is much in the spirit of Bradley's *Principles;* and Josiah Royce (1855–1916) who was very influential in this country. The third general line of development of modern logic attempts to reduce mathematics to a comparatively few logical principles and to express logical inferences in the form of a highly abstract symbolism. Important names and works representative of this tendency are: George Boole, *An Investigation of the Laws of Thought* (1854); John Venn, *Symbolic Logic* (1881); Bertrand Russell, *The Principles of Mathematics* (1903), and *Principia Mathematica* (1910–1913, with A. N.

Whitehead). There is much in this development that is of common interest to the mathematician and the logician, and the movement is still relatively young. A survey of the field will be found in the first chapter of Lewis, *Survey of Symbolic Logic*.

Chapter IV. Questions and Exercises

1. Distinguish the following groups of sciences: physical, biological, social, and formal. Give examples of each group.

2. Indicate the difference between normative and descriptive sciences.

3. Show how the sciences tend to overlap, and explain briefly why this should be.

4. Indicate the several sciences that would be concerned in the complete explanation of the following phenomena:
   (*a*) The poet's vision of a flower.
   (*b*) The destruction of a city by earthquake and fire.
   (*c*) The declaration of war between two states.

5. Give your understanding of Bacon's statement: "The divisions of the sciences are not like different lines that meet in one angle, but rather like the branches of trees that join in one trunk."

6. Read Thomson, *Introduction to Science*, Chapter IV, and answer following questions:
   (*a*) What distinction does he draw between *abstract* or *formal* and *concrete* or *descriptive* sciences? Give examples of each group.
   (*b*) What is his definition of *applied* science? Give examples.

CHAPTER V

PHILOSOPHY AND THE SCIENCES

Thus far in our discussion we have been interested primarily in the sciences. We have seen how science is a necessary outgrowth of common sense, supplementing with its precision the latter's superficiality and inadequacy. We have also noted some of the main features of the scientific method, have learned something of the several groups into which the different sciences fall, and have glanced at a few of the details incident to the progress that the sciences have made. We come now to inquire concerning the relation between philosophy and the sciences. But first it may be well for us to notice briefly that there is what may be called a philosophy of common sense.

§ 1. *Philosophy and common sense*

Everyone, however innocent he may be of scientific lore, has a certain sort of philosophy. He has his views concerning the nature and meaning of life, growth and decay, minds and bodies and their relation to each other, the nature of cause and luck and chance, existence after death, God and His relation to the human individual and to the world, knowledge and belief, truth and error, and the like. Such views are generally based upon vague and unanalyzed inferences, and are usually defined in terms of traditional beliefs. But, however poorly defined and unreasoned they may be, they are nevertheless potent factors in the mental life of the average individual and are held by him as in some sense basal. This is a sort of philosophy which we may call the philosophy of common sense.

This philosophy of common sense is unsystematic and largely unreflective. Like the common sense on which it is based, it is partly inherited by the individual and is full of inconsistencies. It is vague, dogmatic, superficial, and ultimately unsatisfactory. What is needed is that such a philosophy be, not thrown away and utterly discarded, but deepened and systematized, reasoned out in the light which the results of scientific achievement alone can shed upon the intricacies of our environment. And, until it is so reshaped, it can lay no legitimate claim to validity. In last analysis, thus, the question which confronts every normal individual is, not whether he shall have a philosophy, but rather what sort of philosophy he shall have. Some sort of philosophy each one necessarily entertains; the only choice is as to the kind of philosophy one shall hold as satisfactory. And the only philosophy ultimately worth having is that which is constructed on the foundations laid by the very best thought and experience of the race.

So it happens that we must pass from the type of philosophy based upon common sense alone to that founded upon the more substantial basis of scientific achievement if we would approach the goal of our intellectual journey. We must exchange the slipshod, rough-and-ready conclusions that common sense suggests about life and its mysteries for the more sober and rigorously derived conclusions of scientific inquiry. We must, in short, pass from the philosophy of common sense to the philosophy of the sciences. And the purpose of our further study is to suggest the broad features of the foundations and the superstructure of such a philosophy.

§ 2. *Characteristics of the sciences giving rise to philosophical problems*

There are certain aspects of scientific inquiry which generate the problems that are of interest to a reasoned philosophy. Here we shall note three: the assumptions of the sciences, the selective character of the sciences, and the progress of the sciences.

(1) THE ASSUMPTIONS OF THE SCIENCES. All of the sciences make certain assumptions in common, two of which are important for our present purpose. These are: (*a*) that human reason can truly comprehend the nature of the environment, and (*b*) that there are causal relations existing within the environment the discovery of which is the chief end of reason. When the physicist or the chemist or any other scientist sets out on his inquiry about the world he assumes, in the first place, that he can by reasoning truly discover the nature of that aspect of the world in which he is interested and, in the second place, that every particular situation which he investigates is a phase of a causal nexus.

Now it is obvious that these assumptions are absolutely necessary to the procedure of the scientist. They constitute his starting-point; apart from them he could not advance. He must assume that the environment is amenable to reason and that explanation of particular objects is possible, or he could never get under way. But however obviously necessary these assumptions are, it is equally obvious that they *are assumptions* and that a study of their justification and implications is demanded. For the question is inevitable whether they are justified and, if so, what is their ultimate significance. A critical analysis of these assumptions is thus demanded by our intelligence, and we cannot shirk the responsibility which this demand places upon us if we would pursue our intellectual journey to its end.

(2) THE PROGRESS OF THE SCIENCES. All of the sciences change. They are never perfected and finished, but there are always problems ahead to be solved. Each science has its history, and its history is the story of its achievements; but these achievements are never equivalent to the accomplishment of its task, since there is always something to be accomplished. This continuous solution and pursuit of solutions of problems is what we call the progress of the sciences.

There are two aspects of scientific development, two sides of the progress which characterizes the sciences. On the one side scientific progress consists in discovering new facts, adding new information to that already acquired; on the other side it consists in harmonizing this new information with the old by developing general laws which include many facts that before were isolated and disconnected. In short, scientific progress consists in *discovery* and *generalization.* As knowledge grows it adds to itself new bits of information and it becomes more general and systematic. This dual nature of scientific development can easily be illustrated by the history of any of the sciences.

(3) SELECTIVE CHARACTER OF THE SCIENCES. Even such a cursory survey of the procedure of the sciences as we have given in the preceding chapters is sufficient to show that each science has a definite point of view which is peculiar to itself and from which it approaches its problems. Where physics and chemistry, for example, are interested in essentially the same content they study it from different points of view; their over-lapping does not destroy

their differences. And the same is true of all the other sciences. Each is selective: it looks out on the world of fact from a special angle of vision.

This selective character of the sciences is essential to their progress. The human mind cannot attack and solve all problems at once; it is compelled to isolate its problems in order to deal successfully with them. But however necessary for progress in discovery, this selective interest of each science limits its scope and leads it to neglect in its investigations genuine and important, but *for its purposes* irrelevant, aspects of the phenomena with which it deals. From the standpoint of physics color is a light-wave. It is obvious, however, that color is something more than a light-wave, since we experience it as something very different. But this 'something more' is for the physicist irrelevant; *from his point of view* color is a light-wave and nothing more. What is true of the physicist in the case of the color is true of him generally, is true of his science, is true of every science. Each science converges attention upon a particular aspect of the world and excludes rigidly from consideration whatever other aspects are from its own special standpoint irrelevant. It selects. Selection always involves neglect; what is not selected is neglected.[1]

[1] This selective character of the sciences is sometimes expressed by calling each science 'abstract.' If this term is used in this connection, however, its meaning should be clearly understood. As so used it is taken in its literal sense of 'drawn apart' and means only that any given science has its own special point of approach to the environment and is thus 'drawn apart' from the other sciences. This word of warning is necessary because of the vagueness attaching to the term 'abstract' and because it is employed in popular speech as a term of reproach. To call a science 'abstract' in the sense of the term here indicated is to say nothing derogatory about the science in question; all that is meant is that it is selective in its procedure.

§ 3. *From the sciences to philosophy*

Each of the characteristics of the sciences mentioned in the preceding section forces the mind on into the field of philosophy.

(1) THE ASSUMPTIONS OF THE SCIENCES. None of the sciences enters upon a critical analysis of their common assumptions that the human mind can truly know the nature of its environment and that phenomena are causally connected. To undertake such an analysis would carry the sciences beyond the scope of their several fields. The assumptions are for them an indispensable starting-point of inquiry; and, having made these assumptions, the sciences pass on to a detailed consideration of the problems emerging in the course of their investigations. But, since the assumptions themselves raise inevitable questions as to their validity and significance, they must be critically examined. Such a critical examination of these assumptions of the sciences is the discipline sometimes called 'epistemology,' that is, a theory of knowledge, which is a special division of the general subject of study called philosophy. An examination of the justification and implications of the assumptions made in common by the sciences is, thus, a philosophical problem.

(2) THE PROGRESS OF THE SCIENCES. That side of the progress of the sciences which we called above 'generalization' is of special interest to the philosopher. For to the extent that the sciences make progress in generalization to that extent they become more and more philosophical. Each science in a sense has its own philosophy within itself; the generalizations which it develops to explain the results obtained in the course of its investigations consti-

tute the content of this philosophy. In this sense philosophy is interested in connecting up the results of a given science by formulating the general laws in terms of which such results can be explained. And in this sense every scientist, whether he be a physicist, or chemist, or biologist, or psychologist, or any other, who aims at the formulation of such general laws may be called a philosopher. The very progress of science, thus, leads always and inevitably into the field of philosophy.

(3) THE SELECTIVE CHARACTER OF THE SCIENCES. The selective character of the sciences would have no consequences of importance if our environment in its totality could be explained in piece-meal fashion. But apparently it cannot be so explained. When the physicist tells us that a given color is a light-wave of a certain length and rapidity of vibration and that the colors of the rainbow are numerous light-waves refracted at different angles by the drops of rain, we accept his explanation but we feel that it is only partial. There still remain many questions untouched by his explanation, such as, for example, why the particular light-wave should appear to us as *red* or *green* or *blue* and how the inside reds of the rainbow are related to the outside blues and violets in so far as these are psychological experiences. Our environment seems to be such that its various aspects cannot be sharply sundered from each other and explained each in terms of itself alone. So it happens that no special science, taken in its isolation, gives us a complete account of even that part of the environment in which it is particularly interested. Facts criss-cross from the field of one science to that of another and so in an important sense transcend the boundaries of any given science.

Nor do the reports of all the sciences taken in lump fully meet the demands of our intelligence. Intelligence demands that the various reports made by the several sciences be thought in relation to, and if possible harmonized with, each other. The results that are obtained by the physical and biological sciences, for example, have an important bearing upon those obtained by the social sciences; and our intelligence demands that the rational connection of these two sets of results be determined. The generalizations of the physical and biological sciences and the generalizations implicit in human conduct, institutions, and values demand *adjustment;* they cannot be left lying loosely side by side as if they were logically independent. And so it happens that the sum-total of the results achieved by the sciences, both in the way of discovery and in the form of generalizations, cannot, without critical comparative study, be accepted as our final knowledge of the world.

It thus turns out once again that the procedure of the sciences drives the mind on to a consideration of the problems of philosophy. Intelligence demands that a critical study of the interrelations of scientific results be undertaken and the effort made to determine whether, and to what extent, these results are consistent and harmonious. And such a study is another side of the discipline called philosophy.

(4) FROM THE SCIENCES TO PHILOSOPHY. The analysis of the assumptions underlying the procedure of the sciences, the generalization of results obtained through scientific discovery, and the critical comparative study of the results of such generalization within the fields of the several sciences — such is the task of systematic philosophy. Systematic philosophy, as opposed to the non-systematic philosophy of common sense, grows thus directly out of the procedure and results of the sciences. So in passing from the sciences to philosophy, as in passing from common sense

to the sciences, we are not entering upon a wholly new and untouched territory; on the contrary, we are still dealing with the same environment and are only pressing on in our efforts to comprehend its meaning. For in systematic philosophy we are concerned with those problems that arise when we definitely undertake to make the most sweeping generalizations warranted by the discoveries of science, to reduce our assumptions to the fewest possible number, and to comprehend the necessity and significance of those assumptions which at the last we may be compelled to make.

And from this it should be evident that philosophy is no mere pedantic and vain searching after answers to more or less arbitrary and trivial questions, as is sometimes supposed by those who are not acquainted with the nature of philosophy as an intellectual discipline. Unfortunately there are abroad in the world and parading under the name of philosophy many 'isms' that are thus empty and nonsensical, just as there are many absurdities abroad marching under the banner of religion. But for the former true philosophy should no more be held responsible than sane religion should be held responsible for the latter. Systematic philosophy is quite different from a mere logomachy or a flouting of personal idiosyncracies as eternal and immutable principles. It is a necessary aspect of man's cultural development, an inevitable stage in his intellectual enterprise.

The above discussion should also have emphasized another point on which the reader must be clear, namely, the precise sense in which it may truly be said that philosophy supplements the sciences. It is no part of the function of philosophy to call in question the findings of any of the sciences on matters of fact. Philosophy accepts at their face value the discoveries made by the sciences, and then proceeds to make use of these results in the formulation and solution of its own problems. Thus philosophy can be said to supplement the sciences only in the sense that it undertakes to deal critically with the problems that emerge from the discoveries of the sciences and from the procedure through which these discoveries are made. The sciences are the pioneers of intellectual progress; philosophy follows in the rear, as it were, and organizes the territory gained.

§ 4. *The problems of philosophy*

From the preceding discussion it would appear that we might with fair accuracy say that the main problems of philosophy fall into two general groups: those connected with the assumptions of the sciences, and those emerging from the discoveries and generalizations of the sciences. Within the first group are to be found those problems that arise out of the intellectual enterprise itself. For the purposes of our introductory study of these problems, they may be summarized under three heads as follows: the nature of the intellectual enterprise, the certainty of the intellectual enterprise, and the venture of the intellectual enterprise. The first is the problem of the way in which knowledge of the environment is acquired, the second is the problem of truth, and the third is the problem of causation. Within the second general group are those problems that result from the generalizations and selective character of the sciences when the effort is made to see what generalizations are warranted and how these various generalizations bear upon each other. For purposes of this summary statement we may enumerate these generalizations under the headings of the larger working notions — technically called 'categories' — which the sciences are forced to use in their interpretations of the environment. Of these categories there are four of fundamental importance for our survey, namely, matter, life, mind, and value. So in our second set of problems we find four main groups; the problems of matter, the problems of life, the problems of mind, and the problems of value. As we shall see in our discussion below, these problems are not sharply sundered; but this preliminary division is at least suggestive of the field we are to traverse, and may be accepted by the student as provisionally accurate.

In outline, then, our problems are as follows:

I. Problems arising out of the Intellectual Enterprise
  1. The Intellectual Enterprise — Its Nature
  2. The Intellectual Enterprise — Its Certainty
  3. The Assumption of Intelligence — Causality

II. Problems arising from the Categories of the Sciences
  1. Problems of Matter
  2. Problems of Life
  3. Problems of Mind
  4. Problems of Value

The details of this outline will be filled in and subdivisions of problems suggested in the course of our further study.

§ 5. *The method of philosophy*

There are two points of view at present held concerning the method of philosophy, and a word on the question is necessary. On the one hand, there are those who insist that philosophy, like the sciences, must depend upon intelligence for the solution of its problems and that, consequently, the method of philosophy is in principle identical with the method of science, the method of reasoned observation and explanation. According to this group, which for convenience of reference we may designate as the *intellectualist* group, the method of philosophy is purely a rational method of procedure and does not essentially differ from the method of science. In direct opposition to this group stands the group of the *intuitionists,* who hold that the method of philosophy is, or should be, radically different from the reflective method of science. According to the intuitionists the solution of philosophical problems must be attained, not through the activity of intelligence, but through a unique sort of knowing activity which some exponents of the point of view name 'intuition.' From the standpoint of this group philosophy is essentially nonrational — *not irrational* — in its method; it is more closely akin to art than it is to science.[1]

A complete consideration of the problem raised by this difference of opinion as to the method of philosophy involves so many complexities that it lies beyond the scope of our study at this stage. We shall content ourselves with noting three objections that lie in the way of accepting the account offered us by the intuitionist. The first objection is that, if the point of view of the intuitionist be accepted, then it would seem that no philosophy could be true in the sense that it demands general acceptance. Rather philosophy would be a matter of individual preference, varying with temperaments and even with prejudices. On the intuitionist theory there is apparently no standard for testing the validity of philosophical knowledge. The

[1] The famous French philosopher, Henri Bergson, is the most outstanding living proponent of this point of view. If the reader is interested in pursuing the matter beyond the elementary discussion of the text, the following works should be consulted in the order named: Bergson, *Introduction to Metaphysics;* H. W. Carr, *The Philosophy of Change,* particularly Chapter I; Cunningham, *A Study in the Philosophy of Bergson,* especially Chapters II–IV; and Bergson, *Creative Evolution,* see Index under 'Intuition' and 'Intelligence.'

second objection is that this view makes the break between the sciences and philosophy too sharp — so sharp, indeed, that it becomes difficult to understand what precisely the relation between them is and of what possible value the results of scientific knowledge could be to the philosophical enterprise. The third objection arises from the consideration that the intuitionist invariably feels it incumbent upon himself to justify his philosophical doctrines, the insights of his 'intuitive' type of knowing, by appealing to arguments in support of them — a procedure which ought not to be necessary, and which in fact is unjustifiable, if the method of philosophy, 'intuition,' be wholly non-intellectual in its nature. To state the three objections summarily: the intuitionist makes of philosophy a body of knowledge that is neither true nor false, because he gives us no standard by which validity can be tested; he makes necessary a sharp break between philosophy and the sciences, and so divides human knowledge into two parts separated by an impassable chasm; and he finds himself at the last forced to contradict himself by appealing to intelligence for justification of the results obtained by that non-intellectual 'intuition' which he holds to be the exclusive and final source of philosophical knowledge.

In the face of these objections to the intuitionist's conception of the method of philosophy — objections that seem to be unimpeachable — we shall give it up and accept the view of the intellectualist. Henceforth our discussion will proceed upon the assumption that the only method open to the philosopher is the method of reasoned reflection — the method of observing facts and interpreting them through the use of hypotheses. For us philosophy offers no short-cut to truth; it attains its end, as does science, by the hard method of reason, by analysis and synthesis.

§ 6. *Summary of Chapter*

However ignorant one may be of the results of scientific inquiry, some sort of philosophy every one must entertain. Common sense has its philosophy; but the philosophy of common sense is, like common sense itself, superficial and unsatisfactory. Common-sense philosophy needs to be brought into touch with the results of science and revised in the light of these results. And the very procedure and results of the sciences necessitate a more genuine type of philosophy. For the assumptions made by all of the sciences as fundamental to their procedure give rise to certain important problems, while the selective character necessary to the development of the sciences forces each science to leave out of account many important aspects of the environment which are for its purposes irrelevant. Furthermore, the results achieved by all of the sciences taken in sum can hardly be set down as final knowledge of our world. For the various aspects of the environment dovetail in such a way as to force a reasoned consideration of scientific results in juxtaposition; and so we are driven on to attempt to bring together these results in the form of a system of knowledge binding from all points of view. To do this requires a special discipline, and this special discipline is called philosophy. Philosophy, thus, is a necessary outgrowth of the sciences and not a merely pedantic debate of questions that are trivial. It is an essential stage in man's intellectual journey through his world. Nor can it be outgrown. It is always necessarily present at whatever stage man's knowledge may have developed; and the further that knowledge expands and the more specialized it becomes, the more important, as well as the more complex, does the task of philosophy grow. The main problems of reflective philosophy arise, on the one hand, from the assumptions of the sciences and, on the other, from the meaning and implications of the basal scientific categories. The method of philosophy is the prosaic method of reasoned reflection, since the assumption to the contrary leads us into fundamental difficulties and even into an absurdity.

Chapter V. Questions and Exercises

1. What do you understand by a philosophy of common sense? Why is such a philosophy necessarily unsatisfactory?
2. Show in general how the problems of systematic philosophy emerge out of the results and procedure of the sciences.
3. Into what two general groups do the problems of philosophy seem naturally to fall? Explain briefly.
4. Study the account of the relation between philosophy and the sciences given in Thomson, *An Introduction to Science*, Chapter V, and compare with the view developed in the text.
5. State the basal difference between the 'intuitionist' and the 'intellectualist' as regards the question concerning the method of philosophy as compared with the method of science. Which view are you inclined to accept, and why?
6. So far as you are able to follow his argument, make a short summary of Bergson's conception of the method of philosophy as developed and defended in his *Introduction to Metaphysics*.

PART III

PART II

PROBLEMS OF THE INTELLECTUAL ENTERPRISE

CHAPTER VI

THE INTELLECTUAL ENTERPRISE: ITS NATURE

In the first part of our study we have been concerned with the relation which philosophy bears to common sense and science, and with the genesis of the problems of philosophy. We have seen how the inadequacies of the common-sense view of the world lead on to the scientific point of view, and how the problems of philosophy grow out of the selective character and the progress and assumptions of the sciences. We turn now to a consideration of some of the problems with which philosophy is concerned, and we begin with those that cluster around the intellectual enterprise itself. In this chapter we shall inquire into the nature of the process whereby the human mind gets what we call knowledge of its environment. The chapter following will be devoted to a consideration of some of the more prominent characteristics of this process; while the certainty and the assumptions of the process will concern us in the two chapters following. What, then, is the nature of the process which we call 'knowing'?

§ 1. *Locke's theory of knowledge*

We may advantageously begin our consideration of this question by glancing briefly at the answer suggested by Locke in his famous *Essay Concerning Human Understanding* (1690).[1] The advantage of beginning with Locke's

[1] John Locke (1632–1704) is a very influential thinker in the development of philosophy. His writings cover many fields — political science,

view is two-fold: it is relatively simple, and in many respects it is closely connected with the common-sense view of to-day.

(1) THE SOURCE OF IDEAS. Locke's first thesis is that the mind of each human being is at birth a blank tablet, an unwritten page, wholly devoid of ideas, and that all ideas acquired by it come from experience. We must let Locke explain this thesis in his own straightforward manner. To begin with, he tells us, there are in the mind no trace of ideas; whence, then, does it derive its ideas? "To this," Locke says, "I answer in one word, from experience; in that all our knowledge is founded, and from that it ultimately derives itself. Our observation employed either about external sensible objects, or about the internal operations of our minds, perceived and reflected on by ourselves, is that which supplies our understanding with all the materials of thinking. These two are the fountains of knowledge from whence all the ideas we have, or can naturally have, do spring. . . . The understanding seems to me not to have the least glimmering of any ideas which it doth not receive from one of these two. External objects furnish the mind with the ideas of sensible qualities, which are all those different perceptions they produce in us; and the mind furnishes the understanding with ideas of its own operations. . . . Let any one examine his own thoughts, and thoroughly search into his understanding; and then let him tell me, whether all the original ideas he has there, are any other than the objects of his senses, or of the operations

---

education, religion, as well as philosophy. He was trained as a physician, and he held several positions of state under William of Orange. His political writings were potent factors in the growth of the spirit of democracy in government during the eighteenth century, particularly in France; they influenced our own Constitution through Thomas Jefferson who was apparently a student of Locke's views.

of his mind, considered as objects of his reflection: and how great a mass of knowledge soever he imagines to be lodged there, he will, upon taking a strict view, see that he has not any idea in his mind, but what one of these two have imprinted. . . ."[1] In short, the source of all our ideas is experience; experience is of a two-fold nature; on the one side, it is sensation (what we should now-a-days call *perception*), and, on the other, it is reflection (synonymous with one meaning of our term *introspection*); all ideas, therefore, are derived from sensation alone, or from reflection alone, or from the two combined. This is Locke's answer to the problem of the source of ideas.

(2) THE NATURE OF KNOWLEDGE. Having accounted for the presence of ideas in the mind, Locke proceeds to his famous definition of knowledge. The mind has the capacity to compound, compare, and contrast ideas; and from this compounding and comparing ideas our knowledge springs. Knowledge, therefore, as Locke conceives it, lies precisely in those relations of agreement or disagreement (consistency or inconsistency) among ideas in so far as these relations can be discovered by the understanding. Locke's statement of the matter is this: "Since the mind, in all its thoughts and reasonings, hath no other immediate object but its own ideas, which it alone does or can contemplate, it is evident that our knowledge is only conversant about them. Knowledge, then, seems to be nothing but the perception of the connection and agreement, or disagreement and repugnancy, of any of our ideas. In this alone it consists. Where this perception is, there is knowledge; and where it is not, there, though we may fancy, guess, or believe, yet we always come short of knowledge."[2]

[1] *Essay Concerning Human Understanding*, Book II, Chapter I, sections 2–5.

[2] *Essay*, Book IV, Chapter I, sections 1, 2. The reader should bear

Knowledge, then, is the discernment of the agreement or disagreement among our ideas. Examples of each process would be: 'A horse is a quadruped' (agreement); and 'A circle is not a square' (disagreement).

(3) SUMMARY STATEMENT OF LOCKE'S VIEW. Knowledge arises from comparing our ideas (some of which agree and some disagree with each other) and discerning their agreement or disagreement; all ideas come from experience; experience is either sensation or reflection; these, therefore, separately or conjointly, are the source of our ideas, and so of our knowledge. This is in barest outline Locke's answer to the question concerning the nature of knowledge.

§ 2. *Difficulties in Locke's view of knowledge*

At first glance Locke's analysis of the nature of knowledge may perhaps seem simple and correct. The mind receives impressions from the outside and observes its own operations of willing, desiring, thinking, and the like; from these sources we get ideas about our environment and ourselves; and by comparing and contrasting these ideas we derive knowledge that certain of our ideas agree, and certain others disagree, with each other — this may at first glance, perhaps, be taken as a satisfactory account of the intellectual enterprise. It certainly in many respects is identical with the common-sense view. But systematic reflection upon it reveals that it is encumbered with certain difficulties that prevent its being accepted as a satisfactory statement of the origin and nature of knowledge. Three of these difficulties we shall here definitely formulate.

(1) THE MIND AS PASSIVE. The first difficulty in

---

in mind that in the above quotation Locke means by 'perception' what we should probably call *discerning* or *judging*. This is necessary if one is to grasp Locke's definition of knowledge.

Locke's view which makes it unacceptable is that it is based upon the assumption that the mind is passive in the acquisition of its ideas, particularly its ideas about the external environment. The mind, Locke says, is a 'blank tablet' upon which experience writes; its ideas come to it independently of its own initiative — indeed, it can assume initiative, become active, only after it has obtained ideas which it may compare and compound with each other. Ideas are, as it were, poured into the mind from the outside; the mind passively receives its ideas. Now reflection since Locke's day has led to the conclusion that this is not the case. Ideas are not poured into the mind, they are acquired by the mind in its efforts to react to the environment; the mind is not a receptacle of ideas, it is rather the crucible in which ideas are formed. In short, the mind is not passive in the attainment of ideas; it is active, and the results of its activity (its 'reaction' to the environment, we have called it in our introductory chapter) are its ideas. On this score, then, Locke's view is seen in the light of later developments to be erroneous.

(2) IDEAS AS DISTINCT FROM KNOWLEDGE. A second difficulty in Locke's theory of knowledge as viewed in the light of later developments is the sharp distinction which is drawn between 'ideas' and 'knowledge.' According to Locke's view, ideas must exist in the mind before knowledge is possible; and knowledge supervenes upon ideas as the result of the mind's comparing them with each other. Thus, for example, the idea 'horse' and the idea 'black' must be in the mind before it is possible for the mind to have knowledge that a particular horse is, or is not, black; the mind must already have the ideas before it can discern their relations. Now there is an element of truth in this view, but the error is greater than the truth. Into the details,

however, we need not trouble ourselves to go; the essential point which we want to emphasize is that 'knowledge' and 'ideas' grow together in the mind, that the acquisition of 'ideas' is at the same time the acquisition of 'knowledge.' When one has the idea of a given horse, one knows that the horse is black or not; that is, the idea of the particular horse is not merely an abstract and skeleton-like notion of 'horseness' to which later is to be added the abstract notion of 'blackness,' but the idea of the horse is the notion of an object with certain qualities among which is that of color. So Locke's sharp distinction between 'ideas' and 'knowledge' cannot stand in the face of the results of later psychological and philosophical inquiry.

(3) IDEAS AS DISTINCT FROM OBJECTS. Another sharp distinction, which later thought has been prone to deny, constitutes a third difficulty in Locke's theory of knowledge. And that is the distinction between 'ideas' and the 'objects' for which they stand. Ideas, according to Locke, exist in the mind and represent or symbolize objects which exist outside of the mind. Now this gives rise to the difficulty that we cannot know anything about objects, since our knowledge is by hypothesis conversant only about our ideas and ideas are distinct from objects. And with this we are face to face with the problem as to how we can distinguish real knowledge from pure fiction. If we know only relations among ideas and if ideas are wholly different from objects within the environment, then why is not 'A centaur is not a mermaid' as real and genuine knowledge as 'Material bodies are heavy'? How distinguish, in other words, between real and purely fantastical knowledge, if Locke's separation between ideas and objects be accepted? The problem of truth and error we shall consider at length in a later chapter; the point of emphasis

here is simply that Locke's separation of ideas from objects lands us in an apparently insoluble difficulty. And later thought on the nature of knowledge has been led to surrender this distinction along with that between ideas and knowledge, of which it is in point of fact simply the other side.

§ 3. *Judgment the element of knowledge*

The difficulties inherent in Locke's theory of knowledge compelled subsequent thinkers greatly to modify Locke's view and to develop a conception of knowledge which in many respects is radically different. The nature of this other view it is the purpose of this section briefly to describe.

(1) MIND AS ACTIVE. The first radical difference between the later view of knowledge and the view of Locke lies in the conception of mind as active rather than passive. Locke, as we have seen, supposed the mind to be passive in the reception of its ideas; ideas are 'imprinted' on it from some source outside itself. We now know, thanks to the philosophical and psychological studies that have been made since Locke's day, that mind is active in the acquisition of its knowledge. The very nature of mind is to be active; mind is activity, a way in which certain organic forms (such as human beings) react to their environment. And the knowledge which any mind has comes through this activity of it. For the modern view mind is an activity, a type of reaction to the environment, whereas for Locke mind is a sort of receptacle into which ideas somehow come — this is perhaps the basal difference between the new and the old views.

(2) JUDGMENT AS THE ELEMENT OF KNOWLEDGE. The activity of mind through which its knowledge arises is

interpretation of the environment. Through our various senses we come into direct contact with the environment; the eye, the ear, the skin, and the other senses with which the human body is endowed are so many points of contact between the environment and mind. But the senses by themselves alone can hardly be said to give us knowledge of the world. It is only when the reports of the senses are interpreted and their meaning or significance grasped that knowledge arises. "Suppose that one were sitting in one's room very much engaged with some study, or wrapped up in an interesting book, and suppose that at the same time the sound of a drum should fall upon one's ears. Now, the sound sensations might be present to consciousness without calling forth any reaction on the part of the mind. That is, we might be so intent on our book that we should not wake up . . . to the meaning or significance of the drum-taps; or perhaps not even to the fact that they were drum-taps at all. But if the mind did react upon the sound sensations, it would try to interpret them, or put them together so as to give them a meaning. As a result, some conclusion would be reached, as, for example, 'the drum is beating'; or sufficient intellectual work may have been done to give as a conclusion, 'that is the Salvation Army marching up the street.' In any case, it is of the greatest importance to notice that the conclusion does not come into our minds from without, but that it is the product of the mind's own activity. . . . It is not true, in other words, that knowledge passes into our minds through the senses; it is only when the mind wakes up to the meaning of sensations, and is able to put them together and interpret them, that it gains any knowledge." [1] This 'waking up' to the meaning of experiences is gen-

[1] Creighton, *Introductory Logic,* new edition, pp. 322–323.

erally called *judgment*. Judgment, thus, is the mind's interpretation of its environment. And it is the source of our knowledge of the world, whether that knowledge be common-sense knowledge, as in the above quotation, or scientific and philosophical. The act of judging is the essence of the intellectual enterprise in its simplest, as in its most complex, stages.

(3) SUMMARY OF SECTION. The later view of knowledge is, in short, that knowledge results from the activity of mind, the reaction of mind upon its environment; judgment is the element of knowledge, the source whence all knowledge springs. This view is opposed to Locke's not only because it denies the passivity of mind, but also because it does away with the sharp distinction which Locke draws between 'ideas' and 'knowledge' on the one hand, and between 'ideas' and 'objects' on the other. According to this view, 'ideas' and 'knowledge' are alike forms of judgment, and 'ideas' are only the interpretation of 'objects.' When one interprets the light in the distance to mean an on-coming train or automobile, one judges (has an idea or knows) that a train or automobile is approaching; and the idea (judgment) is inseparable from the object. Ideas, objects, and knowledge are merely different sides of judgment, which is the basal act in the intellectual enterprise.

§ 4. *Judging and perceiving, conceiving and reasoning*

A further comprehension of the main thesis (and its justification) of the view of knowledge described in the preceding section may be gained by a brief consideration of the cognitive processes commonly known as perceiving, conceiving, and reasoning, in their relation to the mental activity above called judging. It is sometimes supposed that these processes are different from judging; but this would seem to be a mistake. There is very good reason for holding that they are only different forms of judging. The purpose of this section is to indicate concisely how this is so.

(1) PERCEIVING AS A FORM OF JUDGING. By perceiving is meant, technically, the act whereby the mind acquires immediate information concerning the external environment. We see colors, hear sounds, smell odors, and feel surfaces; these are acts of perceiving. Are they different from the act of judging? If they involve interpretation, they are forms of judgment; if they do not involve interpretation, they are different from judging. Do they, then, involve interpretation? In a sense it may possibly be true that these experiences do not involve interpretations; in so far as the color is a bare color (something seen, but not named) or the sound a mere noise having no special significance, perhaps the perception of the color or sound may be said not to involve judgment. But in so far as the color or the sound means something, in so far, for example, as the color means an apple or the sound a whistle, interpretation is unquestionably involved. Now, since our acts of perceiving are practically always meaningful, we may say that acts of perceiving involve interpretation and are, therefore, forms of judging. When in perception we get beyond the bare 'something' which is given through our sense organs and acquire information about our environment, learn, in other words, that certain experiences of color and temperature and sound and the like signify objects, we are judging these experiences — they then are by us interpreted. Perceiving (in the sense in which it gives us information about our physical environment) and judging, then, are not radically distinct; the former is a type of the latter. Instead of speaking of perception as if it were a cognitive

process standing by itself, it would more accurately be described as *perceptual judgment.*

(2) CONCEIVING AS A FORM OF JUDGMENT. By conceiving is meant the act through which objects are classified and grouped into meaningful contexts. Balls, apples, some stones, the earth, all have something in common in respect of their shapes; we therefore classify them as round objects, or as objects having the common quality of roundness — this grouping of the objects is conceiving, and the common quality of the objects is a concept. Other examples are numerous; every classification is an example. Now it is fairly obvious that conceiving is impossible apart from interpretation; it is precisely interpretation. No one ever directly *finds* a concept; it must be 'thought,' as the popular saying goes. The common quality on the basis of which the classification is made must be discovered, and it can be discovered only through interpretation. All trees that are evergreens, for example, or all animals that are vertebrates, have a common quality; but this must be discovered through interpretation of the particular specimens before classification is possible. When the common quality on the basis of which the grouping is made is a more or less superficial and accidental one, the classification is perhaps not of very great significance; when the common quality is more fundamental and far-reaching in its scope, the classification gains in importance and may even be called scientific. Thus, the classification of objects as 'round' is more superficial, and hence less significant, than the classification of them as 'gravitating'; to say that certain objects are characterised by the quality of roundness gives us less information about them, broadly speaking, than to say that they are subject to the laws of gravitation. But the important point for us is that either

classification gives some information and involves interpretation; it requires interpretation of objects to classify them in terms of their roundness just as truly as it does to classify them in terms of their attraction in respect of their relative masses and distances. And this is universally the case in conceiving; all concepts result from interpretation. Hence conceiving is really a form of judging, and not something radically different from it; in point of fact, conceiving is judging the common qualities of objects.

(3) Reasoning as a form of judging. Reasoning is sometimes supposed to differ sharply from judging, but the same line of inquiry which we have followed in connection with perceiving and conceiving will lead to the conclusion that reasoning also is a way of judging. 'This stick is dry, and therefore will readily burn' is nothing but an interpretation of the significance of the stick in the light of my past experiences with sticks and fire. I merely judge that the dryness of the stick means that it is inflammable. Reasoning is the interpretation of the bearing which some present fact of experience has with reference to the broader field of my experience in its totality. 'A is B, because A is C,' or, 'A is B, and it is therefore C,' resolve themselves on analysis into the judgment that the proposition 'A is B' stands in a certain supposedly necessary relation to other parts of my experience, to my other judgments. Reasoning, then, is a complex form of judging — but a form of judging, nevertheless.

(4) Summary of section. Perceiving, conceiving, and reasoning are merely different forms of judging. They are not sharply sundered from each other; they are ways in which the mind interprets the meaning of its environment. To be sure, it is convenient at times (as is frequently done in books on psychology, for example) to keep them separate

for purposes of detailed consideration; they have peculiar features that necessitate this. But it is important to bear in mind that, after all, they are only different ways in which the mind reacts to its environment when it is trying to grasp meanings: they are types of judgment. Judgment is the basal form of intelligence, the irreducible minimum of the intellectual enterprise.

§ 5. *Conclusion*

The conclusion of the whole matter, then, is that Locke's view of the nature of knowledge and the acquisition by the mind of its material, its 'ideas,' is erroneous. The mind is not a blank tablet which has its 'ideas' imprinted upon it from without; nor is knowledge the discernment of the agreement or disagreement among these 'ideas.' The mind (as cognitive) is an activity, an activity of interpretation, or reaction to the meaning, of its environment; and knowledge is the mind's acquisition of this meaning. Perceiving, conceiving, and reasoning are different ways of judging, modes in which the interpretative activity of the mind expresses itself. For purposes of practical convenience in considering details, these three forms of judgment may be kept distinct from each other and dealt with separately; but the fact that they are all alike forms of judgment must not be overlooked, or the unity of mind in its capacity as a knowing or cognitive principle will be ruptured. Perceiving, conceiving, and reasoning are all alike judging, varying in complexity, to be sure, but not in kind.

Chapter VI. Questions and Exercises

1. Show in some detail how interpretation or judging is involved in:

   (*a*) The perception of an apple when you smell its odor.
   (*b*) The perception of a distant train when you see the headlight.
   (*c*) The classification of a plant or animal as belonging to a certain species.
   (*d*) The vision of a red flag which is taken to be indicative of a dangerous crossing.
   (*e*) The conviction that a boat adrift will float down stream.

2. Study the account of the nature of 'ideas' and 'knowledge' given by Locke in his *Essay Concerning Human Understanding*, Book II, Chapter 1, and Book IV, Chapters 1–4. Does the account seem to you satisfactory? Discuss as definitely as you can.

3. Compare the account of the concept, judgment, and reasoning given in Pillsbury, *Essentials of Psychology*, Chapter IX, with that given in the text.

4. Make a brief comparison between Creighton, *An Introductory Logic*, 4th edition, Chapter XXI, and Russell, *The Problems of Philosophy*, Chapter V.

5. Outline main points developed in Dewey, *How We Think*, Part II, Chapter IX.

CHAPTER VII

THE INTELLECTUAL ENTERPRISE: CHARACTERISTICS OF JUDGMENT

In the preceding chapter we have seen reason to hold that the act of judging is fundamental in the acquisition of knowledge. In our further study of the nature of the intellectual enterprise we now turn to a consideration of some of the more important features of judgment.

§ 1. *The objective reference of judgment*

Since each judgment is in inseparable touch with the environment, being only an interpretation of its meaning or significance, the judgment is said to have an objective reference — that is, each judgment refers to an object. When, for example, I interpret the sounds from the streets as the taps of a drum, my judgment refers to the sound which is its object. Obviously, this particular judgment could not exist if the sound were not there; in that event, there would be nothing to judge and the judgment consequently would never take place. And this is true universally. Every judgment is turned towards an objective situation, something (whether in the physical or social environment makes no difference, of course) which is the object of the judgment in question; and apart from this objective situation the judgment simply would not exist. Every judgment, therefore, has an objective reference, and is inseparable from it. No object, then no judgment.

A short digression for the purpose of emphasizing this point is justified because of its importance. The question is sometimes raised, and has not infrequently been debated, how the mind can know external objects.[1] If objects are outside of mind, how can they ever be known by it. This, it can easily be seen, is based upon the assumption that the mind is sharply sundered from objects, that knowing is something which goes on in the submerged mind wholly apart from the environment. Now, when once this separation between mind and objects is made, the question concerning the possibility of knowledge of objects becomes inevitable. And it is also unanswerable; if mind is sundered from objects, there is no logical bridge possible between them. Our conclusion that judgment is the element of thinking and that judgment always has an objective reference, however, offers a satisfactory way of escape by disclosing the fact that the supposed difficulty is really no difficulty at all since it rests upon a false assumption. For the objective reference of judgment means that, in the act of knowing, mind and object are bound together and are not separate and distinct. Knowledge, then, is primarily a relation between mind and objects, and exists only when that relation obtains. No object, then no judgment; no judgment, then no knowledge. How can the mind know objects? is a question which thus seems to be meaningless; it is impossible for the mind to know anything else but objects. In judging, the mind is in contact with objects. Thus the assumption of the scientist which we noted in Chapter V above, namely, that all knowledge is knowledge of the environment, is, we now see, precisely the assumption that is necessitated by an analysis of the nature of judgment as the activity through which knowledge is acquired. A sharp division between judgment and the environment makes the acquisition of knowledge of the environment an insoluble

[1] See the Appendix to this chapter.

mystery and contradicts the very nature of judgment as an act of interpretation.

§ 2. *Judgment as sharable*

In the second place, every judgment is sharable by several minds. The judgment of one person has a meaning which is the same for the person who entertains it and for all other persons who understand it — that is, assuming that the judgment is clearly and unambiguously expressed. In this respect a judgment differs from other mental experiences, such as a feeling of pain for instance. If I tell you that my tooth aches, you can understand what I mean and so share with me my judgment in a way in which you cannot possibly share the ache of the tooth. My judgment that it is my tooth which aches and not my ear or my throat you can experience, but not my pain. The pain is my own unique experience, non-sharable with anyone else; even should your tooth ache also, it would be your pain which you experience and not mine. But my judgment you can share; it may literally become yours also. It is a bridge, so to speak, between your mind and mine. Judgment, thus, is social; it can be shared between mind and mind. It should be noted in this connection that sharing one's judgment is not at all identical with agreement that the judgment is true. I may share your judgment that your watch is worth fifty dollars without agreeing that such is the case. I share the judgment when I understand its meaning; I agree with the judgment when I assent to it and accept it as true. The problem of the distinction between true and erroneous judgments we shall consider in the next chapter. The point here to be emphasized is simply that one mind may enter into another mind through the gateway of judgment.

§ 3. *Judgment as analytical-synthetical*

In Chapter III above attention was directed to the fact that scientific observation is analytical-synthetical, and that the same dual characteristic belongs to scientific explanation. We can now understand better why this is so. Scientific observation and explanation are nothing but ways of judging, and a fundamental characteristic of every judgment, whether simple or complex, is that it is analytical-synthetical. So in discussing here this feature of judgment we shall be repeating what we have already said there. But repetition will perhaps aid clarity.

By way of example let us take the simple judgment, 'This is a typewriter desk.' It is obvious on a little reflection that this judgment is, on one side, analysis and, on the other, synthesis; it is analytical-synthetical. If I do the work necessary to the creation of this judgment, that is, if I really judge that a given object is a typewriter desk, then I do two things. On the one hand, I distinguish the desk from other objects that are not desks as well as from other desks that are not used for the specific purposes of a typewriter desk; and this means that I note the characteristics of this object which mark it off from other objects. From this point of view, the judgment is analytical. On the other hand, I not only distinguish the object from other objects, but I also classify it; and this means that certain characteristics which it possesses in common with other objects — other desks of a similar kind or class — are noted and the objects grouped accordingly — as a desk of a particular class. From this point of view the judgment is synthetical. Now there are two important points to notice here. First, this analysis and this synthesis are precisely identical with the judgment. The judgment is essentially analyzing and synthesizing, noting individual characteristics and classifying. These two processes exhaust the nature of the judgment. And the second point is practically the same thing said in a different way: analysis and synthesis are only two aspects of the same process. When I note the distinguishing marks of the desk I am at the same time and in the same act noting the features which refer it to its appropriate class or group. In being aware that the desk has such and such distinguishing marks I am also aware that these distinguishing marks set it off into a certain class of desks.

Now what is true of this particular judgment holds in principle of all judgments. Every judgment is identical with analysis and synthesis; and analysis and synthesis are two sides or characteristics of the judgment, just as anabolism and catabolism are two sides of the same biological process called metabolism. Of course, in some judgments analysis is emphasized, while in others synthesis is the more important aspect. But every judgment is in some genuine sense analytical-synthetical.

§ 4. *Types of judgment*

Judgments fall generally into two classes which, despite the fact that they are not mutually exclusive, should nevertheless be distinguished from each other. These are what we shall call the class of *factual-judgments* and the class of *value-judgments*. Factual-judgments interpret objects as mere existences in the environment; while value-judgments appreciate or evaluate objects. To illustrate: the judgment, 'This is a typewriter desk,' is a factual judgment; it merely interprets certain experiences as actually existing parts of the environment. And if one should go on to judge that the desk is of such and such a size, weighs so much, and is colored mahogany or golden-oak, all these judgments are still merely descriptive of certain actually existent experiences and consequently are factual-judgments. If, however, a person of aesthetic taste were to insist that the desk is ill-proportioned or that its golden-oak finish harmonizes poorly with the other furniture of the room, such judgments would be value-judgments; because they are concerned, not primarily with the desk as an actually existent fact, but rather with what it might be and is not. In short, such judgments are appreciative and not descriptive of the desk. Value-judgments appraise, while factual judgments describe.

As suggested in the preceding paragraph, these two classes or groups of judgments are not mutually exclusive. A factual-judgment may appraise or evaluate, as 'That ugly man yonder is a friend of my brother-in-law'; and all value-judgments are in some sense descriptive. So the difference, after all, is largely a difference of emphasis. But the difference is important nevertheless. It is the basis upon which rests the distinction between normative and descriptive sciences noted in Chapter IV above. And the primarily value-judgments give rise to a group of philosophical problems most intimately connected with the chief interests of life, as we shall see in some detail later on in our study. It is important, therefore, that the student keep the distinction in mind.

§ 5. *Genesis of judgment*

The psychological situation that gives rise to judgment has been defined by Professor Dewey as a doubt-situation. So long as experience runs smoothly without any hitch it calls forth only reflex and habitual responses; judgment is not operative. But let a doubt arise concerning conflicting alternatives and judgment immediately becomes active. "A moving blur catches our eye in the distance; we ask ourselves: 'What is it? Is it a cloud of whirling dust? a tree waving its branches? a man signaling to us?' Something in the total situation suggests each of these possible meanings. Only one of them can possibly be sound; perhaps none of them is appropriate; yet *some* meaning the thing in question surely has. Which of the alternative suggested meanings has the rightful claim? What does the perception really mean? How is it to be interpreted, estimated, appraised, placed? Every judgment proceeds from some such situation."[1] Of course, this doubt-situation may spring from manifold sorts of conflict. It may arise from a conflict among the practical needs of life, or it may be created by inconsistencies within the more theoretical side of experience. But, in any case, it is the healing of a conflict within experience which constitutes the unique function of judgment.

In addition to what is said above, it must be remembered that experience, in so far at least as it can be said to involve knowledge, is itself the product of the activity of judging. Consequently, to say that judgment emerges from a conflict within experience is equivalent to saying that any given judgment is generated by conflict among the funded results of previous judgments. In Professor Dewey's example of the moving blur, it is obvious that the questions which he asks about it would not be possible unless one had had previous judgments relevant to 'whirling dust,' 'signaling men,' and 'waving trees'; only the funded results of previous judgments could now suggest these possible meanings of the object of perception, the 'moving

[1] Dewey, *How we Think*, p. 102. The student will find this book very suggestive and enlightening. It is an elementary but penetrating discussion of the nature of the thought-process.

blur.' So judgment really emerges from previous judgments. But this does not change Professor Dewey's main contention. It still remains true that the generating situation of every new judgment is a situation involving a question to be answered, a problem to be solved.

And the practical significance of this fact is very great. The mind that is constantly meeting problems is the mind that is intellectually alive. It is therefore no cause for pessimism that the solution of one problem ends in the creation of other problems to be solved; this only means that the work of intelligence is apparently unending. Puzzle-headedness is indicative of a healthy intellectual growth, if the problems concerned are worth puzzling over; and in any case, it is indicative of a certain sort of intellectual activity. One very good test of intellectual vigor is to be found in the number and persistency of the problems with which one is confronted, provided the problems are significant problems and not idle fancies or empty dreams. If one is to grow in intellectual stature, one must meet and solve problems.[1]

§ 6. *Growth of knowledge*

Growth of knowledge means the building up of a *system* of knowledge, that is, making judgments more and more consistent with each other and noting their interconnections. The rays of light, for example, which have little if any specific meaning in the dawning of consciousness gradually assume a more definite significance as the child grows and at last come to signify definite objects, such as the lamp on the table or the moon in the heavens. The

1 Incidentally, it may be noted that, if what is said above is in principle sound, the intellectual value of a book or a course of study may be sought largely in the number and type of problems issuing from it.

experiences have become more orderly by growing more definite and precise; systematization of meanings has taken place. The various judgments of the youth are more consistent and interrelated than are those of the child, and those of the mature individual still more so. In the experience of humanity writ large in the historical process the same truth is illustrated. Every science, as we have seen, is a systematic arrangement of bits of information concerning the environment; and as it becomes more scientific the systematic character of its information becomes more marked. Growth in scientific knowledge, that is, is identical with making that knowledge more and more coherent, more and more interconnected. Now this is precisely what we should expect to be the case, since knowledge of our environment comes through judgment. For one of the fundamental features of judgment, as we have seen above, is systematization or synthesis; and it is therefore inevitable that progress in the acquisition of knowledge should mean, on the one side, greater systematization.

But there is another side to the process which must not be overlooked. Growth of knowledge means, not only the development of a system, but also the expansion of the circle of knowledge. The individual, as he grows, not only systematizes his judgments but he also adds to his stock of information. A science, as it develops, enlarges the boundaries of its field endlessly as well as orders and arranges the results obtained. But, once more, this is precisely in accordance with the nature of judgment. Judgment always converges towards some problem or novelty. It is concerned with the new as much as with the old. New facts are through judgment brought into relation to the already known, and the boundaries of knowledge are extended in consequence; the new facts are ordered in the light of that which is known, while that which is known is expanded, and it may even be reshaped, so as to make room within the total system for the newly acquired information. Progress in knowledge is thus inevitably the interpretation of new aspects of the environment in the light of an ever-expanding and self-modifying system of knowledge.

And here, once more, be it noted, we are confronted by a fact of far-reaching significance. For it is a fact that is fundamental to all discussion of the relation between radicalism and conservatism in whatever field of human endeavor. Thinking is both radical and conservative; it is always interested in conserving achieved results and yet, on the other hand, it is persistently in search of the undiscovered. The claims of both the old and the novel it recognizes fully and tests impartially; and it willingly bows to those claims which stand its tests. But each is tried in the light of the other; the radicalism of reason is forced to weigh with all due deliberation the claims of its conservatism, and *vice versa.* Do we not here have the key to the age-old controversy? The old is not necessarily the best, though the fact that it is old may weigh in its favor; and its claims cannot be ignored. Nor is the novel necessarily mere fantasy and illusion; but it must show itself worthy of acceptance, and the trial of its claims is all the severer if it is in conflict with the old. Such seems to be the verdict of reason.

§ 7. *Summary of chapter*

Judgments have an objective reference in the sense that each judgment is an interpretation of some part of the environment. Furthermore, judgments are sharable between mind and mind. Every judgment is analytical-synthetical, analytical in so far as it discovers parts or aspects of the environment and synthetical in so far as it classifies and organizes these parts into wholes. Judgments are factual in so far as they aim merely to describe existent aspects of the environment; they are value-judgments in so far as they undertake to appreciate or evaluate the environment. Any given judgment emerges out of the funded results of previous judgments through conflict and doubt. Knowledge grows by means of the discovery of new facts and of systematization of the new and the old. Growth in knowledge is growth in systematic arrangement of judgments, that is, the removal of inconsistencies and the discovery of new interrelations among judgments.

APPENDIX TO CHAPTER VII

One interesting, and very enlightening, side of the historical development of modern philosophy touches upon the problem hinted at in the first section of this chapter concerning the possibility of the mind's acquiring knowledge of objects. A brief reference to some of the high points in the historical controversy may be valuable for those who wish to pursue the matter further.

It is easy to see that the problem is precisely that which confronted Locke when he drew his sharp distinction between 'ideas' and 'objects' as noted in the preceding chapter. If 'ideas' are in the mind and different from objects, then a difficulty immediately arises in the form of the question: Do we know ideas or objects? If it is said that we know only ideas, then it obviously follows that objects lie beyond the scope of knowledge; if we know objects directly, then 'ideas' are rather useless ornaments apparently. Locke sensed the difficulty here involved in his sundering of ideas and objects, but he never squarely faced it. It gave his successors, however, particularly Berkeley, Hume, and Kant, great concern. Berkeley argued that the only way out of the difficulty was baldly to identify objects with 'ideas' and to hold that all objects, "the choir of heaven and furniture of the earth," are nothing but "collections of ideas." This led him to his famous theory of idealism as expressed in the phrase "to be is to be perceived"—that is, the doctrine that existence means being present to a mind. Hume, for his part, could find no way out of the difficulty at all, and ended in a sort of scepticism or subjectivism; that is, he frankly admitted that we can know nothing but our impressions and ideas and therefore all knowledge about the environment reduces to probability. Kant tries to take a middle course between the idealism of Berkeley and the scepticism of Hume, though with doubtful success. He denies, with Hume, that we can ever attain knowledge of objects as they actually and really are in themselves; but he is not willing to agree with Berkeley that we know only 'ideas.' His constructive suggestion is that we know something (called by him 'phenomena' or 'appearances') which is other than mere ideas and yet is not the real environment; and so he seems to be in danger of falling between two stools. Kant, however, suggests a way out of the difficulty, even though he does not pursue it very persistently. This suggestion of Kant's Hegel took up and developed in dead earnest. It was to the effect that the way out of the difficulty is the way we have followed in the text, namely, through denial of the separation between mind and objects from which the difficulty arises; in other words, the solution of the problem that Hegel offers is a denial that the problem is a real problem. This way out is not all smooth sailing, since the fact of error and illusion stand in the way of it. But, whatever other difficulties it may lead into, it at least gets around the impasse into which the separation between mind and environment had brought Hume, and into which it inevitably leads. So later thinkers have generally followed Hegel's suggestion here, though these other difficulties lying along this route are still troublesome and are much in debate between contemporary realists and idealists.

A word on the classical literature of the controversy may not be amiss. Berkeley stated the essence of his argument in the first thirty-three sections of his *Principles of Human Knowledge;* a critical review of this argument will be found in Perry, *Present Philosophical Tendencies,* Chapter VI, particularly pp. 122 ff. Hume's views are developed in his *Treatise of Human Nature,*

Book I; the fourth Part is devoted especially to the difficulties he feels in connection with the problem, and these he summarizes in the last section. The works of Kant and Hegel are too difficult for the beginner, and so the commentaries here must be largely depended upon. Any history of philosophy (such as that by Thilly, or Rogers, or Weber) will give general information concerning their views. For the details of Kant's thesis and the elaborate arguments by which he supports it the *Critique of Pure Reason* must be consulted; Watson's *Selections from Kant* contains a good translation of the salient passages. Hegel's discussion of the problem is embedded in his exceedingly difficult *Phenomenology of Mind* and *Logic*. These are, of course, impossible for the beginner, but something of their content may be learned from the commentaries. Caird's *Hegel* is one of the best of these. The author has tried to simplify Hegel's position on the special problem here under consideration in his *Thought and Reality in Hegel's System*, Chapter I. The opening chapters of Russell's *The Problems of Philosophy* offer a recent elementary survey of the problem.

Chapter VII. Questions and Exercises

1. Explain fully and illustrate the objective reference of judgment.

2. 'This machine needs oiling.' Show how this judgment is at once analytical and synthetical.

3. Distinguish between factual-judgments and value-judgments, and illustrate each type.

4. What is meant by the statement that judgment arises out of a doubt-situation? Illustrate. Show how any such situation presupposes previous judgment. What bearing has this upon the function of problems in the development of intelligence?

5. Indicate the two main aspects of the growth of knowledge as outlined in the text. Give an example in illustration.

6. Outline the main points developed in Dewey, *How We Think*, Part II, Chapter VIII.

CHAPTER VIII

THE INTELLECTUAL ENTERPRISE: ITS CERTAINTY

It is an ordinary fact of experience that some of our judgments are true while others are erroneous. If I assert that all material bodies gravitate, my judgment is commonly accepted as true; if, on the other hand, I hold that all men are trustworthy, I make a judgment which by common consent is erroneous. Furthermore, some of our judgments are more certain than others. We are certain of the judgment concerning gravitating bodies; but of the judgment that the weather will clear tomorrow or that the train will arrive at the time scheduled we are not equally certain. When we are certain of the truth or error of a judgment we say that we know or have knowledge; those judgments of whose truth or error we are not certain do not strictly speaking fall within the field of knowledge, but constitute what we ordinarily call beliefs. These distinctions between true and erroneous judgments and between knowledge and belief give rise to certain perplexing problems which it is our purpose in this chapter briefly to study. We shall consider these problems under three questions: (1) What do we mean by truth and error? (2) What tests may we employ to distinguish between judgments that are true and judgments that are erroneous? and, (3) What is the relation between knowledge and belief? These three questions we shall take up in the order given.

§ 1. *The meaning of truth and error*

There is a confusion in the popular usage of the terms 'truth' and 'error' arising from the fact that the terms have various meanings. It is therefore necessary that we define precisely the meaning in which the terms are to be employed in this discussion and to keep this definition clearly in mind throughout the discussion. Otherwise confusion is inevitable.

Preliminary to this definition let us recall what was said in the preceding chapter concerning the objective reference of judgments. Every judgment, it was there pointed out, is an interpretation of a certain environmental situation. If one judges that the waving object yonder is a man signaling, the judgment has reference to a definite environmental situation — the object seen in the distance. And this is true of every judgment; always there is the 'something,' judged about. Now by 'truth' as the term is used in this discussion is meant agreement between the judgment and the environmental situation of which it purports to be an interpretation; by 'error' is meant disagreement between the judgment and the relevant environmental situation. In other words, a judgment is true in so far as it agrees with its object; it is erroneous in so far as it fails to agree. The judgment, 'All material bodies gravitate,' agrees with its object and is therefore true, since material bodies do in objective fact obey the law of gravitation; but the judgment, 'All men are trustworthy,' does not agree with its object and so is erroneous, since there unfortunately exist some men in whom we cannot with assurance place our confidence. In the twilight I see at a distance something which I judge to be a horse: my judgment, 'There is a horse yonder,' is true or erroneous according as the 'something' is or is not an actual horse standing there in the relations I suppose it to be. If the 'something' is a horse actually existent, then my judgment is true; if the 'something' turns out to be a bush or a cow, then my judgment is so far erroneous. Thus to the question, What do we mean by truth and error? the answer is: Correspondence or lack of correspondence between the judgment in question and the actual environmental situation judged about. And this meaning of the terms should be kept definitely to the fore in the following discussion.[1]

It is interesting to note in this connection that a given judgment may be partly true and partly erroneous. 'That ugly man yonder is the friend of my brother-in-law' would be an example of such a judgment in case the man in question were actually ugly but not a friend of my brother-in-law. Of course, if one were to insist that this judgment is really two judgments — 'That man is ugly' and 'That man is a friend of my brother-in-law' — and that every such judgment is similarly resoluble into a number of simple judgments, then one might perhaps argue that every judgment is either true or erroneous and that no judgment could be both. This would be a questionable position to take, however, involving as it apparently does a confusion be-

[1] The above definition of the term 'truth' must in particular be distinguished from another meaning of the term which is commonly attached to it. We not infrequently mean by truth that feeling of certainty which accompanies a judgment of which one is fully convinced. This is the meaning of the term which we have in mind when we say, as we often do, that whatever one accepts as true is *for him* true. Thus, for example, a traveller on the desert sees an oasis and dies in the conviction that an oasis was there in front of him; in this sense of the term, his judgment might be called true even though what he saw was only a mirage. This meaning of the term 'truth' is very different from that defined in the text and should be kept distinct from it. In this meaning truth is merely a psychological feeling of certainty or conviction, and need have no objective significance at all. The delusions of an insane man might be called true in this meaning of the term — in so far, that is, as his delusions could be brought under judgments.

tween the judgment as an act of thought and the expression of the judgment in language. The expression of the judgment — called in logic a 'proposition' — is undeniably complex; but the question whether the judgment as an act of interpretation is so seems decidedly debatable. At any rate, it must be realized that most of our judgments are such that they cannot be expressed except in complex propositions, and as such they may be partly true and partly erroneous.

§ 2. *Tests of truth and error*

How do we proceed to test the truth or error of a given judgment? If a judgment is true in so far as it agrees with the relevant environmental situation and erroneous in so far as it fails so to agree, what tests can we apply to determine its agreement or non-agreement? This is the most important question in connection with the general problem of the validity of judgments. Unless we can determine when judgments agree or fail to agree with the objective situation judged about, we are still far from a satisfactory solution of the problem of truth. The information that truth lies in such agreement and error in such non-agreement carries us only a very little way in our inquiry concerning the validity of the intellectual enterprise. We want to know whether, and how, this agreement or non-agreement can be determined. And to this inquiry we now turn.

In the history of reflection on the problem three main tests have been proposed. The first is *obviousness,* and the theory which advances this test is called the self-evidence theory. According to this theory true judgments bear on their own face, so to speak, evidence of their verity and to doubt them is impossible. The second test proposed is that of *satisfactory working,* and the theory proposing this test is known as the pragmatic theory. The thesis of the pragmatist is that true judgments are those which work satisfactorily within the body of our experience. The third test is that of *consistency,* and the theory advocating this test is called the coherence theory. According to it the truth of a judgment is to be determined by its consistency with other judgments; a judgment which harmonizes with the main body of our knowledge is to be accepted as true, while a judgment that contradicts the main body of our knowledge is to be rejected as erroneous. Let us study these tests separately.

(1) SELF-EVIDENCE THEORY. According to the self-evidence theory the main test of the truth of judgments is obviousness or indubitability. There are some judgments, it holds, which are so obviously true that they cannot be doubted, and these judgments must be accepted as true. Examples are: the judgment that the moon is shining when one actually experiences it, the mathematical axiom that a straight line is the shortest distance between two given points, and the like. In addition to these judgments which are thus self-evidently true, the upholder of this theory is willing to admit that there are other judgments which are not obviously true but of whose truth we may still be certain; these are judgments which may by obvious logical steps be connected with those judgments whose truth is indubitable. Thus, for example, the mathematician by reasoning from axioms — as in geometry — can show that certain judgments whose truth is not obvious are still necessarily true. But obviousness is the test of our starting-point and of each step in the process of reasoning. It is the foundation, then, upon which all of our true knowledge — knowledge, that is, which is known to be true — is

built; it is the final criterion of truth. Such is the theory of self-evidence.

Among modern philosophers Descartes has perhaps laid greatest stress on this theory; though the view has been advocated by others, notably by Locke. In drawing up a code of rules for the guidance of his reason, the very first rule Descartes set down was to accept nothing as true unless it were self-evidently so. "The first rule was, never to receive anything as a truth which I did not clearly know to be such; that is, to avoid haste and prejudice, and not to comprehend anything more in my judgments than that which should present itself so clearly and so distinctly to my mind that I should have no occasion to entertain a doubt of it."[1] Indubitability is the test of truth.

(2) THE PRAGMATIC THEORY. According to the pragmatic theory a judgment is true when it works satisfactorily in experience, that is, when it proves to be both intellectually and practically satisfying. What difference, intellectual or practical, does the judgment in question make in my experience? — this is the question to be asked in testing the value of a judgment. Utility is the criterion of truth. Two aspects of the theory should be differentiated in order clearly to understand its basal tenets. In the first place, the theory holds that a true judgment is one which works satisfactorily in experience, and its utility is the only test of its truth. In the second place, truth is held to be something that *happens* to a judgment, a judgment is *made* true by being verified and apart from its verification it cannot in any intelligible sense be said to be either true or erroneous.

[1] *Discourse on Method,* Part II. This *Discourse* is an admirable discussion, as well as example, of precise and rigorous thinking. It should be read in its entirety. See also Locke's *Essay Concerning Human Understanding,* Book IV, especially Chapters II and V–VII.

The pragmatic theory is of recent development in philosophical thought, though it is said by its proponents to be merely a new name for old ways of thinking. The theory is most closely associated with the name of Professor William James who, perhaps more than any other thinker, is responsible for its early formulation. According to Professor James the way to test the truth of any given judgment is to ask, if it be true, "what concrete difference will its being true make in any one's actual life? How will the truth be realised? What experiences will be different from those which would obtain if the belief were false? What, in short, is the truth's cash-value in experiential terms?" And a little later in the same context he states positively that a true judgment is one which "is only the expedient in the way of our thinking, just as the 'right' is only the expedient in the way of our behaving."[1] And in these words Professor James has expressed the first side of the pragmatic doctrine of truth: utility is the criterion of truth. The other side of the doctrine he puts in the following emphatic phraseology: "Truth *happens* to an idea. It *becomes* true, is *made* true by events. Its verity *is* in fact an event, a process: the process namely of its verifying itself, its veri-*fication.* Its validity is the process of its valid-*ation*. . . . Truth for us is simply a collective name for verification-processes, just as health, wealth, strength, etc., are names for other processes connected with life, and also pursued because it pays to pursue them. Truth is *made,* just as health, wealth, and strength are made, in the course of experience."[2] Professor Dewey, the leading living exponent of the pragmatic theory, says essentially the same thing in

[1] *Pragmatism,* pp. 200, 222. *The Meaning of Truth* contains Professor James's most detailed statement of the pragmatic theory.

[2] *Pragmatism,* pp. 201, 218. The italics are all those of Professor James.

other words: "The true means the verified and means nothing else."[1] This is the other side of the pragmatic doctrine: a judgment is made true by being verified, apart from verification truth is a meaningless term.

(3) THE COHERENCE THEORY. The coherence theory holds that the test of a judgment's truth is to be sought in the consistency between the judgment whose truth is in question and other relevant judgments. According to it a true judgment is one which is consistent with or is implied by the body of our knowledge, and this consistency is an index to the judgment's verity. To illustrate: the judgment that 'all material bodies gravitate' is known to be true, because it is consistent with our general knowledge about bodies as material; while the judgment that 'all men are trustworthy' is known to be erroneous, because it is inconsistent with the rest of our knowledge about human beings. The consistency upon which the coherence theory lays emphasis is of two sorts: consistency among judgments about abstract or formal relations and consistency among judgments about concrete or factual situations. The first of these we may, for brevity's sake, call *logical* consistency and the second *factual* consistency. A brief consideration of each of these types will help us to understand better the main characteristics of the theory.

(*a*) *Logical consistency.* This sort of consistency is illustrated most clearly in purely deductive reasoning. Simple examples of it are the following propositions in their logical interrelation: 'All X's are Y's' is consistent with 'No X's are non-Y's' and 'Some Y's are all of the X's'; it is inconsistent with 'No X's are Y's' and 'Some

[1] *Reconstruction in Philosophy*, p. 160. This book is a very interesting and suggestive survey of the field of philosophy.

X's are not Y's.' The first three propositions are not identical, and yet their meanings are so involved, the judgments they formulate are so interwoven, that they are consistent with each other; they stand or fall together. But the last two propositions express judgments which are antagonistic to the preceding ones, so that if the one set of judgments is true the other set is necessarily false; the two sets are inconsistent with each other. The same sort of consistency is illustrated in the traditional syllogism of formal logic, in the more elaborate symbolism of the mathematical logic, in the long chains of ordinary geometrical or mathematical reasoning, and in all types of deductive reasoning. If we agree for the purposes of this discussion to call this sort of consistency 'implication,' then the coherence theory holds that if any judgment, X, be true whatever is 'implied' by X is also and for that reason true.

(*b*) *Factual consistency.* By factual consistency is meant the agreement between any judgment and a definite environmental situation. The most common illustration of this sort of consistency is found in what is generally called inductive reasoning. Yesterday the river was low and the water clear; while to-day the water has risen several feet, is muddy, and is laden with drift-wood. There is an agreement between these observations and the judgment that at some very recent time a heavy rain fell within the radius of the watershed drained by the stream. This is a case of factual consistency. It is illustrated copiously in the procedure of the inductive sciences, such as physics, chemistry, biology, and the like. If we call this sort of consistency 'inference,' then the coherence theory may be stated in the following terms: if X, Y, and Z, as definite aspects of the environment, involve the 'inference' that a given judgment, W, is true, then judgment, W, is known to be true.

Summarizing the main features of the coherence theory brought out by this discussion of it, we may say that the coherence theory holds that any judgment which is *implied* by knowledge or is *inferable* from knowledge is known thereby to be a true judgment. Or, more shortly, any judgment reached by implication or inference on the basis of the funded results of other judgments is to be accepted as true. Consistency with the known is a mark of truth; the lack of consistency is the mark either of error or of emptiness.

In modern thought the coherence theory is most closely associated with the name of Hegel among classical philosophers. More recently the theory has been elaborated and defended by the British philosophers, Bradley and Bosanquet, and in this country by Josiah Royce.[1]

§ 3. *Value of the self-evidence, pragmatic and coherence theories*

There are difficulties in each of the theories summarized above. We now turn to a consideration of these difficulties for the purpose of dealing critically with the claims of the conflicting views.

(1) OBJECTIONS TO THE SELF-EVIDENCE THEORY. There are in the main two objections to the self-evidence theory. In the first place, many judgments generally admitted to be true are not obviously so, and consequently obviousness cannot be admitted to be the *only* test of truth. In the

[1] Josiah Royce (1855–1916) at the time of his death was professor at Harvard University. His writings have greatly influenced American thought in many fields. In point of view he is closely allied to Bradley and Bosanquet. Like them, he was much under the influence of Hegel.

second place, many judgments which were at one time or another supposed to be obviously true have turned out later to be erroneous.

(a) *Obviousness not the sole test.* The first objection, that many judgments generally accepted as true are not obviously so, does seem to have considerable weight. The judgment that all material bodies are gravitating, for example, is generally held to be true; but it is not obviously so. The fact is, long reflection was necessary before the truth was discovered. And there are innumerable judgments like this one — true and known to be true, but not self-evidently true. And this fact seems to be sufficient to establish the conclusion that, even granting that self-evidence or obviousness is a test of truth, it cannot be regarded as the only test. We are constantly accepting as true many judgments that do not bear on their face any guarantee of their verity. This objection, however, is not an adequate criticism of the self-evidence theory. For the upholder of that theory can evade the objection by pointing out that he does not contend that *all* judgments known to be true must be self-evidently so. The other side of his theory must not be forgotten, namely, that certain judgments may be known to be true by being shown to be obviously connected with other judgments that in themselves are obvious. This reply is not wholly satisfactory. It tends to identify 'obviousness' with 'consistency' and so passes from the test of self-evidence to that of coherence.

(b) *Obviousness not an adequate test.* A more fundamental objection to the self-evidence theory is that many judgments at one time accepted as obviously true have on further reflection been discovered to be erroneous. It was once regarded as obviously true that the earth is flat, that the earth is at the centre of the universe with the sun and stars revolving around it in circular orbits, and that if the earth were round one travelling around its periphery must sooner or later plunge off into empty space; but such judgments are now known to be false in spite of their apparent obviousness. Even the axioms of mathematics, such as, 'parallel lines cannot meet,' are many of them now seen to rest upon certain general assumptions apart from which they are not true however obvious and indubitable they appear. The fact is that *all* judgments which we are convinced are true seem obvious to us, and if obviousness were the test of their verity we could never be mistaken; all judgments believed would by that fact be true. To contend that obviousness or clearness is the test of truth, Hobbes [1] says, "is metaphorical, and therefore not fitted for an argument; for whenever a man feels no doubt at all he will pretend to this clearness, and he will be as ready to affirm that of which he feels no doubt, as the man who possesses perfect knowledge. This clearness may well then be the reason why a man holds and defends with obstinacy some opinion, but it cannot tell him with certainty that the opinion is true." Obviousness by itself alone is, thus, not an adequate test of truth; with reference to any particular obvious judgment the question is always pertinent whether it is true even though obvious.

(2) Objections to the pragmatic theory. In attempting to estimate the value of the pragmatic theory it is best to consider its two aspects separately.

(a) *Truth as the product of verification.* The pragmatist's contention that truth happens to a judgment in the course of experience, that a judgment is "*made* true by

[1] Thomas Hobbes (1588–1679) was interested chiefly in social philosophy. His greatest work, *Leviathan*, is an elaborate discussion of problems of political philosophy, and exerted a wide influence upon the political thought of the time.

events," cannot stand if the view of truth taken above in the first section of this chapter is correct. That the verity of a judgment "is in fact an event, a process: the process namely of its verifying itself, its veri-*fication*," as Professor James holds, is directly antagonistic to the thesis that any given judgment may be true whether it is known to be true or not. Of course, the contradiction here must be resolved in the light of the relevant facts. And it does seem to be a meaningful statement that the judgment, 'Mars is inhabited by intelligent beings,' is now either true or erroneous despite the fact that we cannot know which it is. And if this is so, then its verity does not depend upon our verification of it. A judgment's being true, then, is independent of our knowledge that it is true. This aspect of the pragmatic theory must therefore apparently be given up.

(b) *Satisfactory working as the test of truth.* The objection most generally raised with reference to the pragmatic test of truth turns upon its vagueness. To say that a judgment is true when it works satisfactorily in experience is to say nothing precise unless 'satisfactory working' and 'experience' are further defined. What precisely is meant by working satisfactorily, and whose experience is in question? If by 'working satisfactorily' is meant simply producing agreeable consequences, then it is clear that many judgments which work satisfactorily are nevertheless erroneous and many true judgments do not work satisfactorily. Again, if by 'experience' is meant individual experience, then by the pragmatic test one and the same judgment may be both completely true and completely erroneous, since one and the same judgment may work satisfactorily in the experience of one individual and not in that of another. Pragmatists generally recognize these as possible objections to their view, but they insist that the above definitions of 'satisfactory working' and 'experience' are not what they mean by those terms. By experience, they say, is meant socialized experience, experience 'in the long run'; and by working satisfactorily is meant producing consequences that are intellectually as well as practically satisfying.[1] If, however, experience is enlarged to include the experiences of all individuals and working satisfactorily is defined so as to embrace logical and factual consistency as well as agreeableness of consequences, then the pragmatic test apparently differs only verbally from the coherence test. For now 'utility' virtually means satisfying the demands of human reason for consistency, which is precisely identical with coherence. Thus it would seem that utility is either an unsatisfactory test of the verity of judgments, or it differs from coherence by such a narrow margin that the difference is hardly distinguishable.

However it is well to retain the pragmatist's notion of workability as a test of truth because of the emphasis which it places upon empirical results. Judgments that are true will in some sense work satisfactorily within experience, even if it be very questionable whether judgments that work are on that account true. And so the insistence upon the necessity of taking into consideration the concrete consequences of judgments in our search for truth is important; it at least fixes attention upon definite situations and starts us in the right direction. Particularly in the field of conduct and religion is the value of the pragmatic test felt. We must perform moral acts and we must entertain religious beliefs in circumstances where doubt is inevitable; and in

[1] In this connection see the discussion of what the pragmatist means by the 'practical' by Professor Dewey in *Essays in Experimental Logic,* Chapters XII, XIII.

so acting and believing consequences are of great importance. Consequently the suggestion of the pragmatist is a valuable one. If he has not given us a satisfactory standard of truth, he has at least indicated a method by which we may perchance discover how it is prudent for us to act and what it is prudent for us to believe in those cases where we cannot be sure what the truth is. Furthermore, his insistence upon results emphasizes the important bearing which facts have upon the outcome of our quest for truth. And for this emphasis his criterion of truth should be kept in the list as separate and distinct from the others.

(3) Objections to the coherence theory. Like the other two theories of truth, the coherence theory is not without its difficulties. The chief objections to it are perhaps three, which may be put in the form of the following questions: (*a*) Is it not possible to construct a consistent system of erroneous judgments? (*b*) Is it not the case that many judgments, finally accepted as true, are at first inconsistent with judgments generally assumed to be true? (*c*) Is not the coherence theory forced to admit that there is at least one truth which cannot be tested in terms of consistency, namely, the principle of consistency itself? If all of these questions are to be answered in the affirmative, then apparently the criterion of consistency is untenable. Let us notice each of the questions separately.

(a) *Consistency among erroneous judgments.* Is it possible to construct a consistent system of erroneous judgments? This certainly seems possible. One may, for example, if one arbitrarily conceives of a possible world in which space has only two dimensions, build up a system of judgments which are consistent with each other and all of which are false. That is to say, one may construct a geometry of flat-land which, though coherent and consistent, is nevertheless false. Fiction may be consistent with itself. But does this show that consistency cannot be a test of truth? The upholder of the coherence theory maintains that it does not, but on the contrary tends to establish his contention. In the first place, he argues, the only 'truth' which can be said to attach to judgments within such a system is to be defined precisely in terms of their consistency; the events in *Alice in Wonderland* happen 'truly' only when they happen in such a way as to be in some sense consistent with the way in which other events in the same world are supposed to happen. A geometry of flat-land can be tested as regards its verity only by appeal to the consistency existing among the various propositions that make it up. Truth in a fictional system means nothing but consistency. In the second place, the advocate of the doctrine of coherence insists, we call these fictional systems erroneous only because they are in the end inconsistent with other judgments that we make about the world we call real. Any imaginary system of judgments is finally tested by reference to its consistency with those judgments that are concerned with the real nature of the world. The geometry of flat-land may not involve us in inconsistency so long as it is concerned with mere *logical* consistency built upon the arbitrary assumption that space is only of two dimensions; and in so far it may be called true. But such a geometry is apparently not *factually* consistent with the rest of our knowledge about our physical environment; and so we call it arbitrary, imaginary, erroneous. So it turns out that the wildest flights of imagination are checked by the test of consistency: the system of judgments resulting can be called true only to the extent that they exemplify an internal consistency among themselves, and they are 'fictional' to the extent that they are inconsistent with the main body of our judgments about the environment.[1]

(b) *Judgments, inconsistent with generally accepted knowledge, finally called true.* It often happens in the course of the development of knowledge that judgments which are apparently inconsistent with other generally accepted judgments are at last admitted to be true. The judgment that the earth is round when first proposed seemed to contradict other supposedly true judgments concerning the nature of the earth; but in spite of that fact it was finally accepted as true. Likewise, the judgment that the earth swings in an orbit about the sun, now commonly admitted to be true, was at first contradictory of traditional beliefs. Does this fact prove that consistency cannot be a test of truth? The advocate of the coherence theory argues, and correctly it would seem, that it proves precisely the contrary. It shows that consistency is the main test of truth. For, be it noted, such judgments as those mentioned in illustration above are accepted as true because they introduce into the main body of judgments a greater degree of consistency than was possible through the acceptance of the judgments which they contradicted. The rotundity of the earth harmonized better than did its flatness with the other judgments gained by man of its nature, and so the principle of consistency forced man to accept the judgment that the earth is round as a true judgment. Likewise, the helio-centric (sun-at-center) conception of the solar system was substituted for the geo-centric (earth-at-center) because the former view was consistent, while the latter view was inconsistent, with growing knowledge of the nature of the sun and the planets and their rela-

[1] In this connection it is interesting to inquire concerning the test we apply to the 'truth' of dreams. In last analysis, it appears to be consistency (or the reverse) with our waking experiences.

tion to each other. And this can be shown to be the case in every situation where a judgment, though contradictory of the traditional, is finally accepted as true. Thus the fact that judgments are frequently accepted as true in spite of their inconsistency with traditional knowledge tends to support, rather than to disprove, the coherence theory. The final acceptance of such judgments depends upon their capacity to introduce into the main body of judgments a consistency not obtainable apart from them. Consistency among judgments is thus the dynamic element within the growth of knowledge.[1]

(c) *Principle of consistency cannot be tested by itself.* The coherence theory proceeds upon this assumption: that two inconsistent or contradictory judgments cannot at the same time be true. And the objection is: this truth at least, namely, that inconsistent judgments cannot both be true, cannot be tested by the criterion of consistency. This objection to the coherence theory seems to be of fundamental importance. Of course, the supporter of the theory may reply that, unless such an assumption is made, then no criterion of truth is possible. And this reply is correct, but largely irrelevant. The fact still remains that the assumption cannot be tested by the principle of consistency itself. There thus seems to be one truth at least that falls beyond the reach of the coherence theory, and this means that consistency is not the *sole* test of truth. We seem here to be driven back to the tests of obviousness and utility: it appears obvious that judgments which are inconsistent cannot be true together, and unless such an assumption is made then the whole structure of science falls to the ground. The principle of consistency is both obvious and useful.

(d) *Summary of section.* The conclusion of the whole

[1] See section 5 of the preceding chapter.

matter, thus, seems to be that in our actual reasoning we employ all three of the tests above proposed. Obviousness is often the starting-point of our inquiries and we frequently return to it as the test of our inferences; though, it cannot be denied, many judgments that appear obvious turn out to be erroneous, and so we cannot say that self-evidence alone is a sufficient test of truth. Utility is, likewise, of invaluable assistance in distinguishing true from erroneous judgments; though here again we have a test which is not by any means infallible and which, apart from very careful definition, is not sufficiently precise even to be of very great practical value. And an attempt to define utility as a test of validity leads us directly into the coherence doctrine which therefore would seem to be fundamental. This is the test which science always employs in determining the value of its theories, though the test of self-evidence is indispensable here in so far as these theories are traced to 'facts' which are accepted without question as a result of direct observation and analysis and in so far as the principle of consistency itself ultimately rests upon obviousness. So all three of our tests are inextricably bound up with each other.

§ 4. *Belief and knowledge*

When our judgments are proved to be true or erroneous we are said to possess knowledge. There are many judgments, however, which cannot be tested completely and which constitute what we ordinarily call beliefs. What then is the relation between belief and knowledge? and how may we test beliefs? To a brief consideration of these questions we turn in conclusion.

(1) Two types of belief. There are two meanings of belief which, for purposes of this discussion, should be

clearly distinguished from each other. In the first place, there is belief based upon knowledge and logically linked with it. Every scientific hypothesis before it is definitely proved is belief in this meaning of the term. Franklin's guess that lightning is identical with electricity, for example, was a belief until he succeeded in establishing its validity; it grew directly out of what he knew about lightning and electricity. Any belief which can be argued about on the basis of what is known is an example of this type. In the second place, there is a type of belief which is not logically connected with knowledge. The belief that the inhabitants of the planet Mars have a language with forty characters in its alphabet would, if one could imagine it seriously entertained by any mind, be an example of this type. Such a belief is wholly sundered from the present body of our knowledge and has no conceivable relation to it. This type of belief is not ordinarily entertained by a normal mind, except in those cases where belief is based upon some supposedly infallible and unquestionable authority.

(2) TESTS OF THE VALIDITY OF BELIEFS. In discussing the tests of the validity of beliefs one must have clearly in mind the type of beliefs one is dealing with. Beliefs of the type first defined above are subject to the ordinary tests of all judgments, since they are nothing but judgments whose validity is still in question and since they are logically bound up with the body of knowledge. In the nature of the case, no belief could be self-evident; it would then be knowledge. But the test of coherence certainly applies here; at least the probability of the belief may be established. In those cases where the belief so far outruns knowledge that the criterion of coherence cannot be applied, the pragmatic test would have to be de-

pended upon to determine the worth of the belief. That beliefs of this type are subject to the ordinary criteria of validity is evident when we consider that growth in knowledge really consists in transforming such beliefs into knowledge; the body of knowledge expands precisely through the validation or disproof of such beliefs.

Beliefs in the second sense above defined, however, are different. Strictly speaking, their validity cannot be tested and the acceptance of them has no logical compulsion. We do make tests of them in practice, because we cannot do otherwise; but when we do so, we do so by applying precisely the tests of ordinary judgments. In other words, we insist in practice upon weighing the value of such beliefs and we do so by converting them into, or treating them as if they were, beliefs logically linked with our knowledge. That the language of the inhabitants of Mars has forty characters in its alphabet has no point of contact with our present knowledge, and strictly speaking its validity cannot be determined by us. If, however, one insists upon seriously entertaining such a belief we regard him as abnormal, that is, we virtually say that the lack of coherence between the belief and our knowledge of our world makes it impossible for any but an abnormal mind to accept the judgment or belief as true. Thus in practice we condemn such a belief, and our condemnation is based upon the test of coherence. In cases of beliefs based upon authority we estimate their value in terms of the authority upon which they rest; that is, we bring the authority into question and test its validity by the application of our ordinary standards. Thus, in those cases where beliefs are sharply sundered from the body of our knowledge either we treat them as purely arbitrary and lacking logical compulsion, or we deal with them as if they were beliefs of the first type.

What, then, is the reasonable attitude with reference to beliefs? It is not unreasonable to entertain beliefs linked with knowledge. On the contrary, reason is always entertaining such beliefs; in fact it is through the trying out of beliefs that reason develops its results into the form of knowledge. Beliefs of this type therefore are essential aspects of judgments. They are essential aspects of judgments, however, only in the sense that they point the way to further inquiry and investigation. Whether they point in the right direction remains always to be determined by this further inquiry; the checking up of beliefs is the other side of the intellectual enterprise. Therefore all such beliefs must be held only provisionally as hypotheses, subject to revision — and, if need be, even to rejection — in the light of advancing knowledge. Beliefs sundered from knowledge are arbitrary, and one entertains them at one's risk.

Chapter VIII. Questions and Exercises

1. Explain what is meant by the statement that a judgment is true when it agrees with its object.

2. Explain and illustrate each of the three tests of truth mentioned in the text. Indicate the objections to each test.

3. Which of the tests proposed seems to you most immediately applicable in each of the following cases?

   X voted the Republican ticket at the last election.
   The soul is immortal.
   The earth moves around the sun in an elliptical orbit.
   Caesar crossed the Rubicon and was finally murdered on the Ides of March.

4. Is it possible to construct a completely consistent system of erroneous judgments? Discuss.

5. Indicate the distinction between belief and knowledge. How may the validity of beliefs be tested?

6. Summarize Russell: *The Problems of Philosophy,* Chapters XII and XIII, and compare with the account given in the text.

7. Outline the main points in the rules for correct thinking formulated by Descartes in his *Discourse on Method,* Part II.

8. Summarize the pragmatic theory of truth as outlined by William James in his book, *Pragmatism,* Chapter VI. Compare with the view developed by Dewey, *Essays in Experimental Logic,* Chapter XII.

9. Summarize, and briefly discuss, the points stated by Locke in the *Essay Concerning Human Understanding,* Book IV, Chapter II, sections 1–7.

CHAPTER IX

THE ASSUMPTION OF INTELLIGENCE: CAUSALITY

In the three chapters immediately preceding we have been concerned with the problems that arise in connection with the nature and certainty of the intellectual enterprise. We have seen that the intellectual enterprise may be defined in terms of judgment, and we have studied the tests or criteria that have been proposed for distinguishing between true and erroneous judgments. We turn now to a consideration of the assumption upon which the whole intellectual enterprise seems to rest — the assumption, namely, that the events and objects which constitute the environment are tied together in causal connections. Nothing in the environment, so the assumption runs, happens or exists without a cause. The winds blow, water freezes and thaws, vegetation blooms and withers, the earth and the heavenly bodies sweep through the depths of space, life appears and progresses on the earth in manifold forms, generations of organisms are born and grow old and die, nations arise and fall, civilizations flourish and fade away — all in definite causal sequences whether known to the mind of man or not. Some of these causal sequences are known, others are being discovered, and all are within the possible reach of the human mind. The aim of the present chapter is to study some of the more important philosophical questions that arise from this assumption of causality.

§ 1. *The nature of a cause*

The word 'cause' has so many meanings that hopeless confusion will be our lot unless we take pains at the beginning of our study to gain a clear comprehension of the meaning in which we shall understand it. So we must first try to analyze the notion and give to it a precise definition. To this end we shall briefly study the meaning of a causal situation as science conceives it.

One characteristic of our environment is that the things and events that make it up are found to exist within an intricate network of relations. The problem of any given science is to unravel certain aspects of this network of relations, and to find out what objects invariably go together. This constant conjunction of things and events is what science means by a causal situation. And by a cause it means a particular set of things and events which is found invariably to accompany something else, some object or event, called the effect. Thus, the scientific cause of the moving billiard ball is the set of conditions that accompany it — the stroke of the cue, the smoothness of the table, the resiliency of the cushion, etc. As science conceives it, a cause is not something that exerts a force (push or pull) which brings the effect into existence; it is not a sort of secret power which now and again jumps out like a Jack-in-the-box and produces an effect, remaining inactive meanwhile. It is nothing but a certain set of conditions (ordinary things and events) which exist as a supposedly indispensable aspect of another set of conditions called the effect.

If a cause is defined, as is frequently done, as the 'antecedent' set of conditions surrounding the effect, care must be taken that 'antecedent' be not understood in an exclusively temporal sense. It is not necessary that the cause of an event or of an object precede it in time. In the case where friction causes heat, for example, it is fairly clear that friction is not antecedent to the heat in the temporal sense; the two are strictly simultaneous. And the indentation of a cushion caused by a heavy ball resting upon it is in no sense subsequent to its cause. Furthermore, there are numerous cases of a causal situation where time is wholly irrelevant. In the case, for example, where the shape of an object is a cause of its peculiar motion no temporal significance can be attached to the cause-effect relation. So time should be eliminated as an essential item in a causal situation; a cause may be temporally prior to its effect, but it is not necessarily so. It will aid clarity, therefore, if we are to speak of a cause as an 'antecedent' set of conditions, to think of antecedence in logical rather than in temporal terms. A cause is antecedent to its effect more nearly in the sense in which premises are antecedent to a conclusion. We should, consequently, perhaps make our definition of the scientific conception of causation clearer by stating the matter thus: a cause is any set of conditions which we are logically forced to posit as necessary to the existence of another set of conditions known as the effect.

It is important for the student to note that the scientific conception of causation differs from the popular conception in this regard: in the popular conception a cause is supposed to exert a force, to do something, whereas this notion of force is foreign to the scientific view. For the scientist a cause is not an 'agent' or activity which produces an effect; it is merely a set of conditions by which the effect is accompanied and in terms of which the effect can be partially, at least, explained. This is the conception which we shall have in mind henceforth when speaking of causes.

§ 2. *Plurality of causes*

One problem of interest that arises in connection with causality may be put in the form of the question: Does every effect have one, and only one, cause, or may there be more than one cause for any given effect. The problem thus stated is known as the problem of the plurality of causes.

It seems at first glance as if there could be no doubt that an effect may have more than one cause. Death, for example, may be caused in sundry ways — by the ravages of various kinds of disease, by drowning, by strangulation, by electrocution, by a gun-shot wound, and so on indefinitely. Heat may be produced by combustion, by friction, by radiation, and the like. And one might proceed at length with examples illustrating the point. Why, then, should there be any question in the matter? For this reason: in every case where it is said that an effect may be produced by manifold causes, more accurate analysis discloses the fact that such a statement is very doubtful. Death as an abstract occurrence may be variously caused, but a specific instance of death is always traceable to a definite set of conditions: death by drowning is not death by strangulation or electrocution or disease, but is the result of a precise set of conditions describable in set physiological terms. Likewise, heat by combustion is very different from heat by friction so far as its causal conditions are concerned. In other words, a specific case of death and a specific instance of heat each has its special cause; in neither case is there a plurality of causes present. Taken generally, then, and without reference to specific things and events, a plurality of causes is possible. But actual causal situations are always tied to specific things and events, and here analysis shows that there is no plurality of causes; for every set of conditions called an effect there is always another, and only one, set of conditions called the cause.

A cause, however, may be very complex, so complex in fact that it is practically impossible to discover all of its elements and give an itemization of them. This is particularly true where personal responsibility is involved. The firing of a projectile on the battle-front, for example, is an event whose cause involves not only structure of gun, powder, and projectile, but also human purposes reaching beyond the individual gunner into the vast unknown of the policies and prejudices of the warring nations. And so it is often necessary in practice to distinguish *proximate* and *remote* aspects of the total causal situation, otherwise the very complexities of many causal situations would defy analysis. But which aspect of the causal situation should be regarded as proximate and which as remote depends upon, and varies with, the point of view of the inquirer. "Take an inundation as an illustration. Someone has broken the dam, or left open the sluices which were committed to his charge. He is the responsible cause of the damage which the water does. We thus take the two forms of causality together in one phrase, but we cannot ignore the fact that from the physical point of view the water is the principal cause and the release of it at a given point is a subsidiary cause; but that from the legal point of view, which has to do with human acts, it is the breaking of the dam or neglect of the sluice which is the responsible and principal cause. On the same lines run the historical controversies in regard to great events: as Thucydides, in the introduction to his *History of the Peloponnesian War,* raised the question what was the cause of it and what the occasion. To this day we still dispute in the same way about Bismarck's Ems telegram."[1] Despite the practical necessity, however, of distinguishing between principal and subsidiary, or proximate and remote, aspects of the causal situation, it must not be forgotten that it is still one situation with which we are dealing. But it is this practical necessity that gives rise to the notion of a plurality of causes, except where the notion can be explained, as above, in terms of abstract generalization.

§ 3. *Causal pluralism and causal monism*

Closely connected with the problem of the plurality of causes, and constituting in fact another side of the same general question, is the problem of causal pluralism versus causal monism.

(1) STATEMENT OF THE PROBLEM. The number of causal situations in the environment is indefinite and presumably can never be exhaustively known by human beings. Every event has its cause, so at least we necessarily assume, and no complete list of events seems possible. But if one begins with any causal situation one finds that that particular situation is only an aspect of a larger situation, and that of a larger, and so on without any apparent stopping-place. As Schopenhauer[2] remarked, every cause is

[1] W. Windelband, *An Introduction to Philosophy,* 1914, McCabe's translation, p. 132.

[2] Arthur Schopenhauer (1788–1860) started in business as a boy, but he soon found a business career distasteful and entered the teaching profession. For a time he was connected with the University of Berlin while Hegel was there. He met little success as a teacher, became especially embittered against Hegel, whom he called a "windbag of philosophy," retired to Frankfort-on-the-Main where he devoted his time to thinking and writing. Plato and Kant were his favorite philosophical writers. His masterpiece, *The World as Will and Idea* (1819), still stands as the classic exposition of the pessimistic view of life.

itself in turn an effect; one can always, apparently with reason, inquire concerning the cause of a cause. For instance, in a case where heat is caused by friction, the friction itself exists under a definite set of conditions, which, if we undertake to analyze it fully, leads us on to very general physical and chemical laws. But, on the other hand, there is frequently no obvious causal connection among different causal situations. To illustrate: there is a cause why a certain species of fish appears at a given depth of the sea, and there is a cause why a man's hair should be red; but there is no obvious, and apparently no conceivable, causal connection between the existence of the fish at this precise depth and the red hair of the fisherman who goes in search of them. Such considerations as these give rise to the problem whether there are many absolutely independent causal situations in the environment, or only one total causal system of things and events of which all particular instances of causation are incomplete and fragmentary phases. Those who accept the first alternative are called pluralists, and their point of view is that of *causal pluralism.* Those who accept the latter alternative are called monists, their view being known as *causal monism.* We turn now to a statement and a critical estimate of the arguments advanced in support of each of these points of view.

(2) THE CASE OF CAUSAL PLURALISM. Causal pluralism holds that there are many — the number is indefinite — causal situations in our environment, each totally independent causally of all the others. The chief reasons advanced for this position are two. First, there are many events, like the red hair of the fisherman and the existence of the fish at a given ocean-depth cited in the previous paragraph, between which there is no conceivable causal relation. Secondly, particular objects and events cannot be

deduced from, or explained in terms of, general principles and laws of reason. "No psychologist could deduce the biography of a man from general psychology. No breeder of animals could deduce from mendelism all the traits found in a given litter. No physicist could deduce from general physics whether a tossed penny will fall heads or tails. In short, the particular entity seems infinitely complex, baffling all attempts to put it completely under any assignable number of laws. . . . Hence from the standpoint of causation the world has an infinitude of ultimate and independent causes. They are ultimate and independent because no amount of knowledge of other details of the world would furnish us enough information from which to deduce this total nature."[1]

(3) THE CASE OF CAUSAL MONISM. Causal monism is the view that the environment is one all-inclusive causal order, of which all particular cases of causation are fragmentary and incomplete aspects. The world is not "an infinitude of ultimate and independent causes"; on the contrary, all special causal situations are merely proximate phases of one total causal situation, parts of one all-inclusive system. According to this view there is only one true cause, namely, the universe; every particular causal situation is a fragmentary aspect of the totality of things. One argument advanced in support of this view is the empirical consideration, suggested above, that every cause which one can observe is in its turn the effect of another cause, which is the effect of another cause, and so on in an infinite regress. This seems to be a fact of ordinary observation, and it appears to be substantiated more and more by our developing knowledge of the world — the further our explanation of things progresses, the more interconnected do they appear

[1] Marvin, *A First Book in Metaphysics*, pp. 122, 123.

to be. The conclusion to which we are driven by such considerations as these, so the argument before us runs, is that all things are bound together in one universal causal system; the adequate comprehension of any given causal situation logically involves the nature of the environment as a whole.

Flower in the crannied wall,
I pluck you out of the crannies,
I hold you here, root and all, in my hand,
Little flower — but *if* I could understand
What you are, root and all, and all in all,
I should know what God and man is.

A second argument in support of monism is based upon the so-called 'internal theory of relations.' This theory and the argument founded upon it are rather technical, and so a general reference to them here must suffice. The theory, broadly stated, is that every entity or object stands in relation to other entities or objects and that these relations enter into and modify the things related (the *relata*). An individual human being, for instance, stands in certain relations to other human beings; he is a father, brother, son, husband, a member of a society, club, political organization, and the like; and these relations in which he stands enter into his nature and make him different from what he would otherwise be. And the same is true, so the theory of internal relations holds, of all objects: they exist in relations, and these relations constitute their nature. The argument built upon this theory is that, since terms thus stand in relations which modify them, every term or object is a part of every other term, every real fact or entity is inseparably connected with every other real fact or entity. The world, in short, is a one system.[1]

[1] The problem of relations has been discussed at length by various writers. A brief elementary discussion will be found in Marvin, *A First*

(4) CRITICAL ESTIMATE OF ARGUMENTS. The arguments advanced by both the monist and the pluralist have merit. On the one hand, it seems clear that the pluralist is justified in his contention that there are many causal situations between which no relation is at present conceivable by us and that particulars cannot logically be deduced from general laws. On the other hand, the monist seems equally justified in his contention that there is no apparent stopping-place in the search for boundaries of any given causal situation; no logical Chinese Wall separating one causal situation from all others is ever discovered. Furthermore, the argument which he erects on the internality of relations is not without considerable weight. But if each of the contestants be granted what he claims his case still is questionable.

That we cannot at present conceive what sort of connection could exist between two given facts (as the appearance of fish at a certain ocean-depth and the red hair of the fisherman) does not justify the conclusion that no connection exists between them. They might be connected and we be so ignorant of the connection that it seems to us inconceivable: it was at one time regarded as inconceivable, for instance, that there is any causal connection between ocean tides and the moon, or between climatic conditions and civilizations. Again, the fact that the multitudinous things and events in the world cannot be deduced from general laws and principles seems hardly to prove that the environment is a complex of an indefinite

Book in Metaphysics, Chapter VIII. A more detailed discussion is presented in Spaulding, *The New Rationalism,* pp. 176 ff. For more advanced material the reader may consult the following: James, *Pluralistic Universe,* Lectures II–III; Russell, *Philosophical Essays,* pp. 150–169; Bradley, *Appearance and Reality* (see Index), and *Essays on Truth and Reality* (see Index); and Joachim, *The Nature of Truth.*

number of independent and ultimate causes. It might very well be that the environment is one causal system and our ignorance of it be so great that it would still be impossible for us to deduce one part of it from another. This argument of the pluralist rests, in last analysis, upon the assumption that the type of consistency which in the preceding chapter we called 'implication' is the only type that can be identified with the causal nexus, that the causal relation is identical with the type of relation that exists between two propositions one of which logically involves the other. But, as we have seen also in the preceding chapter, there is a factual consistency or 'inference' as well as logical consistency, and it is still possible to urge that 'inference' can reveal causal connections as readily as 'implication' can; that, in other words, causal relations may be revealed by inductive reasoning as well as by deductive. As matter of fact, inference reveals many causal connections that could not possibly have been disclosed by mere logical consistency or implication. That heavy bodies fall, for example, is a matter of 'inference,' not of 'implication'; deductive reasoning alone could not possibly have discovered the causal situation here exemplified. So we may very legitimately conclude that the environment might be one total system of interpenetrating causes, that is, one big causal situation, and yet many particular aspects of it not be deducible from others. The case of the pluralist, thus, is not established.

But the case of the monist also leaves some questions unanswered. Grant that, so far as our present knowledge of the world will enable us to go in the causal series, every particular causal situation is conditioned by a larger system of which it is only a part. What conclusion follows? Certainly not that there exists one, and only one, system of causes. It is still conceivable that in this broad universe there are other causal systems besides the one in which we human beings live; and it is conceivable also that the system in which we do live may not itself be one system, despite the fact that we never discover an impassable chasm between any given causal situation and others. Our ignorance alone may be responsible for our inability to discover within the part of the world we know a set of conditions which falls short of the whole and yet is itself unconditioned and, so, causally independent of the rest of the whole. So far as the argument which the monist builds on the internality of relations is concerned, all that can here be said is that the argument is as weighty as is the theory upon which it is founded. If relations are internal and if all terms or objects must exist in relation, then monism would appear to be logically proved. If relations are not internal but external, if, that is, relations may exist without altering the objects between which they exist, the theory of internality falls to the ground and the monist's argument with it. Whether relations are internal or external cannot be discussed here, since the technicalities involved lie beyond the proper boundaries of this elementary text. The student who is interested in the problem is urged to consult the references named in the preceding footnote and the cross-references there to be found.[1]

The upshot of the whole matter would seem to be that neither causal pluralism nor causal monism is proved beyond question. Pluralism has much to appeal to in support of its thesis, and so has monism. There is not enough

[1] Professor Royce's arguments for monism offer an interesting and suggestive variation of the traditional formulation of the doctrine of internality. See his *Religious Aspect of Philosophy,* Chapter XIII, and his *Conception of God,* especially the first Part.

empirical evidence, evidence, that is, resulting from the achievements of knowledge, to pronounce a verdict in favor of either. The argument for monism based upon the nature of knowledge itself would seem to stand or fall with the doctrine of the internality of relations.

§ 4. *Two types of causation*

A distinction is sometimes drawn between two types of causation which it will be worth while to note in conclusion of our discussion. These two types are: *mechanical* causation and *teleological* causation.

(1) MECHANICAL CAUSATION. It is a matter of common observation that lifeless objects continue to exist without change in the same state in which they are unless acted upon by influences from the outside. It is also a matter of observation that such objects always behave in precisely the same manner under the same conditions; they behave with a regular uniformity. A stone remains at rest always in the same place unless its state of rest be interfered with by conditions outside itself, and it always behaves in the same way under the same conditions. A machine continues in its same condition except in so far as it is worn by friction or disintegrated by moisture, temperature, and the like; and furthermore, its behavior is marked by a regular uniformity, and every similar machine will behave in precisely the same manner under identical conditions. The behavior of the stone and the machine is said to be *mechanically* caused. In mechanical causation, thus, there is a rigid uniformity such that, given a certain set of conditions, the same consequences invariably follow and follow in precisely the same order without variation. There is here no element of spontaneity within the total system;

there is only a precise uniformity of behavior in which each stage is determined by the preceding one.

(2) TELEOLOGICAL CAUSATION. In the case of living objects the matter seems to be different. A plant or an animal apparently differs from a stone or a machine in certain important respects. Among these the most important one, perhaps, is the *organization* of the living object. The plant or the animal is not passive like the stone, but possesses a certain initiative of its own; it acts, not like a blind machine, but as a result of its own impulse to live and grow. Stimuli make an appeal to it of attraction or repulsion, and whether a given stimulus attracts or repels depends upon whether it is such as to aid or hinder its life-processes. Now the behavior of the living individual is said to be *teleologically* caused. In teleological causation, thus, there is an element not found in mechanical causation, namely, the organization of the individual itself; there is present a sort of initiative inherent in the organism which is lacking in the non-living object and which apparently is not wholly determinate in its nature — or, at least, not determinate in precisely the same sense in which the activity of the machine, for example, is determinate. This new element in the living object is the 'teleological' factor in the causal situation.

The point here under consideration is sometimes expressed in the statement that life is 'purposive.' If the term 'purpose' is used in this connection, however, one must clearly grasp the limitations in meaning that are essential. As ordinarily understood a purpose is an end or goal consciously entertained and more or less clearly outlined, as when one entertains the purpose of taking a vacation or of pursuing the medical profession as a life's work. Obviously, life as a biological phenomenon cannot be said to be purposive in this sense. Many, by far most, living forms never have purposes of this sort; and even in the case of human beings the activities of life more frequently than otherwise are expressed in tendencies, unconscious desires and impulses, rather than in the pursuit of clear-cut goals. The only sense in which life generally can be called purposive is the sense in which the plant 'purposes' to seek the light or the lion to pursue its prey. And since this meaning is not the one that is ordinarily attached to the word, it is better not to use 'purpose' in this context but rather to employ the more technical and less confusing term 'teleology.' As an end-seeking activity life is fairly accurately described by calling it 'teleological'—from the Greek 'telos' which means 'end.' To speak of all living forms as 'purposive' is to court confusion.

(3) IMPORTANCE OF THE DISTINCTION. This distinction between mechanical and teleological types of causation is important. For the question is raised whether the two types are fundamentally different or the one reducible to the other. This question will concern us below when we come to consider the general problem of life, as a biological fact.[1]

§ 5. *Summary of chapter*

The importance of the problems that center around the notion of causation is commensurate with the importance which the notion itself possesses in the field of scientific inquiry. As a scientific concept, however, causation is quite different from its popular meaning; for by a cause science means nothing more than those conditions that invariably accompany the effect and appear to be logically necessary to its existence. Two problems of great interest to the

[1] See Chapter XIV, section 2.

philosopher emerge out of the scientific notion of causation. These are: the plurality of causes, and causal monism versus causal pluralism. Taken in the abstract, an effect may appear to have a plurality of causes, but for any given concrete effect only one cause would seem to be possible; however, the complexity of causal situations not infrequently makes it necessary for practical purposes to distinguish between proximate and remote causes, which can be determined only with reference to the purpose of the special investigation into the causal situation in question. As regards the point at issue between the causal monist and the causal pluralist, it would seem that there are empirical grounds for both positions and that the problem of relations has an important bearing on the question. A distinction of importance to the debate concerning the fact of life is that between mechanical and teleological causation. By the former is meant a causal situation in which there is rigid determinism; the latter admits a degree of spontaneity and seems to involve a determinism less unyielding. The significance of this distinction for the problem of life will become apparent below in Chapter XIV.

Chapter IX. Questions and Exercises

1. Distinguish clearly between the scientific and the popular conception of cause and effect.

2. Is a cause necessarily antecedent to its effect in the temporal sense? Discuss.

3. What is meant by a plurality of causes? In what sense may a plurality of causes be said to exist? Discuss. Distinguish between proximate and remote causes, and show how they can be distinguished. Show how these vary with one's point of view.

4. What is the point at issue between the monist and the pluralist? Summarize in a few sentences the chief arguments

advanced by each. Which solution of the problem are you inclined to favor and why?

5. Distinguish clearly between mechanical and teleological causation. Give an example of each type.

6. Summarize the main points in Spaulding's chapter on the problem of relations in *The New Rationalism* (Chapter XXVI). Read in connection: Marvin, *A First Book in Metaphysics*, Chapter VIII.

7. Summarize main points in the discussion of causation given in Pearson, *Grammar of Science*, 3rd edition, Chapter IV, sections 1–8.

8. Summarize main points in Hume's discussion of causation in *Treatise on Human Nature*, Book I, Part III, section XIV — the section on the idea of 'necessary connection' (Selby-Bigge's edition, pp. 155–172).

PART III

PROBLEMS OF MATTER

CHAPTER X

MATTER: HISTORICAL SURVEY

As we saw in Chapter V above, certain problems of fundamental importance to the philosopher emerge from the results of the sciences. It is to a consideration of some of these problems that we turn in this part of our study. And we begin with the concept of matter which is one of the basal notions of the physical sciences. In the present chapter we shall undertake a general historical survey of the various meanings that have been attached to the term 'matter' in the course of the development of European thought, reserving for the chapter that follows a critical consideration of the problems that arise from the category.

§ 1. *The concept of matter*

For uncritical common sense, matter is an aggregation of particular things or objects existing in space and directly experienced through perception. It is that panorama of the passing show disclosed through the sense-organs of the body. Or, to employ Berkeley's famous phrase, it is "all the choir of heaven and furniture of the earth, in a word, all those bodies that compose the mighty frame of the world." Reflection, however, discloses certain difficulties in the way of this conception of matter, and has gradually led to the formulation of another conception the analysis of which is here our chief concern.

Particular objects come into being and pass away, they continuously change their form and structure. And when an object has changed its form and structure it, *as that particular object,* has entirely disappeared. The chair that is burnt no longer exists as a chair; the stone that is ground to powder is no longer a stone; the water when evaporated is water no more. We do not suppose, however, that 'matter' has disappeared in these processes of change and transformation. The 'matter' of the chair is not destroyed when the chair is burnt, so at least we suppose; nor do we admit the destruction of the 'matter' of stone or water in those transformations which result in the disappearance of that particular set of qualities, such as color, solidity, heaviness, and the like, which we designate by the name of 'stone' or 'water.' And if the entire "choir of heaven and furniture of the earth" were to change all of their ordinary qualities their 'matter' still, we assume, would remain permanent. Particular objects arise and perish, come into being and pass away; but 'matter' is somehow permanent in the sense that change does not cause it to depart radically from its own nature and become something else.

Matter, thus, is a concept of the human mind, not a percept. It cannot be wholly identified with a particular sensible object or apparently with any combination of sensible objects. It cannot be located as here or there. On the contrary, it is conceived as a permanent something which is somehow universal in its nature and which exists in and through particular objects but is untouched by the fluctuations and changes characteristic of the manifold forms in which it finds expression. To discover the nature of this 'something' has been one chief goal of man's intellectual search from the beginning of scientific speculation down to our own day. A general survey of the different views on the problem held during the course of European thought will serve to put us in touch with one very interesting side of the history of philosophical and scientific reflection.

§ 2. *Views of the early Greeks*

From the standpoint of the history of European civilization the earliest scientific views of the nature of matter appear in Greece dring the late sixth and early fifth centuries B.C. At this time there arose a group of thinkers, called by Aristotle 'physicists,' who discarded the mythological views of their generation and substituted instead views which they themselves arrived at by reflection upon the physical environment. They quit trying to explain natural phenomena in terms of 'spirits' or 'wills,' gods and goddesses, which were supposed to exist in the physical order and control its events, and they undertook to explain these phenomena in terms of the phenomena themselves. They were all of the opinion that there is some sort of ultimate 'stuff' of which the many different objects in the physical environment are composed and by reference to which the events and changes in progress there could be accounted for. But, as was inevitable, they differed widely as to what this 'stuff' is. Their views, however, are not wholly unrelated to each other and, as we shall see in our study of them, the conclusion at which they finally arrived is of considerable significance from the standpoint of later scientific developments.

(1) THE MILESIAN GROUP. Three of the earliest of these thinkers — Thales (one of the reputed Wise Men of Greece), Anaximander, and Anaximenes — are usually grouped together in the histories of philosophy as the Milesian 'school.' Of course, they did not belong to a school in the modern sense of the term. They are referred

to as members of the Milesian 'school' because they were contemporaries interested in the same problem and all lived at the little seaport town of Miletus. As might be expected, their answers to the problem of the nature of matter were vague and largely unsupported guesses. Thales, the earliest of the three, held that the ultimate 'stuff' of the world is water — a thesis suggested to him doubtless by his observations of the important rôle water plays in the processes of nature. Anaximander questioned the validity of the doctrine of Thales, and suggested in the place of it that 'the boundless' must be the ultimate source of all things. Anaximenes, in his turn, urged that 'air' or the atmosphere is the basal substance. In spite of the obvious inadequacy of these answers, there is a certain logical development in theory here which is interesting and suggestive. Water apparently is only a part of the physical environment, and as such cannot be the 'ultimate' substance of all things; the whole of things cannot be explained in terms of one sort of thing. The 'ultimate' must be inexhaustible and infinite. So at least Anaximander argued, and he therefore undertakes to substitute for the finite and limited principle of Thales's theory an infinite and inexhaustible principle. But this principle he did not succeed in describing very clearly; to call it 'the boundless' is to leave it very indefinite. The question naturally arises, The boundless what? And this question Anaximenes thinks he answers by identifying the ultimate stuff with the 'air' or atmosphere that encompasses all; this was the one apparently boundless and infinite thing open to his observation.

(2) Empedocles. The one assumption common to the Milesian trio of thinkers is that the ultimate stuff of the world, whatever it be, is *one sort* of stuff. This assumption, however, Empedocles immediately calls in question. He

was convinced that it is impossible to explain all objects in terms of one ultimate substance; there are so many different kinds of objects in the world we must look for more than one kind of stuff as the source of them. Empedocles discovers four basal elements, namely, earth, air, fire, and water. Everything in the world, he holds, is simply a compound of these elements and all change is the coming together or separation of them in various degrees. "There is no coming into being of aught that perishes, nor any end for it in baneful death, but only mingling, and separation of what has been mingled." "When the elements have been mingled in the fashion of a man . . . or in the fashion of the race of wild beasts or plants or birds, then men say that these come into being; and when they are separated, they call that, as is the custom, woeful death."[1] For Empedocles, then, matter is four-fold: earth, air, fire, water. Particular objects are compounds, and may always be analyzed into these four elements; growth and decay are the commingling and separation of the elements.[2]

(3) ANAXAGORAS. Anaxagoras agrees with Empedocles, against the Milesian school, that the ultimate stuff of the world must be of more than one kind. But he is convinced that Empedocles does not go far enough in the direction in which he starts. In his opinion it is as impossible to explain all the different qualities of objects in

[1] Fragments from Empedocles, and from all these early Greek thinkers, are translated in Bakewell, *Sourcebook in Ancient Philosophy*, and in Burnet, *Early Greek Philosophy*.

[2] This tradition of the four elements was for centuries fixed in European civilization. It was current in Shakespeare's day, and the poet alluded to it frequently. The best known allusion perhaps is found in Antony's statement about Brutus in the last scene of the last Act of *Julius Caesar*.

His life was gentle; and the elements
So mix'd in him, that Nature might stand up
And say to all the world, *This was a man!*

terms of the four elements of Empedocles as it is to explain them in terms of any one of the principles advocated by the Milesian group. He is convinced that a quality cannot be explained by reference to something different from itself; and therefore, he argues, there must be as many elements or basal kinds of matter as there are qualities in the physical environment. For every quality there is a corresponding kind of element: there are blue elements and red elements and all sorts of colored elements, there are hot elements and cold elements, moist elements and dry elements, and so on for each and every quality that can be observed to exist. For Anaxagoras, then, matter is a name for an indefinite number of elements of different kinds, the number of kinds of elements being the same as the number of qualities in the world. This conception is sometimes called *qualitative atomism.*

(4) DEMOCRITUS. Democritus was in his old age a contemporary of Plato and Aristotle and is worthy to be ranked with them in intellectual achievement. He agrees with Anaxagoras that the number of elements is indefinite, and that that number must be very great. But he will not admit that it is necessary to suppose that these elements differ qualitatively. On the contrary, he urges that the only differences among them which we are compelled to admit are purely quantitative differences. Some of them are smooth, round, and light, while others are rough, angular, and heavy; all are in motion through the 'void' (empty space), but some are more mobile than others and travel with a greater velocity. For Democritus, thus, matter is an indefinite number of elements — called by him 'atoms' — different only in size, shape, and velocity of motion. This view is called *quantitative* atomism in distinction from the *qualitative* atomism of Anaxagoras.

(5) Summary of views of early Greek thinkers. The chief significance of the views of these early Greek thinkers is historical: they mark a definite break with the pre-scientific view of the physical order and inaugurate the more rational method of seeking a definite view of matter through analysis of natural phenomena. But the results of their speculations are not wholly without value. Two significant points emerge from them. The first is the conclusion that matter cannot be identified with any particular sensible quality. The second is the conclusion that matter is in some sense granular in structure and that qualities can be quantitatively explained. In short, there emerges from their speculations the two-fold conviction that matter is really a group of elements, and that these elements are to be described in quantitative rather than in qualitative terms. The significance of this conviction lies in the fact that, in general outline at least, it points the direction in which the results of the fuller and more precise investigations of later science have led. Of course, the results actually achieved by these pioneers in science have suffered the fate that was inevitable — they have long since become antiquated. It must never be forgotten, however, that they were brilliant achievements as first stages in Europe's scientific development.

§ 3. *The views of Plato and Aristotle*

Plato and his famous pupil, Aristotle, were both much interested in the general problem of the physical environment. And the views which they suggest have been exceedingly influential in the later development of thought even down to the modern era.

(1) Plato (427–347 B.C.). According to Plato, the objects that constitute the conten' of our physical environ-

ment are particular or individual copies of general types or forms. Thus, for instance, a given stone is a particular example or copy of a certain general class or type of physical objects, a given triangle is a special instance of a certain sort of geometrical figure, and so forth. Every object is a spatial expression of a general type. Now the type which the particular object copies Plato calls the 'Idea' of that object; the special characteristics of the given object arise from the material out of which the object is generated. Thus, any given diamond is a particular copy of that type of precious stones; the unique characteristics of the diamond in question, its special brilliancy, shape, flaws, etc., arise from the stuff or matter out of which it has sprung. So in Plato's view objects are copies of general archetypes or forms; the forms copied he calls 'Ideas,' while the stuff out of which the copies are made is 'matter.' What more precisely this 'matter' is he never succeeds in telling us; it is that something, not further describable, out of which particular objects in the physical environment are fashioned in the likeness of those general 'Ideas' of which they are copies. Any given physical object is only the spatialization of its 'Idea,' that is, the manifestation of its 'Idea' in matter; the perceptual horse is a copy of the 'Idea' *horse* made in matter, the triangle drawn on the blackboard is a copy in space of the 'Idea' *triangle,* and so on for all other physical objects. For Plato, then, matter is the stuff, indefinable because apparently lacking all qualities, out of which copies of general types are made in the process of the world's development; it is formlessness, chaos.[1]

[1] It is difficult to state this Platonic doctrine in brief compass so as to make it intelligible to the beginner. The reader who is not familiar with the doctrine is advised to acquaint himself with the accounts of it given in the general histories of philosophy. He should also read the relevant parts of Plato's *Republic,* especially Books VI–VII. It may help

(2) ARISTOTLE. Aristotle's answer to the problem of matter can be understood only in connection with his doctrine of 'form' and 'matter.' In this doctrine his fundamental thesis is that every particular object in the world is in process of change and that its change is determined by something inherent within it as a sort of potentiality or capacity. Thus, the acorn changes into the oak tree. The nature of the acorn is to change, and to change only into an oak tree; there is in the acorn the potentiality of the oak tree, and no other sort of tree will spring out of it. The acorn changes into something definite, which 'something' is involved within it and determines its development. Now, Aristotle contends, every other particular object is in this respect like the acorn; it is, on the one hand, something which changes and, on the other, it is something into which change inevitably develops. Viewed as something which changes, the object is called by Aristotle 'matter'; viewed as controlled in its changes by an inherent capacity for development along a predetermined line, it is what he calls 'form.' The acorn is 'matter' in the sense that it has within itself the capacity to develop or change into an oak tree; its 'form' is the inherent capacity which predetermines its development into an oak tree, and not into a peach tree or any other sort of tree. Thus in Aristotle's view matter is synonymous with a capacity or potentiality to change. The 'matter' of the stone is the stone's capacity to change; the 'matter' of the child is the child's capacity to grow; the 'matter' of X is X's potentiality, whatever X may be.

---

to remember that Plato's 'Ideas' are somewhat analogous to what modern science means by 'laws,' 'species,' etc., and that his 'matter' is not unlike the 'earth' as described in opening verse of the book of *Genesis:* "And the earth was without form and void."

§ 4. *Some modern philosophical views*

In modern philosophical thought four views of matter have been defended which are of importance for this general survey. These are the views of Descartes (1596–1650), Locke (1632–1704), Leibnitz (1646–1716), and Berkeley (1685–1753).[1]

(1) DESCARTES. In his consideration of the problem of matter Descartes finally came to the conclusion that there is one characteristic of matter, and only one, which we can know with certainty. That characteristic is extension. We know beyond doubt that the world of material objects is an extended world. "We must unhesitatingly conclude that there exists a certain object extended in length, breadth, and thickness, and possessing all those properties which we clearly apprehend to belong to what is extended. And this extended substance is what we call body or matter."[2] Matter and extension, then, are synonymous terms; matter is "extended substance." This is all we can certainly say about it.

(2) LOCKE. According to Locke matter is to us unknown and unknowable. We therefore cannot say anything about it, except that we suppose it exists. What we actually perceive in our physical environment are objects having various sorts of qualities. And matter is "nothing but the supposed, but unknown, support of those qualities

[1] George Berkeley was an Irish philosopher and theologian who developed the philosophy of Locke in the direction of an idealism that has since his day been much discussed. He visited London, France, and Italy. In 1729 he came to the United States on his way to the Bermudas where he had planned to establish a college with the two-fold object of "the reformation of manners among the English in our western plantations, and the propagation of the gospel among the American savages." His plans, however, never materialized. In 1734 he became bishop of Cloyne. His greatest philosophical work is his *Principles of Human Knowledge*.

[2] *Principles of Material Things*, section 1.

we find existing. . . ."[1] We suppose matter exists because we cannot imagine how qualities could exist without something to attach themselves to. An apple, for example, is experienced as a group of qualities such as color, shape, taste, odor, and the like; there must be something for the qualities to *belong to;* that something is the 'matter' of the apple. But we cannot know what that 'something' is, since it lies behind the qualities which alone we can experience. So matter, in Locke's view, turns out to be an unknown X which we assume exists in particular things or objects; and we assume it exists because we cannot imagine the qualities that we directly observe as existing without something in which to inhere. But we cannot say anything at all about its nature.

(3) BERKELEY. Berkeley takes issue with Locke by urging that, if matter is only an unknown X, then there is no justification for supposing it to exist at all. To make such an assumption is purely arbitrary and unscientific. It is simpler, Berkeley goes on to argue, to say that matter is identical with those qualities that we directly observe. Matter is nothing but physical objects, and physical objects are precisely the qualities which we observe in them. "Thus, for example, a certain colour, taste, smell, figure, and consistence having been observed to go together, are accounted one distinct thing, signified by the name *apple;* other collections of ideas constitute a stone, a tree, a book, and the like sensible things. . . ."[2] And this is all there is to these sensible objects; they are simply collections of those qualities observed by us. There is no mysterious and unknown 'matter' lying underneath these qualities and 'supporting' them; such a supposition is, Berkeley

[1] *Essay Concerning Human Understanding,* Book II, Chapter XXIII, section 2.

[2] *Principles of Human Knowledge,* section 1.

insists, both absurd and unnecessary. Matter is the name which we give to the totality of objects in the physical environment, and these objects are nothing but collections of various sorts of qualities; matter, therefore, is the qualities of objects. Such is Berkeley's view on the problem of matter.[1]

(4) LEIBNITZ. Leibnitz agrees with the ancient Greek thinker, Democritus, that there are many elements in the physical world all of which are alike qualitatively. Our analysis of objects, he insists, cannot stop short of such elements. But he is not willing to admit that these elements have any spatial characteristics. They cannot, like the 'atoms' of Democritus or the 'substance' of Descartes, be extended, for if they were extended they would be divisible by analysis and therefore not ultimate. The only unanalyzable element which we can conceive is a non-extended center of force or energy or activity. Such a center of force is the element of matter, and this Leibnitz calls a 'monad.' Since there are many objects in the physical environment there must be many 'monads'; one alone could not be the adequate basis of the multiplicity of things. Matter, thus, for Leibnitz is an indefinite number of centers of activity or energy (monads) organized in such mani-

[1] Berkeley draws a further conclusion from his analysis which has given rise to much controversy. And that is that objects exist only in relation to a mind which perceives them. Objects are nothing but qualities; qualities are nothing but ideas which we experience, such as colors, temperatures, and the like; objects, therefore, are "collections of ideas." But ideas exist only in being perceived or experienced by some mind; objects, therefore, exist only in being perceived or experienced by some mind. "Some truths there are so near and obvious to the mind that a man need only open his eyes to them. Such I take this important one to be, viz., that all the choir of heaven and furniture of the earth, in a word, all those bodies which compose the mighty frame of the world, have not any subsistence without a mind, that their *being is to be perceived or known.*" (*Principles of Human Knowledge,* section 6.) And this truth is 'obvious' to Berkeley because for him objects are nothing but "collections of ideas."

fold ways as to constitute those various groups of qualities which we experience as physical objects.[1]

§ 5. *The views of modern science*

The different conceptions of matter thus far described were not supported by experimental evidence. They were arrived at as a result of the attempt to carry analysis to its uttermost limits, to think matter as an aspect of a consistent view of the world. But since the beginning of the development of modern science the problem of matter has become more and more pressing for the scientist, and experimental investigations during the last century or so have thrown much light upon it. Two main theories have resulted from these investigations. These are: the earlier atomic theory, and the later electronic theory.

(1) THE ATOMIC THEORY. The atomic theory of modern science is that matter is reducible to certain elements, called atoms. A series of experiments begun about the middle of the eighteenth century showed the possibility that material objects can be analyzed into a number of simple particles, that matter is granular as Democritus and Leibnitz had inferred. John Dalton[2] was one of the first among the scientists to make fairly definite suggestions concerning the atomic theory and the measurable weights of some of the atoms; thus the beginnings of the theory are linked with his name. Since Dalton's day chemical analysis has gone

[1] The activity of these 'monads' Leibnitz conceives as mental, basing his inference on the thesis that the only activity or energy of which we have definite knowledge is that which manifests itself in mental work. There is for him, therefore, no sharp distinction between living and non-living matter; all matter is of the same kind of energy. His view has sometimes been called a *spiritual* atomism in contradistinction to the *physical* atomism of Democritus.

[2] Dalton (1766–1844) is famous for his pioneer work in modern science. He is also noteworthy as the discoverer of color-blindness.

far along the path he pointed out and has added to the list of atoms until at present the number of atoms known and measured runs into the eighties. The names of these atoms and their fundamental characteristics the student may easily find in any up-to-date textbook in chemistry.

(2) THE ELECTRONIC THEORY. One assumption concerning the atoms made by the earlier scientists has apparently turned out to be erroneous. And that is the assumption that each atom is simple in structure and impenetrable by further analysis. Recent investigations, particularly in physics, have led to the inference that each atom is within itself a complex universe of electrical energy. It is now said to be composed of a 'nucleus,' or positive electricity, and one or more 'electrons,' or negative electricity, revolving about the nucleus at a very rapid rate of motion. The differences among the atoms bear a definite and measurable ratio to the differences in number and configurations of the electrons composing them. Thus hydrogen is the lightest known atom and it has only one electron revolving about the nucleus; uranium, on the other hand, is the heaviest atom known and it has ninety-two revolving electrons. The other atoms are composed of electrons varying in number between these extremes. So further analysis has shown the atom to be composite in structure and active rather than passive. It is a compound of rapidly revolving electrons which vary in number from kind to kind of atom. It is electrical energy.

(3) SUMMARY. The answer of modern physical science to our problem of matter, then, is that matter is, so far as experimental analysis at present will carry us, electrical energy. "The corpuscle," that is, the electron, "we deem to be the constituent of an atom, the atom the constituent of a molecule, and a molecule the constituent of

a mass of matter, such a[illegible] or a chair. Hence, on this view, the inertia of any material body, and the mass of it as measured by the inertia, is due simply to electrical charges in motion. On this view, then, the to-and-fro motion of a pendulum and the electrical oscillations of the spark from a Leyden jar are simply two manifestations of an identical thing, the inertia of a charged body."[1] But the nature of the electron itself still remains an unsolved problem. "Further than to say that electrons are electricity we cannot go. We can say that matter is molecular, that molecules are composed of atoms, and that atoms are formed of electrons. In finding how the matter of the universe is composed scientists have at last reached the electron. In terms of it they can explain fairly well everything else, or at least there is promise that ultimately everything else will be so explained. But as to the electron itself no explanation can be given. If any explanation is ever obtained it will be in terms of something else which in its turn will be unexplainable and have to be accepted as the fundamental element or beginning from which all other explanations start."[2]

§ 6. *Comparison of views; conclusions*

Looking back over the various views of matter noted in this chapter we discover certain points of importance which

[1] Duncan, *The New Knowledge*, p. 184.

[2] Mills, *Realities of Modern Science*, pp. 88–89. As remarked above in a footnote on this book, its author is always thinking in terms of the physical sciences and primarily in terms of physics. Consequently, his remark in the quotation to the effect that "everything else" can be explained in terms of the electron must be interpreted to mean that matter can be so explained. If he means to include in his "everything else" literally all things in the universe, whether in the physical environment or out of it, then obviously his statement is far from being proved. Certainly it cannot at present be said that there is "promise" that all events in the social environment, for instance, can be explained in terms of electrons, even if matter can be — as there is justification for believing.

may be set down h... ...t summary of results of this historical survey.

(1) In the first place, there is a negative result emerging from Locke's theory which has positive implications of far-reaching significance. That result is the conclusion, emphasized by Berkeley, that matter cannot be identified with something which to the human mind is unknowable. For if it is unknowable it cannot logically be said even to exist, because no reason could then be advanced for its existence. The point may be put in the form of a dilemma: if matter is known to exist, it is not unknowable; if it is not known to exist and no reason can be advanced for its existence, its existence cannot logically be assumed.

(2) A second negative result emerges from the view of Berkeley, and that is that matter cannot be identified wholly with those qualities which are experienced in sense-perception. On the contrary, it is to be discovered, if at all, by elaborate intellectual analysis, by conceptual and not perceptual judgment. On this point there is general agreement against Berkeley.

(3) Finally, in spite of differences of detail, there is general agreement that matter is in some sense atomic or granular in structure, that the physical order of perceptual objects can be resolved by analysis into simple elements. What these simple elements are and what is their structure the results of modern scientific research tell us with fair definiteness and with as great certainty as we can at present attain.

Chapter X. Questions and Exercises

1. State briefly the meaning in which the term 'matter' is used in this chapter.

2. What do you understand to be the views of Plato and Aristotle concerning matter? (In connection with this question consult the histories of philosophy; those by Thilly, Rogers, and Weber are good ones.)

3. Indicate the main points developed by Locke in his discussion of our ideas of substances, *Essay Concerning Human Understanding,* Book II, Chapter XXIII. No exhaustive summary of the chapter is called for, but only a concise statement of your understanding of Locke's view concerning "the ideas we have of substances, and the ways we come by them."

4. Summarize the main points developed in Cooley, *The Principles of Science,* Chapters VI–VII.

5. What do you understand by the atomic theory of matter? How is it related to the electronic theory? (Read in connection with this question the relevant parts of Duncan, *The New Knowledge,* and Mills, *The Realities of Modern Science.*)

6. Give a brief report of the main points developed in Russell, *The A B C of Atoms,* Chapters I–III.

CHAPTER XI

MATTER: APPEARANCES AND REALITY

The results of the preceding historical survey give rise to a problem of great significance for the philosopher. That problem is the problem of appearances and reality, which forms the topic of the present chapter. First we shall attempt to understand the nature of the general problem, and then we shall proceed to study it with special reference to the concept of matter.

§ 1. *The general problem*

One does not have to live long in this world to discover that things are not always what they seem to be. The lines of the railway track stretching away in the distance seem to converge, but we know that they are always approximately parallel; the straight stick thrust in clear water looks bent; the traveler on the desert sees an oasis where no oasis exists; the same water at the same time may seem cold to one hand and warm to the other; the colors of the rug change with changing light and perspective; the pitch of the whistle varies as the rapidly moving locomotive approaches, passes, and recedes. In short, objects in the world about us not infrequently seem to be different from what we must suppose they really are. This fact gives rise to the distinction that we all make between 'appearances' and 'reality.' The converging lines of the railroad, the crookedness of the straight stick, the varying temperatures of the same water at the same time, the changing colors of the one rug, and the varying tone of the one whistle — these we say are 'appearances.' The parallel rails, the straight stick, the constant temperature measured by the thermometer, the actual color of the rug or tone of the whistle — these are 'realities.' The rails 'appear' to converge, but 'really' they are parallel; the stick 'appears' to be bent, but it is 'really' straight; in 'appearance' the water has two temperatures and the colors of the rug and the tone of the whistle change, but in 'reality' there is only one temperature and the colors and tone are constant. In general, then, we seem to mean by 'appearances' objects as they are experienced by us; by 'reality' we seem to mean objects as they exist apart from and independent of our experience of them.

This distinction between appearances and reality we make because we must. We cannot get along without it. Ordinarily we do not notice that there is involved in it a problem of fundamental difficulty. But when once we begin to reflect upon it the question immediately arises: What is the relation between the 'appearances' and the 'reality' of which they are supposed to be appearances? How are the 'converging' railway lines related to the lines as 'parallel'? How are the 'crookedness' of the stick, the different temperatures of the water, the changing colors of rug or tone of whistle related to the 'real' nature of the objects themselves? Broadly: Are 'appearances' wholly unreal, or must they also be given some sort of 'reality'? This is the general problem emerging from the distinction between the apparent and the real.

§ 2. *Limitation of the problem*

The general problem of appearances and reality may, because of its very comprehensiveness, seem to the beginner vague and unmanageable. It can be made more definite, however, by restatement in terms that bring it into direct relation to our problem of matter. This restatement we shall now undertake to formulate.

From the historical survey of the preceding chapter it is clear that matter as conceived by science is quite different from our direct experiences of our physical environment. The table, for example, as we directly observe it has no marks of identity with the table as science pictures it — a multitude of dancing electrons. It is clear, furthermore, that as the scientific view of matter develops it gets farther and farther away from physical objects as they appear to us in perceptual experience. The 'water' of Thales and the red, green, blue, moist, dry, elements of Anaxagoras are much nearer to the physical objects of direct experience than are the atoms of modern chemistry and the electrons of modern physics; and yet rational reflection has driven the mind of man, in its search for a satisfactory notion of matter, from the crude simplicity of the guesses of the ancient Greeks to the tremendously complex hypotheses of the modern scientists. Scientific reflection, thus, leads away from the apparent nature of objects in its search for matter, and so the question is inevitably forced upon us: What is the relation between matter as conceived by science and objects as they appear in direct experience? Is the concept of matter the reality and particular objects of perceptual experience appearances? or is the concept of matter appearance and particular objects real? or are both real? This formulation of the problem of reality and appearances states it in terms that are more familiar to us.

Even this formulation, however, can be further simplified by breaking the general problem into two simpler ones.

Matter appears to us in the form of particular objects, such as trees, tables, mountains, and the like, and these objects we experience as composed of colors, temperatures, shapes, and so forth. A more definite formulation of our problem, then, would concern itself with the question of the relation between the scientific concept of matter and the particular aspects of objects as we experience them. If we agree to designate these particular aspects of objects — colors, temperatures, shapes, and the like — by the term 'qualities,' then our problem would be: What is the relation between matter as conceived by science — the table as a group of electrons — and its qualities — the table as a certain combination of colors, shape, and the like? This is the first side of the general problem. Again, the concept of matter is only one example of many concepts which science discovers about our world; other illustrations are gravitation, evolution, and similar laws or principles. So another formulation of our problem is possible: What is the relation of the general categories or principles of the sciences and the special objects in the physical environment? If we agree to designate these general principles of the sciences by the name of 'universals' and the particular objects of direct perceptual experience by the term 'particulars,' the problem may be stated more briefly still: What is the relation between universals and particulars?

The general problem of appearance and reality, thus, reduces itself to two special problems: matter and its qualities, and universals and particulars. We now turn to a brief study of these two problems.

§ 3. *Matter and its qualities*

We directly experience by means of our senses certain aspects of the environment. These we have agreed to call 'qualities.' Now matter as conceived by science is not identical with these qualities. What, then, is the relation between matter and its qualities, and which are to be called real? This is the problem before us in this section.

(1) MATTER AS WHOLLY DIFFERENT FROM QUALITIES. In the history of reflection on this problem it has been argued by some, notably by John Locke, that matter is something which is entirely different from all the qualities that we experience and which consequently cannot be known by us. It is an unknown X lying back of, and supporting, the qualities that we experience but different from them. It is "nothing but the supposed, but unknown, support of those qualities we find existing. . . ."[1] It is the hidden substrate of qualities.

This view of the problem, however, is very unsatisfactory, as a little reflection will disclose. To say that matter is merely the unknown 'something or other' which we must suppose to exist because it is convenient to do so is to say nothing definite in connection with our problem. It tells us absolutely nothing about the nature of matter or of the relation between matter and its qualities. In fact, it is merely a confession of ignorance, and a confession which lands us in special difficulties. For it inevitably raises in our minds the question why matter should thus be so sharply sundered from its qualities, and how we can be sure, since by hypothesis matter is unknown, it is so sundered. The solution suggested, therefore, is not satisfactory.

(2) DISTINCTION BETWEEN PRIMARY AND SECONDARY QUALITIES. An effort has been made to solve the problem by drawing a division among qualities and distinguishing

[1] See the reference to Locke's view in the fourth section of the preceding chapter.

between *primary* and *secondary* qualities.[1] We shall first try to understand the distinction, and then we shall note its application to the problem before us.

By primary qualities are meant those qualities of the physical environment which we usually call spatial, such as figure, motion, rest, extension, solidity, and number. By secondary qualities are meant all qualities that are not primary, such as colors and brightnesses, noises and tones, odors, temperatures, and the like. In so far as an object has a certain size, shape, solidity, and is in motion or at rest, it presents primary qualities; in so far as it is colored and is hot or cold, odoriferous, etc., it is characterized by secondary qualities. Now, so the argument proceeds, primary qualities are entirely independent of the mind that perceives them, since they are always the same regardless of the perceiving mind. The secondary qualities, however, vary with the perceiving subject and are therefore dependent upon the perceiver in a way in which the primary qualities are not. Thus, the figure or shape of the rainbow is the same whether or not it is perceived by any mind, and it is the same for all minds that may perceive it; but the colors of the rainbow exist only in so far as they are perceived by some mind, and they may be different for various experiencing subjects — a color-blind individual, for example, would not experience all the colors observed by a normal individual. And from this the conclusion is drawn that primary qualities exist in things, while secondary qualities exist only in perceiving or experiencing minds. If there were no perceiving minds in the universe

[1] This distinction was first drawn in the history of thought by Democritus; in modern thought it was emphasized by Descartes and Locke. Berkeley's criticism of it is classic, as is his criticism of the view above attributed to Locke that matter is sharply sundered from its qualities. See his *Principle of Human Knowledge,* Sections 9–21 (Rand, *Modern Classical Philosophers,* pp. 266–272).

objects would still have shapes, solidity, and extension, and be either at rest or in motion; but with the disappearance of all perceiving minds colors and brightnesses, temperatures, odors, and all the other secondary qualities would vanish utterly from the world. In short, primary qualities are objective, existing in things, while secondary qualities are subjective, existing only in minds that experience them.

The application of this distinction to the problem of matter and its qualities is as follows. Matter, it is argued, is identical with its primary qualities, and these therefore are real. Secondary qualities, on the other hand, are not attributes of matter but merely ways in which minds are affected by matter and they, consequently, are appearances only and not real. Such is the solution of the problem offered by those who accept the distinction between primary and secondary qualities.

But this distinction is not without its difficulties. There are two main objections to it. In the first place, primary qualities no more obviously belong to things than do secondary qualities. Colors, temperatures, sounds, and the other secondary qualities *seem* to belong to things as truly as do solidity, figure, motion, and the other primary or spatial qualities. So it is not obvious that primary qualities are objective (in things) and secondary qualities subjective (in the mind). In the second place, no argument can be advanced for the independent existence of primary qualities which does not equally well apply to secondary qualities. Conversely stated, every reason which can be advanced for the subjectivity of secondary qualities holds equally well in support of the subjectivity of primary qualities. If primary qualities *seem* to exist in the physical environment and independently of the perceiving mind, so do the secondary qualities; if the secondary qualities vary with, and are in some sense dependent on, the sense-organs of perceiving subjects, the same is equally true of the primary qualities. Colors, for example, seem to be as much in objects as does motion; but the size of an object or its motion varies with the eye that perceives it — the angle from which it is seen, the distance at which it is observed, and so forth — just as truly as does its brightness or color. To separate sharply between primary and secondary qualities is, therefore, not justifiable; and the solution of the problem of matter and its qualities based upon the distinction is not satisfactory.

(3) MATTER AND QUALITIES AS FORMS OF JUDGMENT. Perhaps the key to the correct solution of our problem is to be found in the consideration that what we here call 'matter' is nothing but a conceptual judgment and what we call 'qualities' are identical with perceptual judgments. 'Matter' is a general notion or concept which science arrives at in its efforts to *judge* the nature of the physical environment; it is a generalization of the physical sciences. And 'qualities' are likewise judgments we make about the more immediate aspects of the environment; they are, primary and secondary alike, types or forms of perceptual judgment.[1] Now, in our study of the basal characteristics of judgment, we have seen that all judgments have an objective reference in the sense that they are in contact with the environment and express something of its nature. Every judgment is an interpretation of the environment and, in so far as it may be said to be true, it expresses the real nature of the environment. And from this follow certain conclu-

[1] To follow the discussion here the reader must have clearly in mind what has been said above in Chapters VI and VII about judgment as the element of thinking. Unless the points there raised are clear they should be reviewed in this connection.

sions that are important in connection with our present problem. In the first place, it follows that all qualities are alike objective in the sense that they are in things; and there is therefore no justification for the distinction between primary and secondary qualities as being, on the one hand, objective, and, on the other, subjective. Secondary qualities are objects of judgments in precisely the same sense in which primary qualities are, and they have attaching to them the same objectivity. In the second place, it follows that the relation between matter and its qualities is the relation between perceptual judgments and the conceptual judgment, or generalization, that grows out of them. It is, in short, the relation between the universals of science and the particulars of sense-perception. What more precisely this relation is we shall be interested to inquire in the following section. Meanwhile we seem to be driven to this conclusion: qualities are objective in the same sense in which matter is objective, and qualities are attributes of matter in the same sense in which the particulars of perception are attributes of the general notions logically connected with them; both matter and its qualities are real, neither is mere 'appearance.' What, now, shall we say is the relation between the particulars of perception and the generalizations of conception?

§ 4. *The universals of science and the particulars of perception*

As we have seen in our consideration of the progress of science, generalization is an important aspect of the development of scientific knowledge. As science progresses its judgments become more and more generalized. This is illustrated clearly in the development of the physical sciences in so far as they have concerned themselves with the problem of the nature of matter. It is a far cry from the 'water' of Thales and the 'earth,' 'air,' 'fire,' and 'water' of Empedocles to the highly conceptualized 'electrons' of the modern physicist; but the development from the views of the early Greeks to those of the moderns is a development in generalization alone. And this same fact might be illustrated by reference to the historical growth of any of the sciences. Scientific reflection about the nature of the environment leads on beyond the particular objects of the first look to general concepts, principles and laws. From the individual objects of perceptual judgment it carries us into the realm of the general notions of conceptual judgments. Denoting the special objects of perceptual judgments as 'particulars' and the general notions of conceptual judgments as 'universals,' we may say that science emphasizes the importance of universals and is constantly seeking to discover and formulate them through observation of particulars. And so our problem takes another form: What is the relation between the universals of science and the particulars through observation of which they are discovered and formulated? Does science lead us away from or towards reality? This problem is more comprehensive in scope than the one discussed in the preceding section under the heading of matter and its qualities. But, as will appear in our consideration of it, it is in principle the same problem stated in more general terms. As so stated, however, it has peculiarities of its own that call for separate consideration.

In answer to the question: How are universals and particulars related to each other? there are, in the main, three views. According to the first, universals and particulars are related to each other as a copy is related to the original; particulars are the copies and universals are the originals.

This is the answer given by Plato in his doctrine of 'Ideas'; the universals with which science deals are, in his theory, the 'Ideas' which the various objects of perceptual experience more or less faithfully copy in spatial and temporal form. The second answer to the question runs to the effect that the universals of science are related to the particulars of perceptual experience as the name 'John Doe' is related to the individual known by that name. The universals of thought are mere names which are used to denote or point out the various individual objects and groups of individual objects that exist in the physical environment. According to the third answer, universals are merely descriptive of relations obtaining among particulars. Various particulars bear certain definite relations, either qualitative or quantitative, to each other; and the description of these relations are their corresponding universals.

Corresponding to these three views of the relation between universals and particulars there are three views concerning their reality. The 'copy' view of the relation between the two implies the conclusion that universals are real and particulars are appearances of them. According to this view, scientific reflection leads in the direction of reality, and in doing so it leaves behind the particulars as unreal illusions. The 'name' view of the relation between the two implies that the particulars only are real, universals being nothing more than convenient signs or symbols used to indicate groups of particulars and, consequently, nothing more than 'appearances.' This view holds that scientific reflection leads directly away from reality towards appearances, though it may admit that such reflection has practical value in so far as classification of particulars is useful for practical purposes. The 'descriptive' view of the relation between universals and particulars is forced to say that both are real; particulars are real as existent qualities, while universals are real as organizations of particulars. From this point of view, scientific reflection leads in the direction of reality, not by neglecting the particulars, but by penetrating them and describing more completely their nature. The 'copy' theory assumes an external relation between particulars and universals with emphasis upon the reality of universals and the illusory nature of particulars. The 'name' theory, likewise, holds that the relation between particulars and universals is external, but the emphasis here is just reversed: the particulars are real, while universals are fictitious but convenient because of their utility. The 'descriptive' theory insists upon an internal relation between particulars and universals, each being involved in the other, and consequently the reality of both is emphasized. The first theory is historically known as *realism;* and the second, as *nominalism.* For the present elementary discussion we may agree to call the third the doctrine of the *concrete universal.*

Viewed in the light of the actual procedure of scientific reflection, both realism and nominalism appear to be erroneous. The universals of science, on the one hand, are not arrived at by neglecting the study of particulars; on the contrary, the discovery of these universals is always conducted in the light of a very careful scrutiny of particulars. Precise observation of particulars and constant reference to them are, as we saw in our study of the method of science, indispensable to the scientist. On the other hand, there seems not the least justification for calling these universals of science convenient fictions, as the nominalist does. They are discovered by a close and persistent study of particulars, and therefore they must be really connected with them; if by observing particular objects the universal of gravitation is ultimately arrived at, then gravitation must be a real aspect of those particulars through the observation of which it is discovered. Thus both nominalism and realism appear not to harmonize with the actual procedure of scientific reflection. The doctrine of the concrete universal, however, does harmonize with scientific procedure. The scientist discovers the universal through a study of the particulars, and therefore the relation between the universal and the particulars must be a very intimate one. The procedure of the scientist, thus, shows that universals and particulars are involved in each other; and that is precisely the contention of the theory which we have called the concrete universal. This, therefore, seems so far established.

It can be further established by reference to what was said in Chapters VI and VII about judgment. We there learned that every judgment is both analytical and synthetical, and that its analysis and its synthesis are two sides of the same process of judging. Now the universals of science are merely syntheses that scientific reasoning makes on the basis of protracted analyses of particular aspects of the environment. Gravitation, for example, is a synthesis which science has made on the basis of the analysis of objects as having mass and bearing to each other spatial relations of distance and motion. To say, then, that the universals of science are involved in the particulars of which they are the synthesis is to say over again what we have already argued is true of all judgment. And from this it seems to follow that the theory of the concrete universal, rather than either realism or nominalism, is the true account of the relation between the particulars of perceptual experience and the universals of scientific reflection.

What, then, is the relation between the universals of

science and the particulars of sense-perception, and which are real? The answer is: universals and particulars are involved in each other, and both are real. A given universal, such as gravitation or matter or evolution, is involved within the particulars relevant to its discovery and formulation. Reality is organized particulars; and scientific reflection — all genuine reflection — is the account of this organization and is based upon analysis of the particulars involved in the system. Neither the particular alone nor the universal alone is real; reality is their systematic interpenetration, and this it is the business of reasoning to unravel through the analytical-synthetical function of judgment.[1]

§ 5. *Reality and appearance*

In the preceding discussion of the problem of matter and its qualities and the problem of universals and particulars we arrived at the conclusion that, in each case, both are real, neither is mere appearance. But no effort was made in that discussion to define what we are to understand by 'reality' and what by 'appearance.' This we must now in conclusion undertake to do, and so we are finally led back to the general problem with which the chapter began. The intervening discussion may have shed light upon the question that will help us to an answer.

The assumption upon which we have proceeded in our discussion is that whatever exists is real. Matter and its qualities, particulars and universals, we have argued, are

[1] While the above discussion has been stated in terms that apply most directly to particulars and universals of the physical environment, the principles advanced are applicable to all phases of the environment. All universals of thought, whether in the physical or the social environment, bear this internal relation to their corresponding particulars; and the reality in each case is the *system* of particulars. We shall have to go over this again later when studying problems in other fields.

real because they exist; and this obviously assumes that whatever exists is real. Now this assumption we all inevitably make. Tables, trees, mountains, human beings, the earth, the solar system — these exist, that is, they are real. Reality and existence, thus, are synonymous terms. Whatever can be said to exist must, for that reason, be granted reality.

To say that the real is whatever exists, however, does not get us anywhere in our definition of reality unless we can indicate the distinguishing marks of existence. We have only changed the form of our problem from, What is real? to, What can be said to exist? But the change in form is helpful. What exists? is a question more easily answered than, What is real? Now the only means by which we can determine what exists is that interpreting activity of the mind which we have called judgment and the basal characteristics of which we have noted in our discussion of it. Whatever judgment forces us to say exists does, we have to assume, necessarily exist. If my judgment, 'This before me is a typewriter desk,' is a necessary judgment, that is, if its assertion and acceptance involves less contradiction of other judgments than does its denial and rejection, then the typewriter desk exists and must be called real. Of course, some judgments that at one time are supposed to be necessary judgments turn out later not to be necessary at all, and so we are not always sure of the existence of objects of judgment. But this means nothing more than that some of our judgments are erroneous. Judgments forced upon us by our experiences, that is, by other judgments, we cannot but suppose are indicative of existence; if some of these judgments turn out to be erroneous and so not necessary, that is only a proof of what we all know, namely, that the human mind is not infallible.

But are not so-called 'appearances' necessary judgments also, and must they not therefore be called real? When I see the stick bent in the water, for example, or the railway lines converging in the distance, are not the judgments, 'The stick is bent' and 'The lines are convergent,' necessary judgments? In a certain sense they undoubtedly are necessary. In respect of the laws of refraction of light in the one case, and of the laws of optics in the other, each judgment is a necessary judgment and is as valid and true as any other judgment could possibly be. When I say that because of the laws of refraction of light the stick in the water is bent, or because of the laws of optics the perspective of the railway lines is convergent, in each case my judgment is true and the object of judgment exists and is real; under these conditions the 'bentness' of the stick and the 'convergence' of the lines are real. If, however, I judge that the stick is bent out of the water, or that the railway lines converge outside of the field of vision, then in each case the judgment is not a necessary judgment, is, in fact, erroneous, and the object of judgment does not exist but is only an 'appearance.'

What, then, is the distinction between appearance and reality? If our analysis is correct, the reply must be: it is the distinction between erroneous and true judgments. The objects of true judgments exist and are real; the objects of erroneous judgments do not exist and have appearance only. Of course, it is difficult, frequently, to distinguish between true and erroneous judgments. This difficulty we have already considered in our chapter devoted to the problem of the validity of the intellectual enterprise, and we have there suggested what tests seem available. The intellectual enterprise is a venture, and not infrequently stumbles; it is not surprising, therefore, that we should often mistake an 'appearance' for a 'reality.' But the venture we make willy-nilly, and the consequent risk is inescapably ours.

Chapter XI. Questions and Exercises

1. State clearly the problem of appearance and reality, and show how it arises.

2. Indicate the two special problems into which the general problem of appearance and reality may be divided when it is stated in terms of the concept of matter.

3. State the distinction between primary and secondary qualities, and indicate its bearing on the problem of matter and its qualities. (Consult Locke's discussion as found in the *Essay Concerning Human Understanding,* Book II, Chapter VIII.)

4. Summarize the main points in Berkeley's criticism of the distinction between primary and secondary qualities in his *Principles of Human Knowledge,* sections 9–21.

5. Distinguish the three views mentioned in the text concerning the relation between universals and particulars.

6. State in your own words the general conclusion of the chapter with reference to the problem of appearances and reality.

7. Read Hoernle; *Matter, Life, Mind, and God,* Lecture II. Summarize main points developed.

CHAPTER XII

SPACE AND TIME

As we saw in our introductory chapter, the physical environment presents three sides or aspects; these we called matter, space, and time. In the two chapters immediately preceding we have made a short study of the concept of matter and some of the problems to which it gives rise. It remains for us to glance at some of the problems attaching to the notions of space and time before passing on to a survey of the problems of life, mind, and values.

§ 1. *The notion of space*

Particular objects in our physical environment, as we have noted, bear to each other certain relations which we designate as 'above' or 'below,' 'outside of' or 'inside of,' 'nearness' or 'remoteness,' 'larger' or 'smaller,' and the like. Such relations we call spatial relations. Space, then, may be roughly defined as the apparent relations of position, size, and shape among physical objects. Some further analysis of the main features of space may help us to get a bit clearer notion of its nature.

(1) Perceptual and conceptual space. In the first place, we must note a distinction sometimes drawn between what we may call two types of space. The first is perceptual space, by which is meant those spatial relations that we seemingly experience in the uncriticised judgments of sense-experience. The distances between objects, the rela-

tive sizes of objects, the directions of objects from given points of reference, the interiority or exteriority of objects in respect of each other — these as they present themselves to our sense-awareness constitute the data of our perceptual judgments of space. The second type is conceptual space which is in important respects different from perceptual space. Here we think of the above relations as in a sense idealised, conceived, that is, without reference to particular objects. The data of our conceptual judgments of space are not specific relations of size and position which physical objects bear to each other in direct experience; they are the general concepts of points and lines, surfaces and solids — in short, such spatial relations as the science of geometry studies. To state the two types of space summarily, then: perceptual space is the space of direct awareness of material objects as having positions and masses relative to each other; conceptual space, on the other hand, is the more abstract or idealised space of the sciences, particularly geometry and physics.

(2) SPACE VERSUS SPACES. At times we speak of *space,* as if there were only one; at other times we speak of *spaces,* as though there were many. 'The spaces of the world,' 'The depths of space' — these are common expressions. The apparent inconsistency of speech here exemplified arises from the two-fold nature of space outlined in the preceding paragraph. When we speak of *spaces* we are thinking of the perceptual type; *space,* on the other hand, usually means the conceptual type. The spaces of perceptual judgment are relations among the multitudinous objects of the physical environment — their varying distances, sizes, and positions. The space of conception is 'pure,' more or less independent of material objects, and so is readily thought of as one.

(3) THE DIMENSIONS OF SPACE. Whether perceptual or conceptual, space is commonly regarded as having three dimensions. In reference to perceptual spaces, these dimensions are length, breadth, and depth or thickness; the dimensions of conceptual space are essentially the same in principle but are defined more accurately as the line, the plane, and the solid. With all of these the reader is, of course, familiar.

§ 2. *The notion of time*

The objects that make up the material order of the world bear to each other another sort of relations besides the spatial. To this other sort of relations we give the name of time. These relations obtain among objects as changing; examples of such relations are 'precedence,' 'simultaneity,' 'succession,' 'duration,' and the like.

(1) PERCEPTUAL AND CONCEPTUAL TIME. As in the case of space, the distinction between the conceptual and perceptual types is supposed to hold in regard to time. And the distinction is in principle the same in the two cases. Perceptual time means those changes which we appear to experience directly within ourselves and in the objects about us as we live from day to day. The changes that we undergo as we run our course through life, the transformations that are bodied forth in objects as they move from place to place or arise and perish — these are the data of our perceptual judgment of time. Conceptualized, time is the 'stream' in which these changes take place, but thought of as more or less independent of the events themselves; it is rather the bare succession of instants of which our arbitrary divisions (seconds, minutes, hours, days, years) are fragmentary and incomplete parts. Conceptual time is idealised duration.

(2) Time versus times. Like space, time is apparently one or many as we please; stretches of duration vary from individual to individual and from situation to situation, but the clock informs us that they are constant. And here, once more, the apparent inconsistency is explicable on the basis of the distinction between perceptual and conceptual time. As perceptual, time is primarily pluralistic in its connotation; in a sense there are as many times as there are individuals who experience it, since duration varies with psychological attitudes and the circumstances that engender them. As conceptual, however, time is one ceaseless flow of duration, so the common assumption runs, which is 'pure' and untouched by the vicissitudes of human fortune and which, consequently, is absolutely constant.

(3) The dimension of time. Space, we have suggested, appears to be tri-dimensional; time, it would seem, has only one dimension, namely, succession. Past, present, and future are only three stages in the one continuous flow of succession, which runs in one direction. The 'present' is in a state of unstable equilibrium, continuously tumbling into the future and as constantly lapsing into the past. Moreover, this direction of time cannot be reversed; it is from past to present, from present to future, and not *vice versa*. Time runs in one direction, and its direction is irreversible. It is to be noted, however, that past, present, and future are more sharply sundered in conceptual, than they are in perceptual, time. Where temporal facts are concerned (some temporal facts at all events, such as human personality), the past and future are not sharply separable from the present; in such cases the present is, in Professor James' striking phrase, a 'saddle-back,' its edges are ragged and sinuous, and it overlaps both the past and the future. In conceptual time, on the other hand, the present

is regarded as clean-cut, an instant which is neither past nor future, and which, when past, is gone forever.

§ 3. *The infinity of space and time*

It is commonly supposed that both space and time are in some sense infinite. The purpose of the present section is to inquire briefly into the meaning and justification of this assumption.

(1) Infinite extension of space and infinite duration of time. If one imagines an object moving away from the earth in a straight line, there is no conceivable end to its journey; it may go on indefinitely, and still there is always a 'beyond' yet untraversed. Thus it seems necessary to conclude that there is no end to the extension of space. If one "takes the wings of the morning" and flies with the speed of light into the abyss of the heavens, space spreads yet before him. Space is infinitely extended. And the same seems true of the duration of time. However far into the recesses of the past or the vistas of the future one may allow his imagination to sweep, there is no conceivable instant at which there is not a still more remote past or a still more distant future. Time is infinite in duration. By the infinity of the extension of space and of the duration of time, then, is meant that there is no conceivable end to either: space lies and time flows — both without end.

(2) Infinite divisibility of space and time. On the other hand, if we look toward the 'here' of space and the 'now' of time, we find the same bewildering boundlessness apparently present. There is no point of space, however small, which cannot conceivably be smaller; a line of any length may be broken into halves, each half into quarters, each quarter into eighths, and so on indefinitely. Likewise,

there is no instant of time so short in duration that it cannot be conceived as shorter just as long as one pleases. Seconds are not the irreducible minimum of duration; why not tenths, hundredths, thousandths, of seconds? Science, indeed, frequently finds this further subdivision necessary; and the only justification for stopping the sub-division at any fraction is the consideration of practical convenience or the imperfection of instruments of measurement. Theoretically there is no limit. Thus space and time are infinite in divisibility, apparently, just as they are infinite in extension and duration. And by infinity is meant here, once again, *without end:* the point of space or the instant of time is never so small that it could not conceivably be smaller.[1]

(3) DIFFICULTIES CONNECTED WITH THE INFINITY OF SPACE AND TIME. It has long been known that there are certain peculiarly puzzling difficulties connected with the infinity of space and time, particularly with their infinite divisibility.[2] These difficulties turn around certain apparent contradictions that arise in connection with the effort to conceive space and time as actually infinite and at the same time as holding of the observed world of objects. A simple illustration (adapted from Zeno's arguments) may be set down as a sample of the nature of these difficulties.

1 Compare the lines of Swift:

> So naturalists observe, a flea
> Has smaller fleas that on him prey;
> And these have smaller still to bite 'em,
> And so proceed *ad infinitum.*

2 The old Greek philosopher, Zeno of Elea (490–430 B.C.) was among the first to call attention to these difficulties, and he did so in the interest of this theory that motion cannot be real. His formulation of the difficulties is varied; the best known of his arguments are the paradoxes of Achilles and the tortoise, and the moving arrow. These and others of his arguments may be found in convenient form in Bakewell, *Sourcebook in Ancient Philosophy,* pp. 22–25.

We ordinarily observe objects moving through space, and there seems to be nothing unusual or difficult about such an observation. But if one takes in earnest the notion that space is infinitely divisible and exists as an absolute entity in the objective order, the fact of motion presents logical difficulties of great proportions. For consider: A point (or an object) cannot conceivably move along a line (of any given length) because (*a*) it cannot start moving, (*b*) it cannot continue in motion even if it should somehow start, and (*c*) it cannot arrive at the end of the line even if it continues to move indefinitely. (*a*) It cannot start moving, because, by hypothesis, there is always an infinite number of points along the line between the position it occupies before it starts and any position it might take after starting; thus there is no position *first after the starting point,* and so it cannot begin to move. (*b*) Again, assume it to be in motion, it could not continue to move because there is no position *next to* the position it any moment may occupy along the line, and for the same reason, namely, there is always an infinite number of points between any position occupied and any other possible position; so it cannot continue to move, since there is no *next position* into which it may move. (*b*) Finally, it can never reach the end of the line because there is no *last* point or position in the series of points through which it must go before it can reach the end, and, once more, for the same reason — between it and the point at the end of the line there is always an infinite number of points. In short, the infinite divisibility of space seems to invest motion with contradiction and so reduces it to a logical impossibility; motion appears to be genuinely inconceivable in the sense that it is self-contradictory. This is only one among the many puzzles that appear to attach to the conception of the infinity of space and time; but it illustrates the fact that there are logical difficulties here, and so for our present purpose it is sufficient.

(4) EFFORTS TO REMOVE THE DIFFICULTIES. Two paths have been suggested along which it is thought escape from the difficulties attaching to the infinity of space and time may be found. One of these, according to some thinkers, lies through a fuller understanding and a more rigorous application of the principles involved in the numerical conception of infinity and continuity. For recent inquiries into the nature of numbers show that infinity means, not endlessness, but system definable by reference to a certain law which characterizes the series; and that an infinite series may be *continuous* and *dense,* that is, *one whole* of parts that merge into each other and not a collection of an indefinite number of discrete and sharply sundered parts. Applying these principles to space and time, those who follow this way of escape urge that the puzzles about motion seem to vanish. For the infinity of space and time does not mean that they are broken up into an infinite (that is, never-to-be-completed) number of sharply sundered points or instants, but it rather means that they are self-contained wholes which are possessed of certain unique characteristics, among which are those of *continuity* and *density.* Now it is these characteristics, we are assured, that make motion intelligible; indeed, these characteristics of space and time are ultimately definable only in terms of motion. The rigorous analysis of the conception of number, thus, seems to some to offer a clue whereby the riddle of motion may be solved. This is, of course, a very technical way out of the difficulty, and we cannot here presume to follow it farther.[1]

[1] Those who have the inclination to go farther in this direction and the mathematical training sufficient to enable them to do so will find a

The other way out of the difficulties connected with the infinity of space and time is less difficult, perhaps, but how far satisfactory remains questionable. It lies through the distinction drawn above between perceptual and conceptual space and time, though it also touches upon the points involved in the mathematical way out. As perceptual, it is suggested, neither space nor time is infinite; as conceptual, both are infinite. But the infinity of *conceptual* time and space, it is supposed, does not involve us in the difficulties suggested above, since space and time as conceptual are by their very nature partly at least removed from the world of sense-perception and cannot logically therefore throw any stumbling-blocks in the way of the concrete ranges of experience. Motion, to take the case mentioned above, is a fact within perceptual, not within conceptual, space; therefore the infinity of conceptual space presents no logical difficulties to a moving object.[1]

§ 4. *Objectivity of space and time*

Are space and time objective in the sense that they are actually existent entities as physical objects are, or must they be described in some other fashion? To this question different answers have been proffered, three of which we may here set down.

(1) SPACE AND TIME AS ENTITIES. It is commonly assumed that space and time have an objective existence in the same sense in which physical objects have. They are supposed to be forms, so to speak, in which matter moves

convenient starting-point in Spaulding, *The New Rationalism,* pp. 451–469. The references there given will point the way still farther.

[1] The following references may be consulted for further discussion: Fullerton, *Introduction to Philosophy,* Chapters VI–VII. Sellars, *The Essentials of Philosophy,* Chapters XVII–XVIII. Fletcher, Introduction to *Philosophy,* Chapters XXXI–XXXII. Pearson, *Grammar of Science,* 3rd edition, Part I, Chapter VI.

about and changes from state to state. This is the common-sense notion of space and time. It is the view which has been handed down as a tradition from Galileo and Newton, both of whom were convinced that space and time are objectively existent frameworks of the material order.[1] And, until quite recently, this was the view of the physical sciences generally. But recent developments in these sciences have led to the formulation of another theory, as we shall see below.

(2) SPACE AND TIME AS FORMS OF PERCEPTION. Opposed to the notion of space and time as objective and absolute entities is the view which regards them simply as necessary forms of perception. According to this view space and time are nothing more than ways in which the human mind experiences objects, spectacles, as it were, through which the mind looks out on its environment. Were all human minds and all other minds similarly constructed (if there be any) blotted out, space and time would forthwith cease to be. They are not in things, but in the mind that experiences things. They are, to be sure, necessary forms of perception or experience, not idle fancies to be dispensed with at pleasure; but they are of the mind nevertheless.[2]

[1] Newton's conception is as follows: "Absolute, true and mathematical time flows in virtue of its own nature uniformly and without reference to any external object." "Absolute space, by virtue of its own nature and without reference to any external object, always remains the same and is immovable." Quotations taken from Schlick, *Space and Time in Contemporary Physics* (translation by H. L. Brose), p. 2.

[2] Among classical philosophers Kant most vigorously advocates this view of space and time (see the division of the *Critique of Pure Reason* called "The Transcendental Aesthetic"). His thesis is: "space is nothing at all, if its limitation to possible experience is ignored, and it is treated as a necessary condition of things in themselves"; and "in abstraction from the subjective conditions of sensible perception, time is simply nothing, and cannot be said either to subsist by itself, or to inhere in things that do so subsist" (Watson, *Selections from Kant,* pp. 29, 34). Pearson (*Grammar of Science,* 3rd edition, Part I, Chapter VI)

(3) SPACE AND TIME AS ABSTRACT CONCEPTS. A third view of space and time regards them as general notions or conceptions derived from particular experiences. On this view, space and time are abstract ideas and have significance only as such. Perhaps the clearest expression of this view is to be found in that admirable discussion of ideas by John Locke, the famous *Essay Concerning Human Understanding,* to which we have already had occasion several times to refer. Space, Locke tells us, is an idea that we get by contemplating either the distances between objects or their bare extension. When we think of the extension of objects (length, breadth, and thickness) without any reference to the objects themselves, or of the distance between objects when there is nothing in it, we are thinking of pure space. Time, in its turn, is nothing but duration broken into various lengths (hours, minutes, seconds, etc.); while duration means the distance between any parts of that succession of ideas which we experience as they come and go in our minds. Time, thus, is measured duration, and duration is an idea we get from the succession of our mental experiences. So, for Locke, space and time are the ideas we derive from the contemplation of distances between objects or different parts of objects on the one hand (space), and between ideas as they run their course in our minds on the other (time). And this account by Locke may be taken as a statement of the third view of space and time which we desire here to contrast with the other two views previously defined.[1]

---

advocates a view somewhat similar to Kant's, though he would apparently explain space and time in terms much more psychological than Kant would be willing to employ. For Pearson "Space and time are not realities of the phenomenal world, but the modes under which we perceive things apart" (*Grammar of Science,* p. 218).

[1] Locke's full account of the matter will be found in the *Essay,* Book II, Chapters IV, XIII–XV.

(4) Critical estimate of the three views above stated. It is clear that the three views of space and time above outlined cannot all be accepted, since they are not consistent with each other. If space and time be absolute entities, then neither the second nor the third view is acceptable. Each of the views has an element of truth in it; but there is reason to hold that none of them is entirely satisfactory. (*a*) Taken as absolute entities, space and time force upon us those paradoxes about infinity which we have already noted; furthermore, recent investigation has disclosed that such a conception of space and time cannot explain certain important facts in the physical environment and it is consequently being abandoned by scientific thought as we shall see in the next section. (*b*) If we think of space and time as mere forms of perception, ways in which the mind experiences objects as extended and changing, we cannot help but wonder why objects in the world about us and we ourselves behave so persistently as if space and time were somehow objective realities. (*c*) And the explanation of space and time as general notions derived from special experiences which we have with distances of extension and duration seems no explanation at all; for 'extension,' 'duration,' and 'succession' are themselves apparently only space and time under other names. So it would appear that neither of these three views is a wholly satisfactory description of these basal notions of our experience.

§ 5. *The theory of the relativity of space and time*

Recent scientific developments, particularly in the fields of mathematics and physics, have led to a new conception of space and time which promises to overturn a good many assumptions that hitherto have seemed established. Apparently we are on the eve of a new theory which certainly has far-reaching implications. The technicalities involved in the formulation of this new view forbid any attempt here to outline its arguments, even in their more superficial aspects. Some mention of the view must be made, however, if only to call attention to its existence and to give some references in connection with it. The attempt will be made merely to state two of its theses.

(1) THE WELDING OF SPACE AND TIME. The views discussed in the preceding section all alike assume that, whatever space and time may be, they are at least radically different from each other. The new theory holds, on the contrary, that, so far from being disparate, space and time are inseparably linked with each other as two sides or aspects of the same reality, namely, motion, and that the full consideration of the one necessitates a consideration of the other also. In short, it holds that space and time are connected in an intimate manner. Instead of speaking of space *and* time, as has been the custom hitherto, we should be much nearer the truth if we spoke only of space-time; they are in nature hyphenated.[1]

[1] "The mutual structural relations between events are both spatial and temporal. If you think of them as merely spatial you are omitting the temporal element, and if you think of them as merely temporal you are omitting the spatial element. Thus when you think of space alone, or of time alone, you are dealing in abstractions, namely, you are leaving out an essential element in the life of nature as known to you in the experience of your senses" (Whitehead, *The Concept of Nature,* p. 168).

"The idea that there is an absolute framework of time and a quite independent absolute framework of space is not easy to avoid. For we have been schooled to it, and the idea works well for the purposes of everyday life on our globe. But if both space and time are stripped of what is unessential, and presented in their bare nakedness, they look different. If there were no succession in time, and everything appeared as at one instant, a little reflection shows that we could not apprehend the positions of points in space. Their reality depends for us on their separation, which itself depends on transition, and this on succession in time. On the other hand, if, in the absence of all separation in space, there were only one spatial point in which existence centered for us as time elapsed, it is equally clear that intervals of time would have no

(2) THE RELATIVITY OF SPACE AND TIME. A second thesis of the new view, and the one which for us constitutes its chief importance, is that space and time are wholly relative to the motion of observers and the measuring systems they employ. The Newtonian conception of space and time as absolute entities existing everywhere the same as the framework of the world is given up; for the new view space and time taken as absolute are wholly without meaning. They have meaning only when referred to moving systems of objects, and they vary with those systems. Suppose, for example, an observer on the earth and another observer on the sun to be watching the same event; the spatial and temporal relations of that event will be different for the two observers since they belong to two different systems of reference one of which is moving and the other relatively at rest. "Big Ben [a London clock] strikes one and, an hour later, two. For me, sitting hard by in Queen Anne's Gate, the strokes appear to occur at the same place, and to be separated by an hour. This agrees, too, with what my own watch says. But an observer situated on the sun would consider that the strokes had occurred at different situations in space of Big Ben, for he would have seen that the earth had moved in the hour about 70,000 miles along its orbital track with respect to the sun, from which he is observing. In resolving the result of his observation into the space component of the position, he thus resolves it with a different result from mine, for whom, Big Ben being at rest for me, the change is *nil*. If he resolves the space by a different standard of reference, he has also to resolve the time component differently, for space and time . . . in-

meaning. Duration would be immeasurable, for it is by spatialising, as on the dial of a watch, that we measure it. Space and time are really abstractions from a reality which includes both in mutual implication" (Viscount Haldane, *The Reign of Relativity*, p. 46).

volve each other. The watch of the observer on the sun may be constructed on the same principles as my own, but the measurement of time by the units marked on the watch on the sun, though apparently analogous, will have a different meaning. Its apparent agreement with mine will not be real, for the spaces on its dial, to which reference has to be made for measurement in looking for the simultaneities belonging to correspondence in time as indicated on the dial spaces, will not be in reality corresponding spaces, the measurement being made on a different basis of reference. There will thus be two different local time systems, just as there are two different local space systems, and the observer in each will measure with reference only to the coordinates of his own system."[1] Thus both space and time are entirely relative to the standards of measurement used by observers, and these standards will vary as the relative movement of the systems in which the measurements are made vary.[2] Simultaneity, succession, length, and such similar relations of space and time have, for the new view, no absolute meaning which is eternally and immutably the same everywhere in the universe; on the contrary, these change from system to system of reference.[3]

---

1 Haldane, *The Reign of Relativity,* p. 86. The chapter in which this passage occurs is a comparatively simple statement of the theory of relativity. Another formulation of the point of the above quotation, which is slightly more abstract, will be found in Schlick, *Space and Time in contemporary Physics,* English translation, 1920, pp. 13-16.

2 Compare spatial relations as they appear to an observer in a swift moving train with the same spatial relations as an observer standing the track would experience them.

3 For example, at some inconceivable distance from us there events co-present with us now and also co-present with the birth Queen Victoria. If A and B are co-present there will be some system which A precedes B and some in which B precedes A. Also there be no velocity quick enough to carry a material particle from A and or from B to A. These different measure-systems with their divergencies of time-reckoning are puzzling, and to some extent affront our common sense. It is not the usual way in which we think of the Universe. We think of one necessary time-system and one necessary space. Accord-

Time and space, in short, are wholly relative to the circumstances under which they are experienced.

This looks like a direct return to one of the views of time and space noted above, the view, namely, that they are nothing but forms of perception. In a sense this may be said to be … . At least it is closely connected with the facts up an older view was based, such as the varying size of objects when seen under different conditions, the speculiarities of moving objects according as the observer is moving or at rest relative to them, and the like. But the new theory differs from the old in at least one important respect: it holds that space and time are in some sense objective, that is are real characteristics of the world of objects, and not merely forms of perception dependent exclusively upon the observer. The striking confirmation of the theory by the results obtained from observation of the total eclipse of the sun, May 29, 1919, seems clearly to show that it is in principle correct, and it is probably tined to play an important role in the immediate future of the physical sciences.[1]

The new theory, there are an indefinite number of discordant time-** indefinite number of distinct spaces" (Whitehead, *The … "Nature,* pp. 177-178).

1 The Theory of relativity is associated primarily with the name of Professor Einstein (born 1874), who is chiefly responsible for its mathematics proof. His researches can, of course, be understood only by those have a sufficient comprehension of the higher mathematics to follow reasoning. There are relatively simple expositions of the theory, at … of its general conclusions, couched in fairly untechnical language. There exposition of it is easy of comprehension, largely because of the indistinct difficulty of the subject but partly because the theory runs so counter to our traditional views. One who wants to understand the theory, even as regards its conclusions, must first learn to unthink much of what seems to him obvious about space and time.

Some of the relatively simpler expositions are: Albert Einstein, *The Special and General Theory of Relativity;* H. A. Lorentz, *The Einstein Theory of Relativity;* H.L. Brose, *The Theory of Relativity;* Steinmetz, *Space and Relativity.*

The more philosophical bearings of the theory are discussed in the two following books: H.W. Carr, *The General Principle of Relativity in*

6. *Conclusion*

From the discussion of this chapter at least one result should stand out clearly: space and time are very difficult notions. They are basal conceptions within our environment, but they stoutly defy any offhand analysis. For both the scientist and the philosopher they present pressing problems — problems which the philosopher has long been cognizant of and busy with, but which the scientist (at any rate, the physicist) has only comparatively recertify attacked as of fundamental importance in his own special field. And it is clear, also, that these problems are far from complete solution. The theory of relativity has solved some of them, and has thrown light upon many others; but from it arise still other problems whose solutions remain to be found. And here, once more, we have a concrete illustration of the principle which we have from time to time noted, namely, that the intellectual enterprise consists partly in making new problems grow out of the solutions of the old.

It is no part of our undertaking to presume to survey the special problems of the various sciences. But it is not amiss here to remark that the doctrine of the relativity of space and time, if accepted, presents to the physical sciences the task of restating many basic principles. For the current formulations of these principles presuppose the Newtonian view of space and time, and the new theory is a direct denial of certain aspects of this traditional view.[1] But into such matters we could not here presume further to enter, even if they were relevant to our task.

---

its Philosophical and Historical Aspect; Viscount Haldane, *The Reign of Relativity,* especially Chapters III-V.

[1] Note, for instance, the formulation of the law of gravitation which rests upon the Newtonian tradition. Whitehead, *The Concept of Nature,* pp. 179 ff., calls attention to the difficulty here involved, and suggests a reformulation.

The philosopher has long been troubled by the puzzling nature of space and time, and since the days of Zeno he has tried in his own way to deal with them. Particularly has he felt that space and time as absolute entities conceived 'without reference to any object' present difficulties that are very great.[1] So the new doctrine of relativity is not wholly new to the philosopher; not infrequently in the history of philosophy something like it in principle has been insisted upon, though with different emphasis.[2] But recent developments in the scientific conception of space, time, and motion have an important bearing on the philosophical side of the controversy, and shed much light upon it. The new view of space and time seems to the philosopher a special case of a more general problem, the problem of the relation between knowledge and reality. Is not all of our knowledge, and not merely our knowledge of space and time, relative to the observer? And does this mean that knowledge of the objective order of things is impossible? Just because the special case of space and time seems to the philosopher to be linked in principle with this larger question, the new doctrine of relativity throws much light on the more general question. It at least suggests that that which is 'relative' to the observer need not on that account be deemed 'unreal'; and it may even suggest that reality can be defined only in terms of knowledge, that reality and truth are synonymous terms.[3]

[1] Kant, particularly, emphasized the difficulties in his famous analysis of space and time. He even went so far as to hold that much of our mathematical knowledge would be wholly impossible if space and time were such absolute entities.

[2] See Haldane, *The Reign of Relativity*, Chapters III and VI for a brief survey of the matter.

[3] See section 5 of the preceding chapter. Lord Haldane's *The Reign of Relativity* should be read by those who want a scholarly discussion of the general philosophical bearings of the new doctrine of relativity.

CHAPTER XII. QUESTIONS AND EXERCISES

1. Define briefly space and time. Distinguish between perceptual and conceptual space and time. State main points developed by Pillsbury, *Essentials of Psychology*, pp. 162–176.

2. What is meant by the infinity of space and time?

3. Distinguish the following views of space and time:
   (*a*) As 'entities'
   (*b*) As 'forms of perception'
   (*c*) As 'abstract notions'

4. Can you answer satisfactorily to yourself the arguments about composition and division of matter and about motion advanced by Zeno? (For the arguments see Bakewell, *Sourcebook in Ancient Philosophy*, pp. 22–25.)

5. So far as you are able, make a study of any of the books mentioned at the end of section 5, and give a brief report on the theory of relativity explained in them.

PART IV

PROBLEMS OF LIFE

CHAPTER XIII

EVOLUTION: ITS MEANING AND TYPES

One of the basal characteristics both of ourselves and of our environment is change. Time, we have seen in the preceding chapter, is apparently universal in its scope, everything seems to be bitten by its tooth; and time is change. Nothing seems to be fixed and stable; we ourselves and all about us are in process of transformation. As the old Greek philosopher, Heracleitus, expressed it: "Everything flows."[1] Confronted by this universal fact, science has through centuries of reflection busied itself with the problems involved in it. In explanation of it the general theory of evolution has been developed; and, though still in process of being defined in details, this theory has come to be one of the basal categories in contemporary thought. It is a category which is applicable to other fields than that of the biological environment, as we shall see in our study of it; but, as we shall also see in our further inquiry, the category has special application in the biological field, and one of the most pressing of the philosophical problems to which it gives rise lies within its application to this field. Hence we may be justified in considering it under the head-

[1] Heracleitus (flourished about 500 B.C.) was a native of the city of Ephesus and is said to have been descended from the line of the Ephesian kings. Because of his somber view of life he is sometimes referred to as the 'weeping philosopher.' He is fond of stating his views in paradoxes, and many of his observations are very keen (see Bakewell, *Sourcebook in Ancient Philosophy*, Chapter III, for a translation of some fragments of his writings). In the history of philosophy he is noteworthy chiefly because of the great emphasis placed by him in his general view of the world upon the sweep and ultimate significance of change.

ing of the problems of life, though, strictly interpreted, it should not be so limited; really it is one aspect of the general problem of time. This limitation of the subject we may, however, be permitted to make for the purposes of our study. Our task is the two-fold one of learning something of what the general theory of evolution means and of inquiring into the problems connected with it. The meaning and types of the theory form the subject of the present chapter; the problems will be considered in the chapter that follows.

§ 1. *General meaning of evolution*

Stated in general terms, the category or theory of evolution is the thesis that the various complex forms of the world as they at present exist have grown by gradual stages from much simpler and less complex beginnings, which growth can be traced, in general outline at least, by piecing together evidence that falls within the limits of our observation and so can be scientifically defined or described. Literally, to 'evolve' means to 'unroll,' being derived from the Latin verb *evolvo* which is compounded of the two words *e* or *ex* ('out') and *volvo* ('to roll'). Taken generally as applied to the world at large or the universe, then, evolution is the process of the world's 'unrolling.' With reference to any special subdivision of the world (such, for example, as a planet or a species of animal or plant life) evolution is the 'unrolling' of that particular eddy within the gigantic stream of the world's ongoing. And the theories of evolution (for, as we shall see, there are different types) are the stories of how this unrolling, whether of planets or plants, has taken place told with as great precision and in as great detail as the scientist can command.

The notion that evolution is a fundamental feature of the world is practically as old as our Western science. The ancient Greek thinkers were all somewhat acquainted with it; and some of them, particularly Empedocles, Democritus, and Aristotle, developed fairly well-defined, though, from our present point of view, quite crude views concerning it. In the fragments of the writings of Empedocles one may find the modern doctrine of 'natural selection' rather clearly hinted at, though of course vaguely and even absurdly conceived in detail. The general doctrine of the development of the universe out of the primitive elements or 'atoms' is the fundamental thesis of the Democritean world-view. In the philosophy of Aristotle, likewise, the doctrine of the 'unrolling' of things is of fundamental importance, and his special biological studies anticipate with considerable clarity some of the basal aspects of the modern evolutionary view of life. But the main work in connection with the theory of evolution has of course been done in the modern period, and more particularly in the last two centuries. Among the great names here may be mentioned: Kant, Herschel, Lamarck, Laplace, Lyell, and Darwin. For the details concerning the work of these thinkers, and of numerous others who labored with them, the reader should consult the histories of the different sciences.[1]

[1] Libby's *History of Science,* H. F. Osborn's *From the Greeks to Darwin,* Thomson and Geddes' *Evolution,* and Merz's *History of European Thought in the Nineteenth Century,* Vol. II; Chapter IX, contain much information in easily accessible form. The more important works of the thinkers named above with their dates are: Kant, *General Natural History and Theory of the Heavens* (1755). Herschel, *The Construction of the Heavens* (1787). Lamarck, *Natural History of Animals* (1816-1822). Laplace, *Exposition of the Solar System* and *Celestial Mechanics* (1825). Lyell, *Principles of Geology* (1830–1833). Darwin, *Origin of Species* (1859).

Kant, Laplace, and Herschel were interested in the evolution of the stellar world primarily; and with their names is associated the beginning

The general fact of evolution naturally divides itself into three special types. These are: the evolution of inorganic matter, the evolution of life, and the evolution of human society. A brief survey of the meaning of each of these will help us to grasp the meaning of the general concept.

§ 2. *Biological evolution*

At present when evolution is mentioned one thinks immediately of biological evolution, or the evolution of life. This is probably due to two facts. The first is that Charles Darwin, a biologist interested exclusively in the facts of life, by his masterful presentation of evidence in his epoch-making book, *Origin of Species* (1859), ultimately convinced the scientific world. The other fact is that the biological sciences have been constantly discovering such evidence of the validity of the evolutionary view as is in the main readily intelligible to the lay mind. However that may be, evolution at present primarily connotes biological or organic evolution. So we consider this type first.

(1) TYPES OF BIOLOGICAL EVOLUTION. As the name indicates, biological evolution means the unrolling of organisms, the growth and transformation of organic forms, from relatively simple beginnings through various stages of increasing complexity. Of biological evolution there are two types which must be distinguished, namely, *ontogenetic* and *phylogenetic*.

(a) *Ontogenetic evolution.* By this is meant the evolution of the individual organisms of any given species from their beginning in a simple cell to their mature and

of the nebular hypothesis (see Berry, *Short History of Astronomy*). Lyell was chiefly concerned with the problem of the evolution of the earth. Lamarck and Darwin devoted their attention primarily to the evolution of life on earth.

complex forms. The chick, for example, grows from a simple beginning in the egg through various stages of complexity up to the mature individual with fully developed organs, muscles, and bones. The story of this 'unrolling' of the chick is a study in ontogeny. This is the sort of evolution which the embryologist investigates in his laboratory by taking individual organisms of the same species at different stages of their development and through comparative study working out their life history. It is a type of evolution with which we are all familiar through our ordinary casual observation of plants and animals; it is illustrated in the growth of every organism, including our own.

(b) *Phylogenetic evolution.* Phylogenetic evolution is the name given to the evolution of species. Like any individual organism, a given species, such as the horse or dog, is supposed to have had its beginning in relatively simple forms and from this simple beginning to have 'unrolled' through multitudinous types of varying complexity until the form in which it at present is commonly known was attained. The story of this development or unrolling of a species is a study in phylogenetic evolution. This is the type of evolution in which the comparative anatomist is interested. The horse of to-day can thus be traced back through generations of different types to a pigmy quadruped (called the eohippus) eleven inches in height and with several toes in place of a hoof. In the same way, different species are observed to have similarities of structure which are supposed to be indicative of some sort of common origin. Phylogenetic evolution, thus, calls our attention to facts farther removed from common-sense observation than are those studied in ontogeny; but these facts are none the less significant on that account.

As held by scientists of to-day, then, biological evolution means that life has in the course of the world's ongoing sprung from simple organic forms and has developed through different stages and in various directions according to discoverable laws; and that the development from simple beginnings to complex maturity of individual organisms such as we see going on around us every day is an illustration of the more general development of species.

(2) AGENCIES IN BIOLOGICAL EVOLUTION. The main factors operative in the evolution of life as defined by Darwin are three: struggle for existence, heredity, and variation.

(a) *Struggle for existence.* A fundamental characteristic of every living creature is the tendency manifested by it to take care of itself and, to the extent of its ability, to make use of its environment for the gratification of its own needs. This tendency drives the organism to strive both to continue in existence and to enlarge its sphere of influence. Self-preservation and self-development is its goal, towards which it is driven by its very nature as a living being. Thus there arises a struggle among living beings for existence; those that win in the struggle survive, while the losers perish. The struggle is one of 'tooth and claw'; life is the issue at stake. Such in bald outline is Darwin's conception of the struggle for existence and the necessity for it.

(b) *Variation.* In the struggle for existence, Darwin further maintained, some individual organisms have the advantage over others because they happen to possess characteristics favorable to the conflict which the others lack. Darwin explains these as chance variations; variations, that is, which occur in the course of the struggle but which cannot be explained in the light of our present knowledge of the structural organization of individual organisms. Such variations he regards as potent factors in the evolution of life.

(*c*) *Heredity.* But, if those variations which happen to appear in the individual organism and prove advantageous to it in its struggles to exist are to prove advantageous to the species as well, they must obviously be transmitted from generation to generation of organisms. This transmission of characteristics from an individual organism to its offspring has been shown to be an actual fact, and to it is given the name of heredity.

These three factors constitute the fundamental elements within the general principle which Darwin named 'natural selection.' And it was upon this principle that he relied to account for life's evolution. This principle is obviously potent in the development of life as we observe it around us in forest and field; it is therefore reasonable to assume, he argued, that it is operative in the evolution of life generally. And on the basis of this assumption he built his explanation of the origin of species. The details of these three factors within natural selection, particularly the factor of heredity, are very differently conceived to-day and many changes have been, and are being, made in Darwin's account. But the evolutional factors themselves are still accepted by biologists generally as in principle correct.

§ 3. *Social evolution*

Social evolution is that part of the general evolutionary process in which human beings participate, and which is due largely to their behavior. The development of moral customs, religious beliefs and practices, types of civic or governmental organization, industrial enterprises, systems of thought, etc., are examples of the sort of evolution here under consideration. It is, in short, the evolution characteristic of the social environment.

(1) Types of social evolution. There are as many types of social evolution as there are distinguishable aspects of the social environment. And so we might summarize these types under the six headings mentioned above in Chapter I as different sides which the environment as social presents. It will be simpler, however, and for our present purpose sufficient, to group these different aspects of the social environment under the two heads of *institutions* and *convictions*. And so we shall here mention only two types of social evolution, namely, the evolution of institutions and the evolution of convictions. These two with fair accuracy include the main phases of the development of the social environment.

(a) *Evolution of institutions.* On the one side social evolution is evident in the development of institutions. By 'institutions' are here meant the more or less permanent embodiments of various sorts of relations obtaining among the individuals that make up the social group. In illustration may be mentioned the important institutions of the family, the church, the state, civic and industrial organizations, and color, class, and race traditions. Such institutions are constantly undergoing changes, and the changes to which they are subject constitute that aspect of social evolution we here call institutional.

(b) *Evolution of convictions.* The other side of the changing social order is to be found in developing convictions. By 'convictions' here are meant beliefs or judgments reflectively arrived at and accepted as true. These, also, are constantly changing, and, as in the case of institutions, there is a certain continuity in the midst of the changes. This side of social development finds its chief expression in man's cultural life — in his artistic, scientific, and philosophical systems; but it is also inherent within his institutional development. Within his arts, sciences, and philosophies it stands out in bold relief; in a less conspicuous, but no less significant, manner it is present deep within the current of the evolution of institutions.

Of social evolution there is, and can be, no serious question. Each of its aspects is a fundamental side of human history. And each is inextricably bound up with the other. Carlyle has emphasized this sort of evolution in the fourth lecture of his *Heroes and Hero-Worship:* "I do not make much of 'Progress of Species' as handled in these times of ours. . . . Yet I may say, the fact itself seems certain enough. . . . No man whatever believes, or can believe, exactly what his grandfather believed; he enlarges somewhat by fresh discovery, his view of the Universe; and consequently his Theorem of the Universe. . . . It is the history of every man; and in the history of mankind we see it summed up into great historical amounts — revolutions, new epochs. . . . So with all beliefs whatsoever in this world — all Systems of Beliefs and Systems of Practice that spring from these."

(2) THE NATURE OF SOCIAL EVOLUTION. The thesis of the theory of social evolution is that the institutions and convictions that constitute the content of the social environment always evolve from simpler social forms. As in the field of the phenomena of life, so here, the process has been from the simple to the more complex. "Civil law and political institutions, industrial, commercial and banking customs, methods of transportation and numberless machines have evolved by stages that are known in detail; and some of these stages have been gone through almost be-

fore our very eyes. And if the new has grown out of the old when progress has been so largely the result of reflective thought, how surely must it have so grown in the early days of history! The evidence that it did so is abundant. The anthropologists and the students of the dawn of history are revealing to us everywhere the growth of early civilization out of primitive culture, for example, in the political and social organization of peoples, in their religion and speculations, in their buildings, and in their tools and industries. Even such sciences as medicine, chemistry, astronomy, and history grew directly from primitive magic and myths." [1] The social environment is in process of change; it has unrolled from, and out of, previous simpler institutions and beliefs, and ultimately out of primitive 'folkways.' The new emerges out of the old by continuous stages. This is the theory of social evolution at present generally accepted by the historians of human civilization. Abundant evidence is at hand to establish the thesis; and every discovery relating to social organization, both in the present and in the immediate and remote past, adds strength to the evidence at hand. The social environment unrolls: it is, as is life itself, an evolution.

(3) AGENCIES IN SOCIAL EVOLUTION. Social evolution consists largely in those changes within the existing order demanded by reflection; apart from reflection, the existing order would remain practically static. Changing convictions, then, are the dynamic element within the changing social environment; upon them depend the transformation of institutions. As Carlyle says in the above quotation, it is because "no man believes, or can believe, exactly what his grandfather believed" that change in the social environment is inevitable. Any agency, therefore, which de-

[1] Marvin: *The History of European Philosophy*, p. 7.

velops reflection and thought is an agency in social evolution. There are many of these, but only the following can here be noted as of special importance.

(a) *Work.* The necessity that the human race finds forced upon it to make provisions for its continuance in existence, to supply itself with food and shelter, makes thinking in its turn a necessity. In the primitive forms of occupation, hunting and fishing, alertness is of great importance; mere brute force and physical prowess do not here guarantee success, cunning is also essential. In the later forms of occupation, agriculture and commerce, mental alertness is indispensable. Work, thus, necessitates thought and so is a potent factor in social evolution.[1]

(b) *Conflicts of interests.* Conflicting interests constitute another important factor in social evolution, since thinking is absolutely necessary to resolve them. Mental alertness, inventiveness, the capacity to guess another's plans or to understand another's point of view — these are essential if one mind is to meet another mind and gain the victory at stake. And this is true whether the conflict is purely mental, as in a business transaction or a difference of belief, or physical, as in battle. "Not to the strong is the battle, nor to the swift is the race" — at least, not always. Strategy is an element of no mean importance.

[1] It is true that since the modern industrial revolution which has resulted in very great specialization of labor many of the workers have little to do but watch machinery and see that it does the work properly; and thus little demand is made of the worker that he *think.* He threatens to become little more than a machine himself. Two points here, however, are to be noted: this reduction by modern industrial organisation of many laborers to mere watchers of machinery constitutes one pressing social problem for the present generation; and, secondly, the more complex industrial organization becomes the more thought is required on the part of somebody. Specialized work has not eliminated the necessity of thought, it has rather emphasized it; but it has placed the necessity upon the shoulders of a few — the managers and planners — and threatens to convert the majority of workers into mere tools.

And, of course, in mental conflicts, strategy alone is important.

(c) *The outstanding individuals.* Perhaps the most powerful single factor in social evolution is the outstanding individual, the individual who thinks beyond his fellows and by so doing becomes a marked individual within the group. The great warrior or hunter at the earlier levels of society shapes to a very large extent the outlook of his group and determines its practices; even if he does not wholly transform the institutions of his group by breaking with tradition, he necessarily leaves his mark upon them and they cannot be precisely as of old. At the later levels the prophets, poets, statesmen, philosophers, and scientists, in short, the *thinkers,* largely dig the channels in which future social change is to run. To ask what would have been the condition of society without its great religious and moral reformers, its leading soldiers and statesmen, its poets and painters and sculptors, its inventors and captains of industry, or its lovers of truth — to ask such a question is, of course, to ask a question that cannot possibly be answered. But the question may serve to emphasize the indispensable function performed by these exceptional individuals in that transformation of institutions and beliefs which we call social evolution. And they are thus powerful because in them reflection, the dynamo of social change, grows incarnate.

§ 4. *Inorganic evolution*

Evolution seems not to be limited in its scope to the organic realm alone. Long ago the Greeks were convinced that the inorganic world has had its history of continuous change from stage to stage of complexity, and modern science has wonderfully justified their conviction. Worlds and suns have also evolved, as have the tiniest elements of matter. Thus the inorganic and the organic alike are apparently involved within one vast sweep of an unrolling universe.

For the purposes of this elementary survey of inorganic evolution a consideration of three types will be sufficient. These are: geologic evolution, astral evolution, and atomic evolution.

(1) GEOLOGIC EVOLUTION. Study of the little planet on which we live reveals to the geologist the fact that it has not always been in the condition in which it appears to us. Only through various stages of change has it finally become the solid ball from which we draw our life. And these stages of transformation have left their traces in ocean, soil, rocks, rivers, and mountains, traces which the geologist pieces together as the string of evidence upon which he rests his story of the earth's development through aeons of time unimaginable. And the process, he tells us, is still going on before our very eyes in the formations that are being built up and the changes that are taking place all around us on the surface of our planet. The earth as it now appears is the result of infinitely gradual changes which have run their course in the ages gone and which even now are working irrevocably at their unending task. This, the geologist informs us, no one can doubt who has eyes to see and an understanding to appreciate the significance of what is observed.

(2) ASTRAL EVOLUTION. But terrestrial evolution, the growth of this little planet of ours, is only a short chapter in the gigantic book of nature and her ways. The astronomer bids us look abroad into the starry heavens above, and there he assures us we may see the process of evolution taking place on an infinitely larger scale. Our solar sys-

tem, too, has had its history, he informs us, and in his view the stars in their courses are but different manifestations of a universal evolution which includes within its scope the whole material universe. Through the use of spectroscope and telescope he discovers that these stellar bodies fall into three main groups of gaseous stars, metallic stars, and carbon stars. And in these groups he finds different chemical elements present. In the group with the highest temperatures, the gaseous stars, he discovers comparatively few chemical elements; and he discovers, further, that with a decrease in temperature from the gaseous through the metallic to the carbon stars more and more chemical elements appear with an ever-increasing complexity of organization. And so he concludes that those numberless stars yonder in the azure deeps are, like our little planet and the system to which it belongs, caught in the evolutionary whirl.

(3) ATOMIC EVOLUTION. But this is not the end of the story, wonderful as it seems. The chemist and the physicist, intent upon analyzing the elements of matter, urge us to turn our gaze towards the infinitesimal and see what wonders there nature reveals. In the infinitely small as in the infinitely large, they tell us, continuous change is at work. The very elements themselves, so long regarded as immutable and eternally fixed, are it now appears touched by transformation. Some of them at least are now known to be capable of transmutation into other elements, nor does the result of the transmutation seem to be any more 'ultimate' than the element from which it springs. Both uranium and thorium may be transmuted into new elements which in their turn may also change, as the emanation from radium, with a wholly new spectrum, changes into helium. If some of the elements change, then why

not all? Thus those bits of matter which have been supposed to be the unchanging foundations of the mighty frame of the world may be mere stages in the turn of the evolutionary wheel. They too, there is reason to suppose, are only particular aspects of the kaleidoscopic panorama of the world.

Thus throughout the material order nothing seems permanent. From molecules and atoms to whirling systems of suns and planets evolution holds sway. As in the realm of life and mind so in the realm of the inorganic, change is the rule. The old Greek was right: "Everything flows."

Chapter XIII. Questions and Exercises

1. What is the meaning of 'evolution'? What is the meaning of a theory of evolution?

2. Distinguish the following types of evolution: Biological, Social, Geological, Astral, Atomic.

3. Distinguish between 'ontogenetic' and 'phylogenetic' evolution. Illustrate each.

4. Indicate the main agencies in: Biological evolution. Social evolution.

5. Summarize the main points in: Cooley, *The Principles of Science,* Chapter X; Columbia Associates in Philosophy, *Introduction to Reflective Thinking,* Chapter VII; Thomson, *Bible of Nature,* Chapter III.

6. For supplementary reading, see Thomson and Geddes, *Evolution.*

CHAPTER XIV

EVOLUTION: ITS IMPLICATION

As indicated in the preceding chapter, scientific inquiry seems to lead to the conclusion that evolution is a fundamental feature of our world. It is also universal in its scope; nothing seems to escape it, neither suns and systems nor atoms nor the mind of man. What precisely are the details of the story science alone can inform us; upon such matters only the expert can speak with competency. But we are not here interested in the details; our inquiry is rather concerning the philosophical implications of these different types of evolution which we have already briefly surveyed. What is the meaning of it all? This is the general question which the philosopher finds confronting him as a result of the detailed studies of the sciences, and it is this general question which we are briefly to consider in this chapter. It may be made more specific by division into two questions: (1) Are all of the different types of evolution causally bound up with each other, or are they separate and distinct stories? and (2) Can the evolution of life be accounted for wholly in terms of mechanical causation, or must the process in some sense be deemed teleological? [1]

§ 1. *Evolution versus evolutions*

Is the universe in its totality to be considered as one evolutionary process including as eddies within its current

[1] The distinction between mechanical and teleological causation has been discussed in Chapter IX above. This distinction the reader should have clearly in mind throughout the present chapter.

the various types of evolution mentioned in the preceding chapter, or are these several types fundamentally different from each other? Is there only one evolution, which is the stream of the world, or are there many evolutions? To this question two answers are possible, and both have been urged. The first is the contention that there is one all-inclusive development of which both organic and inorganic evolution are only aspects or stages; this is the answer of monism. Over against this stands the answer of pluralism, which holds that the several types of evolution are sharply sundered from each other, and so are not definable as aspects of one fundamental type. For the monist there is only evolution; for the pluralist there are evolutions.

(I) THE THESIS OF MONISM. Science seems to have shown us that the whole physical environment is a gigantic process of evolution which reaches back into the unimaginable past and always goes forward in accordance with inviolable laws. As a relatively insignificant chapter in this process our solar system, like millions of others perhaps, has slowly evolved. Through various geological epochs the crust of one body within this system, our little planet, has gradually formed, and upon it there has emerged protoplasm endowed with the functions of a living thing. In numerous gradations higher organic forms have appeared, the most complex of which is the human organism whose mind and social institutions have developed through centuries of slow, halting, and painful effort. Brooding upon these results of science the monist finally arrives at the conclusion that all these different sorts of evolution are really one. They merge into each other through imperceptible stages, and each therefore is only a part of the universal flow of things. Starting from ourselves and attempting to trace the changes out of which we have come, we are at last driven to the conclusion that we are products of the same evolutionary process which runs through the formation of the earth on which we live, the solar system of which our earth is a part, and the other systems stretching out and out into the reaches of space beyond our sun. "This animal kingdom cannot exist without the vegetable kingdom; this again cannot arise before the stony crust of the earth has been disintegrated into loose soil by physical and chemical influences. We must further presuppose that this soil is watered by rains from time to time. The rain can fall only on condition that the water has previously been absorbed by the air, that it has been carried to a higher stratum and then condensed by a change of temperature. The water, again, cannot rise unless the earth is heated by the sun's rays. Hence the smallest blade of grass really calls into play the entire planetary system with all its arrangements and movements, and all the laws of nature."[1] "More and more do we see that we are the last result of a series of consecutive changes running back without any sudden break in continuity to a time when the stars were young. Organic evolution is the last stage in inorganic evolution and we are akin to the stars."[2] There are not *evolutions,* there is only *evolution;* and this evolution is the entire universe of things and events, both organic and inorganic. Such is the thesis of monism.

(2) THE THESIS OF PLURALISM. Against the thesis of the monist the pluralist enters the objection: 'Not proved.' Many parts of the environment have no evident connection with other parts, and it is consequently easy to view the totality of things and events as disparate systems of change

[1] Quoted — not with approval — from v. Baer by Paulsen: *Introduction to Philosophy,* English translation, second edition, 1907, pp. 225–226.
[2] Duncan: *The New Knowledge,* p. 214.

rather than as one all-embracing sweep. "The world is full of partial stories that run parallel to one another, beginning and ending at odd times. They mutually interlace and interfere at points, but we cannot unify them completely in our minds. In following your life-history, I must temporarily turn my attention from my own. . . . It follows that whoever says that the whole world tells one story utters another of those monistic dogmas that a man believes at his risk. It is easy to see the world's history pluralistically, as a rope of which each fibre tells a separate tale; but to conceive of each cross-section of the rope as an absolutely single fact, and to sum the whole longitudinal series into one being living an undivided life, is harder. . . . The great world's ingredients so far as they are beings, seem, like the rope's fibres, to be discontinuous, cross-wise, and to cohere only in the longitudinal direction. Followed in that direction they are many."[1] The pluralist, thus, is willing to admit that there are points of contact among the different evolutions within the environment. But he insists that what these points of contact are must be discovered by observation, and that there is no justification for holding, at least so far as our present knowledge extends, that all of the 'stories' of the world are only different chapters within *one* story. At least the probability is, he urges, that there are many evolutions and not one only.

(3) Critical estimate. The student will doubtless have noted that the problem here in debate is in principle identical with the problem discussed in Chapter IX under the heading of 'causal monism and causal pluralism.' The

[1] W. James: *Pragmatism,* 1907, pp. 143–144. Professor James is one of the most vigorous defendants of plu.alism among recent writers. See his *Pluralistic Universe.*

critical remarks there made are consequently equally applicable here. To repeat them here in detail, however, is unnecessary. The main points may be briefly recalled as follows: there is empirical evidence in support of each side in the debate, the merging of the different types of evolution by imperceptible stages supporting monism and the 'partial stories' within the world-order supporting pluralism; while the general argument based upon the nature of relations turns upon the answer to the question whether all relations are 'internal' or whether some of them at least are 'external' and more or less arbitrary.[1] The controversy between the monist and the pluralist, then, would appear to be in the following status: either further empirical evidence bearing upon the issue must be awaited, or a solution of it be reached through a detailed study of the general problem of relations among terms. Doubtless both lines of procedure may be followed to advantage in the future discussion of the issue, as they have been in the past.

§ 2. *Evolution of life: mechanism versus vitalism*

In more recent discussion the controversy turning about the notion of evolution has been limited in its scope to that type of evolution with which we are perhaps most familiar, namely the evolution of life or biological evolution. As thus limited the problem reduces itself to the question: Can the structure and behavior of organisms be completely explained in essentially those terms (physical and chemical) by which the structure and behavior of nonliving matter (the crystal, for instance) can be explained, or is there something, some principle or activity, in the organic not found in the inorganic? Or, put in terms of our previous distinction between mechanical and teleolog-

[1] See above Chapter IX, section 3.

ical causation: Can life in its development be satisfactorily accounted for in terms of mechanical causation, or is teleological causation also a factor within it? The two main answers to this question represented among contemporary scientists and philosophers are known as *mechanism* (which lays the emphasis upon mechanical causation) and *vitalism* (which insists that teleological causation is a factor).

(1) MECHANISM AND VITALISM. The mechanist holds that the living organism is only a physical-chemical machine and that its behavior can be resolved by analysis into physico-chemical processes. For him there is no fundamental difference between organic and inorganic matter; the chief difference between them which he admits is that of complexity, the organic forms being much more complex in their structure than the inorganic. The vitalist objects to this position, and urges that the organism is not a physical-chemical machine differing from the inorganic only in complexity of structure. He insists, on the contrary, that organic forms are radically different in kind from inorganic forms, that there is in the organism something *new* which is not found in inorganic or non-living matter. We shall let each of these contestants speak in some detail concerning his thesis, and then we shall attempt to estimate the status of the debate.

(2) THE CASE OF THE MECHANIST. The evolution and activity of all organic forms, the mechanist contends, can be satisfactorily explained in terms of mechanical causation. The arguments which he advances in support of this thesis are in the main four.

(a) *Life not mysterious.* It is a rather common assumption that life is something more than the ordinary processes of change and activity that take place in the living organism. Life, so it is sometimes supposed, is a mysterious entity which is radically different from these observable processes. Now the mechanist is unreservedly opposed to this assumption; there is, he holds, no justification for it. It is only a superstition reminiscent of the primitive conception of life as separable from the body. The truth of the matter is that life actually and exclusively *is* precisely what life *does*. Study the behavior of the organism and you study its life; its life is not something different from its activities and the processes going on within it. If these activities and processes can be explained in terms of mechanistic causation, then life can be so explained; for life is identical with them.

(b) *Progress towards mechanistic explanation of phenomena of life.* It is a matter of history that the biological sciences have in recent years made considerable progress in explaining the activities of organisms mechanically. Many phenomena, such as movements of organisms in response to stimuli and the development of muscles and organs within the organism, have been partly at least explained in mechanistic terms, despite the fact that only a short while ago it was supposed to be impossible so to analyze them. And every advance made by these sciences results in analyses of this sort. There is, therefore, every reason to believe that all vital phenomena, even though many of them at present can not be so analyzed, will sooner or later yield to such analysis; the historical progress of the biological sciences warrants this belief.[1] This is a second line of argument that seems to support the mechanist's position.

(c) *Method of science mechanistic.* A third line of ar-

[1] For evidence in support of this argument the reader should consult such a detailed consideration as that of Professor Loeb in *The Organism as a Whole* and *Forced Movements, Tropisms, and Animal Conduct.*

gument the mechanist bases on the method of scientific explanation. The argument is as follows: The most exact inductive sciences that we have developed, namely, physics and chemistry, now formulate their explanations in terms of mechanistic causation. And the more any given science develops in precision and accuracy, the more mechanistic does it become. When organic chemistry, for instance, found it possible to prepare organic compounds synthetically, the concept of a 'vital principle' was discarded and mechanical principles substituted in its place. It is therefore natural to assume that the method of science is essentially mechanistic; explanation in terms of mechanical causation is its ideal or goal. The more scientific the study of the phenomena of life becomes, therefore, the more will emphasis be placed upon mechanism as the correct interpretation of life. The inevitable goal of the biological sciences, *as sciences,* is a mechanistic view of the evolution of life.

(d) *Intelligibility synonymous with mechanistic explanation.* Finally, the mechanist contends that in so far as we succeed in giving a mechanistic account of life we make it intelligible; and, contrariwise, in so far as we fail to give such an account we leave life mysterious and vague. Physical and chemical processes we know in our laboratories; we can make them objects of direct experimental observation. Consequently, in so far as we can reduce life to such processes we make it understandable; to the extent that life is anything more than such processes it is merely a question-mark. Digestion as vital, in the sense of a complex of chemical processes, we know; digestion as vital in any other sense is a mystery. Mechanism as theory of life, therefore, looks in the direction of intelligibility.

(e) *Summary.* This, then, is the case of the mechanist: Life is not something different from the activities and processes of living organisms; many of these phenomena of life can be mechanistically explained, more of them are constantly being so explained, and there is reason to believe that all can be; the more precise the biological sciences grow in their analyses the more mechanistic they must inevitably tend to become, since precision in analysis is essentially synonymous with mechanistic explanation; causation as mechanistic is alone intelligible. As over against this brief of the case of the mechanist what has the vitalist to say?

(3) THE CASE OF THE VITALIST. On his side of the debate the vitalist asks acceptance of his thesis for the following reasons:

(a) *The organization of the living being.* Every living object is an organized whole and as such it has characteristics which, the vitalist thinks, do not fall within the scope of the mechanist's explanation. For the organism behaves in a way in which the non-living object does not; its behavior is an *adjustment,* that is, an attempt to right itself with the environment so that its well-being is taken care of. The movement of the amoeba towards food or away from an injurious substance, for example, is in the service of the individual's life as a whole; its activity has some sort of reference to its future welfare. An engine, on the contrary, will as readily tear itself to pieces as preserve itself intact by its behavior. If the organism is to be called an engine, then, it must be remembered what sort of an engine it is: it is " a self-stoking, self-repairing, self-preservative, self-adjusting, self-increasing, self-reproducing engine."[1] It is, in short, a teleological engine, whose every activity

[1] J. A. Thomson: *Bible of Nature,* p. 100.

in some sense serves, or is meant to serve, the 'end' of the organized whole.

(b) *Indeterminate activity of organisms.* In the case of inorganic matter one can predict with precision what will happen under given circumstances, while there is a certain indeterminateness in the behavior of an organism which is unpredictable. A stone on the hillside if loosened will roll until it reaches the bottom or meets an obstacle that interferes with the motion of it; and if it does meet an obstacle which brings it to a stop, it makes no effort to proceed on its journey. Its motion is not of its own impulsion. But the organism is different. The ant or the bee or even the plant seems driven by some sort of inner compulsion which causes reaction to stimuli such that it cannot be accurately predicted. If the ant meets an obstacle in its journey, it goes around or under or over it; the bee disturbed will fly away, but in one of an infinite number of possible directions; and the plant tries one type of reaction or another according as its environment places one or another sort of demand upon it. The organism is indeterminate in its behavior, whereas the behavior of inorganic matter is fairly predictable.

(c) *Some vital processes can be explained only teleologically.* Recent experimentation has shown that there are certain vital processes, such for example as that of breathing, which cannot be explained in terms of mechanical causation, but demand rather some sort of teleological causation. "The idea which gives unity and coherence to the whole of the physiology of respiration is that of the organic determination of the phenomena. The same idea has to a greater or less extent already given, or is in process of giving, unity and coherence to the phenomena of nutrition, secretion, and circulation. It is an idea which guides us at every turn in physiological work, and constantly suggests new lines of investigation. . . . By regarding the structure and activities of a living organism as the expression of organic unity we arm ourselves with a theory which is just as useful in biology as the idea of mass is in chemistry." [1] The teleological view of life, thus, is necessarily involved in the actual experimental procedure of the biologist; the phenomena of life cannot be explained otherwise than through teleological causation.

(d) *Inconceivability of biological mechanism.* Finally, the vitalist has at times been inclined to argue that it is inconceivable how life can be explained in purely mechanistic terms. From the insensible stone tumbling down the hillside to the complex and exceedingly varied behavior of organisms, particularly the more highly developed organisms such as the vertebrate animals, is indeed a far cry. And to suppose that the behavior of these organisms can be explained in precisely the same way in which the course of the stone down the hillside can be accounted for is simply inconceivable. Biological mechanism, therefore, is absurd on the face of it; it undertakes to account for the phenomena of life in an inconceivable manner.

(e) *Summary.* This, then, is the case of the vitalist: living beings are characterized by a unique sort of organization whose activity serves the welfare of the whole, and such a characteristic no machine possesses; the activity

[1] J. S. Haldane, *Mechanism, Life and Personality,* p. 88. This book and the same author's *Organism and Environment* advocate the vitalistic view of life and offer evidence in support of it. The position taken by Professor Haldane is in direct opposition to that taken by Professor Loeb in *The Organism as a Whole* and *The Mechanistic Conception of Life.* A comparison of these books will serve to introduce the reader to the scientific side of the controversy. References for further study are given in the exercises at the end of this chapter. See also the article by Jennings in *The American Naturalist,* Vol. XLVII, pp. 385 ff, and the papers by Lovejoy there referred to.

of organic forms is indeterminate and unpredictable, and so is markedly different from the behavior of non-living matter; the phenomena of life are by experimental observation shown to be such that a scientific attempt to explain them necessitates the use of teleological causation; and, finally, it is inconceivable that the complex behavior of organisms, particularly of the higher organisms, can be mechanically accounted for.

(4) SOME CRITICAL REMARKS ON THE DEBATE. The following remarks may be helpful by way of a critical estimate of the debate between the vitalist and the mechanist.

(*a*) The first argument of the mechanist is indicative of a truth of great importance. Certainly life is not something different from the observable processes which we call vital; it is not a hidden and mysterious entity behind these processes, any more than the mind is a mysterious 'substance' which thinks and wills and feels. But this truth is as compatible with the vitalist's view as it is with that of the mechanist. Life may be identical with the vital processes (digestion, contraction of muscles, circulation of the blood, etc.) and still the main contention of the vitalist be true. The real problem is: How explain those processes with which life is thus identified?

(*b*) The second argument of the mechanist has considerable weight, if it is true in fact. That the biological sciences have, with improvement in the technique of experimental observation, progressed steadily in the mechanical interpretation of life appears to be a strong reason for holding that mechanism is on the right track. However, not all biologists are agreed that progress in biological research shows progress in the mechanistic explanation of life. As we have seen above, Professor Haldane holds just the opposite view, and there are other investigators in the field who agree with him in principle. There is thus a question of fact at issue which must be settled by the actual procedure and accomplishments of the biological sciences. Generally speaking, this much seems to be fairly certain: if the phenomena of life (meaning thereby the particular vital processes such as digestion, reproduction and the like, special processes as well as the activity of the organism as a whole) show themselves to be more and more amenable to mechanistic analysis as the technique of the biological sciences is refined, then the case of the mechanist is strengthened; if the reverse is true, then the claims of the vitalist are strengthened.

(*c*) The last two arguments of the mechanist do not seem to have any great value. That physics and chemistry formulate their explanations in terms of mechanical causation is no reason for supposing that biology must do so, unless it can be positively shown that physics and chemistry in their procedure exemplify what is necessarily true of all sciences. This must be proved, not assumed. Until it is proved there still remains the possibility that the phenomena of life necessitate the conception of a different type of causation from that which is applicable to the phenomena with which physics and chemistry deal. The last argument of the mechanist is really a restatement of the third in slightly different terms and with different emphasis. And it is open to the same criticism. If it is *assumed* that there is only one type of intelligibility of *all* phenomena, namely, intelligibility in the sense of mechanical causation, and if this assumption is made the basis for an argument designed to show that the phenomena of life are only thus intelligible, then obviously the question in debate has been 'begged'; the argument, that is to say, assumes what it is designed to prove.

(*d*) The first two arguments of the vitalist have great weight in support of his position. The 'organization' 'indeterminate activity' characteristic of living things are phenomena which present to the mechanistic theory quite formidable obstacles. That these are characteristic of life seems true; and to many minds they dispose of the mechanistic hypothesis as an adequate account of vital phenomena.

(*e*) The third argument of the vitalist would seem to be crucial in the controversy. If there are some vital phenomena, such as breathing, nutrition, heredity, and the like, which cannot be explained except in terms of teleological causation, then the case of the vitalist is, it would seem, practically established. But, as indicated in paragraph (*b*) above, there is not general agreement among biologists as regards the phenomena here in dispute. Further progress in biological research can alone, therefore, speak decisively.

(*f*) The last argument of the vitalist, if, indeed, it is seriously advanced, proves nothing at all. Many hypotheses which when first advanced have to many seemed inconceivable have, in the course of the later development of science, turned out to be not only not inconceivable but necessarily true. Thus, at one time it was held to be inconceivable that the earth should be round or should swing free in space and revolve around the sun; men have been burnt at the stake and otherwise persecuted for believing such 'absurd' hypotheses. But these are matters of common-sense acceptance now-a-days. An hypothesis, therefore, cannot be ruled out of consideration because of its 'inconceivability'; too many 'inconceivable' hypotheses have been proven true. The simple truth is that an hypothesis, unless it is flatly self-contradictory, cannot be regarded as inconceivable apart from a detailed investigation of its claims and the testing of those claims in the light of relevant facts.[1]

(5) CRITICAL ESTIMATE OF THE CONTROVERSY BETWEEN THE MECHANIST AND THE VITALIST. In attempting to estimate the status of the debate between mechanism and vitalism as regards the phenomena of life, four points of importance should be noted:

(*a*) In last analysis the debate turns on the question as to whether the type of organization that characterizes living beings is in any way such that it differs fundamentally from the sort of organization which is found in any non-living complex, such as an internal combustion engine, a crystal, or the myriad bubbles in the frothy surface of a dish of soap-suds.[2] Does the organism behave in a manner radically different from the way in which a non-living complex behaves, and does the internal structure of the living possess a quality which the non-living complex does not have? This is the basal question at issue.

(*b*) The vitalist is willing to admit that the explanation of the phenomena of life offered by the mechanist is a legitimate account of certain aspects of these phenomena, namely the mechanisms through which life expresses itself in organic forms; he contends, however, that such an explanation is not wholly and completely adequate, since certain aspects of these phenomena lie beyond the scope of the explanation offered. But the mechanist, on his side, main-

[1] The student should connect the discussion here with what was said above on the method of science. See Chapter III, particularly section 5.

[2] This illustration is emphasized by Professor Thompson in his paper published in the *Proceedings of the Aristotelian Society,* Volume XVIII, as a contribution to the symposium held in London, 1918, on the subject: "Are Physical, Biological, and Phychological Categories Irreducible?" Other contributors to the symposium are Professors Haldane, Mitchell, and Hobhouse.

tains that the vitalist's account can lay no claim to any scientific value and is thus without justification. Here, it would appear, the burden of proof falls on the mechanist.

(*c*) In so far as the vitalist urges that within the organic forms we find something which is not present in the inorganic he lays himself open to the legitimate question: What, precisely defined, is this 'something'? And until he answers this question satisfactorily he must remain embarrassed by the accusation, frequently brought against him, that he is indulging himself in a vague and mystical hypothesis which lacks scientific precision; that he is, in short, not explaining life scientifically.[1] It should be noted, however, that the vitalist is under no obligation to define this 'something' in terms of the mechanism of the body, since his very thesis is that it cannot be so defined. It is by his hypothesis in some sense non-bodily.

(*d*) Finally, it is clear that the outcome of the debate between the mechanist and the vitalist has a very important bearing upon the more general problem concerning the evolution of the world-order with which this chapter began. If the mechanist is right, then monism would seem to be the more probable hypothesis; if the vitalist is right, then, whether monism or pluralism be accepted, the evolutionary process itself must be differently conceived from what it would be if mechanism is the satisfactory solution of the problem of life. Biological evolution thus appears to be in an important sense crucial.

[1] This 'something' is given different names by vitalists. Bergson in his *Creative Evolution* calls it the 'vital impulse'; 'entelechy' is the term commonly used by Driesch in his *Science and Philosophy of the Organism;* while McDougall in his *Body and Mind* speaks of it as the 'soul.'

§ 3. *Emergent versus repetitive evolution*

As suggested in the last paragraph of the preceding section, there are two radically different views of the evolutionary process which emerge when one attempts to apply the notion of evolution to the world as a whole. And it is necessary in dealing critically with the notion of evolution to keep these views distinct.

(1) Emergent evolution. The first of these views is what we may call *emergent* evolution. This view of evolution holds that in the ongoings of the world-order something 'new' is being continuously created as the process goes from level to level of existence — from the inorganic to the organic, and from the biological or vital to the psychological or mental. Thinking of the world as one universal sweep of evolution, this view would hold that out of one level grows something novel, which in its turn emerges into something else novel, and so on through whatever levels of existence we may discover, or may exist undiscovered, within the world-order. Or, put in more specific terms, it holds that the novelty of life grows out of inorganic forms and that the novelty of mind grows out of organic forms, the higher levels being real additions, and not mere duplications without additions, to the lower; when life appears in the process something 'new' is created, and with the appearance of mind another 'new' element is added which before was not explicitly present within the process. This is the conception of evolution as *emergent*.

(2) Repetitive evolution. Over against this view of the evolutionary process stands the *repetitive* view. This view holds that nothing 'new' appears in the process of the world's development, but that every level is a bare repetition of the preceding level. When in the ongoings

of the world-order matter passes from the inorganic to the organic level and from the biological or vital to the psychological or mental, there is according to this view no 'creation' involved; on the contrary, there is only another but more complex ordering and arrangement of the same elements which in simpler relations were explicitly present from the beginning. Mind is merely a different and more complex expression of life, life is merely a different and more complex expression or product of matter, and matter is the ultimate form of existence or reality; and all of these are linked within one continuous and repetitive series of causal sequences which we call the evolution of the world — such is the view of evolution as *repetitive.*

(3) Facts relevant to the two views. That there is a wide difference between the emergent and the repetitive views of evolution is clear. It is clear also that both views cannot be true; the one excludes the other. Which is true? We can here do no more than call attention to the main sets of facts that are relevant to the answer to this question. And it requires little reflection to disclose that these facts are those of life and mind. If the vital and mental phenomena can be held to be merely more complex repetitions of those elements that antedated their appearance in the world-order, then repetitive evolution is the true account of that order; if, on the other hand, the facts of life and mind must be looked upon as something 'new' in the ongoings of the world, if, that is, they cannot be explained as links within a merely repetitive causal series of events, if mind cannot be reduced to biological processes and life in its turn to physical and chemical processes, then it would appear that — if we are to think of the world as one evolutionary process and not many — emergent evolution is alone tenable. We have already dealt

critically with the more important side of the facts of life in our survey above of the controversy between the vitalist and the mechanist; the vitalist is in principle contending for the view of emergent evolution, while the mechanist is insisting upon the repetitive view of evolution. What we have there said, thus, bears upon the point at issue here. The facts of mind we shall survey in the next Part of our study, particularly in Chapter XVII.

Chapter XIV. Questions and Exercises

1. State clearly the point at issue between the monist and the pluralist on the general problem of evolution. Indicate the bearing of the problem of relations (see Chapter IX, section 3, above) on the debate. Which position seems to you more acceptable and why?

2. Distinguish between the vitalistic and mechanistic views of life. State in outline the arguments for each view as presented in the text.

3. Distinguish between emergent and repetitive evolution.

4. Read and briefly summarize Hoernle's discussion in *Matter, Life, Mind and God,* Lecture III.

5. State concisely the main points in Thomson, *The Bible of Nature,* Chapter IV.

6. References for further study on mechanism and vitalism: Loeb, *The Organism as a Whole;* Loeb, "Mechanistic Conception of Life," *Popular Science Monthly,* 1912 (reprinted in Loeb, *The Mechanistic Conception of Life,* pp. 3–31); Haldane, *Organism and Environment;* Henderson, *The Fitness of the Environment;* the symposium by different writers in the ***Philosophical Review***, 1918, Vol. XXVII, pp. 571–645.

PART V

PROBLEMS OF MIND

CHAPTER XV

MIND: HISTORICAL SURVEY

We turn now to a consideration of the problems connected with mind, the category which is basal to the social sciences. A study of these problems will bring us into touch with some of the more important aspects of our social environment. We begin with the problem of the nature of mind.

§ 1. *Problem of the nature of mind*

The word 'mind' is constantly on our lips and our very familiarity with the word is apt to stand in the way of our comprehension of its meaning. The fact that we make use of the word so frequently leads us to suppose that we know precisely the nature of that for which it stands. A little reflection, however, is sufficient to convince us that mind is a very complex affair and that the problem of its nature is far from easy of solution. The problem itself is difficult to grasp; so difficult, in fact, that our first step in discussing it must be an attempt to state it with precision.

(1) Some preliminary definitions. As a preliminary to the statement of the problem of mind we shall first fix the meaning of certain terms that must be used in the formulation of it. These terms are chiefly two: *experiences* and *consciousness*.

(a) *Experiences*. During waking moments every normal individual observes lights and shadows and colors, hears noises and tones, undergoes pleasures and pains, joys and sorrows, entertains hopes and fears, pursues ends, solves problems. In other words, each individual is constantly feeling, willing, and judging. Now any specific instance of feeling or willing or judging we shall define as 'an experience.' The numerous acts of feeling, willing, and judging constitute the individual's experiences.

(b) *Consciousness.* Of these various experiences the individual is, or may be, aware. One may be aware that one has perceived the table, felt the hurt, made the decision, or solved the problem. Now this being aware of experiences is what we may call being 'conscious' of them; consciousness is awareness of experiences. It is to be noted that consciousness as thus defined is limited to the passing moment and is constantly changing; it comes and goes with the passing of experiences.

(2) FORMULATION OF THE PROBLEM OF MIND. From what has just been said it is obvious that mind as ordinarily understood cannot be identified with conscious experiences. Mind is commonly supposed to be inclusive of consciousness, but more than consciousness and different from it. The momentary loss of consciousness, as in normal dreamless sleep or the still deeper sleep resulting from an anaesthetic, does not at all mean the loss of mind. Furthermore, something may be said to be in mind without at the same time being in consciousness. One has in mind, but seldom in consciousness, the multiplication table, the names of one's friends, and the entire body of what one may be said to know. Mind, thus, appears to be more comprehensive than consciousness, and also more permanent and enduring; consciousness includes relatively few experiences at a time and is continuously shifting, sometimes disappearing entirely, while mind includes a very much more

complex content and remains in some sense constant. Now it is through mind that the various experiences of the individual grow into what we popularly call the character or personality of the individual; indeed, mind and personality are not ordinarily distinguished. So the problem of mind might be stated in the form of the question: How is the creation of personality — one continuous experience — out of many experiences possible? Or, perhaps more definitely; What is the explanation of the relatively persistent [1] unity that attaches to the manifold experiences of the individual? If we arbitrarily use the term 'self' to designate this unity, our problem can then be stated more briefly: What is the self? [2]

(3) ORDER OF DISCUSSION. The remaining part of this chapter will be devoted to a brief survey of the more important views that have been held on the problem of mind in the course of European thought. In the following chapter the attempt will be made to evaluate the points of view outlined in this historical inquiry.

§ 2. *Primitive conception of mind*

It would be unwarranted to suppose that primitive man persistently reflected on the problem of mind. The problem doubtless caused him no sleepless nights. But he did entertain beliefs which we may with proper precaution piece together as his view of mind. He seems to have

[1] I say 'relatively persistent' because there are certain types of mentality — such as insanity, multiple personality, and similar abnormal types — which cast suspicion on the assumption that this unity is wholly above transformation or disruption. For a study of multiple personality, see Prince, *The Dissociation of a Personality*.

[2] Throughout this discussion of mind it is to be understood that the human mind alone is under consideration and that, unless expressly stated to the contrary, the normal human mind is meant. The vexed question as to the mind of the lower animals is left on one side as not manageable within the present introductory survey.

imaged himself as of a two-fold nature. On the one hand, he naturally thought of himself as a physical body occupying space and suffering its limitations; on the other hand, he believed that there was within his body and inhabiting it a sort of shadowy duplicate of it. This shadowy duplicate of the body he thought of as independent of the body in the sense that it might be separated from it either temporarily or permanently, and also as untouched by those limitations to which his natural or physical body was subject. "The belief most widely current among the peoples of lower culture is that each man consists, not only of the body which is constantly present among his fellows, but also of a shadowy vapour-like duplicate of his body; this shadow-like image, the animating principle of the living organism, is thought to be capable of leaving the body, of transporting itself rapidly, if not instantaneously, from place to place, and of manifesting in those places all or most of the powers that it exerts in the body during waking life."[1] Sleep, it is supposed, is due to the temporary separation of this ghostly duplicate from the body, while death means its permanent separation. Primitive man's view of what we call mind, then, is that mind is a shadow-duplicate of the body which lives within it and animates it but is independent of, and separable from, it. This is his explanation, in so far as he may be said to have had any explanation, of himself as mental.

Language clearly shows the close connection which originally existed between mind and the shadow or breath of the body. In many languages words which now mean mind originally meant breath or shadow. And it is not difficult for us to understand this association. The body always has its accompanying shadow which in some vague fashion

[1] McDougall, *Mind and Body*, p. 1.

is a duplicate of it. When one lies down in sleep this shadow disappears from view, and in dreams one may have actual experience of its floating away from the body and roaming at will in other places. While the breath, which comes and goes through the mouth and nostrils while the body is a living thing, takes its permanent departure at the moment of death.

§ 3. *Views of the early Greek thinkers*

Just as the early group of Greek thinkers discarded the primitive conception of matter and undertook to replace it by a more definite conception, so they set aside the primitive view of mind and sought in its place a less vague hypothesis. On the whole they were inclined to think of mind as a sort of attenuated matter. Perhaps it would be more accurate historically to say that they drew no sharp distinction between mind and matter; on the contrary, they were prone to think of matter as living and to explain mental phenomena by that same original stuff which they conceived to be basic in the material or physical order. "Anaximenes of Miletus . . . says that 'our soul, which is air, rules us' . . . Anaxagoras, who accounts for the ordering of elements into a system of things by referring to the activity of Mind or Reason, calls mind 'the finest of things,' and it seems clear that he did not conceive of it as very different in nature from the other elements which enter into the constitution of the world. Democritus . . . developed a materialistic doctrine that admits the existence of nothing save atoms and empty space. He conceived the soul to consist of fine, smooth, round atoms which are also atoms of fire."[1] And the same holds true in principle of the other Greek 'physicists.' Each

[1] Fullerton: *Introduction to Philosophy*, pp. 101–102.

of them identified mind with matter and explained it in terms of that primitive stuff, however conceived by him, which he regarded as the eternal substance out of which all things have come.

§ 4. *Views of Plato and Aristotle*

Plato and Aristotle teach a theory of mind which became traditional in European thought during the Middle Ages and which has been influential even in modern times.

(1) PLATO'S VIEW. According to Plato, the mind or 'soul' of the individual expresses itself in three fundamental types of experiences very much like what by later thinkers were named thinking, willing, and feeling. Of these the last two are the baser activities of the soul and belong to it only in so far as it is connected with the body. The rational element, however, is the divine element within the soul; it is the soul or mind in its true being and is wholly independent of the relation which the soul bears to the body it inhabits. As rational the soul of each individual existed somewhere before it became attached at birth to the particular body it now inhabits, and at death it will depart from the body into another state of existence. This is the famous theory of the pre-existence and transmigration of souls taught by Plato in his dialogues.[1] In its true essence, then, the soul is independent of the body and capable of existing by itself alone as pure rationality.

(2) ARISTOTLE'S VIEW. Aristotle insists upon a much closer connection between mind and body than did Plato. For him the soul is the organization of the body; or, to

[1] In this connection the student will find interesting the myth of the charioteer in the *Phaedrus,* the tale of Er, son of Armenius, in the tenth book of *The Republic,* and the arguments for the immortality of the soul in the *Phaedo.* Wordsworth gives a beautiful poetical expression of the Platonic doctrine in his *Ode on the Intimations of Immortality.*

use his terms, the soul is 'form' to the body which is its 'matter.' However, when Aristotle speaks of the soul or mind as the *organization of the body,* he does not wish to be understood to use the term 'organization' in the sense of physiological organization; he rather thinks of the soul or mind as an entity, partly at least separable from the body, which makes possible the organic whole that we know as the body. In other words, the soul is the organizing principle of the body but it is not identical with bodily organization; mind is the non-bodily principle within the body which, though it constitutes the essential nature of the body, may be said to "stand to it in the same separable relation as a sailor to his boat." Despite his effort to bring mind and body into closer relation than Plato succeeded in doing, therefore, Aristotle is in principle agreed with Plato: mind is after all something different from the body and exists in its own right. And he agrees with Plato, further, that the essence of mind or soul as thus separable from body is rationality; the reasoning element is the non-bodily, and presumably immortal, part of mind.

(3) SUMMARY OF VIEWS OF PLATO AND ARISTOTLE. Stated in the terms defined in the first section of this chapter, the answer of both Plato and Aristotle to the problem of the nature of mind is briefly this: Mind is a unity of the manifold experiences of the individual; that which binds these experiences together in one totality, their cement so to speak, is a non-bodily entity or principle, called by them the 'soul'; the soul owns these various experiences, very much as the ranchman owns his cattle, and the soul's ownership is the linkage among them; the fundamental activities of this soul are thinking, willing, and feeling — in Plato's phraseology, the 'rational,' 'spirited,' and 'appetitive' elements; in so far as the soul

is rational it is wholly independent of, and separable from, the body to which it is related "as a sailor to his boat." In short, mind or soul is a non-bodily entity, a spiritual substance, which *does* the various and sundry experiences of perceiving, judging, feeling, and willing that make up the content of the individual's mental life.

§ 5. *Two modern criticisms of the Platonic-Aristotelian view*

The Platonic-Aristotelian view of mind early became traditional and continued to dominate psychological and philosophical thought until well down into the modern era. It was accepted in principle by all of the thinkers of the Middle Ages and also by some of the representatives of modern thought, notably Descartes, Locke, and Berkeley. It is true that the traditional view was stated from time to time in different phraseology and even changed in some of its important details, but no change was made in its basal features. The mind was still conceived as an immaterial non-bodily entity, a spiritual substance, which was capable of having various experiences but which could not be identified with any particular experience or with any combination of experiences. In the course of the centuries, however, the time came when this ancient view of mind was vigorously attacked and the difficulties involved in it definitely stated. The two thinkers who led the attack were David Hume (1711–1776), one of the keenest thinkers Scotland has produced, and Immanuel Kant (1724–1804), a German thinker of Scottish ancestry and one of the greatest figures in modern philosophical thought.

(1) Hume's criticism of the traditional view. Hume bases his criticism of the traditional view of mind

primarily upon the consideration that there is absolutely no evidence which one can discover in support of the conception. If such an entity or spiritual substance as the traditional view supposes the mind to be really exists, he urges, then one ought to be able to point to evidence of the fact. But, he submits, there is not the slightest evidence of the existence of such an entity. All that one can discover in any given moment of consciousness are numerous experiences — called by Hume 'perceptions' — of pleasure, pain, sights, sounds, thought, desire, and the like. One cannot ever find there anything like this spiritual substance talked about in the traditional doctrine, nor can one observe any experiences upon which to rest an inference concerning its hypothetical existence. There is therefore no justification for supposing that it does exist. "For my part," Hume says, "when I enter most intimately into what I call *myself,* I always stumble on some particular perception or other, of heat or cold, light or shade, love or hatred, pain or pleasure. I can never catch *myself* at any time without a perception, and never can observe anything but the perception. When my perceptions are removed for any time, as by sound sleep; so long am I insensible of *myself,* and may truly be said not to exist. And were all my perceptions removed by death, and could I neither think, nor feel, nor see, nor love, nor hate after the dissolution of my body, I should be entirely annihilated, nor do I conceive what is further requisite to make me a perfect non-entity."[1] Such are the chief reasons which Hume advances against the traditional theory of mind and in behalf of which he asks that it be discarded as not a

[1] *Treatise of Human Nature,* Book I, Part IV, section vi. Selby-Bigge edition, p. 252. By a 'perception' in this quotation Hume means an 'experience' in the sense defined above.

genuinely scientific conception. All we can know within our consciousnesses are sundry experiences; these experiences are constantly changing and hence cannot be identified with that spiritual substance which is supposed to continue the same from day to day, whether connected with or separated from particular experiences, whether sleeping or waking; such a spiritual substance is, therefore, not directly observable, nor is there any evidence that it exists, and so it must be given up as a mythological conception. To what extent this reasoning is conclusive we shall inquire in the further course of our survey.

(2) KANT'S CRITICISM OF THE TRADITIONAL VIEW. Kant's method of attack against the traditional view of mind is different from Hume's, but in the end it leads to essentially the same conclusion. Instead of pointing out, as Hume does, that for the existence of mind as a spiritual substance no direct evidence is available, Kant argues that the traditional view is self-contradictory. For this view holds in effect that each individual knows his *self* as he knows other objects, that he can make his *self* a direct object of knowledge. Now this is impossible, Kant maintains, since it is always the self or mind that does the knowing; the mind is always subject of knowledge and cannot be made object of knowledge. I cannot know *I*, but only *me;* myself as *subject* I cannot know, but only myself as *object.* But myself as object is precisely my various experiences that come and go with passing moments. Thus Kant comes around to Hume's position: all we can know directly are our experiences, hence there is no justification for supposing that the mind as traditionally conceived exists. To suppose that the mind is known as a spiritual substance is not only unjustifiable, but involves a manifest contradiction.

§ 6. *Constructive views of Hume and Kant*

Having denied the validity of the traditional view of the mind, both Hume and Kant proceed to suggest new hypotheses which they contend are more scientific and intelligible. The two hypotheses are in important respects different from each other, and a study of them will open the way for our survey of contemporary theories.

(1) HUME'S VIEW OF MIND. Hume's fundamental thesis is that any individual's mind is exclusively and wholly the sum-total of experiences that fill that individual's life. The joys and sorrows, pleasures and pains, sounds and sights, ideas and deeds that fill the individual's life from day to day — these, and these alone, constitute his mind. In Hume's own words: "The mind is a kind of theatre, where several perceptions successively make their appearance; pass, re-pass, glide away, and mingle in an infinite variety of postures and situations. There is properly no *simplicity* in it at one time, nor *identity* in different; whatever natural propension we have to imagine that simplicity and identity. The comparison of the theatre must not mislead us. They are the successive perceptions only, that constitute the mind. . . ."[1] Hume admits, as he must of course, that these 'perceptions' or experiences, in spite of their wide diversities, constitute *one set,* since they all belong to the same individual. Your various experiences of sights, sounds, sorrows, and the like are all *yours,* however unlike each other they may be and however quickly they may come and go. Each individual mind is, in Hume's phraseology, "a bundle or collection of different percep-

[1] *Treatise of Human Nature,* Book I, Part IV, section vi, Selby-Bigge edition, p. 253. The student must bear in mind that Hume uses the term 'perceptions' in this quotation and elsewhere in his book as synonymous with the term 'experience' as we have defined it above.

tions, which succeed each other with an inconceivable rapidity, and are in a perpetual flux and movement. . . ." But the question inevitably arises: Why should these rapidly changing experiences constitute a 'collection'? What is the 'string' that ties them into a 'bundle'? Why, in plain language, should numberless rapidly passing and radically different experiences hang together as the experiences of one and the same individual mind? This question is of basal importance in any theory of mind. Its justice Hume himself recognizes, and he attempts to answer it. Briefly stated, his answer is this: these various 'perceptions' that constitute the 'bundle' which we call the mind of a given individual are bound together by the laws of association. As Hume understands them, these laws are mainly three: the law of contiguity or nearness in space, the law of succession or nearness in time, and the law of resemblance or likeness. Experiences that are contiguous to each other in space, or are successive in time, or resemble each other, if they are thus joined with each other constantly, tend to become linked together and the one is associated with the other. To illustrate these three types of association: if the dog and its master are seen frequently together, the two are finally associated and the sight of either alone tends to bring the other to mind (association by contiguity); the flash of lightning is always immediately succeeded by the noise of the thunder, and so when we see the flash we expect to hear the noise even before it is actually heard (association by succession); the resemblance which the face of a stranger now before me bears to the face of my absent friend tends to bring to mind an image of the friend (association by resemblance). In these several ways, thus, experiences are linked together and constitute one mind. So the 'string' that binds the manifold experiences of the individual into one 'bundle' is woven out of the laws of association. This, then, is Hume's answer to the problem of mind: The mind is a multitude of different experiences connected with each other by means of the laws of association.

(2) KANT'S VIEW OF MIND. The solution of the problem of the nature of mind proffered by Hume is not acceptable to Kant. And it is not acceptable to him largely because he thinks that Hume failed to probe to the bottom of the question concerning the mind's unity. Kant is willing to admit that the laws of association are operative within experiences, and so far he agrees with Hume. But he insists that these laws themselves would be impossible unless the mind were something more than a mere haphazard bundle of experiences. For these laws of association presuppose memory; contiguous, successive, and resembling experiences are not ordinarily associated unless they are repeated several times, and repetition is identical with memory. Because I see the master and dog together once is no reason why they should become associated in my mind except under very unusual circumstances; ordinarily, I have to see them together several times before the associative link between them is formed. But this means that I must remember having seen them together several times before any association takes place. Memory, thus, is presupposed by association. Now, Kant contends, memory is impossible unless there is some sort of agent to do the remembering. Thus Kant is forced to the conclusion that Hume's view of mind as a collection of experiences tied together by the laws of association does not go to the heart of the matter; there is more of unity within mind, he insists, than Hume admits. This unity he calls by the somewhat formidable appellation of 'synthetic

unity of apperception,' nor is it quite clear what he means by this. He sometimes speaks of it as thought or intelligence — the 'I think' which accompanies all our experiences. But, fortunately for our present purpose, it is not necessary for us here to inquire what precisely Kant means by his 'unity of apperception.' He at least means by it some sort of capacity within the mind to organize different experiences into meaningful wholes either by way of memory and association or by way of inference. For Kant, then, mind is not a 'bundle' of experiences; it is rather an 'organization' of experiences made possible by an actually existent principle or agent of organization. In other words, mind for him is a multiplicity of experiences brought together into meaningful wholes or groups by the activity of an organizing agency, probably conceived by Kant as judgment. Two points in this view need emphasis to distinguish it from the preceding views: (*a*) the first is the insistence upon the necessary existence of some definite principle of unity among experiences — a necessity which Hume denies; (*b*) and the second is the conception of this principle as an active, organizing agency, over against the traditional Platonic-Aristotelian view of it as a passive and changeless entity or thing.

§ 7. *Some recent psychological views of mind*

In recent thought three main views of the nature of mind have been held by psychologists. These we shall now attempt to state in general outline.

(1) THE HUMIAN TRADITION. On the one hand, there is the view of mind which follows, not historically but logically and with variations in detail of course, the line of thought suggested and defended by Hume. Perhaps

one of the clearest expressions of this view is that by Professor Titchener: "Mind is the sum-total of human experience considered as dependent upon the experiencing person . . . the phrase 'experiencing person' means the living body, the organized individual . . . for psychological purposes, the living body may be reduced to the nervous system and its attachments. Mind thus becomes the sum-total of human experience considered as dependent upon a nervous system. And since human experience is always process, occurrence, and the dependent aspect of human experience is its mental aspect, we may say, more shortly, that mind is the sum-total of mental processes."[1] This view of mind is essentially Hume's conception dressed in the terminology of contemporary physiology and psychology. Professor Pillsbury states practically the same view in his definition of mind as "the entire series of conscious states of an individual from birth to death."[2] This is the view of an important school of contemporary psychologists.

(2) THE KANTIAN TRADITION. There is another important group among contemporary psychologists who maintain (agreeing in principle with Kant) that human experiences cannot be made intelligible apart from the assumption that there exists among the experiences some ground of unity other than and different from both the experiences themselves and the central nervous system. For this group mind is a manifold of experiences linked together by a unifying agency which is non-bodily in nature. Professor Stratton has expressed this point of view in the following vigorous passage: "Sensations and judgments and memories, and all things else in our mental life, are to be

[1] *Text-Book of Psychology*, 1910, p. 16.
[2] *Essentials of Psychology*, 1911, p. 6.

conceived, not as self-complete and relatively independent things, but as acts of a living being. . . . The mind can no more be constructed out of small pieces of ideas than the living body can be conceived as resulting from a gradual assembling of scattered heart-beats, with, later, a stray digestion and the rest. . . . The mind is the deeper and more permanent reality, and mental phenomena are its ways of behavior. It has power and activity from within. It is not a mere creature of circumstances — not a mere eddy in the endless stream of sensations, — it is an agent, a person, facing the world, and acting upon it with will and intelligence."[1] And this view Professor Stratton presents as the "ascendant view" of modern psychology.

(3) Behavioristic view. Within recent years, particularly since Professor Stratton's book above quoted was written, there has grown up in psychology another view of mind which, though in some respects novel, bears striking similarity to one aspect of Aristotle's view of mind as 'form' of the body. This view has gained considerable strength during the last decade and is at present a strong

[1] *Experimental Psychology and Culture,* 1903, p. 305. Other interesting expressions of the same point of view are the following:

"The facts of our conscious life, especially the fact of psychical individuality, the fact of the unity of consciousness correlated with the physical manifold of brain-processes, cannot be rendered intelligible without the postulation of some ground of unity other than the brain or material organism." McDougall, *Mind and Body,* p. 356.

"The scientific study of conscious experience leads to a concept of unity and self-consciousness, which is the most fundamental and comprehensive concept which can be formulated in experience." Judd, *Psychology,* 1907, p. 316.

"Psychology may be defined provisionally as science of consciousness — of perception, memory, emotion, and the like. Many psychologists find this definition sufficient as it stands, but . . . it does not go far enough. For consciousness does not occur impersonally. Consciousness, on the contrary, always is a somebody-being-conscious. There is never perception without a somebody who perceives, and there never is thinking unless some one thinks. Bearing this fact in mind, we may define psychology more exactly by naming it science of the self as conscious." Calkins, *A First Book in Psychology,* 1910, p. 1.

contender in the field of psychological theories of the nature of mind. The view is that all experiences are nothing more than bodily reactions to the environment, and that the bodily organism — the nervous system and its attachments — is the only ground of unity among these experiences. Thus, Dr. Watson tells us that 'personality' means nothing but "an individual's total assets (actual and potential) and liabilities (actual and potential) on the reaction side . . . assets are that part of the individual's equipment which make for his adjustment and balance in his present environment and for readjustment if the environment changes. By liabilities we mean similarly that part of the individual's equipment which does not work in the present environment and the potential or possible factors which would prevent his rising to meet a changed environment."[1] By 'equipment' here Dr. Watson means exclusively biological aptitudes such as instincts, impulses, habits, and the like. Mind, thus, is virtually identified with instincts, impulses, and habits as types of response to the environment; it is the body in action. Experiences are organic responses to the environment, and the unifying ground of them is the organism itself.[2]

§ 8. *Summary of views*

This brief historical survey is perhaps sufficient to suggest with fair accuracy some of the more important views

[1] *Psychology from the Standpoint of the Behaviorist,* 1919, p. 397.

[2] The group of 'new realists' — an important group of contemporary philosophers — generally hold in principle to the behavioristic view of mind. Perry's *Present Philosophical Tendencies,* Chapter XII, and Holt's *Concept of Consciousness* are representative books of this group. Professor Dewey is quite sympathetic to the point of view as is indicated by his latest book, *Human Nature and Conduct.* The discussion of that book is based on the belief, as expressed in the preface to it, that "Mind can be understood in the concrete only as a system of beliefs, desires, and purposes which are formed in the interaction of biological aptitudes with a social environment."

of mind held in the evolution of European thought on the problem. For purposes of a summary statement of these views we may perhaps reduce them to three main types.

(1) THE 'SOUL' THEORY. The first type is the conception of mind as a complex of experiences, non-bodily in nature, bound into a unity by some sort of spiritual principle which is distinguishable from the experiences themselves. There are two forms of this theory quite different from each other. The first of these, the traditional view handed down from Plato and Aristotle, looks upon the unifying bond of experiences as a definite entity which is always identical with itself and wholly passive in nature except in so far as it may be said to *have* experiences; this view is usually called the 'spiritual-substance' theory of mind. The other form, associated with the development of the views of Kant and Hegel, looks upon the spiritual bond of experiences as an activity, not a substance or entity, whose essence consists in the organization of individual experiences into meaningful wholes; this form of the 'soul' theory of mind is known by different names, three of the most common being 'transcendental,' 'organic,' and 'personalistic.'

(2) THE 'ACTUALISTIC' THEORY. The second type is the view of mind as an aggregate or collection of experiences, non-bodily in nature, but connected only by certain chance laws of association. For this type of theory there is no spiritual bond of unity among the experiences; from its point of view, if you exhaustively enumerate all of the experiences of the individual from birth to death in their various haphazard groupings, you will have compassed the totality of his mind and its ultimate nature will have been adequately described. This type of theory is commonly called the 'actualist' theory.

(3) THE 'BEHAVIORISTIC' THEORY. The third type practically denies that there are any experiences or any principle of unity among experiences that can be regarded as non-bodily in nature. On the contrary, it holds that all experiences are merely bodily responses to environmental conditions and that the unity among experiences finds its final and complete ground in the neuro-muscular system. Mind is behavior, and the unity among experiences is the behaving organism; hence the name of 'behaviorism' for this type.

CHAPTER XV. QUESTIONS AND EXERCISES

1. Define: experience, consciousness.

2. State clearly the problem of mind. In connection with this question study Pillsbury, *Essentials of Psychology,* Chapters XV and XVI.

3. Indicate the main views of mind held in the development of thought on the problem.

4. Summarize the main objections raised by Hume and Kant against the traditional spiritual-substance theory of the mind.

5. Read Hume's analysis of 'personal identity' in the *Treatise of Human Nature,* Book I, Part IV, section VI. Summarize the main points.

6. State briefly the conception of mind outlined by Perry in *Present Philosophical Tendencies,* Chapter XII.

7. Give the main points developed by Judd in connection with the concept of the self in his *Psychology,* Chapter XII.

CHAPTER XVI

MIND: CRITICAL ESTIMATE OF VIEWS

The historical survey of the preceding chapter, showing as it does a wide variety of views concerning the nature of mind, forces upon us the necessity of attempting something like a critical estimate of their several claims. Before going on to this, however, let us remind ourselves of the main results of the preceding discussion. Four theories were discovered: two forms of the 'soul' theory, namely the spiritual-substance view and the organic or personalistic view; the actualist view; and the behavioristic view. Among these views there is a consensus of opinion that the 'mind' of a person is a complex whole of numerous experiences somehow interconnected; but differences arise in connection with the question as to how these experiences are interconnected. The spiritual-substance theory assumes a definite entity that binds them together by 'owning' them; the organic or personalistic theory puts in the place of this entity an activity — 'subject,' as Hegel says, rather than 'substance' — which is supposed to unify the experiences by expressing itself in and through them; the actualist view virtually denies all unity, save what can be accounted for on the basis of groupings that arise through repetitions of experiences in certain relations; while the behaviorist theory insists that the neuro-muscular system itself is the only ground of unity needed, and any other is superfluous and mythological. What, now, are the relative merits of the claims of these several views? This is the question before us in the present chapter.

§ 1. *The spiritual-substance theory and the actualistic theory*

It has appeared from our historical survey that the spiritual-substance and actualistic theories of the nature of mind have been subjected to vigorous criticism, the former by Hume and the latter by Kant. And this criticism has virtually disposed of the two theories as serious contestants for consideration now-a-days; apparently they must be either given up outright or modified beyond recognition.

(1) THE SPIRITUAL-SUBSTANCE VIEW. So far as the traditional Platonic-Aristotelian theory is concerned, the defects in it which Hume with great penetration disclosed still vitiate it; and they are open to anyone who will stop seriously to consider the matter. These defects may, for summary statement here and without special reference to Hume's exposition of them, be reduced to two. (*a*) One never observes within experiences such a spiritual substance as this theory assumes to exist; therefore the only reason that can be given for the assumption is that it is the most satisfactory hypothesis that can be advanced in explanation of the unity within the mental life whose explanation we are seeking. (*b*) But a little reflection discloses that, so far from being the most satisfactory hypothesis, it does not in the slightest degree render intelligible the unity that exists among experiences. For, be it remembered, this spiritual substance is by hypothesis a changeless passive entity which is the same yesterday, to-day, and (presumably) forever. How, then, it could possibly link itself on to the evanescent and constantly changing experiences in such a way as to bind them together into one whole such that a given experience, which may belong

to the distant past (as, hearing a ghost yarn in childhood), bears a causal relation to a much later experience (as, fear of a cemetery in later life)—how this is possible the theory offers no intelligible solution. It merely asserts that this spiritual substance, this 'ego,' somehow in its purity 'owns' or 'supports' or 'has' the various experiences of hope and fear, pleasure and pain, joy and sorrow, remembering and aspiring, observing and thinking, which make up the content of the individual's life; what is to be understood by the relation of 'owning' or 'supporting' or 'having' is not stated, and apparently cannot possibly be stated, with sufficient precision to make this very important matter intelligible. In short, the theory is so vague as to have no rational value, and its vagueness cannot be removed since it is inherent in the fundamental concept ('spiritual substance') which the theory postulates. As a rational solution of the problem of mind, therefore, the theory is useless; its abstractness and consequent vagueness is its ruin.

(2) THE ACTUALISTIC VIEW. Modern psychologists who seemingly accept the actualistic view of the nature of mind generally accept it as a point of view convenient for the purposes of the psychologist. That is, when they define mind as the sum-total of mental experiences they are thinking of it as something which the science of psychology is interested in analyzing. Now if the psychologist finds actualism a convenient point of view in his work, no one may presume to call him to account for making use of it; that is his privilege. And if actualism be taken simply as a convenient point of departure for the studies of the psychologist, nothing can be said against it. For purposes of psychological observation mind is largely identical with experiences; the business of the psy-

chologist is to find out what these experiences are and to describe them with precision. But taken as a completely adequate account of the nature of mind the view of the actualist is open to serious criticism. The criticism of it which Kant advanced would seem to be fatal. Stated in terms more familiar to us than those employed by Kant in his formulation of it, his criticism amounts to the accusation that this view cannot account for such knowledge as we human beings actually do possess. This knowledge would be impossible if mind were only an aggregation or 'collection' of haphazard experiences. If our minds were nothing more than such a collection, we could not possibly make universal judgments. That 'every effect must have a cause,' that 'the sum of the interior angles of a triangle is equal to one hundred and eighty degrees of a circle,' or that 'the presence of friction implies heat' could never be known from separate and sharply sundered experiences. The fact that such judgments exist and are typical of mind is sufficient proof that mind is not alone a mere collection of experiences. In Kant's own words: "If consciousness were broken up into a number of mutually repellent states, each isolated and separated from the rest, knowledge would never arise in us at all, for knowledge is a whole of related and connected elements." "If each feeling were limited to a single moment, it would be an absolutely individual unit. In order that the various determinations of a perception, as, for instance, the parts of a line, should form a unity, it is necessary that they should be run over and held together by the mind." "If, in counting, I should forget that the units lying before my mind had been added by me one after the other, I should not be aware that a sum was being produced or generated in the successive addition of unit to unit; and as the conception of the sum is simply the consciousness of this unity of synthesis, I should have no knowledge of the number."[1] In other words, Kant is urging here that both reasoning and memory would be impossible if mind were nothing more than a collection of experiences; to make these possible mind must be a unity in a sense in which an aggregation or collection is not a unity. And it must be admitted that Kant's criticism of the actualistic theory is justified. Mind is in some sense an organized whole; any theory which leaves this out of account finds itself in the end, as Kant insists, unable to account for judgment and memory. So we may leave the actualist's theory on one side as an inadequate description of the totality of mind.[2]

Having discarded the spiritual-substance and the actualistic views of mind as unsatisfactory because of the difficulties that attach to them — difficulties exposed long ago, particularly by Hume in connection with the spiritual-substance theory and by Kant in connection with actualism, — we are left with two other theories to consider. So we pass on to a study of the claims of the behavioristic and personalistic views.

§ 2. *Some preliminary considerations*

Before proceeding to a critical study of these two theories, however, it is very necessary that we have clearly before us the more important characteristics of mind which

[1] The above quotations are taken from Watson's translation of the *Critique of Pure Reason* and are to be found in his *Selections from Kant* on pages 56, 57, and 60 respectively.

[2] Even Hume seemed to recognize its inadequacy. In an appendix added to his *Treatise of Human Nature,* he says: "Having thus loosen'd all our particular perceptions, when I proceed to explain the principle of connexion, which binds them together, and makes us attribute to them a real simplicity and identity; I am sensible that my account is very defective. . . ."

any theory of the nature of mind, if satisfactory, must make intelligible. These characteristics are, first, the fact of consciousness or awareness, and, secondly, those special activities of mind which exemplify in an emphatic manner the interconnection, or dovetailing, of experiences.

(1) CONSCIOUSNESS. By consciousness is meant, as indicated in the previous chapter, awareness of something. One may be aware that one's tooth is uneasy, that an important engagement is pressing, or that the book which one desires is absent from its accustomed place and that one is irritated in consequence. This awareness of experiences is consciousness, and it is a characteristic of mind that must be explained by any theory of the mind's nature.

(2) ACTIVITIES EXEMPLIFYING UNITY OF EXPERIENCES. In the second place, there are several activities of mind which exemplify the functional interrelation of experiences; they are simply different ways in which experiences are linked together as complex units or wholes. And these activities must be explained by any adequate theory of the nature of mind. The more important of these activities are the following.

(a) *Habit.* Past experiences of the individual are constantly functioning in the present. For example, if my tooth-brush hangs in a certain place for a number of weeks, my repeated experiences of reaching for it there result in a tendency on my part to continue to seek it in the old place even long after I have moved it to another place in the room. Walking, talking, manipulating machinery, playing games like tennis and baseball, and the doing of a thousand and one similar things are all illustrations of the same sort of activity. In this activity experiences that belong to the past continue to function in the present. To the activity is given the name of habit.

(b) *Perception.* By perception is meant the experience of objects as present to the senses of vision, audition, taste, etc. This is a very common type of experience and at first seems to be quite simple. Analysis discloses, however, that it always involves the linking of present with past experiences. Take, in illustration, one's perception of a friend approaching in the distance. Besides the experience directly present in consciousness, namely, the visual appearance of an object approaching, there are involved in the total experience called *the perception of a friend* a number of recollections (sound of the friend's voice, the color of his eyes, his personal characteristics of jollity, sympathy, and the like) which cluster about the visual appearance of the friend's body as seen from the distance and which are reinstatements of experiences that belong to the past. And, be it noted, these recollections are important elements within the perception of the friend, since without them such a perception would be wholly impossible. And this is true of every act of perceiving: while possessing a core of present experiences connected with the activity of the sense-organs, it is constituted largely of reverberations from past experiences hanging over in the present and functioning there. Thus perception like habit, to which it is in some respects closely allied, is a type of mental activity in which the interrelation of experiences is fundamental; in it present is linked with past.

(c) *Emotion.* The activity known as an emotion, such as fright, joy, anger, or sorrow, is exceedingly complex. It, too, is a functional interweaving of manifold experiences. Suppose you are driving a car on a dangerously narrow and precipitous mountain road and suddenly you discover that the car is gaining momentum in spite of the application of the brake. Your terror is much more complex than your immediate experiences with the racing car. Besides the perceptual complex, the emotion involves numberless reactions growing out of past experiences plus more or less vague forebodings as to the possible outcome of the impending catastrophe. And this is in general true of every emotion; it is a complex of experiences built around a perceptual nucleus and, like habit and perception, it reaches back into past experiences.

(d) *Recollection.* Another important activity of mind is the recall of past experiences by explicitly reinstating them in present experiences through imagery. This is recollection — memory in the narrow meaning. Thus, one may reinstate in consciousness where one was yesterday, the sights one saw during last summer's vacation, the melody one heard sung long ago, and the verse committed in childhood. The essence of this activity is the reproduction in present consciousness of that which actually constituted the content of another consciousness more or less remote in time.

(e) *Thinking or reasoning.* By thinking or reasoning is meant reading the meaning or significance of some content of consciousness and making inferences on the basis of it. Illustrations are numberless. The farmer regards the glow at sunrise and predicts rain for the morrow; the juror hears the evidence and reaches a conclusion concerning the guilt or innocence of the accused; the mathematician infers that, the nature of the triangle being what it is, the sum of its interior angles must equal 180 degrees; by observation of the process going on in the test-tube before him the chemist learns that certain elements are active there; and so on indefinitely. Obviously here we have a very complex activity. It is the linking together of multitudinous experiences in meaningful relations.

(3) Summary of section. We have thus six activities in the light of which the theories of mind we are yet to consider must be tested. Did the mind — as the actualist supposes — consist solely of fading experiences which are discontinuous and so sharply sundered from each other that no one left a trace of its existence upon any other, then neither consciousness nor habit nor perception nor emotion nor recollection nor judging would be possible. But these activities belong to mind and, indeed, constitute its basal features. Mind, therefore, must be said to be a unity of complexes; and if we are to secure a scientific conception of its nature, this unity must be made intelligible. We turn now from this preliminary analysis to an estimate of the two theories of the nature of mind remaining for our consideration.

§ 3. *The behavioristic theory*

Behaviorism undertakes to explain all the activities of mind enumerated in the preceding section — in so far, that is, as they are admitted to be genuine types of activity — in terms of the central nervous system and its attachments.[1] A fundamental characteristic of the neuro-muscular system is what is known as 'integration.' By integration is meant the tendency of the nervous system to function as a whole and not as a collection of independent and

[1] Of course, various exponents of behaviorism differ in the details of their theory. No account can here be taken of these differences. Furthermore, like actualism, behaviorism as a psychological point of view is legitimate; and as such is not open to all of the criticisms developed below in the text. What follows must therefore be understood by the reader to be an attempt to state what seems to be the logical drift of behaviorism taken, not as a provisional psychological point of view, but as a complete and exhaustive account of the nature of mind. For three distinct formulations of behaviorism see the opening pages of the article by Lashley, "Behaviorism and Consciousness," *Psychological Review*, Vol. 30, pp. 237 ff.

detached elements. In other words, the nervous system is made up of millions of elements, called 'neurones'; these neurones are bound together in an intricate network of relations and are functionally connected so that they tend to act together — when one neurone is excited its activity is transmitted to other neurones in such a way that they tend thereafter to function in connection with it; this interfunctioning of neurones ramifies throughout the nervous system, and to this interfunctioning is given the name of 'integration.' Now it is the contention of behaviorism that all the activities of the mind can be satisfactorily explained in terms of integration.[1] Let us attempt to follow his explanation of the activities above enumerated.

To the extreme behaviorist consciousness is a word without an intelligible meaning. He may not deny outright that there is some meaning to be attached to it, but he does insist that to say there is is to make an assumption for which no tangible evidence can be given. The various activities of mind, he thinks, can be satisfactorily and adequately explained without the use of the term 'consciousness,' and he therefore denies that any obligation to explain the nature of consciousness rests upon him. He excludes it from his scientific vocabulary as a useless and superfluous term; and, doing so, he by implication at least denies that consciousness has any real existence.

Habit he explains in terms of the interfunctioning of neurones. My practice of reaching for my tooth-brush, for example, has repeatedly excited conjointly the same set of neurones; as a result a circuit[2] is formed among the

[1] If the reader is not familiar with the general structure of the neuromuscular system and of its element, the neurone, he will find information in the psychological texts sufficiently detailed for the present discussion. If he wishes an exhaustive analysis, he must go to the books on neurology.

[2] The technical name for this circuit is 'reflex arc.'

neurones so that when one acts the others act with it in the same manner in which they have acted with it before. Hence, when I desire my toothbrush, certain neurones are stimulated which communicate their activity to their fellows in the circuit and the movement of my arm in the direction of the old location of the tooth-brush results. Now one such circuit or 'reflex arc' may itself become a part of a larger circuit; so we have systems of reflexes. Habit can be defined, then, "as a complex system of reflexes which functions in a serial order when the child or adult is confronted by the appropriate stimulus. . . ."[1] Habit, in short, is the neuro-muscular system active in specific situations.

Perception, likewise, finds its sufficient explanation, the behaviorist thinks, in precisely the same terminology. Take the case of the child learning to perceive 'the orange.' Suppose that 'the orange' at first means to the child nothing more than what it sees; *then* the act of perceiving will consist in the activity of a certain set of neurones involved in the act of seeing. But let the child have the experiences of taste, odor, and feel in conjunction with his visual experience of the orange, and let this conjoint experience be repeated frequently enough to establish an integration among the various neurones involved in these different experiences, eventually the color of the orange will call up its odor, taste, and feel even when the orange is seen merely and not tasted and smelt and touched. Thus the full-blown percept of the orange as a complex of qualities is born; it is simply an integration of neurones. Perception, thus, is a type of habit.

Emotion is explained by the behaviorist as a complex of nervous processes connected with the perception of a

[1] Watson, *Psychology from the Standpoint of the Behaviorist*, 273.

definite situation through the reflex arcs or circuits concerned. Your fright in the case of the run-a-way car, for example, consists of violent bodily changes caused by integrations initiated by the situation that confronts you but reaching far back into your hereditary past. Or more technically: "An emotion is an hereditary 'pattern-reaction' involving profound changes of the bodily mechanism as a whole, but particularly of the visceral and glandular systems."[1]

Recollection, the behaviorist insists, is nothing but a type of habit, and so can be explained in the same way that all habits are accounted for. It is true that there is a common assumption to the effect that recollection involves mental imagery and so is different from ordinary habits. When we recollect what we had this morning for breakfast we ordinarily suppose that we have in consciousness images of various articles of food. But mental images do not exist, according to the behaviorist's account; what are usually called images are nothing but "implicit language or word habits." Consequently there is no difference between recollection, recall of past experiences, and habit; the explanation of the one is the explanation of the other.

Thinking, as the behaviorist views it, is also a language habit. "It is not different in essence from tennis-playing, swimming or any other overt activity except that it is hidden from ordinary observation and is more complex and at the same time more abbreviated so far as its parts are concerned than even the bravest of us could dream of. . . . When we study implicit bodily processes we are studying

[1] Watsor, *ibid.*, p. 195. "By pattern-reaction we mean that the separate details of response appear with some constancy, with some regularity and in approximately the same sequential order each time the stimulus is presented."

thought; just as when we study the way a golfer stands in addressing his ball and swinging his club we are studying *golf.*"[1] The activity of thinking, thus, is nervous integration; we think with our neuro-muscular system.

§ 4. *The 'personalistic' or 'subject' theory*

According to the personalistic theory of the nature of mind it is impossible to identify the ground of unity among experiences with the neuro-muscular system as behaviorism undertakes to do. Instead, this theory would insist upon a 'subject' or 'self' as the only ground of unity with reference to which the activities above discussed can be understood. Before we undertake to see how it would explain these activities let us note certain questions of fact upon which it joins issue with behaviorism.

(1) Questions of fact at issue. The upholder of the 'subject' theory of mind takes issue with the behaviorist upon three important questions of fact, namely, the existence of consciousness, the existence of images, and the nature of thinking.

(a) *The existence of consciousness.* The behaviorist, as we have seen, tends to deny that any intelligible meaning can be attached to the term consciousness. The personalist, on the other hand, contends that we have direct evidence within immediate experience that consciousness exists since we are directly aware of our experiences. And he contends, furthermore, that this awareness is as intelligible to us as is any particular experience to which it attaches itself.

(b) *The existence of images.* Again, the personalist contends that the behaviorist is wrong in his denial of the existence of images. The flash of lightning seen and the

[1] Watson, *ibid.*, pp. 325–326.

same flash recalled or imaged are, he maintains, two distinct types of experiences as common sense says they are. He agrees with Hume that experiences existing in consciousness as present and images as reinstatements of past experiences "are so very different, that no one can make a scruple to rank them under different heads, and assign to each a peculiar name to mark the difference."[1]

(c) *Nature of thinking.* Finally, the personalist objects that the type of adjustment or learning which the behaviorist identifies with thinking is not exhaustive of all forms of the thought process. The behaviorist holds that there is no essential difference between thinking about a scientific problem and learning to play tennis or golf or to use a typewriter; the personalist denies this and asserts that there is an essential difference between this latter sort of 'thinking' and that which is involved in the solution of a scientific problem. In short, the personalist contends that there are two ways in which one may know: one may know *how,* as in knowing how to play tennis or golf, and one may know *about,* as in knowing the rules of the game or at what angle and with what force to hit the ball in order best to accomplish a certain purpose in playing the game. And these two types of knowing, as well as the types of thinking involved, he insists, are quite different from each other and cannot without violence be identified.

(2) EXPLANATION OF THE ACTIVITIES OF MIND. It is the conviction of the personalist that the several activities of mind which we have been considering in this chapter cannot be explained except upon the assumption that 'subject' exists as the ground of unity among experiences.

In the first place, consciousness, recollection as involv-

[1] *Treatise of Human Nature,* Part I, section 1.

ing images, and thinking in the sense of learning *about* demand for their explanation such a 'subject.' Consciousness is nothing but a unique relation that exists between a given experience and the subject that is conscious; an experience is in consciousness when the subject is 'aware' of it. Recollection, likewise, is the reinstatement in present consciousness of past experiences through the medium of images now present to the subject. And thought in the sense of understanding or comprehending the meaning of experiences can be explained only as a unique activity of the subject by which the significance of logically related experiences is read and interpreted. In other words, consciousness is the subject's awareness of experiences, recollection is the subject's picturing through imagery experiences that are past, and judgment is the subject's interpretation of experiences, both present and past, as having meaning with reference to some problem.

Again, while admitting that the behaviorist's account of habit, perception, and emotion is a valuable description of one side of these activities, the personalist contends that it is not a complete description. In the formation of habit there is always an element of choice which is potent within the process and which can be explained only as the act of the subject; unless this element of choice be taken into account, habit cannot be distinguished from purely instinctive activity. In perception, likewise, the subject is involved, since there must be a 'perceiver' for which the present experience of the color of the orange, for example, is linked up with former experiences so radically different as those of smell and feel and taste; were there no such 'perceiver' the odor and taste of the orange could not become associated with its color. Finally, emotions involve, besides the integration of 'pattern-reactions,' the activity of the subject in appreciating the significance of the total situation that gives rise to the emotion. Habit, perception, and emotion therefore cannot, for the personalist, be satisfactorily explained apart from reference to an active 'subject' whose experiences they are; this, the personalist contends, is the verdict of direct experience as well as a theoretically necessary hypothesis.

(3) SUMMARY OF SECTION. The personalist, in the first place, accuses the behaviorist of unjustly denying the existence of certain aspects of the mental life, and of leaving out of account certain important phases of the basal activities of mind. The description of mind which the behaviorist offers, the personalist agrees, is acceptable if taken as a description of merely one side of these activities; but because of its omission of important features of the activities described it cannot be taken as complete. When the features of mind overlooked by the behaviorist are considered, the personalist contends, we find ourselves driven to posit the neuro-muscular system *plus* a 'subject,' rather than the neuro-muscular system alone, as the ground of unity of the mind.

§ 5. *Evaluation of the two preceding theories*

The following observations would seem to have an important bearing upon the controversy between the behaviorist and the personalist:

(1) INTROSPECTION AS A SCIENTIFIC METHOD. The question at issue between the personalist and the behaviorist with reference to the existence of images and consciousness depends in last analysis upon the answer one gives to the further question whether introspection (in the sense of direct acquaintance with what goes on in one's mind) is to be allowed as a scientific, that is, trustworthy

and objective, method of observation of mental facts. It is by introspection that the personalist thinks he establishes the existence of images and awareness as real elements within mind; but the behaviorist is prone to deny that introspection is possible or, at least, significant. This question will therefore have to be settled before the other one can be answered.

(2) NATURE OF THINKING. In his identification of thinking with such activities as swimming, playing golf, and the like, and in his denial that there is any sense in which thinking is different from these the behaviorist would appear to be at a disadvantage. For the personalist seems to be justified in his contention that there is a difference of considerable importance between *knowing how* and *knowing about*. The first way of knowing may be said to be characteristic of a bird in building a nest, but not the second; the bird knows how to build a nest, but it can hardly be said to understand the principles or value of nest-building. The same distinction seems to hold in the case of human beings. One may know how to put together a machine without wholly comprehending the structure of the machine. At least, it is not obvious that the two types of knowing can be absolutely identified; but the apparent success of the behaviorist's explanation of thinking rests largely upon the assumption that they are not essentially different.

(3) VAGUENESS OF 'SELF' OR 'SUBJECT.' The personalist, however, is not without his difficulties. Perhaps the chief of these is the vagueness attaching to his ground of unity among experiences. The behaviorist here seems to have the advantage in the debate. The structure of the neuro-muscular system we know in part, and when we speak of 'integration' we can understand at least in a

general way what is meant; but the 'subject' of the personalist is a vague notion, and it is not clear precisely how the hypothesis of the 'subject' helps us in making intelligible to ourselves the unity of experiences involved in those activities of the mind that it is invoked to explain. So it is incumbent on the personalist to make this conception more definite, and this task is perhaps his chief stone of stumbling. However, if he can show that the hypothesis of the behaviorist is clearly inadequate to explain the facts, then he is at liberty to insist upon his own view despite its apparent vagueness. And it must be remembered, further, that it is the point of the personalist's contention that the unity of mind cannot be defined exclusively in bodily terms; hence it is unjust to demand of him that he make his 'subject' intelligible and objective in the same sense in which integration among neurones is intelligible and objective. Nevertheless, the demand that he make his ground of unity less vague than it now is is a legitimate demand which he cannot escape.

Chapter XVI. Questions and Exercises

1. Indicate the chief objections to the actualist's conception of mind.

2. Compare section 2 of this Chapter with Chapter XV of Pillsbury, *Essentials of Psychology*.

3. Show how consciousness, habit, perception, emotion, and thinking bear upon the debate between the personalist and the behaviorist.

4. How would the behaviorist explain each of the phenomena mentioned in the preceding question? How would the personalist explain them?

5. What is your estimate of behaviorism and personalism taken as exhaustive accounts of the nature of mind? Discuss.

6. Summarize the main points in Lecture IV of Hoernle's *Matter, Life, Mind, and God.*

7. For further and more advanced study on the problem of mind consult: Hoernle, *Studies in Contemporary Metaphysics,* Chapter VIII; Holt, *The Concept of Consciousness;* Holt, *The Freudian Wish;* Laird, *The Problems of the Self.*

CHAPTER XVII

MIND AND BODY

To one who holds that there is a difference between mind and body the problem of their relation to each other is an inescapable one. And since it is not evident from our preceding discussion that they can be wholly identified, it becomes necessary for us to consider the suggestions that have been offered in connection with the problem.

§ 1. *Facts indicating close connection between mind and body*

Whatever may be the final solution of the problem concerning the mind-body relation, it is evident from the first that the relation is a very close and intimate one. Facts which cannot be denied seem unmistakably to show this.

(1) FACTS OF COMMON-SENSE OBSERVATION. In the first place, there are many facts of every-day occurrence which prove that mind and body are intimately bound up with each other. A blow on the head or an application of ether or chloroform removes temporarily at least all traces of conscious experiences. One's general physical condition affects one's mental outlook; and, on the other side, prolonged mental effort shows its traces in a tired body. Fear is accompanied by a palpitating heart and quaking limbs, anger by clenched fists and set teeth, while laughter usually goes with joy and tears with grief. To such a list the student will have no difficulty in adding at will.

(2) Facts of experimental observation. More subtle facts experimentally determined reveal the same intimate connection. It has been experimentally observed, for example, that the blood-pressure both in the forearm and in the brain perceptibly changes from the normal when one is doing mental work, such as multiplying one number by another, or is laboring under slight emotional excitement, such as embarrassment or chagrin. The effects of certain drugs (cocaine, opium, etc.) are correlated with characteristic changes in consciousness. The result of these experiments and others of the kind "is to bring about the conviction that body and mind are in most intimate connection, and that the intercourse of the two is not occasional, but is constant. . . . It is now generally accepted that the body reflects every shade of psychic operation; that in all manner of mental action there is some physical expression. 'All consciousness is motor' is the brief expression of this important truth; every mental state somehow runs over into a corresponding bodily state."[1]

(3) Facts of anatomy. The facts of anatomy point to the same truth. A disease of the brain affects the mental life. Various types of mental experience are now known to be localized in different parts of the brain, visual experience in the occipital lobe, auditory experience in the auditory center, olfactory experience in still a different region, and so forth; and if a given part of the brain is diseased or seriously injured, the mental experiences connected with that part are seriously interfered with if not eliminated entirely. Furthermore, comparative anatomy conclusively shows that mind grows in significance as the nervous system grows in complexity from the lower to the higher levels of organic forms. Thus, for example, the mind of the

[1] Stratton, *Experimental Psychology and Culture*, pp. 268–269.

horse or dog is less significant than is the mind of man, and the nervous systems — particularly the brain structure — of the lower forms is much less complex than is that of the higher. Development in nervous systems runs concomitantly with the development of minds.

(4) THEORIES CONCERNING THE CONNECTION BETWEEN MIND AND BODY. The preceding observations seem to indicate that mind and body are intimately bound up with each other; such an intimate connection seems proved by the facts of common-sense and scientific observation and by inferences based upon the results of anatomical study. Can this connection between the two be further described? Several theories have been advanced in answer to this question. We shall consider in some detail two of the main ones, namely, parallelism and interactionism; the more important variations of these basal views together with a more recent theory we shall make note of in the final section of this chapter.[1]

§ 2. *The interaction theory*

The interaction theory of the relation between mind and body was advocated in a rather crude form by Descartes.[2] As we have seen in our historical survey of the various views of mind, Descartes accepted the Platonic-Aristotelian conception of mind as a substance; and he gave it a definite location in the pineal gland of the brain at which point it was supposed to exert an influence upon the body and, in turn, to be affected by bodily processes. Since Descartes, the theory has been restated in more subtle terminology,

[1] The reader who is interested in going into the matter more fully should consult Sellars, *The Essentials of Philosophy,* Chapters XX–XXII; Fullerton, *Introduction to Philosophy,* Chapter IX; Paulsen, *Introduction to Philosophy,* pp. 74–111; and Pratt, *Matter and Spirit.*

[2] See his *Passions of the Soul,* XXXIV.

but it has remained in principle the same. Our purpose in this section is to understand the general nature of the theory without reference to any individual thinker's statement of it, and to note some objections that lie against it.

(1) The theory stated. The main thesis of the interaction theory is that the relation obtaining between mind and body is a causal relation. Bodily processes are at times supposed to cause mental experiences, such as perception or feeling, and at times to be caused by them. Thus, according to the theory, the nervous processes in the visual center of the brain are the cause of my perception of a light; and, on the other side, my desire to acquaint myself with the contents of a book is the cause of the contraction of muscles involved in my walking across the room to the table on which the book is lying. In short there is a direct interaction between bodily processes and mental experiences, that is, the mind-body relation is a causal relation.

(2) Objections to the theory. Despite the fact that most of our commonplace observations seem to justify the view of interactionism, the theory is not without its difficulties. Two of the most weighty of these we shall here set down.

(a) *Inconceivability.* The first objection is that, as understood by the interactionist, mind and body are so utterly different it is wholly inconceivable how a causal relation could possibly exist between them. We can fairly readily comprehend how the activity of brain cells can stand in a causal relation to the contraction of muscles; that is, we can understand a causal connection between one bodily process and another. And we can also understand how a desire for food might cause the appearance within mind of an image of the food that will satisfy this desire; that is, we can make intelligible a causal relation between one mental experience and another. But how a nervous process in the brain could cause a mental experience, or *vice versa,* is beyond our powers of comprehension. It is much as if we were asked to comprehend how an image of fire could set the coal on the hearth burning. The two terms, body and mind, are so utterly different that they stare vacantly at each other and refuse to link themselves causally. A causal relation between body and mind is inconceivable — such is the first objection to the interaction theory.

(b) *Violation of the law of conservation of energy.* We find that material objects are capable of doing work; thus, coal is capable of converting water into steam, a storage battery is capable of propelling a car through the streets, and so forth. This capacity for doing work is called in physics 'energy.' The work actually done by an object is 'kinetic energy'; while the power to do work is 'potential energy.' The energy of a storage battery which is inactive is its 'potential' energy; the energy of the same battery expended in driving the motor is 'kinetic' energy. Now it is a general conclusion of the physical sciences that the total amount of energy in the universe as a whole, both potential and kinetic, is constant. In the many transformations of energy that take place within the world energy is neither created nor destroyed; potential energy may be changed into kinetic, or *vice versa,* but the total amount of energy remains constant. Thus, when fire changes water into steam and thereby heats buildings or drives machinery, all that happens is that potential energy is transformed into kinetic energy; no energy is produced, nor is any destroyed. And the same is true of the universe at large: whatever transformations of energy may take place there, the total amount of energy remains constant. This principle is known in the physical sciences as the 'law' or principle of *the conservation of energy*.

Now the objection is raised against the interaction theory of the mind-body relation, that it violates the principle of the conservation of energy. If the interaction theory were true, so the objection runs, and an act of volition, say, caused me to strike with my hand, then there would happen in the physical environment an event — namely, the contraction of muscles in my arm and the consequent movement of my arm through space — for which there is no compensatory transformation of energy, and so there would be added to the physical order a certain amount of energy. Or, on the other hand, if a light wave sets going certain chemical changes in the retina of my eye which are transmitted by means of the optic nerve to the visual center of the brain where the energy terminates in the activity of certain neurones which, in turn, cause a mental experience — namely, my seeing or perceiving the light, — then a physical process ends in mental activity, and so a certain amount of physical energy is apparently lost from the physical order. The hypothesis of the causal relation between mind and body is thus apparently in conflict with one of the fundamental principles of the physical sciences and therefore, according to the objection, must be surrendered.

§ 3. *The parallelistic theory*

The parallelistic theory of the mind-body relation is associated among classical philosophers chiefly with the names of Spinoza and Leibnitz.[1] In one form or another the theory has been held even down to our own day.

[1] Spinoza's statement of the theory is found in his famous work, *The Ethics*. The essence of his view is contained in the two following propo-

(1) Nature of the theory. The parallelist denies that there is any causal connection between mind and body. He admits that every mental experience has its corresponding bodily activity, or, as it has been expressed, every psychosis (mental process or experience) has its neurosis (corresponding bodily or nervous process). But he insists that the bodily and the mental series are not causally connected; they always happen together in a constant order, visual experiences being accompanied by nervous activity in the visual center of the brain, auditory experiences being always accompanied by nervous activity in the auditory center of the brain, and so forth, but neither is the cause or the effect of the other. They are causally independent of each other, though always and necessarily and constantly parallel. Professor Paulsen, a recent advocate of the theory of parallelism, explains it very interestingly as follows: "Let us imagine with Leibnitz the skull of an animal or man to be as large as a mill. Suppose one could walk around in it and observe the processes in the brain as one can observe the movements of the machinery and the cogging of the wheels in the mill. What brain-processes would the observer expect to see? . . . The adherent of the parallelistic theory must evidently expect the following. The physical processes in the brain form a closed causal nexus. There is no member that is not physical in its nature. One would see as little of psychical processes, of ideas and

sitions from that work: "The order and connection of ideas is the same as the order and connection of things," Part II, Proposition VII; and "Even as thoughts and the ideas of things are arranged and associated in the mind, so are the modifications of body or the images of things precisely in the same way arranged and associated in the body," Part V, Proposition I. For Leibnitz, "bodies act as if there were no souls, and souls act as if there were no bodies; and yet both act as though the one influenced the other," *The Monadology*, paragraph 81 — a translation of this work by Leibnitz may be conveniently found in Rand, *Modern Classical Philosophers*, pp. 199 ff.

thoughts, as in the movements of the mill. A man crosses the street. Suddenly his name is called; he turns around and walks toward the person who called him. The omniscient physiologist would explain the whole process in a purely mechanical way. He would show how the physical effect of the sound-waves upon the organ of hearing excited a definite nervous process in the auditory nerve, how this process was conducted to the central organ, how it released certain physical processes there which finally led to the innervation of certain groups of motor nerves, the ultimate result of which was the turning and movement of the body in the direction of the sound-waves. All these occurrences combine into an unbroken chain of physical processes. Alongside of this, another process occurred of which the physiologist as such sees nothing and needs to know nothing, with which, however, he is acquainted as a thinking being who interprets his percepts; there are auditory sensations, which aroused ideas and feelings. The person called heard his name; he turned around in order to discover who called him and why he was addressed; he perceived an old acquaintance and went to greet him. These occurrences accompany the physical series without interfering with it; perception and presentation are not members of the physical causal series."[1] For the parallelist, then, mental experiences are causally connected with mental experiences, and bodily processes are causally connected with bodily processes; but there is no causal connection between the two systems. The two series are parallel, but causally independent of each other.

(2) Objections to the theory. Among the facts that tend to support the parallelist's view of the mind-body relation are the following: reflex acts like jerking the finger

[1] Paulsen, *Introduction to Philosophy*, English translation, 1907, p. 84.

away from a hot object or dodging when a swiftly moving object directly approaches the face; habitual acts, such as walking, talking, etc.; reveries or day-dreams; long trains of continuous reflection; and the facts connected with certain more or less abnormal types such as talking in one's sleep, hypnotism, and the like. Such facts may, apparently, be accounted for on the assumption of parallelism that causal connections exist only among mental states, on the one side, or among bodily processes, on the other. However, there are important objections to the theory that have from time to time been advanced against the acceptance of it. Three of the more weighty of these we may note.

(a) *Sudden experiences*. Suppose one is suddenly awakened from a revery or deep concentration on a problem by the slamming of a door or a clap of thunder. Such an occurrence the parallelistic theory finds difficult to explain. The only explanation of the perception of the sound which it could offer from the mental side would have to refer it to previous experiences, since mental experiences are causally connected only with other experiences. But in this particular case, there seems nothing in the previous experiences that could in any justifiable sense be said to be the cause of the interruption by this particular sound of that which up to its appearance was going on in the mind; and that for the reason that it is an *interruption*. Taken by itself the train of experiences within the revery or the series of judgments bearing upon the problem in hand could not be responsible for the disturbing noise; the noise is an interloper. How then account for it? Before such a question the parallelistic theory seems to be brought to a sharp stop. Sudden and irrelevant experiences stand decidedly in its way. This is the first objection to it.

(b) *Makes mind useless in biological evolution.* One of the basal principles in the theory of organic evolution is that whatever survives in the struggle for existence must be of some service in the struggle, that its survival is guaranteed only by its utility. If the theory of parallelism were true, however, mind would seem to be of no use in the development of life. For, by hypothesis, it could exert no determining influence upon bodily conduct and therefore could have no efficient contact with the appearance and development of bodily characteristics. It is, therefore, difficult to understand why, on the basis of the parallelistic theory of the mind-body relation, the continued existence, to say nothing of the increasing importance, of mind in the development of organic forms can be explained. Mind, as parallelism conceives it, seems to be biologically useless. This is the second objection.

(c) *Parallelism implies panpsychism.* The third objection to the parallelistic hypothesis is that, if it be true, then we are logically driven to the conclusion that mind is present wherever there is bodily activity, whether this activity be in organic forms or in inorganic compounds. If every psychosis has its neurosis, if, that is, every mental experience has its corresponding bodily process, then where are we to stop? Has digestion, for example, its corresponding experience? If not, why not? Digestion certainly is a bodily process, and is intimately connected with those other bodily processes that are known to be accompanied by parallel mental processes. And when once we start on this road, so the objection runs, there is no stopping place short of the general conclusion that all physical processes, organic and inorganic processes, have their parallel mental processes. And so we are driven to the amazing inference that mind is spread out everywhere in the universe parallel with all types of material change and activity; that not only the human body has its experiences, but all bodies, including "the choir of heaven and the furniture of the earth," have theirs. This is the view generally known as panpsychism — 'mind everywhere.' But this view is absurd. Hence the parallelistic theory of the mind-body relation is absurd and must be given up. This is the third objection to the theory.

§ 4. *Critical estimate of interactionism and parallelism*

What now shall we say by way of estimating the value of these conflicting views of the mind-body relation? A brief attempt to answer this question, or at least to view the problem it presents, is necessary.

(1) THE INTERACTION THEORY. The theory of interactionism has *prima facie* evidence in its favor to the extent that it appears to harmonize with what we seem to know most directly concerning the mind-body relation. Mind and body do seem to be causally connected with each other, though, of course, it is still possible that this 'seeming' is an appearance only and not reality. But the objections raised against the interactionist's view do not appear to be wholly convincing, as the following considerations may serve to indicate.

(a) *Inconceivability*. So far as the objection that a causal relation between body and mind is inconceivable is concerned, three points may be noted. In the first place, to say that an hypothesis is inconceivable is to say nothing serious against it, unless it can be shown to be inconceivable in at least one of the following meanings: lacking contact with the main body of human knowledge and, so, arbitrary; or, of such a nature that the affirmation of it involves a greater contradiction of the main body of human knowledge than does its denial; or, finally, such that it is self-contradictory. And the hypothesis of interactionism is inconceivable in neither of these three meanings. In the second place, the assumption upon which the objection rests appear to be that there cannot possibly exist a causal relation between a nervous process and a mental experience; but this is precisely the point at issue and cannot logically be assumed. Finally, there is no greater mystery or unintelligibility in a causal nexus between a nervous process and a mental experience than there is in a causal nexus between, let us say, a purely physical process such as the movement of a light-wave and a neurological process in the optic nerve or the retina — a causal nexus that is admitted by all as a fact.

(b) *Conservation of energy.* In connection with the objection to interactionism based upon the principle of the conservation of energy and the supposed conflict with it, three points are of importance. The first is the consideration that, when two objects are causally connected, there is not necessarily a transference of energy between them. As we have already seen in our discussion above of the nature of the causal nexus, two things are causally connected when they are in some sense necessarily dependent upon each other; transference of energy from one to the other is not at all necessarily involved in their causal conjunction. Hence, in so far as this objection to interactionism assumes that every causal nexus involves a transference of energy, it would appear to rest upon a false assumption. The second point to be noted is that the possibility of transformation of energy is not excluded in the mind-body relation. It is still conceivable that when a nervous process is the cause of a mental experience — as, for example, when the activity of the neurones in the visual center of the brain causes a visual perception of an object — there is a transformation of energy rather than a destruction of it, just as there is when the energy of a light-wave is transformed into the energy of a chemical process in the retina and a nervous process in the optic nerve. If this were the case, then there would be no violation of the principle of the conservation of energy in the mind-body relation.[1] The final point to be noticed is that the principle of the conservation of energy is an hypothesis of the physical sciences and has been formulated without any reference to mind. It is supposed to be expressive of what is true only of *physical systems* of energy, and has no obvious reference to those systems — if there be such — which are not wholly physical in nature. And it is conceivable at least that the mind-body is precisely such a system.

(2) PARALLELISM. We turn now to the objections raised against the parallelistic view of the mind-body relation and ask concerning their significance. Are they sufficient to make the theory untenable, or may the parallelist satisfactorily reply to them?

(a) *Sudden experiences.* At first glance, the objection based upon the undoubted occurrence of sudden perceptions in the flow of experiences, as when the sound of a bell interrupts our meditation, is a formidable one for the parallelist. How account for the mental experience of hearing the bell? It cannot be caused by the experiences into which it unexpectedly comes; it follows upon any sort

[1] This interpretation of the mind-body relation, it should be noted, would imply that mind and body are not so sharply sundered as many statements of the interaction theory would seem to suppose. For the implication of such an interpretation would appear to be that what we here call bodily processes on the one hand, and mental experiences on the other, are in point of fact, like 'kinetic' and potential' physical energy, only two forms of one and the same reality — as Leibnitz long ago supposed.

of experience whatever, and bears no known causal connection to the experiences upon which it does follow. The only way out of this difficulty left open to the parallelist is to say that the occurrence of the perception is caused by psychical processes unknown to the observer. As Professor Paulsen puts it: "The movements which proceed from the bell have as their sole effects nervous excitations and brain states. Sensation, on the other hand, is the effect of the inner processes accompanying these vibrations." "Processes which are unknown to us, but whose physical equivalents are physical or chemical processes, are the causes of these psychical states."[1] Such an answer, however, is unsatisfactory for two reasons: it explains a fairly definite situation within our experience in terms of processes that are unknown, and apparently unknowable; and it assumes that every bodily process has its accompanying mental experience. To explain the known in terms of the unknown is never justifiable if a simpler explanation, that is, one involving less appeal to the imagination, is logically tenable. The assumption involved in this explanation is in principle identical with panpsychism, which we will consider below.

(b) *The objection that parallelism makes mind useless in organic evolution.* There does seem to be evidence that mind plays an important rôle in the development of life to the extent that it may be said to exert a determining influence upon the organism's reaction to its environment. The parallelist would have to deny that mind exerts any such influence, and so he is compelled to take issue with apparent facts. To this objection, however, he may reply that the facts are only apparent, that there is no justification for supposing that mind is influential in organic de-

[1] Paulsen, *Introduction to Philosophy*, p. 91.

velopment. And in support of this contention he can point to recent advances in our scientific knowledge of the way in which life develops, the emphasis being placed upon the cellular structure of the body as the chief factor in organic evolution rather than upon mind.[1] This reply, however, raises an issue of fundamental importance, the issue, namely, which is in debate between the mechanist and the vitalist.[2] And until this issue is settled, neither the parallelist nor his critic can, on the point here under consideration, with assurance be deemed correct in his position.

(c) *Parallelism as involving panpsychism.* This objection rests upon two theses: that parallelism does logically involve panpsychism, and that panpsychism is necessarily absurd. The first thesis seems true; at least it is true unless one stops short at some point and arbitrarily says that beyond this point mind is not found; if some bodily processes are necessarily accompanied by experiences, why not all? The second thesis, however, is not obviously true. Our prejudices, to be sure, run counter to the panpsychist view of the world; we are not in the habit of thinking that all bodily processes, inorganic as well as organic, are accompanied by mental processes, that all bodies have souls. And we are prejudiced against thinking in this fashion. But our prejudice needs to be justified before we discard the panpsychist view as absurd. So the parallelist may here reply to his critic by simply asking him to show that panpsychism is an absurd view of the world and by calling his attention to many considerations that may be advanced in support of it.[3]

[1] For a general survey of the material relevant here the student should consult the articles on 'evolution' in the encyclopaedias and the following books: Thomson and Geddes, *Evolution* and Moore, B., *The Origin and Nature of Life*.

[2] See above, Chapter XIII.

[3] This is precisely what Professor Paulsen does in his discussion of

(3) SUMMARY OF SECTION. Neither interactionism nor parallelism is free from difficulties. On the whole, however, it would seem that of the two theories interactionism is the simpler hypothesis and involves fewer difficulties. The most weighty objection to parallelism is that it seems to involve us in a world-view which is at least questionable, namely panpsychism, and it leaves unanswered the question why there should be that invariable concomitance between bodily processes and mental experiences which it posits.

§ 5. *Other theories of the mind-body relation*

Many thinkers have been so impressed by the difficulties confronting the interaction and parallelistic theories that they are convinced neither view can be accepted. They have, therefore, sought for other explanations. Some of these other views must at least be mentioned in conclusion of this chapter.

Two of the older views which have been developed as ways of escape from the difficulties of the general theories of parallelism and interactionism are: the double-aspect theory, and epiphenomenalism. The *double-aspect* theory, which is in fact a type of parallelism, holds that both mind and body are only two sides of the same reality, just as the concave and convex sides of a piece of curved glass are two sides of the one object. Mind and body, then, are in a sense identical — they are faces of an identical thing, the inner and outer surfaces of it, so to speak. Mind and body "constitute one single process, observable in two ways"; they are, as it were, the same thing "said in two

---

the matter, *Introduction to Philosophy*, pp. 87–111, which should be read in its entirety. While what is there said is not convincing, it is at least suggestive and provocative of thought.

languages." According to *epiphenomenalism* there is a causal relation between mind and body, but it holds only in one direction; mind is an off-shoot of brain activity, and so in a sense may be said to be caused by it, but mental processes cannot function as causes in relation to brain processes. Mind is an *epi*-phenomenon — a phenomenon, that is, which is of secondary importance only. It is produced by the brain, a halo dancing above the brain cells as Bergson poetically puts it; but it is incapable of acting upon the brain in any causal manner. It is not difficult to show that these two theories are only variations of the two theories above considered, and that they do not carry any greater conviction than that which attaches to either parallelism or interactionism. They are, however, historically at least, important variations.[1]

In quite recent discussion another point of view has been suggested which, it is supposed, promises to put the mind-body problem in a somewhat different light. This is the theory of *emergence*. Its main thesis is that the mind 'emerges' out of brain-organization, much as water 'emerges' out of H_2O. The fundamental term to be defined here is, of course, 'emergence.' What precisely is meant by it? It means the appearance in the evolutionary process of something 'new,' something which could not be called the 'resultant' of the elements through whose combination or organization it arises. To illustrate: "When carbon having certain properties combines with sulphur having other properties there is formed, not a mere mix-

[1] Sellars, *The Essentials of Philosophy,* Chapter XXII, gives an elementary account of them with some criticism. Pratt, *Matter and Spirit,* Lectures I–IV, presents a spirited discussion and a vigorous criticism of the whole problem. A more advanced survey will be found in McDougall, *Body and Mind* and Strong, *Why the Mind Has a Body.* This last book contains a very valuable, though for the beginner not easy, criticism of views.

ture, but a new compound, some of the properties of which are quite different from those of either component." Now the unique properties of this new compound, that is the qualities of the carbon bisulphide which differ from the qualities possessed either by the carbon taken alone or by the sulphur taken alone, are 'emergents' from the combination of the two substances. These qualities are 'new' and could not have been predicted in detail before the carbon and the sulphur were combined; in this respect they are different from the weight of the new compound, which could be calculated simply by adding the weights of the components. The weight of the new compound, thus, is not an 'emergent,' it is rather what is called a 'resultant,' of the combination of the two substances. A 'resultant' is that which is predictable on the basis of the nature of the components. An 'emergent,' on the other hand, is unpredictable before the combination takes place and is different from any of the qualities possessed by the separate elements that enter into the combination. The 'emergence' of mind from bodily organization means, then, that mind arises out of bodily organization, but is nevertheless something new or unique; it grows on, or out of, brain states; but it is something added to the brain states in the course of Nature. The mind is not identical with body, nor is it causally connected or parallel with bodily processes as something fundamentally different and sundered from them. Mind rather 'emerges' in the course of biological evolution; the mind-body relation is definable in terms of emergence. Some are convinced that this new conception at least points the direction in which is to be found a satisfactory and final solution of the vexed problem of the mind-body relation.[1]

[1] See the article by Professor Patrick, "The Emergent Theory of Mind," *The Journal of Philosophy*, 1922, Vol. XIX, No. 26. The general meaning and significance of the notion of emergence is discussed at length

Chapter XVII. Questions and Exercises

1. Indicate some of the facts showing close connection between mind and body.

2. What is the interaction theory, and what are the main difficulties confronting it?

3. What is parallelism? Indicate its chief difficulties.

4. Summarize the discussion by Stratton: *Experimental Psychology and Culture*, Chapter XIV.

5. Read and criticize the theory of Paulsen, *Introduction to Philosophy*, pp. 87–111.

6. Summarize the views of Descartes, *Works* (edited by Haldane and Ross), Vol. I, pp. 331–356.

7. Outline the main points in Pratt, *Matter and Spirit:*
   (*a*) Lecture II, on "Parallelism"
   (*b*) Lecture III, on "The Denial of the Problem"
   (*c*) Lecture IV, on "The Difficulties of Interaction"

8. For more advanced study consult: Bergson, *Mind and Energy*, Chapters II, VII; Strong, *Why the Mind Has a Body;* McDougall, *Body and Mind.*

---

by C. Lloyd Morgan in his *Emergent Evolution*, from which (p. 3) the quotation in the paragraph above is taken. The student will note that this notion of 'emergence' is in principle identical with the notion of 'emergent evolution' defined above, Chapter XIV, section 3.

CHAPTER XVIII

THE SOCIETY OF MINDS

In our discussion of mind hitherto we have proceeded as if each individual mind were complete in itself and existed by itself alone. But we know that this is not the case. Every mind exists in relation to other minds. This interrelation of minds constitutes what we call 'society,' and it gives rise to certain important problems of interest to philosophy. The aim of the present chapter is to describe the general characteristics of the development of society, or the community of minds, and to indicate some philosophical problems growing out of it.

§ 1. *Early group-life*

It is a mistake to suppose that primitive man lived in a state of isolation from, and independence of, his fellows. On the contrary, while there is much that is uncertain concerning primitive society, one fundamental fact stands out clearly and unmistakably, namely, that group-life is its dominant feature. Recent investigations have shown beyond question that the life of primitive man is a group-life, that the individual in primitive society derives both his rights and his obligations from membership within the group. Let us notice briefly some of the outstanding characteristics of primitive social organization.

(1) THE KINSHIP GROUP. The unit of primitive social organization is the kinship group. This is a group of per-

sons who think of themselves as having descended from a common ancestor. In some cases the ancestor is believed to be an animal, as in the instances of the North American Indians, of certain African and Australian tribes, and perhaps of the early Semites. In other cases the common ancestor is supposed to be some hero or even a god. But in any event, whether the group ancestor be thought of as animal, man, or god, the assumption on the part of the members of the group is the same, namely, that they are all of one common stock and one blood circulates in them all. There are other types of groups, such as the household or family group in the narrower meaning; but the kinship group is historically the most important type.

(2) THE SOLIDARITY OF THE GROUP. One of the main features of the early group is its feeling of solidarity. Bound together by ties of blood, as they supposed themselves to be, the individuals composing the primitive group thought of themselves only in terms of the group to which they belonged; when one suffered all suffered, when one was injured all felt the wrong and were anxious to avenge it. "The members of one kindred looked on themselves as one living whole, a single animated mass of blood, flesh, and bones, of which no member could be touched without all the members suffering. . . . If one of the clan has been murdered, they say 'Our blood has been shed.'"[1] This sense of solidarity of the group in primitive social organization is much stronger than the feeling of family ties in civilized communities. Speaking of clanship among the Kafirs, Dudley Kidd says: "The sense of solidarity of the family in Europe is thin and feeble compared to the full-blooded sense of corporate union of the Kafir clan."[2] And this is true generally of primitive peoples; everywhere the group

[1] W. R. Smith, *The Religion of the Semites,* 2nd ed., p. 274.
[2] *Savage Childhood* (1906), p. 74.

is the unit, and each individual within the group regards himself as bound by inescapable ties to all other members of his group.

Nor must it be imagined that the individual desired to escape these ties. On the contrary, he could not think of himself as existing apart from them; outside of the group into which he is born the individual becomes an outcast, an 'outlaw' in fact as well as in name. The *natural* condition of the individual is to be within and a part of such a group; to exist within it is not a hardship but a privilege. "The striking thing about this unity of the clan is that it is not a thought-out plan imposed from without by legislation upon an unwilling people, but it was a *felt-out* plan which arose spontaneously along the line of least resistance. If one member of the clan suffered, all the members suffered, not in sentimental phraseology, but in real fact."[1]

(3) THE INDIVIDUAL AND THE GROUP. Whatever rights may belong to the individual among primitive peoples belong to him by virtue of his membership within a group. Generally speaking, the primitive group was communistic in the possession of property, and the individual could be said to own property only as a member of the group. "The land belonged to the clan, and the clan was settled upon the land. A man was thus not a member of the clan, because he lived upon, or even owned, the land; but he lived upon the land, and had interests in it, because he was a member of the clan."[2] His rights, too, whatever rights he has, are determined by his membership within the group. "Justice is a privilege which falls to a man as belonging to some group — not otherwise. The member of the clan or the household or the village community has a claim,

[1] Dudley Kidd, *op. cit.*

[2] Hearn, *The Aryan Household,* p. 212. Quoted by Dewey and Tufts, *Ethics,* p. 24.

but the stranger has no standing. He may be treated kindly, as a guest, but he cannot demand 'justice' at the hands of any group but his own."[1] The man without a clan or group has no rights. "In primitive society the exclusion of a man from his kinsfolk means he is delivered over to the first comer absolutely without protection."[2] In short, primitive man is an individual only in so far as he is a member of the group; apart from the group he is as a beast of the field with absolutely no claims upon his fellows. Whatever rights he has belong to him by virtue of his membership within the group. The 'outcast' is the 'outlaw.'

(4) COLLECTIVE RESPONSIBILITY. Another characteristic of early group-life is that of collective responsibility. The group as a whole is held responsible for the acts of its members when such acts concern any member or members of another group; and the group as a whole holds itself responsible for the avenging of any injury done to one of its own members. Responsibility is of the group rather than of the individual. Survivals of this principle at higher levels are evident in 'blood-feuds' within certain communities and in the dealings of modern States with each other and with savage tribes.[3] But the sense of soli-

[1] Dewey and Tufts, *Ethics,* pp. 27–28.

[2] Hobhouse, *Morals in Evolution,* Vol. I, p. 90. Compare the story of Cain, the murderer of his brother, Abel. Jehovah punished Cain for his deed by separating him from his group and making of him a 'fugitive and vagabond' in the earth. "And Cain said unto Jehovah, My punishment is greater than I can bear. Behold, thou hast driven me out this day from the face of the earth; and from thy face shall I be hid; and I shall be a fugitive and a vagabond in the earth; and it shall come to pass, that every one that findeth me shall slay me." (*Genesis,* Chapter IV, verses 13, 14.)

[3] "If some member of a savage tribe assaults a citizen of one of the civilized nations, the injured party invokes the help of his government. A demand is usually made that the guilty party be delivered up for trial and punishment. If he is not forthcoming a 'punitive expedition' is organized against the whole tribe; guilty and innocent suffer alike. Or

darity attaching to primitive group organization causes this feeling of collective responsibility to be very much more intense among primitive groups than among modern nations.

(5) SUMMARY OF SECTION. Primitive man looks upon himself as a member of a group bound together by ties of blood. The group is largely communistic in the possession of property, and it is membership within the group which gives to the individual whatever rights are his; apart from the group the individual is an 'outlaw' in fact as well as in name. A sense of solidarity, born of the conviction that each member of the group is of the same blood as every other, makes of the group the unit, in a literal sense, of primitive social organization. Competition is between group and group rather than between individual and individual, since responsibility attaches to the group and not the individual as such. This group-life is not imposed upon primitive man by some external authority; it is a natural and inevitable expression of the line of least resistance in man's social evolution. Man by nature is a social animal: group-life is the flowering of his nature.

§ 2. *Evolution of primitive groups*

In the course of man's social development the primitive groups have been transformed into the larger groups of civilized society known as nations or states. From the numberless small groups of primitive society there have

in lieu of exterminating the offending tribe, in part or completely, the nation of the injured man may accept an indemnity in money or land from the offender's tribe. Recent dealings between British and Africans, Germans and Africans, France and Morocco, the United States and the Filipinos, the Powers and China, illustrate this. The State protects its own members against other States, and avenges them upon other States. Each opposes a united body to the other" (Dewey and Tufts, *Ethics*, p. 28). The punitive expedition into Mexico by troops of the United States Army recently carried out (1916) to avenge a foray across the border illustrates essentially the same principle.

grown through the centuries of history a relatively few larger groups and finally the greater nations of the modern era. The transition has been from the status of many small and relatively insignificant groups to the organization of a few great and powerful nations — from primitive group-life to national life.

(1) FORCES IN THIS TRANSITION. This transition has been a natural process brought about by certain agencies working silently but irresistibly within the social order. These agencies are varied in character, but they may be grouped together under relatively few headings. The more important of these are the following. (*a*) Economic forces — such agencies as appear in the development of humanity from the hunting and fishing life to agricultural and commercial undertakings. (*b*) Psychological agencies — such as those of sex, the desire for honor, for private property, for liberty, and the like. (*c*) Intellectual expansion — the critical attitude to the *status quo,* progress in invention and interest in the novel, and the consequent demand for new institutions and ideals. (*d*) Religious forces — conflicting religious interests and cults, with a consequent expansion of the idea of God and of the ideals and worship praiseworthy in His eyes. (*e*) War — conflicts between groups, the consolidation of groups, and the inevitable change in customs, traditions, and ideals. All of these agencies are natural manifestations of that interrelation of minds which we call society, and they inevitably lead to the breaking up of old traditions and beliefs, the removal of barriers between group and group, and the transformation of social organization from the group life of primitive man to the national life of civilized man. Numerous illustrations of these forces at work in history are easily available. And they all show that the primitive group is the

source whence the more highly developed organization of civilized society springs.[1]

(2) TWO ASPECTS OF THE TRANSITION. Of this development of the primitive groups into the larger states of civilized society there are two aspects which should be noted. On the one hand, the development consists in an intensification of individuality, a growth in individualism; on the other hand, it is marked by an expansion of the group both in numbers and in complexity of organization. (*a*) In the primitive group, as we have seen, the individual hardly counts; the group is in fact the social unit. It is in terms of the group that the individual owns property and possesses rights and privileges; apart from the group he is of little significance. But with the progress of social development the individual becomes more and more important, owns property in his own right, and claims rights and privileges which attach to him as an individual and which are inalienable. Thus the individual is progressively emphasized and his importance and intrinsic worth progressively acknowledged in the course of social evolution. (*b*) Again, the primitive groups are small, varying in size from tens to a few hundreds of souls. Social development gradually expands the circle of the group until the great nations with their millions of individuals are created. And with this expansion of the numbers within the group there has run along concurrently an increasing complexity within its internal organization. The early group governed by its relatively few and simple customs and traditions expands into larger groups of greater intricacy of internal organization manifested in types or forms of institutions,

[1] For a somewhat detailed discussion of these agencies from the point of view of moral development see Dewey and Tufts, *Ethics*, Chapter V. In connection with this discussion Myers, *History as Past Ethics*, Chapters I and II, should be consulted.

which in the greater nations are exceedingly complex and all but defy analysis. Thus in social evolution the group grows both in numbers and in complexity of organization.

It must not be forgotten that these are two sides of one and the same process — the process of social growth. As the group to which the individual belongs expands in numbers and grows in intricacy of organization, the individual himself becomes more and more important in his own right, assumes a greater degree of initiative, demands for himself fuller privileges, and consequently involves himself in more numerous and varied obligations. And, contrariwise, as the individual breaks away from the bondage imposed upon him by the solidarity of the primitive group and assumes greater privileges and responsibilities in his own right as a person, the group to which he belongs concomitantly widens its scope and reaches farther out among his fellows both as regards the number of individuals concerned and as regards the complexity of social combinations. "The history of setting free individual power in desire, thought, and initiative is, upon the whole, the history of the formation of more complex and extensive social organizations. Movements that look like the disintegration of the order of society, when viewed with reference to what has preceded them, are factors in the construction of a new social order, which allows freer play to individuals, and yet increases the number of social groupings and the depth of social combinations." [1] In short, the development of *personality* in the individual, progress towards individualism in the sense of the desire and the capacity on the individual's part to take initiative and to assume

[1] Dewey and Tufts, *Ethics*, p. 428. The entire chapter from which this quotation is taken is an interesting account of some of the details involved in the movement here under consideration.

responsibilities, is paralleled by an increasing complexity and intricacy in the individual's social relations and *vice versa*. These are two sides of the same process: social growth takes place through enlarging groups of increasingly significant and self-assertive individuals.

§ 3. *The group-mind*

A fundamental feature of the social order must here be noticed before we pass on to a consideration of some of the problems emerging from it. This we shall call the mind of the group, or the group-mind, as over against the individual minds of particular persons. There are two points of special interest to us: first, what precisely we are to understand by the group-mind; and, second, the relation between the group-mind and the different individual minds that constitute the group.

(1) THE NATURE OF THE GROUP-MIND. Every group organization has its customs and traditions, its beliefs and institutions. In other words, every group has its ways of thinking and acting just as every individual has. Now it is these ways of thinking and acting which the group adopts and adheres to that we mean when we speak of the 'group-mind.' The manners of speech and dress, the moral and religious customs and traditions, the economic and political practices and beliefs, the scientific and artistic convictions and conventions, which any group *as a group* entertains—these constitute the group-mind. These customs, traditions, beliefs, and institutions cannot be attributed to any individual mind or any combination of individual minds; they are expressive of the mind of the group, the *Zeitgeist* as the Germans call it. In some sense they are integral aspects of the social order.

(2) THE GROUP-MIND AND INDIVIDUAL MINDS. A ques-

tion of far-reaching significance arises in connection with the relation that exists between what we have called the group-mind and the individual minds composing the group. Are we to think of the group-mind as an actual mind, a sort of super-mind, existing in its own right apart from, and in a sense superior to, individual minds; or is the relation between them to be differently conceived?

It has sometimes been supposed that the group-mind exists independently of the individual minds within the group and is in a real sense superior to them. This personification of the group-mind is evident in various theories of the state; apparently, something of the sort is accepted by the German philosophers Fichte and Hegel and some of their later disciples.[1] But there seems to be no justification for this interpretation of the matter, certainly not if the definition of the group-mind which we have adopted be accepted. It is true, indeed, that social customs and beliefs and institutions are in a sense independent of individual minds; they do not exist in isolated individual minds. But neither do they exist aloft by themselves, without any connection or contact with individual minds. On the contrary, they appear to be the expression of the *interpenetration* of the different minds that compose the group. Take a given science, like physics, for example: it does not exist in any individual mind or in any combination of individual minds, and yet it is a product of a relatively few individual minds; it has been created in the

[1] See Fichte's *Addresses to the German Nation,* and Hegel's *Philosophy of Mind, Philosophy of Right,* and *Philosophy of History.* See also Dewey, *German Philosophy and Politics* for a criticism of the point of view. In his *Metaphysical Theory of the State* Hobhouse attributes the view mentioned in the text not only to the German philosophers but to so recent a writer as Bosanquet (*Philosophical Theory of the State,* 1899), and he criticizes it vigorously. For an interesting, though somewhat involved, discussion of some of the problems here at issue the reader might consult the above book by Bosanquet.

course of social evolution by different minds each working upon, and adding to, the results achieved by others. And this would appear to be true, in general principle, of all toms and traditions, all institutions and social practices. ctly speaking, then, the group-mind as we have defined s not a mind; it is rather the interconnection of indi- ual minds, their interfunctioning and interpenetration. It he product of separate individual minds acting con- tly.[1]

§ 4. *Problems connected with the society of minds*

Out of the historical development of group life there emerge many special problems of compelling significance. These have been made the problems of the several social sciences, however, and are of no direct concern to us here. They are dealt with in history, anthropology, economics, political science, sociology, psychology, and ethics. But among the numerous problems that arise out of the on-goings of the social order there are certain general ones of great interest to the philosopher. Two of these we shall here indicate, reserving a study of them to the chapters immediately following. These are: freedom of intellectual activity on the part of the individual mind, and the sover-eignty of groups.

FREEDOM OF THOUGHT. As we have seen above, chief features of social development lies in the ressive emphasis that is by it placed upon the individ-

[1] If this be true, then individual minds are not so sharply sundered as is at times supposed. For it is sometimes supposed that each mind is in a water-tight compartment by itself, and exists thus in isolation. If the position in the text is true — and the facts seem to warrant it, — no individual mind lives to itself alone in a world all its own and exclusively its own. This might be the case in sleep or abnormal waking experience; but in normal experience each mind is in a common world with other minds, it penetrates other minds and is of other minds a part.

ual and the consequent tendency to bring the individual mind into conflict with the group-mind. As the importance of the individual within the group grows, he insists upon thinking and acting for himself whether or not what he thinks and does coincides with the group's ways of thinking and doing. This demand for freedom tends, thus, to bring him more or less directly into conflict with his group, and the problem concerning the extent to which, if at all, the individual may legitimately claim freedom from group interference becomes more and more pressing. A fuller statement of the problem and some considerations relevant to its solution will be set down in the following chapter.

(2) Problem of sovereignty. All along in the history of society the group has been the principal unit, particularly in economic and political matters, and each group has acted as if it had the inalienable right to determine its own affairs without interference from any group or combination of groups. Thus another general problem arises: Where within the group does this right reside, and to what extent is the claim of each group that this is an absolute right justified? This is a problem of fateful significance, as the wars of history have tragically shown. We shall look at some of its sides in Chapter XIX below.

Chapter XVIII. Questions and Exercises

1. What is the kinship group? In what sense may it be called the nursery group of primitive society? Indicate some of its main features.

2. Describe the main aspects of the transition from primitive groups to modern states, and indicate some of the chief agencies in the transition.

3. Show how the growth of the social order emphasizes at once the importance of the individual and the complexity of group-organization. (Read in connection with this question Dewey and Tufts, *Ethics,* Chapter XX.)

4. What is meant by the group-mind as used in the text, and how is it related to individual minds within the group?

5. Summarize briefly the theories of the state outlined in Young, *The State and Government,* Chapter II. Compare the summary of theories given by MacKenzie, *Outlines of Social Philosophy,* pp. 145–153.

6. Outline Dewey and Tufts, *Ethics,* Chapters II–III.

7. Summarize the main points in Mackenzie's discussion of human nature in *Outlines of Social Philosophy,* pp. 29–38.

8. What according to Mackenzie (*Outlines of Social Philosophy,* Book II, Chapter VI) are the main social ideals?

CHAPTER XIX

FREEDOM OF THOUGHT

Man's struggle towards liberty has been a long and arduous one. From submergence within the group the individual has come by slow and painful stages to the attainment of privileges and responsibilities in his own right. The history of the race is the story of this arduous struggle. Freedom of thought is the side of this struggle which to us here is of chief concern, and it is of great significance since all other types of liberty are bound up within it. "As a man thinketh in his heart, so is he." What, then, are the main features of the problem which this side of social evolution presents?

§ 1. *Genesis of the problem of freedom of thought*

On the cultural level of primitive group life the problem of free thought does not exist. It is a problem which arises only in connection with that stage of civilization at which it becomes possible for the individual mind to set itself over against the group and to look upon itself as having significance in its own right. A brief consideration of the genesis of the problem may throw some light both upon its meaning and upon the direction in which a solution may be found.

The reason why the problem of freedom of thought never arises within the primitive group is because at that level the individual always thinks as the group thinks. The group-mind, as expressed in the customary and traditional beliefs and behavior of the group, holds undisputed sway over every individual mind within the group. If in any given group it is customary to build houses with only one window, then every individual will build his house after that fashion; if it is customary within the group to condemn certain types of conduct or to accept certain religious beliefs and perform certain rites and ceremonies at stated times, then each individual within the group will so behave without cavil or hesitation. In short, the individual mind within the primitive group follows customary activities and accepts traditional beliefs without question. To do this is as natural for primitive man as to breathe or procreate his kind. Now, so long as the individual thus submits to the traditions and customs of his groups, there cannot possibly arise a problem concerning freedom of thought. When everybody thinks like everybody else there cannot be any question as to whether each has a right so to think; each one thinks as he does because it is being done generally.

But with the expansion of the primitive group into more complex social types and with the emancipation of the individual from total and unquestioning subservience to the group-mind, resultant from an advancing civilization, there inevitably comes the time when a conflict arises between the individual's ways of thinking and acting and those of the group. The individual grows critical of the customs and traditions of his group and raises troublesome questions about the validity of old manners and beliefs.[1] There

[1] A clear historical illustration of this may be found in the appearance of the Sophists in Greece of the fifth century B.C. and the general movement of thought which they represent. They called in question most of the traditional and customary beliefs of their day and subjected them to a vigorous and rather destructive criticism. Any history of philosophy

develops from this a conflict between the individual and his group, between his mind and the group-mind as expressed in the customary and traditional. And it is this conflict which gives rise to the problem of freedom thought. So long as there is no such conflict there can be no problem of free thought, as we have urged in the preceding paragraph, and for the very simple reason that everybody then thinks alike; so long as the individual thinks precisely as the group thinks no one will raise the query whether he has a right thus to think. But just so soon as differences between mind and mind within the group appear, just so soon as traditional ways of acting and believing are called in question, then there immediately emerges the all-important problem as to the right of the individual to oppose himself to the group by doubting the validity of the customary and traditional or by accepting new beliefs at variance with the old. This is a presumption on the part of the individual and the group will not allow it to stand uncontested. What right has the individual thus to set himself against his group? is the question which the group insists on asking. And the individual replies with the counter-question: Why not? And so the battle is on.

The problem of freedom of thought, then, arises out of the conflict between the individual's behavior and beliefs and the behavior and beliefs of the group as expressed in customs and traditions. There are two points in connection with the problem which should be carefully noted. The first is that the problem is an inevitable outgrowth of

---

will give a general account of their views. The Renaissance and the Reformation are historical examples of the same critical attitude towards the past. An interesting survey of mankind's struggle for freedom of thought may be found in Bury, *A History of Freedom of Thought* (Home University Library). This book also contains references for further reading.

an apparently inevitable conflict. It is an ineradicable characteristic of social development. The second point is that the problem concerns something of fateful significance in social organization. The deaths of Socrates, of Jesus of Nazareth, of Giordano Bruno, and of hundreds of others who have suffered martyrdom because of their dissatisfaction with the traditions of their day, bear tragic testimony to the deep-lying importance of the conflict; and the various censorships, economic, moral, and religious, advocated and practiced by the group to-day, as in the days of the Holy Inquisition, give evidence of the same eternal fact.

§ 2. *Significance of the conflicting forces*

From the preceding section it appears that the problem of freedom of thought is created by the conflict between the individual mind and the mind of the group as formulated in customs and traditions. The next step in our consideration of the problem, then, must consist in an inquiry concerning the significance of the contending forces.

(1) THE IMPORTANCE OF CUSTOMS AND TRADITIONS. It is easy to see that what we call customs and traditions are merely concrete expressions of the organization of the group of minds. They conserve the results of the group's previous experiences and function as the memory of group life. They are to the group what habit and recollection are to the individual. Apart from them it is difficult to see how any organized group of minds could possibly exist, since without them group stability would be impossible. They constitute, as it were, the balance-wheel of social life. They express that continuity within group experience which is the basis upon which, from one point of view, all social organization and stability depend.

(2) THE IMPORTANCE OF INDIVIDUAL INITIATIVE. If

all minds within the group were held in slavish subjection to custom and tradition, progress and development would be impossible. The group would be stable, but its stability would be practically synonymous with stagnation. The older China is, among modern nations, a good example of that sort of group. China has seen the rise and fall of many other nations and even civilizations, and has remained stable in the midst of a changing world; but China has been practically stationary for centuries, she has not kept step with the progress taking place in the world about her. Progress depends largely upon the exceptional individual, the individual who breaks away from the beaten paths and blazes new trails for himself and his fellows. The mind that holds beliefs different from those of the group and forces the group to modify its customs in consequence is an indispensable element within any progressive community. Such a mind is the *free* mind, unbound by mere tradition. The free mind is the dynamo of social advancement. "Where there is no vision the people perish" — and there is no vision where no minds are free to see other vistas than those that stretch away into the dim and musty past. Freedom from the trammels and impediments of custom and tradition is an indispensable prerequisite to social progress.

§ 3. *Resolution of the conflict*

Customs and traditions are useful and necessary expressions of group organization; in them lies social stability. Individual minds that are free to entertain beliefs of their own are equally vital to social life; they are essential to progress. The function of the customary and the traditional is conservation; the function of the free mind is creation. Both functions are essential to the social order of minds, neither can be dispensed with. How, then, may the conflict between the two be satisfactorily resolved?

(1) TWO ANSWERS TO THE QUESTION. There are in the main two answers to this question. The first is the answer of the extreme *conservative,* who insists that customary and traditional beliefs are of basal importance in social organization and that where there is a conflict between them and individual beliefs the latter should be set aside. The second is the answer of the extreme *radical,* who urges that the individual mind should be freed from all subservience to the traditional and customary and be permitted, and even encouraged, to entertain its own beliefs regardless of any conflict between them and the beliefs of the group. Of course there are all shades of compromise between these two extreme positions, but these indicate the two main types of answers that have been operative in the actual practice of social life.

(2) ARGUMENTS FOR CONSERVATISM. The conservative advances the following arguments in support of his position: (*a*) In the first place, he emphasizes the important function of traditional beliefs within the life of the group, and he urges the consequent necessity of keeping these, at least the more basal ones, undisturbed by doubts and criticism as the bed-rock upon which to build our social organization. (*b*) In the second place, he points to the dangers involved in the attempt to uproot these beliefs, the chief danger which he sees lurking within such an attempt being the threat of social disruption and anarchy; even serious criticism of them seems to him dangerous, since criticism is the first step in overturning them. (*c*) And, finally, the conservative points to the fact that beliefs which have stood the test of time are more likely to be true than are those generated within the narrow limits of individual experience;

to set individual experience against the experience of the group is a presumption which is not warranted. In addition to these positive arguments, the conservative has in his favor theological prejudices which generally hold to the sacredness of traditional beliefs. But his arguments are chiefly the three mentioned above: the practical utility of tradition as a stabilizing influence, the social danger involved in criticizing the more basal traditions, and the presumption in favor of the validity of traditional beliefs as over against those of the individual.

(3) ARGUMENTS FOR RADICALISM. The radical, on his side, suggests the following considerations in support of his claims: (*a*) Traditional beliefs are, in the nature of the case, expressions of points of view that belong to the past, and they are consequently being continuously outgrown with the acquisition of new knowledge; they therefore need constant revision in the light of new truth, and unless so revised they cease to function satisfactorily within the group. (*b*) Freedom of the individual from the hindering influences of the traditional and customary is the indispensable prerequisite of all social progress; to shackle the individual mind by binding it down by tradition, therefore, is to block progress and bring the group life to a dead stop. (*c*) The prejudice that the older a belief is the more value it has is based upon a false assumption. That a belief has stood the test of time is in itself no guarantee of the validity, or even of the utility, of a belief, unless it can be shown that the test which time has brought to bear upon the belief is such that it meets all the demands of advancing knowledge; many of the most hoary traditions are nothing more than superstitions. These, then, are the three main arguments of the radical: traditional beliefs are necessarily of the past and so are con-

stantly in need of revision, individual freedom is essential to progress, and mere age of a belief is no guarantee of its value. While he admits, as he must, that the religious consciousness is on the whole conservative and so opposed to his position, still the radical may claim that, in its higher reaches at any rate, religious development lends some support to his claims; for he can point to the undeniable historical fact that every great religion has its outstanding free thinkers through whose untrammelled view religious beliefs are from time to time revised and made to square with the demands of advancing experience, that every vital religion, in short, has its prophets (radicals) as well as its priests (conservatives).

(4) Evaluation of the two answers. What shall we say concerning the relative merits of radicalism and conservatism? It is obvious that there is truth on both sides of the controversy, and this is so obvious that most people now-a-days adhere to neither side to the exclusion of the other; a compromise is generally sought, at least in theory. The conservative is unquestionably right in holding that the customary and traditional element within group life is of value and in insisting that that value be preserved. And it is equally clear that the liberal's demand for an open air in which the free mind may breathe and flourish is amply warranted. The conservative pleads for stability, the radical for progress. The error to which each is liable is the error of neglecting the truth in the other's position. To the extent that the conservative emphasizes the absolute importance of traditions and customs and insists that the individual mind be made subject to them without recourse, to that extent his emphasis seems misplaced and his position untenable; traditional beliefs cannot be accepted as the criterion of truth when they themselves are in ques-

tion. Likewise, in so far as the radical belittles the genuine importance of the traditional and accepts individual preferences as more valuable simply because they are novel, his position is both unsatisfactory and dangerous; he then fails to distinguish between a sane critical attitude and mere individual caprice and prejudice. If the conservative, on his side, would admit that, while tradition is valuable, there is nothing sacred about it which forbids its revision, or, in case of necessity, its rejection, in the light of new ideas; and if, on his side, the radical would admit the tentative or provisional value of tradition until newly acquired knowledge forced its revision or rejection — if each participant in the debate would thus compromise with his opponent, apparently there would be no basic difference between them and each would be nearer the truth.

(5) Conclusion. The answer to our question would thus seem to be fairly clearly indicated. Freedom of thought is the breath of life to the society of minds; without it there can be no growth or development within the group. And this freedom of thought must inevitably bring the individual mind into more or less sharp conflict with traditional beliefs. In case of conflict, the age of the belief, its persistence over a period of time within the group, gives it a certain vested right to acceptance until advancing knowledge shows clearly that it stands in need of revision or must be rejected as wholly erroneous. In such a case, new knowledge must have right of way or the society of minds is doomed to stagnation and probably to decay. Any group which deliberately suppresses this freedom on the part of individuals by that act commits spiritual suicide. On the other hand, freedom of thought must be sharply differentiated from mere eccentricity and individual idiosyncracy; otherwise, the group is in danger of disruption and anarchy.

Whoever ventures to set his mind over against the group-mind must test his views in the fire of fact and prove beyond cavil their value before he can legitimately expect his group to be willing to change the old for the new. For such a venture there must be ample justification, since the venture is always of fateful significance to the society of minds that makes it. Free minds acting upon, and gradually transforming, generally accepted beliefs, stability and permanence within progress and change — such would seem to be the ideal of social development.

Chapter XIX. Questions and Exercises

1. State in general outline the genesis of the problem of freedom of thought.
2. Summarize the positions of the radical and the conservative on the problem, and outline arguments in support of each.
3. In a short essay apply the principles developed in the text to one of the following problems:
   (*a*) Freedom of religious convictions
   (*b*) Freedom of the press
   (*c*) Freedom of speech in time of war
4. Outline the main points developed in B. Russell, *Political Ideals,* Chapter IV.
5. State in a few sentences the thought developed by Tennyson in *In Memoriam,* section XXXIII, and give your estimate of its value.
6. Summarize briefly Mackenzie, *Outlines of Social Philosophy,* Book III, Chapter III.
7. Write a short summary of J. S. Mill's essay, *On Liberty,* Chapter II. Compare Bury, *History of Freedom of Thought,* Chapter VIII.

CHAPTER XX

PROBLEM OF SOVEREIGNTY

A second problem arising from the society of minds, a problem that has been much debated in the development of political philosophy, is the problem of sovereignty, to a consideration of which we now turn.

§ 1. *Nature of the problem*

Instead of speaking of the society of minds it would be much nearer historical fact if we should speak of *societies* of minds. For in the historical development of the social environment there have always been numerous groups, more or less sharply sundered from each other and each regarding itself as having complete and final authority over its own affairs. At the primitive level the groups are small and very numerous. Driven by the agencies inherent in human nature these groups were in constant conflict with each other. Out of this conflict came amalgamation and expansion of groups into fewer and larger ones, until through the course of the centuries the many small groups have been supplanted by few large ones; the kinship groups have grown into the great national states which now cover the face of the earth and divide its surface and resources among themselves. Throughout this development the groups have never ceased to look upon themselves as wholly independent of each other. Each group insists upon its right to manage its internal affairs without interference or suggestion from other groups. So all along in the course of history there has been group isolation. It was so in the beginning, as is evidenced by the perpetual conflicts that mark man's early history; it is so at present, as the tragic testimony of the latest and most destructive of international wars bears witness. And it has ever been so. Might is right was the old slogan; and that meant that any group had the right to assert its authority as far as it could by the sword expediently extend it. Self-determination among the nations now seems to be the watch-word of the hour; and by 'self-determination' is usually meant the right of each group to do as it pleases, to determine for itself what shall be its internal organization and foreign policies, so long as its procedure does not contravene the similar rights of other groups.

Now this division of humanity into several isolated and sovereign groups, though natural and apparently inevitable, gives rise to certain perplexing problems that grow more perplexing and insistent as, with advancing civilization and the inventions incident to it which affect communication and travel, the groups become larger and more vitally touch each the activities of the others. Of these problems, the one which has generally been regarded as of fundamental importance and which in modern thought has caused much discussion is the problem of sovereignty: What is meant by sovereignty within the group, and is each group's sovereignty absolute and indefeasible or limited by some higher authority? The persistent discussion centering around this problem is indicative of its basal nature; it concerns something of profound importance in human social organization.

For convenience in our consideration of the problem here we shall break it into the two questions that arise according as attention is fixed upon the internal organization of the group or upon the interrelations of groups. The first of these questions concerns sovereignty within the group and may be formulated thus: What is meant by sovereignty within the group and where does it reside? The second question concerns the outward relations of the group and may be put thus: Is there any sovereignty outside of the group to which its own sovereignty is subject, or is its own sovereignty absolute with reference to itself? Looking upon the government of a group as the visible expression or manifestation of sovereignty, these two questions may perhaps be formulated in more familiar terminology as follows: To whom within the group is the government responsible? and Is the government of one group wholly independent of the governments of all other groups? To a consideration of these two specific questions we now turn, beginning with the first.[1]

§ 2. *Sovereignty within the group*

In discussing the problem of sovereignty within the group there are two main points to be noted. The first is the nature of sovereignty, and the second is the locus of sovereignty. The second problem is, from the standpoint of political philosophy, the more important; but the first is logically prior to the second, since vagueness with reference to it must inevitably introduce confusion into the whole debate.

(1) THE NATURE OF SOVEREIGNTY. By sovereignty is meant the supreme power within the group. In so far as the group has control over its own affairs it is said to be a

[1] An interesting and exhaustive survey of different theories of sovereignty since Rousseau may be found in an essay by C. E. Merriam published in *Studies in History, Economics and Public Law* (edited by the faculty of Political Science of Columbia University), Vol. XII, Number 4. This essay was published in the year 1900.

sovereign group, and its sovereignty lies in this control. Modern discussion of the problem of sovereignty has emphasized two points upon which the reader should be clear.

(a) *Indivisibility.* There has been repeated emphasis upon the indivisibility of sovereignty within the group. "Modern constitutionalism has rated highly the utility of a division of governmental powers, but it has not tended to show that the sovereignty itself is capable of such division. The legislative, administrative and judicial functions are not regarded as militating against the essential and ultimate unity of the principle from which they emanate. Not even in the haziness that has obscured the Federal State has the principle of a divided sovereignty been able to maintain the ground it won, but it has been driven out and replaced by the conception of the one and indivisible sovereignty resident in the State."[1] Sovereignty, then, is one and indivisible: this seems to be the main emphasis of modern theory and practice.

This monistic view of sovereignty is opposed by a group of thinkers known as 'pluralists,' who insist that every state is really made up of more or less distinct subordinate groups, such as different churches and various economic and professional associations, among which the sovereignty of the state is in fact divided. The pluralists are not willing to accept without qualification the view that sovereignty is indivisible. But it is perhaps true to say that their position as yet lacks convincing formulation; in any event, it is in opposition to the generally accepted doctrine that, from the standpoint of its sovereignty, the state is one.[2]

[1] C. E. Merriam, *History of the Theory of Sovereignty Since Rousseau* (1900), p. 223. This is the essay referred to in the preceding footnote.

[2] A vigorous presentation of the pluralist's claims may be found in H. Laski's *Studies in the Problem of Sovereignty*. See also Graham Wallas, *The Great Society;* and Duguit, "The Law and the State," *Harvard Law Review*, November, 1907.

So despite the advocates of pluralism the statement still holds that there is general recognition, in practice at least, of the indivisibility of sovereignty within the group.

(b) *Legal and political sovereignty.* Modern discussion has brought out a distinction that is of considerable importance in connection with the general problem of sovereignty. That is the distinction between the 'legal sovereign' and the 'political sovereign.' By the legal sovereign is meant the supreme power in so far as the interpretation and administration of the laws of the group are concerned; it is the sovereign to which the lawyer, in his capacity as lawyer, appeals and beyond which he does not go. By political sovereignty is meant the supreme power within the state which is the ultimate and final source of all authority, legal or otherwise; it is the authority from whose verdict there can be no appeal. "The legal sovereign is the final and determining power, so far as the legal order or system goes; the political sovereign is that body in the community, the will of which is ultimately obeyed; one is characterized as the lawyer's sovereign, the other that of the layman."[1]

Of these two types of sovereignty the political is the more basal. In the United States, for example, a law is a good law so long as it is constitutional; beyond the constitutionality of the law the lawyer as such does not inquire, its constitutionality is its authority. But the Constitution itself is not beyond question, and when public opinion so dictates it may be amended. Thus legal sovereignty in the United States — and the same is true of all states — is subordinate to political sovereignty; the latter may dictate revision and even radical transformation in the former. "Behind the sovereign which the lawyer rec-

[1] C. E. Merriam, *op. cit.*, pp. 218–219.

ognizes there is another sovereign to whom the legal sovereign must bow." [1] This more basal sovereign is the political sovereign. The problem of political sovereignty is, therefore, the one in which the political philosopher is interested, and that is the problem with which we shall be concerned henceforth in our discussion.

(2) THE LOCUS OF SOVEREIGNTY. Where, then, in the group is political sovereignty located? What is the warrant for it?

(a) *Two answers to the question.* There are two main theories of the locus of sovereignty within the group. These we may for purposes of our discussion call the absolutistic and the democratic theories. By the absolutistic theory of sovereignty is meant the theory which holds that sovereignty within the group resides exclusively in a few — one or several — privileged members. In the actual practice of group organization this theory has expressed itself in three types of government. They are: absolute monarchy — based upon the conception that sovereignty inheres within one individual as the special and unique representative of an hereditary line which for various reasons, in last analysis because of divine appointment, is supposed to have exclusive claim upon this prerogative; autocracy — based upon the assumption that sovereignty belongs to a privileged few in whom it is vested because of certain perquisites of birth or wealth or intellectual ability; tyranny — an application of the doctrine that might is the determinant of sovereignty. Over against the absolutistic view the practice of groups has set another theory which is the antithesis of it. This is the democratic theory which holds that sovereignty is vested in the general will

[1] D. G. Ritchie, "On the Conception of Sovereignty," *Annals of the American Academy of Political and Social Science,* Vol. I, p. 392.

of all the individuals composing the group, or at least of all who can efficiently participate in the generation of such a will. In practice this theory has assumed two forms: limited or constitutional monarchy — the monarch being merely representative of the general will wherein sovereignty is vested and which places upon the monarch whatever limitations it deems best; republic — an explicit recognition that government is of the people and by the people, all law-makers being directly accountable to public opinion and exclusively representative in their capacity.[1]

(b) *Estimate of these answers.* In undertaking to evaluate the absolutistic and the democratic theories of sovereignty the following points should be noted. (1) There is no evident reason why sovereignty within the group should be vested in any individual or any minority of individuals as an absolute and indefeasible right, nor can any reason readily be given. (2) Those forms of absolutism that have not made for the welfare of the group as a whole have been universally condemned, even by the supporters of the absolutistic theory. And this means that the group welfare is generally recognized as in some fundamental sense the determinant of sovereignty within the group. (3) The democratic ideal is more and more applied as humanity develops. (4) The group is nothing but the interpenetration of minds that make up its membership. Each mind, therefore, is an integral element within the whole, at least in so far as it participates in the organiza-

[1] Some of the more important exponents of these theories in modern thought are the following: Hugo Grotius, *The Law of War and Peace,* 1625; Thomas Hobbes, *Leviathan,* 1651; John Locke, *Two Treatises on Government,* 1690; J. J. Rousseau, *Social Contract,* 1762; Jeremy Bentham *Fragment on Government,* 1776; G. W. F. Hegel, *Philosophy of Right,* 1821; John Austin, *Lectures on Jurisprudence,* 1832; J. C. Bluntschli, *General Theory of the State,* 1852; Bosanquet, *The Philosophical Theory of the State,* 1899.

tion of the group. It appears, consequently, that the real sovereignty of the group should, and does, lie precisely in this interfunctioning of minds, that is, in the group as a whole, in the 'general will,' and not in any individual or any minority of individuals. The democratic theory seems logically preferable.

(c) *Some difficulties confronting democracy.* The application of the democratic ideal of sovereignty, however, is beset by certain dangers and difficulties that should not be overlooked. One very real danger arises from the fact that in a democracy the tyranny of an unenlightened majority may be substituted for the tyranny of an enlightened minority. This objection to the democratic ideal has been emphasized by many theorists, particularly by Plato among the Greeks and Nietzsche among the moderns.[1] The only way in which this danger may be averted is for the group to take pains that no majority be permitted to play the rôle of tyrant; and this can be done by keeping the acts and policies of the majority open to criticism and review by the opposing minority.[2] One of the most serious difficulties confronting any democratic group is the difficulty of formulating and giving efficient expression to the general will of the group. The method generally practiced is the method of counting ballots. It is difficult to believe, however, that this method alone gives expression of the real will of the whole; ballots should not only be counted,

[1] Plato's views on the subject are expressed in his *Republic.* Nietzsche's views are scattered throughout his writings; in locating them invaluable assistance may be had from the index volume added to the English translation of his works under the editorship of A. Tille.

[2] "A majority is tyrannical when it decides without hearing the minority, when it suppresses fair and temperate criticism on its own acts, when it insists on restraining men in matters where restraint is not required by the common interest, when it forces men to contribute money to objects which they disapprove, and which the common interest does not demand." Bryce, *The American Commonwealth,* Chapter 84.

they should if possible also be weighed and evaluated. But there is no practical method at hand for doing this, though if it could be done the application of the democratic ideal would be much more surely guaranteed.[1]

(3) SUMMARY OF SECTION. Sovereignty means the supreme power within the group. Political sovereignty differs from legal sovereignty and is basal. Both the absolutistic and the democratic views of the locus of sovereignty have been practiced by groups in their historical development. The absolutistic ideal, however, seems largely arbitrary and has been more and more discarded in practice. The democratic ideal, which seems the logically justifiable conception of sovereignty, makes the 'general will' sovereign within the group. The chief difficulty confronting the practice of democracy is the determination and efficient application of this 'general will.' The great danger involved in the practice of democracy is that the tyranny of the majority will be substituted for the tyranny of the minority; to prevent this, free discussion and open criticism by the minority of the majority's acts and policies are essential.

§ 3. *Sovereignty among groups*

The second general question arising from the problem of sovereignty concerns the relation that each group bears to others. Is each group its absolute sovereign?

(1) TWO ANSWERS TO THE QUESTION. To this question two answers have been suggested by the growth of man's

[1] A criticism of the ineffectiveness and failure of 'ballot-box democracy' and suggestions looking toward a method of giving expression to the real 'general will' of the group may be found in M. P. Follett, *The New State*. Some interesting suggestions on the more theoretical side of the problem may be found in Professor Bosanquet's *The Philosophical Theory of the State*.

social experience. The first is the answer of the *nationalist,* which is to the effect that each group is its own absolute sovereign and beyond it there is no sovereign to which it owes the slightest allegiance. The second answer is that of the *internationalist* who, in opposition to the position of the nationalist, holds that over and beyond the individual group there always stands the ideal group of humanity, the great society of minds, to which all subordinate groups alike owe allegiance and with reference to which their separate authorities are limited. In the actual practice of groups nationalism has been dominant, and still is. Internationalism, in theory, is as old as Stoicism and Christianity; but it has always been an ideal generally regarded as either impractical or undesirable or both. In recent years, however, internationalism has gained considerable strength in theory, and in the Hague Tribunal and the more recent League of Nations it has even seriously threatened to enter directly into practice.

(2) Estimate of these answers. In debating the claims of these two answers to our question two possible misconceptions may cause confusion and should be cleared up. (*a*) In the first place, it is frequently assumed that the internationalist's ideal, if put into practice, would involve the destruction of individual groups and, consequently, the feeling of patriotism and the virtues that spring from it. A little reflection should be sufficient to show that there is not the slightest justification for such an assumption. It is perfectly conceivable that states might be organized in such a way that no existing state would be destroyed by such organization. If individuals can live together in groups and still retain their individuality, if the state does not destroy the family, the church, or such smaller groups falling within its scope, if a nation may be composed of in-

dependent and more or less sovereign states, why may not nations organize themselves into one large group without losing their individual characteristics or negating the allegiance of their citizens? Nations might continue to exist as more or less independent political units within an international grouping; whether or not this would be the case would depend altogether upon the sort of internationalism practiced. The point here is simply that internationalism need not necessarily involve the destruction of national states.

(*b*) The second misconception which offers a difficulty to clear thinking on the subject is the reverse side of the preceding one. It is the assumption that internationalism is indissolubly connected with certain theories of government and social organization on the order of extreme socialism. It may be true that internationalists are frequently found to be socialists and even communists at home; but, if true, it does not prove that socialism and internationalism are synonymous terms. There may be, and there are, internationalists who are far from the socialist's camp. The assumption to the contrary is merely another illustration of the fact that, in popular thinking, false associations are constantly leading into erroneous by-paths. Whether or not socialism and its kindred 'isms' are dangerous doctrines has absolutely nothing to do with the debate as to the value of the internationalist's views concerning intergroup relations. Internationalism and socialism are two very different theories, neither being in any way logically connected with the other. Internationalism, then, does not necessarily involve the destruction of national states, nor has it any logical relation to any form of socialism. This being clear, one is in a better position to face the real issues involved in the nationalist-international controversy.

The following points would seem to be relevant to the debate. They are set down here, not as an exhaustive list of relevant points, but merely as suggestions which may be of assistance to the reader in his efforts to reach some conclusions on his own account concerning the merits of the controversy.

(*a*) The history of mankind's social development shows, as we have already seen, that the many small and weak groups of primitive society have in the course of the centuries grown into a relatively few large groups latterly called states or nations. As the centuries pass and civilization advances the interrelations of the groups become more and more marked and their interdependence emphasized. At present every group is vitally affected by the fortunes, good or ill, of every other group, as was unmistakably evidenced by the last war. This has given rise to the League of Nations, mankind's latest experiment in social organization. Now this historical development would seem to have an important bearing upon the problem at issue, and a fairly strong case may be based upon it for the thesis that the drive of human history is toward a one general and all-inclusive society of minds.

(*b*) Closely connected with the above historical development is the further consideration that any theory of man's group-life which stops short with a few separate and distinct groups regarded as absolutely independent of each other seems arbitrary. History shows no such stopping-place, and no theoretical justification for such a division among groups can be easily advanced. The question always remains, Why should each group have this indefeasible authority over itself? And until this question is answered the theory cannot be accepted as complete. The burden of proof here seems to rest on the nationalist.

(*c*) But the internationalist also has his difficulties. The wide diversities of moral, religious, political, and economic traditions that obtain among the various groups of humanity as at present existing undoubtedly throw numerous difficulties in the way of carrying into practice the internationalist's ideal. Not only is he confronted by political boundaries; he is also confronted by the boundaries that divide religions and civilizations, and these are infinitely more difficult to cross. Many and great are the practical difficulties that stand in the way of his scheme. But there seems no good reason to hold that these difficulties are insurmountable.

(*d*) The nationalist's position with reference to group sovereignty is in principle closely allied to the absolutist's position with reference to sovereignty within the group; while the position of the internationalist is an extension of the democratic ideal to states and nations. And, if this be so, then whatever considerations are relevant to the controversy between the absolutist and the democrat with reference to intra-group organization would seem to be relevant, *mutatis mutandis,* to the controversy between the nationalist and the internationalist with reference to inter-group organization: the latter would then appear to be the former in a different application.

Such are some of the points that have a bearing upon the very fundamental problem of the organization of mankind. There are, of course, many others both theoretical and practical; but those mentioned above seem to touch upon the basal aspects of the problem and may serve to start the reader upon a further course of reflection.

Chapter XX. Questions and Exercises

1. Define the problem of sovereignty and briefly trace its genesis.

2. What is meant by the indivisibility of sovereignty? State clearly the distinction between the monistic and the pluralistic views of sovereignty (Read Haines and Haines, *Principles and Problems of Government*, pp. 53–57). What is the distinction between political and legal sovereignty?

3. Distinguish between the absolutistic and the democratic views of sovereignty, and estimate the value of each.

4. State briefly the points at issue between the nationalist and the internationalist, and outline the argument involved in the controversy. Read in connection with this question Mackenzie, *Outlines of Social Philosophy*, Book III, Chapter I.

5. Summarize the main points in:
   (*a*) Young, *The State and Government*, Chapter III.
   (*b*) Russell, *Political Ideals*, Chapter V.
   (*c*) Mackenzie, *Outlines of Social Philosophy*, Book I, Chapter II; and Book II, Chapter IV.

6. Some references for further and more advanced study: Locke, *Two Treatises on Government;* Hobbes, *The Leviathan;* Rousseau, *The Social Contract;* Kant, *Perpetual Peace;* Machiavelli, *The Prince;* Plato, *The Republic;* Aristotle, *Politics.*

PART VI

PROBLEMS OF VALUES

CHAPTER XXI

THE WORLD OF VALUES

In Chapter VIII above we noted that judgments fall into two general classes which we called factual-judgments and value-judgments. Thus far in our study we have been concerned with problems that arise in connection with the first class and we have purposely neglected to take into account the problems that have to do with the second class. It is now time for us to turn our attention to these problems, and the remaining part of our study will be devoted to a consideration of them. They are the problems of value, and they are of very great importance in human experience. Through a general description of what we may call the world of values, the present chapter will undertake to outline more clearly the nature of these problems of value that are of such interest to philosophy as well as to common sense.

§ 1. *Judgments of value*

As a point of departure in our study of the world of values let us remind ourselves of the nature of judgments of value and note their significance.

(1) NATURE OF JUDGMENTS OF VALUE. As we have already seen, judgments of value differ from judgments of fact in this important respect: they appraise the worth of objects, whereas factual-judgments merely describe objects. For instance, if one judges that the flower or the rainbow is beautiful, or that the deed is generous, one appraises its

worth and deems it valuable. What we have called factual-judgments are different; they do not undertake to evaluate, but only to describe, a given environmental situation. 'The rainbow is formed by the refraction of light-waves,' 'The flower is colored red,' 'The man who did this deed was seen by me' — these are examples of purely factual judgments. Value-judgments appraise the worth of objects, while factual judgments describe the nature of objects; in this lies the important difference between the two types.

(2) OBJECTIVITY OF VALUE-JUDGMENTS. It is sometimes said that values are purely subjective in the sense that they are wholly relative to individual preferences. This assumption has even become traditional and is incorporated in many of our common sayings. "There is nothing good or bad but thinking makes it so" and "There is no disputing about tastes" are examples of the sort of sayings in which this assumption is embedded. There is an element of truth in the view — just enough, in fact, to make it dangerous as an error. The element of truth is that values are in an important sense dependent upon the human mind for their existence. But the error involved in the assumption must not be overlooked. When we judge that an object has value, that the rainbow or the flower is beautiful or the deed generous, we feel that the judgment is by no means an arbitrary one and that there is something in the objects so judged which makes the judgment necessary. We feel that in an important sense the rainbow or the flower is such that we *must* judge it beautiful, the deed is in its own right generous, the parcel of ground has its 'real' value which is independent of the fluctuations of the 'market' value, and so forth. In short, values seem to lie in objects just as truly as do colors and temperatures

and all of the other qualities with which factual-judgments are concerned; values are beyond the arbitrary preferences of individual human beings. Of course, preferences do enter into the situation as an important element of it, as we shall see more fully later; but there is equally an aspect of that which is deemed valuable which is independent of individual preferences, some quality in the object that calls out these preferences.[1] And if this be true then it follows that value-judgments are also in a sense descriptive, for values are in a sense factual; value-judgments are descriptive of those qualities in objects, whatever they may be, which evoke the appreciative response. Thus it is an error to suppose that value-judgments and factual-judgments are sharply sundered. In a sense all judgments are factual, in the sense namely that if they are real judgments they deal with facts. The difference between the two types of judgment is therefore primarily a difference of emphasis, the value-judgment emphasizing appreciation and the factual-judgment emphasizing description. But this difference of emphasis is of great significance and justifies the distinction which we have drawn between the two types.

§ 2. *Types of values*

It is, of course, impossible to make a detailed list of the numberless things which human beings esteem valuable. It is fairly evident, however, that these fall naturally into certain general classes, some of the more important of which we may here set down as an aid to our comprehension of the world of values.

[1] We shall return to this point below in our discussion of moral and aesthetic values. For the general problem of the objectivity of values the more advanced reader might consult Sorley, *Moral Values and the Idea of God*. It is easy to see that the problem is one aspect of the more general problem of the objectivity of judgment itself.

(1) BODILY VALUES. In the first place, many things are deemed valuable because of the relation they bear to bodily health and efficiency. These we may conveniently call bodily values. Here are included all those forms of exercise and activity that make for the increased efficiency and development of the body, all satisfactions of bodily desires and impulses that are concerned with the life and health of the organism. The body is of fundamental importance in life, and as such its demands must be taken into account and evaluated. Some, to be sure, have supposed it to be the 'prison house' of the soul and have, consequently, despised its claims; a whole philosophy of life (asceticism) has been founded upon depreciation of bodily values. Others (for instance, the ancient Greeks), on the contrary, have held bodily values in high esteem, and so have developed a view of life quite different from the ascetic view. With Browning they urge:

> Let us not always say
> "Spite of this flesh to-day
> I strove, made head, gained ground upon the whole:"
> As the bird wings and sings,
> Let us cry "All good things
> Are ours, nor soul helps flesh more, now, than flesh helps soul."
> (*Rabbi Ben Ezra*)

But whether the body be looked upon as a hindrance or an aid in the struggle of life, its claims cannot be ignored. Bodily values are of fundamental importance.

(2) ECONOMIC VALUES. Another important type of values are the economic. The social interdependence of human beings is so intimate that many of their desires cannot be satisfied by isolated effort. One wants what others have, and in order to secure it something he possesses which others want must be given in exchange; so

a system of the interchange of commodities has grown up. This system constitutes the economic order, and the economic values are those which emerge from this order. The logically fundamental concept here is, of course, that of wealth in terms of which other economic values are defined. Like bodily values, economic values are of fundamental importance; they arise from those basal human needs which can be satisfied only through economic wealth. How important they are in daily life is sufficiently evident when one considers what values human beings for the most part keep uppermost in their minds through the waking hours of their three-score years.

(3) Aesthetic values. A third important class of values is the aesthetic. These are the values of beauty in all of the manifold forms which it assumes both in nature and in the works of man. Viewed in the light of purely practical considerations — practical, that is, in the narrow and mean sense of the word — the importance of the aesthetic values of human life is not so obvious as is that of the other values mentioned above. And yet their importance is tremendous, and grows with the advancement of civilization. What life would be without these values one shudders to think: they are perhaps the purest joys that human frailty is capable of.

(4) Moral values. The last type of values which we shall here mention is the group of moral values. Both because of their utility in the life that now is and because of their implications relevant to the hope — entertained by many — of another and better life, these moral values are of exceeding great importance. The basal concept here is the concept of goodness. Some things appeal to us as good and some as evil, some as right and others as wrong; and our evaluations of objects in terms of good and evil,

right and wrong (broadly, in terms of goodness) constitute our moral values. Moral judgments appear to be limited to human conduct and human relationships. We do not ordinarily appraise objects or events in the physical environment as good or evil in the moral sense, nor do we evaluate the conduct of animals with reference to goodness. Ordinarily only human conduct and institutions are objects of moral judgment. How important this type of values is within human experience may be seen from a study of the rôle it plays in the creation, preservation, and transformation of social traditions and institutions; the whole history of the human race bears witness to its basal significance.[1]

§ 3. *Intrinsic and extrinsic values*

Some of the values of life are desired for their own sakes alone, while others are desired as a means to an end. The beauty of the rainbow, for instance, is valued on its own account; but the parcel of land, the bank-account, or the automobile is valued because of what it will enable one to acquire in the way of the satisfaction of further desires. The rainbow's beauty is an example of what is technically called an 'intrinsic' value. The parcel of land, the automobile, and the bank-account, on the other hand, are illustrations of what technically are known as 'extrinsic' or 'instrumental' values. By an intrinsic value, then, is meant any value which claims appraisal in its own right; it is (or claims to be) of absolute worth, an end in itself. Extrinsic values have worth, not in their own right, but because of what they can bring in the way of other values; they are of instrumental worth only, a means to an end.

[1] See the opening chapters of Myers, *History as Past Ethics*. The entire book exemplifies the point.

Precisely what values are intrinsic and what instrumental or extrinsic is a question of considerable difficulty. Are all bodily values, for example, intrinsic or extrinsic? Are any economic values intrinsic, or are all of them instrumental? How would aesthetic and moral values be classified? We need not here enter upon a detailed study of these matters, though the attempt to answer such questions would serve to put the distinction between intrinsic and extrinsic values in bolder relief. For our present purpose it is sufficient to note that aesthetic and moral values (at least the logically fundamental ones) are generally held to be intrinsic, and that most if not all of the other types of value are instrumental only. It may be stated, by the way, that one of the most difficult problems of the practice of living is to place values in their proper relations to each other; the reasonable coördination of values — 'first things first' — is one way of defining the ideal life, but it is an ideal that is hard to attain and in fact is never attained except approximately even by the best.

The introduction of the distinction between intrinsic and extrinsic values is important for our further study, because it serves as a convenient means of delimiting our field. For it is out of the intrinsic values, whatever they may be, that the philosophical problems arise in the world of values; extrinsic values are of no special concern to the philosopher. Henceforth in our discussion, therefore, when we speak of values we shall be thinking primarily of intrinsic, not of extrinsic or instrumental, values; and thus the scope of our inquiry is brought within more manageable limits. And we may still further narrow the field by arbitrarily confining attention to those intrinsic values (beauty and goodness) that fall in the classes of aesthetic and moral values. And this is not wholly arbitrary; for within these types we find, if anywhere, values that are genuinely intrinsic and, furthermore, values that are of special concern to the student of philosophy. Our further study, then, will turn upon the problems of aesthetic and moral values.

§ 4. *The problems of aesthetic and moral values*

What, then, are the problems to which the value-judgments of the aesthetic and moral experience give rise? The present section will attempt to answer this question in general outline; a somewhat detailed study of the problems will be undertaken in the chapters following.

(1) PROBLEMS OF AESTHETIC VALUES. Aesthetic value-judgments, as we have seen, appraise objects according as they possess, or do not possess, that peculiar something called beauty. There are, of course, manifold forms of the beautiful, but it is in some real sense supposed to be the same in all; so the basal aesthetic concept is that of beauty. There are mainly three problems clustering about this basal idea which we shall consider. These are: (*a*) What is the nature of beauty? (*b*) What is the nature of the experience which we call 'appreciation' and 'creation' (in art) of beauty? and (*c*) What is the relation between beauty and goodness? The first of these problems is, strictly speaking, largely a problem of the science of aesthetics, though not wholly so; it touches upon a certain general question that has philosophical implications of considerable importance. The second problem is primarily a psychological one, though here also the problem leads naturally and inevitably out into the field of philosophy. The third problem is strictly philosophical, since it is concerned with the interrelation of two sciences — namely, aesthetics and ethics. These problems we shall consider in order in the next chapter.

(2) Problems of moral values. Moral values are more fundamental in human experience than is any other type of values. They seem to touch the very depths of human hopes and fears, and they body forth the highest human ideals. Consequently, the problems connected with them are far-flung in their scope; they are among the most perplexing as well as the most persistent problems with which the mind of man has busied itself during the centuries of its intellectual endeavors. Stated briefly, these problems may be formulated as follows: (*a*) What is the nature of goodness? (*b*) What are the conditions of the creation of goodness? and (*c*) What are the conditions of the conservation of goodness? The traditional formulations of these problems, with which the reader may perchance be more familiar, are as follows: (*a*) What is the chief end of life or the highest good (*Summum bonum* is the Latin phrase)? (*b*) Is there such a thing as a free will, or are all wills determined? (*c*) Can the human soul be said to be immortal or does it die with the body, and what can we know about the existence and nature of God? Though stated in less familiar terms, the first formulations of the problems emerging out of the moral experience of mankind are perhaps clearer. They at least have the advantage of directing our attention to the fact that the different problems center around the basal notion of goodness, and they thus more clearly indicate the common point of departure for a reasoned consideration of the problems in question. In any event, these formulations suggest the lines along which our own later study of the problems will run, and so they should be kept in mind by the reader. What is goodness, how is it created or made possible in human experience, and how (if at all) is it conserved as a fundamental characteristic of the world-order? — this

three-fold question states concisely what we shall have in mind to answer as we proceed in the discussion of Chapters XXIII–XXVII below.

Chapter XXI. Questions and Exercises

1. Distinguish value-judgments and factual-judgments, and give examples of each.

2. Give at least two examples of each of the four classes of values mentioned in the text.

3. What types of values besides those mentioned in the text does Everett suggest in his *Moral Values,* Chapter VII? Be prepared to explain the nature of, and illustrate, each of these classes.

4. Differentiate clearly between intrinsic and extrinsic or instrumental values.

5. Are economic values intrinsic or extrinsic? Discuss briefly.

6. Is the value which education possesses intrinsic or extrinsic? Discuss.

7. Summarize the main points gathered from the discussion of the objectivity of values by DeLaguna in his *Introduction to the Science of Ethics,* pp. 335–339.

CHAPTER XXII

PROBLEMS OF AESTHETIC VALUES

The aesthetic type of reaction is a practically universal characteristic of human experience. Even primitive man aspires towards the beautiful; he expresses this aspiration in decoration, ornamentation, dance, and music. And civilized man objectifies this aspiration in his more advanced artistic creations. Wherever a civilized society is found the aesthetic interest ramifies profoundly through the warp and woof of it. "The plastic arts, with poetry and music, are the most conspicuous monuments of this human interest, because they appeal only to contemplation, and yet have attracted to their service, in all civilized ages, an amount of effort, genius, and honour, little inferior to that given to industry, war, or religion. The fine arts, however, where aesthetic feeling appears almost pure, are by no means the only sphere in which men show their susceptibility to beauty. In all products of human industry we notice the keenness with which the eye is attracted to the mere appearance of things: great sacrifices of time and labor are made to it in the most vulgar manufactures; nor does man select his dwelling, his clothes, or his companions without reference to their effect on his aesthetic senses. Of late we have even learned that the forms of many animals are due to the survival by sexual selection of the colours and forms most attractive to the eye. There must therefore be in our nature a very radical and widespread tendency to observe beauty, and to value it."[1]

[1] Santayana, *The Sense of Beauty*, 1896, p. 1. For a simple and interesting account of the primitive arts and a brief introductory study of the "Science of Art" see Grosse, *The Beginnings of Art.*

This universal interest in the beautiful gives rise to certain problems that constitute an interesting corner of philosophy. What can we definitely say concerning the nature of beauty, and what are some of the main features of the aesthetic judgment — the appreciation of the beautiful? And how does the activity of the aesthetic judgment stand related to those moral valuations that touch perhaps even profounder depths in the society of minds? These are the questions that grow out of man's aesthetic attitude towards his world, and they are the questions which we shall briefly consider in the present chapter. Even though no satisfactory solution of them be forthcoming, we shall have done well to have forced our minds to impinge upon them. At least something of their significance may be grasped.

§ 1. *The nature of beauty*

The problem of the nature of beauty is a difficult one, and many theories concerning it have been advanced in the course of man's speculation.[1] Its adequate treatment would demand a separate volume. Here we can only touch upon certain fundamental aspects of the problem, and what is said will be little more than a syllabus to be supplemented by further reading and study on the student's part. We shall undertake primarily an analysis of the elements of the problem.

(1) Beauty as objective. It has at times been held that beauty is objective in the sense that it exists in things and would continue so to exist even if there were no minds to appreciate it. This view is expressed by Richard Price, for example, in his contention that beauty is an attribute

[1] Surveys of the greater theories will be found in E. F. Carritt, *The Theory of Beauty;* and Knight, *The Philosophy of the Beautiful,* Part I. This last book contains valuable bibliographies.

or quality so "*inherent* in objects that it would exist in them whether any mind perceived it or not."[1] The locus of beauty is in the environment, and not in any sense in the mind of the one who appreciates it.

As we shall see below, there is an element of truth in this view. But there are difficulties in the way of it which forbid its unconditional acceptance. The chief of these perhaps is the fact, easily verified, that notions of beauty vary from age to age and from race to race; this is particularly evident in works of art, as a survey of different types of music, painting, or sculpture will show. It is not easy, for instance, for one trained in the traditions of European art to appreciate beauty in the art of the Chinese and the Japanese. The Hottentot Venus, it has been affirmed, is extremely ugly in the eyes of the foreigner; while the statues in Buddhistic temples, and even the temples themselves, do not spontaneously impress the mind of the alien with a sense of their beauty. And even modern Europeans find difficulty in discovering the beauty hidden in some examples of the art of mediaeval Europe; in fact, some of these examples may to the modern mind appear hideous. Such facts as these would seem to be inconsistent with the theory of the extreme objectivity of beauty. If beauty be objective and in no sense dependent upon the mind that experiences it, why should it not universally be the same for all minds? Why these variations? Again, the appreciation of beauty requires, not infrequently, a certain period

[1] Quoted by Raymond, *Art in Theory,* p. 127. Richard Price was a Unitarian minister and a thinker of note of eighteenth century England. He was a forerunner of a view of ethics that later came to be known as the 'intuitional' view; he held that right and wrong are directly perceived by an 'intuition' of the understanding. This, obviously, is in keeping with his view of beauty as expressed above. His most important work is *A Review of the Principal Questions of Morals* (1757; revised and enlarged edition, 1787), from which the quotation in the text is taken. In addition he wrote several works on political questions.

of training on the part of the mind that would observe it. In all the higher forms of art this is true, as the appreciation of classical music abundantly illustrates. And this fact also seems hard to reconcile with the doctrine of the objectivity of beauty in its extreme form. For these reasons, therefore, among others that may occur to the reader, the doctrine seems hardly satisfactory. Beauty is apparently in some sense relative to the mind that observes it, and not wholly independent of it.

(2) BEAUTY AS SUBJECTIVE. There is another view of the locus of beauty which is the opposite extreme from that described above. This is the view that beauty exists, not in the environment, but wholly in the mind. It is a peculiar way of feeling that human beings entertain about the world, a "light that never was on sea or land" but exists only in the heart of man.

> They have no song, the sedges dry,
> And still they sing.
> It is within my heart they sing,
> As I pass by.
>
> Within my breast they touch a string,
> They wake a sigh.
> There is but sound of sedges dry;
> In me they sing.[1]

Here, once again, there is an undoubted element of truth. Such facts as those above mentioned seem to lie in support of it. That beauty is relative to traditions and training and cannot be defined in isolation from them would seem to imply that it is embedded in the psychology of the society of minds. But, granting this, there are other

[1] George Meredith, "Song of the Songless," quoted by Langfeld, *The Aesthetic Attitude*, p. 26.

facts that will not permit us to say that beauty is wholly a matter of subjective feeling. On this side it must not be forgotten that, broadly speaking, beauty exists for all minds alike and that adequate training tends to bring aesthetic judgments towards a common standard. "It is notorious that the verdicts passed by the human race as to Beauty are as various as the nations, and almost as the families of mankind. But such statistics . . . cannot disprove the fact . . . that, given an adequate education in Beauty, these scattered judgments and verdicts will approach toward a common standard; and that the crude taste of the savage will yield, in a perfectly normal way, to the insight of the civilized. . . . It is an undoubted fact . . . that wherever education has advanced beyond the elementary stage, there is a consensus of opinion as to what things are beautiful and what are not. Minor or secondary differences remain, and always will remain; but the radical difference in the judgments as to Beauty is between those adopted by the savage and the civilized, not between those which are entertained by the latter. Further, we can only explain artistic progress in a nation if there be a standard towards which that progress normally tends."[1] And such facts as these cannot be easily accounted for on the basis of the assumption that beauty is wholly subjective and exists only as a psychological fact in the mind of man. The difficulty here is as great as that which would arise were one to essay a purely subjective explanation of the nature of truth and the growth of the sciences.

(3) Beauty as subjective-objective. If, then, the locus of beauty is neither exclusively in objects nor exclusively in the mind, where may it be said to be? The

[1] Knight, *The Philosophy of the Beautiful,* Part II, p. 8.

most obvious answer is: In the environment *and* in the mind of man, in the mind as a special sort of reaction to the environment. And this would seem to be the truth of the matter. Beauty is definable only in terms of objects of a certain sort standing in a peculiar relation to perceiving minds: it is the way minds are affected by certain objects. It is "neither totally dependent upon the person who experiences, nor upon the thing experienced; it is neither subjective nor objective, neither the result of purely intellectual activity, nor a value inherent in the object, but a relation between two variables — the human organism and the object."[1] This view of the matter seems to fit in well with all the facts, and so is empirically sound. It is also consistent with the general principles above developed in our study of judgment. The values of beauty are the objects of the aesthetic judgment; and every judgment, we have seen, is precisely the reaction of mind to an environmental situation. These objects are beautiful which are of such qualities as to arouse in an observing mind that peculiar response called 'aesthetic' — the judgment of beauty.

What further can be said as to the qualities of those objects that act as stimuli to the aesthetic response, and what are some of the main characteristics of the response so aroused? What are the objective conditions of the beautiful, and what are the distinguishing marks of the aesthetic judgment? These questions are forced upon us by the immediately preceding considerations, and we shall try in the next two sections to look in the direction in which their answers would seem to lie.

[1] Langfeld, *The Aesthetic Attitude*, p. 108.

§ 2. *The objective conditions of beauty*

An introductory word is necessary here to bring to the reader's mind a distinction with which he is already familiar. Every one knows that beautiful objects fall into two general classes: objects of nature or natural objects, and the creations of man's genius or the objects of art. Within the first class there is a great variety of objects which we call beautiful. The laughing cascade and the surging sea, the rolling valley and the towering mountain, the moonlit heavens and the clouds at sunset — these and a thousand other objects in nature produce within us the aesthetic response. No detailed enumeration of them is, of course, possible.[1] But we can note certain general types of beauty exemplified in the objects of nature, and classify them as sublime, majestic, graceful, and the like. With the classification of objects of art all are familiar under the headings of the arts themselves: painting, sculpture, architecture, music, and poetry.[2]

What now are the chief qualities of objects, whether natural or artistic, that give rise to the aesthetic response? Why does the rainbow make the heart 'leap up' when one beholds it, and what has the rainbow in common with other beautiful objects that it and they should evoke the aesthetic judgment? What are the objective conditions of beauty?

[1] Note St. Paul's classic statement: "There are celestial bodies, and bodies terrestrial: but the glory of the celestial is one, and the glory of the terrestrial is another. There is one glory of the sun, and another glory of the moon, and another glory of the stars; for one star differeth from another star in glory." (I *Corinthians,* Chapter XV, verses 40, 41.)

[2] Knight, *The Philosophy of the Beautiful,* Part II, Chapters VIII–XIII, gives a general survey of the several arts; and to each chapter he appends a rather extensive bibliography which will be helpful for further reading and study. Brown, *The Fine Arts,* deals in an interesting way with sculpture, architecture, and painting. Primitive art is touched upon in the book referred to above: Grosse, *The Beginnings of Art.*

To this question many answers have been offered.[1] And this is inevitable, since the conditions themselves are so very complex. We can only attempt here to suggest a general statement with reference to the matter. In the first place, it is obvious that the arrangements embodied in the object are of great importance in the aesthetic attitude. The framing and arrangement of pictures, the setting of the statue, the order and combination of colors, the scenic arrangement of the drama, the form of the poem, the order of rhythms in music — these are illustrations in point. It is difficult, and perhaps impossible, to give an exhaustive characterization of these objective conditions of beauty, since mind is an indispensable element within the relation and different minds are affected in various ways and by varying qualities in objects. However, considering the objective conditions of beauty by themselves alone and without reference to the perceiving mind, we may perhaps say that there is one characteristic always to be found exemplified in them; and that is unity. The beautiful object is the unified object. "It is through this unification of the object, this relating of its parts to one another, that it is grasped by the mind. There is in this an economy of effort which is essential to mental development.[2] Therefore, it is reasonable to expect that an arrangement of the elements of an object of contemplation which aids this unification will meet the requirements of the mind better and be more acceptable than an arrangement which does not do so. Unity can, therefore, be considered a firmly estab-

[1] The books by Carritt and Knight, mentioned in a footnote at the beginning of this chapter, present a good introduction to the main views. Bosanquet, *History of Aesthetic,* gives a more advanced survey of the same field. The sundry references in these books, particularly the bibliographies by Knight, open doors innumerable for the curious.

[2] Compare what was said above, Chapter VII, about judgment as at once analytical-synthetical.

lished principle of beauty."[1] This condition of beauty is particularly marked in the greatest works of art, as is abundantly exemplified by the products of the artistic genius at its highest; any of the works of Shakespeare, the paintings of Michael Angelo, the statues of Pheidias, or the great cathedrals of mediaeval Europe may be taken as examples. The point is well put by Browning in *Abt Vogler:*

> But here is the finger of God, a flash of the will that can,
> Existent behind all laws: that made them, and, lo, they are!
> And I know not if, save in this, such gift be allowed to man,
> That out of three sounds he frame, not a fourth sound, but a star.
> Consider it well: each tone of our scale in itself is nought;
> It is everywhere in the world — loud, soft, and all is said:
> Give it to me to use! I mix it with two in my thought,
> And, there! Ye have heard and seen: consider and bow the head!

This unity expresses itself mainly in three ways: unity of form, unity of content, and unity of form with content.[2]

Here we seem to have the basal characteristic of the objective conditions of the aesthetic judgment in its purest and highest type, in so far as those conditions can be described apart from the aesthetic response itself. But, obviously, the subjective response of the mind to the objective conditions is of indispensable importance in the complete understanding of the beautiful; and to a consideration of that we now turn.

[1] Langfeld, *The Aesthetic Attitude*, p. 31.

[2] To fill in details here the student should refer to the discussions of the point and illustrations of it taken from the arts as given by Langfeld in *The Aesthetic Attitude,* Chapters VII and VIII. For a study of the principles involved see particularly pp. 169–190.

§ 3. *The aesthetic judgment*

What are the main features of the aesthetic judgment? This is the second question that confronts us in our quest for the comprehension of beauty.

Two answers to this question have been proffered. One (called 'intellectualism' or 'rationalism') holds that aesthetic appreciation is merely an intellectual judgment that a given object is beautiful, and that, in order to create beautiful objects, such and such rules must be followed. The other ('romanticism' or 'sentimentalism') emphasizes the emotional or feeling element in aesthetic appreciation, and denies that set rules can be laid down for the creation of the beautiful. According to the intellectualists the aesthetic judgment is exclusively rational, and differs in no important respect from such purely factual judgments as 'Heavy bodies fall' or 'A straight line is the shortest distance between two given points.' According to the romanticists, on the other hand, the purely rational element is of minor importance in aesthetic judgments, if, indeed, it can be said to be present at all; the aesthetic judgment is merely a feeling for beauty, an 'intuition' that leads directly and immediately into the heart of the objects experienced as beautiful. For the one the aesthetic judgment is a rational process; for the other it is an immediate feeling.

The truth apparently lies between these two extremes. Certainly the aesthetic judgment cannot be identified with a formal process of reasoning; it involves an emotional or feeling quality which is a primary characteristic of it. One does not ordinarily reason that the picture or poem or sunset is beautiful because of such and such attributes that belong to it; one is rather directly impressed with its beauty. On the other hand, the aesthetic judgment is not merely a matter of feeling, otherwise it would not be educable nor could reasons be advanced in support of it once it had made its deliverance as to beauty or the lack of it; beauty then would be exclusively a matter of 'taste.' After all, the aesthetic judgment is a *judgment;* it grows out of an intellectual background and expresses an intellectual point of view. This background and this point of view are necessary for the perception of beauty even in natural objects, and still more so for the appreciation of objects of art. Unquestionably there is an immediate feeling in the aesthetic response; the beauty of the object is directly experienced, and that is the primary fact.

> Consider it well: each tone of our scale in itself is nought;
> Give it to me to use! I mix it with two in my thought,
> And, there! Ye have heard and seen: consider and bow the
> head!

But one must not forget that it is mixed in 'thought.' What immediacy there is results from previous training and experience, just as the 'immediate' solution of the scientific problem, as it were by a flash of intuition, results from, is the fruition of, previous prolonged reflection by the scientist on the elements of the problem under consideration.

The aesthetic response, then, involves both intelligence and feeling, both reason and emotion. It is a judgment with a pronounced feeling-tone. Those most keenly endowed with the aesthetic sense, the great creative artists, are at once highly intellectual and profoundly emotional. " If we glance through the history of art, we shall find that those who have produced the most enduring works were men of great intellect as well as of deep feeling. Perhaps one of the best examples is Leonardo da Vinci, who excelled in science as well as in art. With him as with others of the immortals, we find that there was always a balance between the two sides of his nature. Great art has not been produced upon a purely emotional background, nor upon a purely intellectual one. The latter is unfortunately less often found than the former, but given a great intellect, there can then be as much of the emotional side as even the extreme Romanticist can desire. The combination is rare, but so is genius."[1] And if this be true of the immortals in art, we may be fairly certain that it is true of the aesthetic response generally.

A more detailed survey of the characteristics of the aesthetic judgment need not here be undertaken. The problem, after all, is largely psychological, and for an exhaustive study of it the reader should consult the special texts.[2]

§ 4. *Beauty and goodness*

We come now to the last of the questions which in the beginning of the chapter we decided to consider. What is the relation between beauty and goodness? To what extent should the principles of morality enter into the determination of the beautiful?

Once more we find two extreme views with reference to the questions before us, and, as usual, we shall probably discover that the truth lies in a synthesis of the extremes.

[1] Langfeld, *The Aesthetic Attitude*, p. 10. The entire discussion from which this quotation is taken (pp. 6–13) should be read. For an important contemporary point of view somewhat different from that developed in the text, see Croce, *Aesthetics*.

[2] The following references are given as offering a beginning of such a study: Langfeld, *The Aesthetic Attitude*, particularly Chapters III–VI inclusive; K. Gordon, *Aesthetics;* E. D. Puffer, *Psychology of Beauty;* Babbitt, *The New Laokoon*, especially Chapters IV and V; E. F. Carritt, *The Theory of Beauty*.

On the one hand, there are those who are inclined to insist that the beautiful should always be judged with reference to its bearing upon the principles of conventional morality, and that nothing which contravenes these principles can in the end be truly beautiful. On the other hand stand those who are convinced that moral considerations have no place in the evaluation of the beautiful; 'art for art's sake' is their way of stating their thesis. Those who advocate the first position would place the ban upon everything which is risqué or questionable on moral grounds; while those who advocate art for art's sake would admit any subject provided it is artistically conceived. Which of the two views is correct?

Clarity of discussion may be aided by a distinction in meaning between two possible interpretations of the point at issue. To hold that art (for it is artistic objects, not objects of nature, with which the problem before us is concerned) is subject to morality may mean either that truly beautiful art must point a moral, or that the products of artistic creation are rightfully subject to ethical considerations in our final appraisal of them. Keeping this distinction in mind, we can perchance see our way more clearly. There seems no justification whatsoever for the first contention. The fact is that the highest art does not aim at edification, or, if it does so at all, it does so only in an indirect manner. Didactic productions are not the highest creations of the artistic genius.[1] "Of all these anti-aesthetics, which reduce the value of that pleasant thing called beauty to the moral lesson imparted by an artist, we must barely say that they do not describe our aesthetic experience. . . . It is not impossible, but it is rare, to find a quite satisfactory work of art to which we can assign its edifica-

[1] Note, in illustration of this sort of poetry, Pope's "Essay on Man."

tion. Milton does not really justify God's ways to men, but we perhaps care more for him than those who thought he did. Dr. Johnson saw that Shakespeare 'seems to write without any moral purpose' and 'is not always careful to show in the virtuous a disapprobation of the wicked.' As Scott said: 'The professed moral of a piece is like the mendicant who cripples after some splendid and gay procession, and in vain solicits the attention of those who have been gazing on it.'"[1]

The thesis that the objects of art are rightfully subject to moral considerations in our final appraisal of them is on a different footing. It is true that many works of art may transgress the boundaries of conventional moralities and shock sundry sensitive souls in consequence; and they are none the less works of art for all that. But true art cannot claim for itself absolute freedom from contact with the deeper principles of a scientific ethics; for a scientific ethics is concerned with the basal laws of the whole social order, and art, no more than economics or politics, can presume to demand exemption from its realm. "Art is subject to moral criticism, because morality is nothing more nor less than the law which determines the whole order of interests, within which art and every other good thing is possible. It will scarcely be denied that art is an expression of interest, that both its creation and its enjoyment are activities, moods, or phases of life; and it follows that before this specific interest can be safely or adequately satisfied, it is necessary to fulfill the general conditions that underlie the satisfaction of all interests. It is as absurd to speak of art for art's sake as it is to speak of drinking for drinking's sake, if you mean that this interest is entitled to entirely free play. Art, like all other interests, can flourish

[1] Carritt, *The Theory of Beauty*, pp. 64–65.

only in a sound and whole society, and the law of soundness and wholeness in life is morality."[1] The very comprehensiveness of morality is its warrant for presuming to include within its proper field the standards of the aesthetic judgment. And this presumption is no impertinence; for the standards of the moral judgment are more fundamental than are those of the aesthetic.

Chapter XXII. Questions and Exercises

1. Distinguish between beauty as subjective and beauty as objective.

2. Indicate in general terms the main elements in the problem of the nature of beauty.

3. Summarize the chief points in the discussion of unity by Langfeld, *The Aesthetic Attitude*, pp. 169–190.

4. Summarize the main points in the discussion by Langfeld of "Intellectualism versus Emotionalism," *The Aesthetic Attitude*, pp. 6–13. Read in this connection Babbitt, *The New Laokoon*, Chapter IV.

5. State the problem of beauty and goodness, and indicate the general lines of its solution.

6. Outline Perry, *The Moral Economy*, Chapter V.

7. Write a short summary of Langfeld's chapter on "Empathy" (*The Aesthetic Attitude*, Chapter V).

8. What is Plato's view of the relation between morality and art as developed in the *Republic?* (See particularly the first part of Book III.)

9. State briefly the main points of Croce's theory of beauty as summarized by Carr in *The Philosophy of Benedetto Croce*, Chapter IX.

[1] Perry, *The Moral Economy*, p. 174. The entire Chapter V should be read in this connection.

CHAPTER XXIII

THE NATURE OF GOODNESS

We are constantly evaluating human conduct and institutions as good or bad, right or wrong. The good we approve and the bad we condemn. These moral judgments constitute the content of the science of ethics, and a detailed study of them falls within the field of that special discipline. One problem connected with them, however, is the seed-plot out of which grow certain other problems of philosophical interest. That problem concerns the nature of goodness — the basal ethical concept. On what basis do we make these distinctions between good and bad, right and wrong? What is the standard with reference to which the good and the bad may be differentiated? What, in short, is the nature of goodness? This question we must here briefly consider as a preliminary to our further discussion of the problems of value.

§ 1. *Views of the nature of goodness*

Broadly speaking, the answers to the question before us fall into two classes. On the one side, it has been held that goodness is to be defined with reference to certain general laws or principles which somehow exist in their own right without reference to particular experiences and that, consequently, the standard of goodness is absolute and unchangeable. On the other side and in opposition to this position, it has been argued that good and bad, right and wrong, are only ideas which the human mind gradually acquires as a result of the consequences that experience brings; goodness and its opposite, therefore, are created in the course of human experience and so are relative to time and circumstances, at least in their creation and, perhaps, in their significance. We may, for the present discussion, call the first view the *intuitional* theory, and the second the *teleological* theory. Let us consider each in some detail.

§ 2. *The intuitional theory*

There are two forms of the intuitional view, according as the standard of goodness is supposed to be external to the human mind or inherent within it.

(1) THE STANDARD AS EXTERNAL TO THE NATURE OF MIND. The view has at times been held that the standard of goodness is an immutable principle which exists outside the human mind and is wholly independent of it. Here, once again, a division arises. Those who hold the general thesis are not agreed as to the locus of the standard. It exists outside the human mind, but where? One group answers: In the nature of things. Another answers: In the will of God. The first answer was put very clearly by a British thinker, Cudworth,[1] in his famous book entitled *A Treatise Concerning Eternal and Immutable Morality.* Early in that book we find him saying: "It is not possible that anything should be without a nature, and the nature and essences of things being immutable, therefore upon supposition that there is anything really just or unjust . . .

[1] Ralph Cudworth (1617–1688) was one of the leading members of the so-called Cambridge Platonists — a name given to a group of thinkers who flourished at Cambridge in the late seventeenth century. He published one philosophical book during his life-time, *The True Intellectual System of the Universe* (1678); but he left a mass of manuscript some of which was published after his death.

there must of necessity be something so both naturally and immutably, which no law, decree, will, or custom can alter."[1] And towards the conclusion of his argument he reiterates his thesis and holds it proved: "Wherefore the result of all that we have hitherto said is this, that the intelligible natures and essences of things are neither arbitrary nor fantastical, that is, neither alterable by any will whatsoever, nor changeable by opinion . . . so that if moral good and evil, just and unjust, signify any reality, either absolute or relative, in the things so denominated, as they must have certain natures, which are the actions or souls of men, they are neither alterable by mere will or opinion."[2] In short, the standard of goodness exists in the nature of the world, is absolute and eternal, and not relative either to the will of man or the will of God. The contrary view is stated very clearly in the words of Gerson: "God does not require actions because they are good, but they are good because He requires them: just as others are evil because he forbids them."[3] The standard of goodness exists, not in the nature or essences of things, but in the will of God; for the will of God there is no standard, save that will itself.

(2) THE STANDARD AS INHERENT IN THE MIND. The other form of the intuitional view holds that the standard, while absolute and in a sense immutable, nevertheless is

[1] Book II, Chapter I, section 1.

[2] Book IV, Chapter VI, section 3. Descartes holds something of the same view. See his reply to the sixth set of objections raised against his *Meditations* in *The Philosophical Works of Descartes,* translated by Haldane and Ross, Vol. II, p. 251.

[3] See Janet, *Theory of Morals,* p. 167; and Lecky, *History of European Morals* (third edition, revised), Vol. II, pp. 17 ff. There were other thinkers during the Middle Ages who agreed in principle with Gerson, notably the much greater philosopher, Duns Scotus. St. Thomas Aquinas, the greatest representative of the Church of the late Middle Ages, opposed this view and taught a doctrine somewhat akin to that of Cudworth.

inherent in the human mind itself. Good is good, evil is evil, as man wills — not individual men, be it noted, but humanity, the mind of *man*. The standard of moral values lies within the will of mankind. The classical formulation of this point of view is found in the ethical writings of Immanuel Kant.[1] According to Kant there is inborn in every normal mind a moral law which is the same for all and about which there need be no dispute. This moral law he calls the 'categorical imperative' and of it he gives this formulation: "Act in conformity with that maxim, and that maxim only, which you can at the same time will to be a universal law."[2] This, Kant argues at length, is a necessary law of human reason, and it is the foundation upon which rest all our moral judgments. Goodness, according to him, is definable only in terms of this universal law of the mind — the categorical imperative. "Duty consists in the obligation to act from *pure* reverence for the moral law. To this motive all others must give way, for it is the condition of a will which is good *in itself,* and which has a value with which nothing else is comparable."[3] Consequences have no significance with reference to the determination of the goodness of conduct; results are morally indifferent. "A man's will is good, not because the consequences which flow from it are good, nor because it is capable of attaining the end which it seeks, but it is good in itself, or because it wills the good. By a good will is not meant mere well-wishing; it consists in a reso-

[1] In previous notes something has been said about the life and historical significance of the works of Kant. His main ethical works are: *Fundamental Principles of a Metaphysic of Morals,* and *Critique of Practical Reason.* The first was published in 1785, and the second in 1788. The two have been translated by Abbott in a volume entitled *Kant's Theory of Ethics.*

[2] Watson, *Selections from Kant,* p. 241. Note the other formulations of the law given on pp. 242, 246.

[3] Watson, *op. cit.,* p. 231. Compare pp. 225–226.

lute employment of all the means within one's reach, and its intrinsic value is in no way increased by success or lessened by failure.[1] A good will is a will which, regardless of consequences, obeys the moral law, that is, acts in such a way that the resulting conduct might appropriately be done by everybody else; such a will is intrinsically good — "a jewel which shines by its own light," — and it is the only thing that is intrinsically good. Every other good has only instrumental value.

(3) SUMMARY OF SECTION. The intuitional view holds that the standard of the good is absolute and immutable, wholly untouched by the vicissitudes of human frailty. There is not agreement among the intuitionists as to where precisely this standard may be said to exist; some hold that it exists in the nature of things, others that it exists in the will of God, and others that it is embedded deep in the nature of human reason. All do agree, however, that consequences are of no moral significance and cannot logically play a part in the definition of goodness. Goodness is in no sense subservient to our weal or woe; in the last analysis it determines our weal and woe.

§ 3. *The teleological theory*

The teleological theory lays the emphasis precisely upon the point which intuitionism denies. So far from minimizing the moral significance of consequences as the intuitionist does, the teleologist insists that consequences are of great moral significance, that they, indeed, are alone of ultimate moral value. The standard of goodness is to be found in the results or 'ends' following upon the object whose moral value one is seeking to determine. There are three main forms of this view, according as the nature

[1] Watson, *ibid.*, pp. 225–226.

of the 'ends' made basal vary. These are *hedonism, energism,* and *asceticism.*

(1) HEDONISM. Hedonism is the theory that pleasures are the end in terms of which goodness is to be measured. That act is good which produces a preponderance of pleasure over pain; it is bad if the reverse is true. There have been many representatives of hedonism from the Greeks to the present, prominent among whom may be mentioned Epicurus and his school, Bentham, and J. S. Mill. These differ among themselves on various points in the formulation of the theory, but we cannot here discuss these differences. Their common thesis is of more concern to us, namely, that pleasure is the standard by which the goods of life are to be distinguished. Mill's statement of the theory may be regarded as classic: "The creed which accepts as the foundation of morals, Utility, or the Greatest Happiness Principle, holds that actions are right in proportion as they tend to promote happiness, wrong as they tend to produce the reverse of happiness. By happiness is intended pleasure, and the absence of pain; by unhappiness, pain, and the privation of pleasure. . . . Pleasure, and freedom from pain, are the only things desirable as ends; and all desirable things . . . are desirable either for the pleasure inherent in themselves, or as means to the promotion of pleasure and the prevention of pain."[1]

(2) ENERGISM. This is the theory that the end by which goodness is to be measured is the full expression and development of the capacities of human beings. The ca-

[1] J. S. Mill, *Utilitarianism,* Chapter II (fifteenth edition, published by Longmans, Green, and Company, 1907, pp. 9–10). Some other great texts of the hedonistic theory are the sayings of Epicurus and some of the writings of Lucretius (see Bakewell, *Sourcebook in Ancient Philosophy*), and Jeremiah Bentham, *Principles of Morals and Legislation.* For an exhaustive historical survey, together with penetrating criticism of the several formulations of the theory, see Albee, *History of Utilitarianism.*

pacity of enjoyment is one of these capacities, but only one; the hedonist, therefore, according to this view, is guilty of emphasizing one aspect of human experience to the exclusion of many other capacities — the capacity to grow, to acquire knowledge, to give one's all in loyalty to a cause, to cherish memories, to love one's fellows, to create art, and to do innumerable other things — which are equally valuable and worthy ends. So the energist would urge that, not pleasure alone, but all of the multitudinous capacities of man's nature constitute the foundation of morals, the standard of goodness. There are two formulations of this theory according as the capacities of the individual human being are conceived in social or biological terms; the one is altruistic, the other is essentially selfish or, at least, individualistic.

(a) *Altruistic energism.* Here the capacities of the individual which are supposed to be expressed and developed through good conduct and by reference to which good conduct is distinguished from bad are conceived primarily in their social significance. The self that is to be succored and developed is thought of as a self which lives and moves and has its being only and inevitably in a society of selves; the capacities that are to be given free play are those that are turned in the direction of attaining the interests of the group, either directly through social activity or indirectly through the development of a loyal individual.[1]

(b) *Egoistic energism.* This form of the theory holds that the standard of goodness is the expression of the individual's capacities without any regard, or with only sec-

[1] This conception of the good has been advocated by many thinkers from Plato and Aristotle down to our own day, though with differing emphases. Two typical and relatively simple formulations of it may be found in: Paulsen, *A System of Ethics,* Book II, Chapter II; and Wright, *Self-Realization,* Part II, Chapters IV and V.

ondary regard, to social consequences. Here capacities are conceived primarily in biological terms, and the effort is made to found a theory of morals upon the biological concepts of a struggle for existence and the survival of the fittest. Nature works through self-assertion and individualistic tendencies, and so should man; goodness, in the only sense in which it has intrinsic value for human beings, is self-aggrandizement.[1]

(3) Asceticism. Asceticism is largely a negative theory of goodness. It looks upon the natural desires of the individual, particularly those that are primarily connected with the body, as ignoble; and it conceives goodness as arising from the elimination or, if that be impossible, the curbing of such desires. In its extreme form asceticism indulges in the mortification of the flesh; practiced in greater moderation it may be content with the withdrawal of the individual from indulgence in the ordinary comforts of life, with the renunciation of all social relations and obligations, or with a refusal to participate in those types of pleasure which many people pursue as a matter of course. As a general theory of the good, however, it seeks its standard in some form of self-denial and self-discipline, whatever may be the variations in practice that result.

Generally this view of life is closely connected with religious convictions, though this is not universally the case. The Cynics of ancient Greece advocated the theory in the interest of purely moral considerations; and so did the Stoics, though in a greatly modified form. The religious mo-

[1] The writings of F. Nietzsche present the most persuasive account of this ego-centric view. These works have been translated from the German under the editorship of Tille, and so are available to English-reading students. They have been widely read, and have exerted a very appreciable influence upon contemporary social thought. Opposed to Nietzsche and his views stand most of the other classical philosophers. For a simple introduction to Nietzsche see Wright, *What Nietzsche Taught.*

tive is prominent, however, in the practices of some parts of the Christian community of the early Middle Ages, the monastic orders, and in the similar groups of Buddhist priests. Where the religious note is prominent the notion of other-worldliness assumes paramount importance in the theory; that is, the motive for the denial of present desires and the delimitation of interests is for the sake of the life to come. Tennyson has vividly portrayed this motive, which the history of religious asceticism amply illustrates, in "St. Simeon Stylites":

Let this avail, just, dreadful, mighty God,
This not be all in vain, that thrice ten years,
Thrice multiplied by superhuman pangs,
In hungers and in thirsts, fevers and cold,
In coughs, aches, stitches, ulcerous throes and cramps,
A sign betwixt the meadow and the cloud,
Patient on this tall pillar I have borne
Rain, wind, frost, heat, hail, damp, and sleet, and snow:
And I had hoped that ere this period closed
Thou wouldst have caught me up into Thy rest,
Denying not these weather-beaten limbs
The meed of saints, the white robe and the palm.[1]

Such in principle is the aspiration of the religious ascetic. But whether religious complications are involved in asceticism or whether the theory be founded exclusively upon morality, the essence of it remains: goodness lies in restraining, curbing, and, it may be, mortifying the ordinary needs and desires, both bodily and mental, and in persistent refusal to gratify them.

(4) SUMMARY OF SECTION. The teleological view of the

[1] This poem is a biting criticism of the ascetic ideal of life. It is also a subtle study in the psychology of asceticism; the insidious manner in which self-mortification metamorphoses itself into a refined and unconscious egoism is skillfully pictured. The poem deserves careful study.

nature of goodness seeks the standard within the vicissitudes of human experiences. The hedonist finds the criterion in pleasures and pains, either of the individual mind (Epicureanism) or of the society of minds (Utilitarianism). The energist denies that pleasure alone is a satisfactory criterion and enlarges the standard so as to include all of the ends which human beings normally hold to be valuable as a means to the maintenance and development of the entire personality conceived either in ego-centric (selfish or individualistic) or altruistic (social) terms. The ascetic, finally, hopes to attain goodness by the negative standard of self-abnegation and self-denial, which is regarded as a good in itself and valuable on its own account (Cynicism) or valuable only as a means to the attainment of a better life in the hereafter (religious asceticism).

§ 4. *Critical review and transition*

Looking back over the theories of goodness outlined in the present chapter, one can see that some of the sub-forms of each theory are open to easy criticism. That the standard of goodness exists external to the human mind, whether in the nature of things or in the arbitrary will of God, is, in the first place, not easily proved; and the thesis involves so many difficult implications that one is not willing to accept it if a simpler hypothesis be possible. Likewise, hedonism, both egoistic and social, can hardly be accounted a satisfactory view of the nature of intrinsic goodness; for many pleasures are deemed bad by us just as many pains are good, and some pleasures are held to be better than other pleasures, not because they are more intense or last longer, but because they are what they are. The pleasure one gets from loyalty to a noble cause, for example, even though it perchance be less intense, is better than the pleasure one might derive from lazily indulging oneself in idle fancies. And in the light of such facts it is difficult to see how pleasure, or its privation, could possibly be the ultimate criterion of intrinsic moral worth. Again, any theory of goodness which would identify it with individual interests exclusively, or even primarily, is open to question because it fails to take into account the society of minds of which each individual is a part; it forgets that the interests and welfare of the individual are inextricably bound up with the interests and welfare of the group. Finally, asceticism is unsatisfactory both practically and theoretically; it fixes too much attention upon the 'temptations' of life, it violates human nature by suppressing its tendencies, and it is a purely negative conception of goodness.

Taking into account only the main tenets of intuitionism and the teleological view of goodness without any reference to the variations in their formulation, two observations stand out fairly clearly. (*a*) In the first place, there would appear to be an element of truth in each theory which no sound view of life can afford to neglect. On the one side, the intuitionist's contention that the standard of goodness is somehow independent of the contingencies of human experience must be accepted in principle; otherwise the standard of morality degenerates into prudence and expediency, and a moral theory is rendered impossible. On the other side, the teleological theory makes goodness a matter of genuine concern in the practical affairs of human beings and gives to morality a precise content that can be concretely defined and scientifically observed. (*b*) And, in the second place, neither the intuitional nor the teleological view, taken by itself and in its extreme form, is ultimately satisfactory; each contains an element of truth which the other neglects. Intuitionism leaves the concept of goodness high and dry, so abstractly conceived as to prove baffling both in theory and practice; while the teleological theory, untouched by the principles of the intuitionist, tends to rob morality of that absolute authoritativeness which it undoubtedly possesses.

Further criticism of these theories, however, rightfully belongs to the science of ethics. For details the reader will have to consult the textbooks on ethics.[1] It remains for us here only to indicate that the problem of goodness is the seed-plot out of which other pressing problems grow. For we inevitably question concerning the conditions, the conservation and ultimate significance of goodness. Assuming that human beings may attain unto it, how is this possible? And of what significance is the fact of morality with reference to the continued existence of the individual and the ultimate nature of his environment? The former problem is the problem of free will. The latter brings us into the field of the religious consciousness and face to face with the age-old questions of immortality and the existence of God. These we shall consider in the following chapters.

Chapter XXIII. Questions and Exercises

1. Distinguish between the intuitional and the teleological views of goodness.

2. Indicate the chief sub-forms of: (*a*) The intuitional view; (*b*) The teleological view.

3. Give a brief interpretation and estimate of the thought of Tennyson's " St. Simeon Stylites."

[1] The following texts may be listed for further study: Wright, *Self-Realization,* especially Part II; Paulsen, *A System of Ethics,* Book II, Chapters I, II and VI; Everett, *Moral Values,* Chapters II–VI; Dewey and Tufts, *Ethics,* Part II, especially Chapters XII–XVIII; Palmer, *The Nature of Goodness;* Hyde, *Five Great Philosophies of Life.*

4. State concisely the arguments for, and the objections to, the several views of the standard of morality outlined in the text. (Read in connection with this question as many as possible of the references mentioned in the footnote to section 4 above.)

5. Make an outline of Paulsen, *A System of Ethics,* Chapter II of Book II. Compare with the point of view developed in Wright, *Self-Realization,* Part II, Chapters IV and V.

6. State briefly the main points in the conception of goodness defended by Miss Calkins in *The Good Man and the Good,* pp. 32–50, and 67–79.

7. Outline Rogers, *The Theory of Ethics,* Chapter I.

CHAPTER XXIV

CREATION OF GOODNESS: THE PROBLEM OF FREEDOM

The problem of human freedom is an ancient one in philosophical debate. The Greek philosophers, to be sure, were not generally concerned with it; they assumed that man is a free agent without greatly troubling themselves to inquire precisely what such an assumption implies. But with the beginning of the Christian era in European thought the problem assumed great importance, and from that time to the present it has been emphasized in debate upon the fundamental aspects of the moral and religious consciousness. And its persistence is indicative of the fact that it touches upon something of basal significance.

§ 1. *The problem of freedom and theology*

It is doubtless true that whether human freedom exists is a matter of considerable religious importance. Were man not in some genuine sense free, one cannot readily understand how the religious consciousness would be possible.

"Our wills are ours, to make them thine."

And this intimate connection between freedom and religion has, naturally enough, resulted in a logical connection between the problem of freedom and theological dogmas. A thoroughly comprehensive discussion of the problem appears to be inextricably bound up with theological speculations concerning God, man, and their relation to each other. And so it has happened, not infrequently in the historical development of the controversy, that discussion of the problem of free-will has wandered off into a labyrinth of questions about creation, predestination, and the like.

This is clearly illustrated in the writings of the thinkers of the Middle Ages. In the early centuries of the Christian era there was a group of thinkers, known as the Church Fathers, who were much interested in rationalizing the then new faith. This indeed was a necessity, since they found themselves compelled to bring their religious beliefs into harmony with the intellectual point of view which had been bequeathed by Greek thought to the Romans. In the course of their speculations the Fathers met, as was inevitable, many pressing problems. The problem of the origin of evil was one of these, and they rightly regarded it as of fundamental importance in a reasoned consideration of the doctrines basal to the Christian faith. They therefore discussed it at length and with considerable fervor. Two assumptions, or, rather, two theses which they supposed finally settled, lay at the bottom of the controversy. One of these was that man, having been created by God, must have been originally good and only good; the other was that man, as he now is, "is as prone to evil as the sparks are to fly upwards." How, then, did man come to be evil? The only answer that seemed to these thinkers logically possible was: Man himself is responsible. When God breathed into his nostrils the breath of life and man became a living soul, he was pure and spotless, untouched by sin, innocent of evil ways; through a free act of will Adam, the first man, disobeyed the command of God and fell, and with him fell the entire race of mankind. Evil is sin; sin is transgression of God's will, disobedience to God's commands; man's will transgressed. Thus came evil into the world; the free will of man is its gateway. The postulate of freedom is therefore necessary as an explanation of the fact of evil. This solution of the problem of freedom was, of course, not original with the Church Fathers; it is more or less clearly outlined in various passages of the epistles of St. Paul, particularly in those passages whose aim is to rationalize the atoning sacrifice on Calvary. But it was accepted, defended, and expanded by the early Fathers, especially St. Augustine; and it made its way into the views of St. Thomas Aquinas, Luther, Calvin, and a host of other theologians of the centuries following. Gradually it ramified through popular theology and has at last become so deeply rooted in it that to many minds a separation of the problem of freedom from its theological context seems impossible in any serious discussion of it.

It would be interesting and profitable to study these farther reaches of the debate, and we shall briefly return upon them later on when we come directly to discuss the religious consciousness. For a first approach to the problem of freedom, however, it is better to eliminate such considerations from the scope of our inquiry. Indeed, it is necessary to do so. Enmeshed in its theological setting the problem is practically hopeless from the beginning. There are here so many by-paths not clearly marked, so many labyrinths of traditional feelings and preconceptions, so much vagueness in short, that a straight-forward following of the main problem is rendered practically impossible. So we shall arbitrarily leave aside the religious bearing of the problem and endeavor to fix attention upon its simpler and more immediate phases. If by so doing we lose in comprehensiveness, we shall at least gain in definiteness. What is the empirical evidence that man is free, and in what sense may his freedom be defined? This is the question now before us.

§ 2. *The moral situation*

Before going on to a consideration of the question whose answer we are seeking, we must briefly enter upon a further preliminary statement which may serve to impress upon us the significance of our problem. In the preceding chapter we said that goodness is the seed-plot out of which the problem of freedom grows. Let us inquire a bit further into the meaning of this.

Many aspects of our environment we do not judge morally. The events of the physical order do not ordinarily fall within the scope of our moral judgments; though we may regard an earthquake as a tragic calamity, we do not say that it is bad in the moral sense of the term. It, like all natural events, is morally indifferent. And the same is true of the animal kingdom below man. We may for one reason or another hold the brute creation in esteem or disesteem, but it lies beyond the reach of our moral approbation or disapprobation. In their immediate application moral values belong exclusively to the social environment; they have to do only with human conduct and human institutions. But even here there are exceptions. The child that has not, as we say, reached the age of accountability, the permanently insane person, and the person momentarily deranged by the stress of extraordinary emotional excitement — these are not commonly regarded as strictly moral agents; we do not evaluate their acts or their character by reference to a moral standard. In short, there are some things we judge morally, and others we do not so judge; some persons are moral agerts, and others are not. Why these differences? Where do the boundaries of morality lie? What are the distinguishing marks of a moral situation?

Only a summary answer to the question will here be attempted.[1] It is commonly agreed that moral goodness, or the reverse, is present where responsibility (*moral*, not *legal*) is present. And by moral responsibility is meant such a relation between the agent and his deeds that he can be censured or praised because of them. Now this relation is commonly supposed to be conditioned by a certain initiative or spontaneity on the agent's part usually denoted by the phrase 'freedom of the will.' Thus freedom seems, in general opinion, to be the distinguishing mark of a moral situation; at least, it is apparently an indispensable element within the moral situation. No freedom, no goodness! — this is the common assumption. And there is reason to hold that it is more than an assumption. It would appear to touch something fundamental in the creation of moral values, and some of the greatest minds have attempted to establish its foundational character.[2] It might perhaps be more appropriately called — as Kant called it — a necessary postulate of morality than an assumption; certainly it is not an unsupported assumption.

Thus it is that the problem of freedom grows directly out

[1] For a detailed analysis of the moral situation see Dewey and Tufts, *Ethics*, Chapter X. This analysis is very suggestive; but the question is raised whether the definition of the moral situation resulting from it is comprehensive enough, since the definition excludes habitual responses which we commonly suppose are elements of the moral situation. The definition is: "Conduct as moral may be defined as activity called forth and directed by ideas of value or worth, where the values concerned are so mutually incompatible as to require consideration and selection before an overt action is entered upon." (p. 209.) Compare: De Laguna, *op. cit.*, Chapter III.

[2] The classic argument here is that advanced by Kant in his *Metaphysic of Morals* and *Critique of Practical Reason*. The argument is difficult, but it well repays study. The relevant parts of Paulsen's *Immanuel Kant* will prove helpful as a commentary.

of the concept of goodness. A consideration of the problem therefore is of extreme importance from the standpoint of the group of moral values.

§ 3. *The denial of freedom: fatalism*

The first view of freedom that we shall consider is an outright denial of it. This is the view of the fatalist who holds that every event in the universe, the human will included, is bound by the iron grip of eternal and immutable laws. There is no freedom anywhere, only an unbending necessity.

(1) STATEMENT OF FATALISM. Two emphases of fatalism should be distinguished, though in principle they are the same.

(a) *Natural events fixed absolutely.* On the one side, fatalism insists that every natural event — particularly death — is predetermined both as to the manner in which it shall occur and the time at which it shall take place. All events are bound to happen in a certain way and at a certain moment, and there is no possible interference with this necessity. "Thus a woman believed that she was fated to be drowned at sea; and when a steamer in which she had taken passage was wrecked, she refused to enter a life-boat, because, as she said, she would only bring disaster to the others in the boat. A Filipino quack doctor made the most extravagant claims with regard to his healing powers. When a number of his patients died, he was not in the least disconcerted. He had been perfectly able to cure them, he said, but *their time had come* — as, indeed, the fact of their death proved. And when a man's time has come to die, nothing can prevent it!"[1] This is one emphasis of fatalism.

[1] De Laguna, *Introduction to the Science of Ethics,* p. 57.

(b) ***Human destiny predetermined.*** **On the other side, fatalism emphasizes the thesis that the destiny of human beings is eternally fixed by the forces of the universe. The deeds one does, the sufferings one undergoes, the ideals one entertains, the character one has — these are the products of the external order of nature. What is to be in a man's life will be, down to the minutest details; his destiny is written in the stars, and nothing he or anybody else can do will change it in the least degree.**

> The Moving Finger writes; and, having writ,
> Moves on: nor all thy Piety nor Wit
> Shall lure it back to cancel half a Line,
> Nor all thy Tears wash out a word of it.

"Whatever may happen to thee, it was prepared for thee from all eternity; and the implication of causes was from eternity spinning the thread of thy being, and of that which is incident to it."[1] This is the strictly moral side of fatalism.

(2) ESTIMATE OF FATALISM. If the fatalist's contention be true, then clearly man's freedom is an impossibility; his world and he as a cog within it are rigidly bound by the iron laws of an unyielding necessity. That this contention contains some truth there need be no question. Every event in the universe presumably stands somehow related to other events;[2] and the finite individual is immersed in an engulfing environment which, as we have already urged, is of compelling significance to his life and character. There is in the fatalist's view, however, a deep-seated error. And that lies in his failure to take cognizance of the fact that in the ongoings of the world new events are

[1] Marcus Aurelius, *Meditations,* Book X, section 5. See the selections from the translation by Long given in Rand, *The Classical Moralists,* pp. 144–160.

[2] See the chapter above on causation.

continuously happening and that the destiny of each individual is to a very great degree dependent upon what the particular individual is and does. In other words, the fatalist overlooks the true significance of time. "There is nothing new under the sun" expresses an important truth, but it is an unwarranted exaggeration; there is also novelty, the continuous transformation of the old into the new. "Character is determined by environment" is, in its turn, not wholly erroneous; but it is only a half truth. The individual's ways of thinking and feeling are determining factors in the social order. "Dependent upon a cosmic Power we all indeed are, but the fact that this Power accomplishes certain ends only in and through our thinking and willing, is disregarded by fatalism."[1] For these reasons, then, it would appear that fatalism is an unsatisfactory view of man and his place in his world. The denial of freedom in any and every sense of the term flies in the face of facts, namely, moral values; the conception of the world as so rigid that in it moral values cannot bud and grow must in the end show itself to be unworthy of our intellectual allegiance.

§ 4. *Indeterminism and determinism*

Among those who insist upon freedom and so stand opposed to fatalism, there is a rather sharp difference of opinion concerning the meaning that is to be attached to freedom. In the main two views have been held, namely, indeterminism, or libertarianism, and determinism. In this section we shall try to understand what these views are; the section that follows will be devoted to a study of the arguments usually advanced in support of them.

(1) INDETERMINISM. This is the view that man's will

[1] Everett, *Moral Values*, p. 364.

is free in the sense that it is *uncaused*. At the moment of action, so the indeterminist holds, there are real alternatives before the will; one or the other may be chosen indifferently. To be sure, the agent's character, his past history and present purposes and impulses, exert an influence upon the will by delimiting the possibilities open to him in the moment of choice. What the indeterminist primarily insists upon is that there are always real possibilities open and that the choice might very well have been different. He finds freedom, thus, in a genuine spontaneity of the will that expresses itself in an undetermined choice within a limited field of possibilities.[1]

(2) DETERMINISM. The determinist maintains, on the other hand, that the agent's will is always determined in the moment of willing, not by wholly external forces as the fatalist claims, but by the tendencies, the impulses and purposes, that belong to the agent's character. The act of choice is not uncaused; like any other event, it is always an element within a causal situation. It is the result of conflicting forces, namely, the motives present in the moment of choice. These forces are not external to the agent's character, but are elements within it. Hence the individual is in a sense free — free, that is, to follow the bent of his own nature and to express in conduct tendencies that belong to him as a rational being. For the determinist, then, freedom is not to be sought in an uncaused spontaneous act of choice among alternatives, but in the capacity inherent in each moral agent to determine the bent of his own character. Freedom, in short, means for him, not indeterminism, but self-determinism — self-expression and self-development.

[1] This point of view is developed and defended by Professor James in an essay entitled, "The Dilemma of Determinism" published in the volume *The Will to Believe*.

(3) SUMMARY STATEMENT. The main point of difference between the indeterminist and the determinist is that the former insists upon an uncaused act of choice which the latter denies. Both agree that freedom is predicable of human experience. For the indeterminist, however, this freedom lies in a spontaneous and uncaused power to choose among given possibilities; whereas, for the determinist, freedom means the power which the individual has (the power of reason) to appreciate and consciously to follow the deeper demands of his own nature.

§ 5. *Arguments for the two points of view*

We pass now to a brief statement of the arguments usually advanced in support of the two views of freedom outlined in the preceding section.

(1) ARGUMENTS FOR INDETERMINISM. The arguments which the indeterminist advances in support of his thesis are mainly three:

(a) *Direct consciousness of freedom.* At the moment of choosing everyone feels that the act of choice is undetermined, and that the result of the choice might very easily have been different; if the choice were made over the opposite alternative could readily be accepted. This immediate (or 'intuitive') feeling that the act of choosing is arbitrary, which all of us experience in moments of decision, is one of the facts upon which the indeterminist builds his theory of an uncaused will. We feel that our will is uncaused, and it must be so.

(b) *Moral responsibility presupposes an undetermined will.* It is an ordinary fact of experience that moral agents are held responsible for their choices; that is, their choices are praised or censured *as their own.* The philanthropist is praised for his benevolence; the murderer is censured and punished for his crime. This attribution of responsibility would be wholly unreasonable, so the indeterminist argues, if man were not free in the moment of decision, that is, if it did not lie in his power to have decided otherwise. The fact of moral responsibility on the agent's part is, thus, a second pillar in support of indeterminism.

(c) *Indeterminism or fatalism.* Finally, the indeterminist argues that if his view is erroneous fatalism is necessarily true. Either freedom is impossible, or freedom means uncaused choice; there is no other alternative. Determinism is an unsatisfactory position which can be accepted only so long as it is not completely thought out; think it through and it will be seen to be logically indistinguishable from fatalism. The denial of freedom is implied in it. Indeterminism, therefore, is the only intelligible view of freedom.

(2) Arguments for determinism. On his side of the controversy the determinist presents the following arguments:

(a) *Psychological analysis of volition proves his case.* An unbiased analysis of the so-called act of choosing as it takes place in human experience reveals the fact that it always results from a given set of conditions and has no existence apart from these conditions. Every choice is motivated, and the strongest motive wins. To be sure, these determining factors are not external to the nature of the agent; they are elements within his character, *his* motives, and the neglect of this fact is the basal error of fatalism. But it is equally clear that they are causally related to the act of choice; they are the set of conditions out of which it springs and apart from which it simply would not happen. The philanthropist and the murderer choose as they do, because they are as they are; being as they are they could not do otherwise.[1] Psychological analysis proves determinism; it reveals no unmotived or uncaused act of choice, and hence there is none.

(b) *Moral responsibility presupposes determinism, not indeterminism.* That we attribute responsibility to moral agents for their deeds the determinist does not wish to deny. What he does deny is the indeterminist's claim that this is an argument for indeterminism as a view of freedom. If one could choose indifferently, without reference to what one has been in the past and to the motives or tendencies present at the moment of choice, one could hardly be held responsible for the results; for one could then claim, and with justice, that the deed after it is done is not his very own but only the product of the arbitrary will or choice of the moment. To be responsible for a deed, the deed must be mine. But how could a deed be mine now, if it was done in the past and was at the time the product of an arbitrary choice? Does it not belong exclusively to that arbitrary choice, and might I not now choose the exact opposite if it were to be done over again? So far from its being true, then, that indeterminism is implied in responsibility, responsibility is a difficulty in the way of the theory. Determinism alone offers a basis upon which to rest an intelligible justification of moral censure or praise.

(c) *Determinism in keeping with scientific assumptions concerning causation.* The scientific enterprise of mankind, as we have seen above, is based upon the general assumption that events are always found as elements within a causal situation. While it is true that this assumption cannot be specifically proved beyond question, it seems to

[1] Compare the famous statement of Luther at the time of his trial: "*Ich kann nicht anders.*"

be a fundamental postulate of reason and is justified by the progress of the sciences; it can therefore be taken as a reasonable hypothesis. Now, indeterminism stands in flat contradiction of it, since the will of man is made by this theory an exception to the law of causation. Determinism, on the other hand, stands in harmony with the postulate; the act of will is, as this view conceives it, like every other event in the world enmeshed in the causal nexus. And this fact, the determinist urges, is a strong support of his conception of freedom: it does not do violence to the scientific attitude of mind.

§ 6. *Critical estimate of arguments*

No attempt will be made in this section to award the decision in the controversy about free will. The student must think the matter through for himself, and arrive at his own decision. In his efforts to do this the following points may prove helpful:

(1) The first argument of the indeterminist is weak and inconclusive. Granting that there is a universal feeling of freedom (in the indeterminist's sense) at the moment of choice or decision — which is psychologically questionable, — it does not necessarily follow that freedom in this sense exists. The feeling that will is uncaused may signify nothing more than our ignorance of the causes actually operative within the decision.[1]

[1] Spinoza's statement on this point is classic. Let us assume, he says, "what ought to be universally admitted, namely, that all men are born ignorant of the causes of things, that all have the desire to seek for what is useful to them, and that they are conscious of such desire. Herefrom it follows that men think themselves free [in the indeterminist's sense] inasmuch as they are conscious of their volitions and desires, and never even dream, in their ignorance, of the causes which have disposed them so to wish and desire." (*Ethics,* Appendix to Part I; *Spinoza's Works,* Elwes' translation, Vol. II, p. 75.) In his correspondence he illustrates the point thus: "Conceive, I beg, that a stone, while continuing in motion, should

(2) As regards the argument from responsibility, this much seems evident: we do not ordinarily attribute responsibility to persons who are of such a nature that their present conduct is uninfluenced, consciously and selectively, by their past experiences. This is precisely the reason why we do not hold the immature child or the lunatic responsible morally; their activity is not called forth and directed by ideas of value or worth. Now is not any will, conceived as the indeterminist conceives it, in exactly this status? It would seem that a will which by hypothesis is totally uninfluenced *in its choice of the moment* is by definition irresponsible. The determinist scores here rather than the indeterminist.

(3) The indeterminist's argument that the disjunction confronting us is 'either indeterminism or fatalism' is not logically sound if the determinist can indicate *one* important difference between his view and that of the fatalist and at the same time keep from falling back into the in-

---

be capable of thinking and knowing, that it is endeavoring, as far as it can, to continue to move. Such a stone, being conscious merely of its own endeavor and not at all indifferent, would believe itself to be completely free, and would think that it continued in motion solely because of its own wish. This is that human freedom, which all boast that they possess, and which consists solely in the fact, that men are conscious of their own desire, but are ignorant of the causes whereby that desire has been determined." (*Spinoza's Works,* translation by Elwes, Vol. II, p. 390.)

Benedict Spinoza (1632–1677), of Jewish descent, was trained for the profession of a rabbi. He early decided, however, to devote his life to philosophical inquiry, and he carried out this decision despite poverty and persecution. The purity of his ideals and his unreserved loyalty to the search for truth make him one of the most picturesque figures in the history of philosophy. He was early excommunicated from the synagogue, and shunned by Jews and Christians alike. He has sometimes been called an atheist; the truth is he taught that God is the only reality. He lived the larger part of his life in solitary retirement in Holland. For an interesting account of his life see Pollock, *Spinoza: His Life and Philosophy,* Chapter I; a translation of the sentence of excommunication is given on pp. 17–18.

determinist's thesis. For an exclusive disjunction is logically valid only if it exhausts the possibilities in the situation.

(4) The determinist's appeals to the universal principle of causation and to concrete psychological analysis of motivation would appear to be strong points in his favor. In his first appeal he has behind him the postulate and procedure of all the sciences; in his second appeal the psychologist is with him, at least so far as specific acts of choice are concerned, since the psychologist admits no undetermined acts of choosing. From these two points of approach the position of the determinist would seem to be stronger than that of the indeterminist.

(5) Finally, the main significance of indeterminism, the element of truth within it, lies probably in its insistence that man is in some sense master of his destiny and is not merely the helpless sport of his environment. The significant points in determinism are: (*a*) its opposition to the notion that 'chance' is anything more than an expression for our ignorance of causal sequences; and (*b*) its insistence upon the rôle played by an individual's character, his tendencies to react, in the determination of his present conduct. As opposed to fatalism both views are right. Does determinism leave room for the element of truth emphasized by the indeterminist? — this is the question finally at issue in deciding between the relative merits of these two views of freedom.

Chapter XXIV. Questions and Exercises

1. Briefly explain why the problem of freedom of the will should so commonly be discussed in connection with theological questions.

2. Make a brief summary of the main points developed in the discussion of the moral situation in Dewey and Tufts, *Ethics,* Chapter X. Do the same for the discussion in De Laguna, *Introduction to the Science of Ethics,* Chapter III, Compare the two points of view.

3. Briefly explain fatalism. Wherein lies its basal error?

4. Distinguish clearly between the theories of indeterminism and determinism.

5. Give as concisely and definitely as possible your opinion as to the controversy between the two points of view, and the reasons why you think as you do.

6. Give a brief summary of the contents of the essay on "The Dilemma of Determinism" by Professor James in *The Will to Believe.* Compare the view of Rogers, *The Theory of Ethics,* Chapter V.

7. Summarize the main points in Paulsen, *A System of Ethics,* Book II, Chapter IX.

8. Analyze as completely as you can some important decision you have recently made; is there any sense in which it seems to you the decision was undetermined? Explain.

9. Study the psychology of volition as presented in any up-to-date text in psychology (see, for example: Dunlap, *A System of Psychology,* Chapter XV; Pillsbury, *The Essentials of Psychology,* Chapter XIII; or the chapters on volition in any other recent texts available to you), and indicate the bearing of the results of your study on the problem of free will.

CHAPTER XXV

ULTIMATE SIGNIFICANCE OF GOODNESS: BELIEF IN GOD

We turn now to a consideration of the problems of value directly connected with the religious consciousness of mankind. Religious beliefs are the most far-reaching beliefs of the human mind, and the problems to which they give rise are consequently among the most difficult to envisage. But they are inevitable problems emerging as they do from the deepest needs of the soul of man; and consequently, despite their baffling nature, they have been persistent in the course of man's intellectual enterprise. Two of these problems are of special concern to us in this introductory study of the problems of philosophy, namely, the problem of God and the problem of immortality. A survey of the latter will be undertaken after the first has been considered.

§ 1. *The idea of God*

It has been truly said that mankind is incurably religious. Wherever on the face of the earth man is found and at whatever level of civilization he may happen to be, he commonly has his religious beliefs and practices. Basal among these is the belief that there exists in the world something supra-human which works for man's weal or woe and which demands of him an attitude of reverence and worship. Such a belief seems indispensable to religion; it is a universal belief in mankind's religious experience, at least so far as the unreflective development of that experience is concerned. It is, of course, conceivable that one might formulate a religious code from which is omitted belief in God. This in fact has been done.[1] Such a formulation would naturally identify religion with morality and would identify God with Humanity, as is done by Comte. In what sense, if at all, this could be called a 'religion' we need not stop here to inquire. It is fairly clear, however, that this conception of life is pretty far removed from that which is usually called the religious view and which finds its expression in the great religions of the race; in the religious view as ordinarily understood the concept of God as in some real sense supra-human is fundamental. Whatever may be the genesis of the idea [2] or its justification, it is historically deeply embedded in all stages of progress from savagedom to civilization as a basal concept of the religious consciousness.

(1) SIGNIFICANCE OF THE IDEA IN SOCIAL EVOLUTION. The idea of God has been of tremendous practical significance in the social development of mankind throughout the ages. It has kept pace with the growth of moral ideals and has reacted powerfully upon them. A clear illustration of this is the story of the Hebrew people from the time of their nomadic wanderings in the wilderness of Sinai to the dawning of their national life in Palestine, as portrayed in

[1] See the religions of Positivism as formulated by Auguste Comte in his *Politique positive* (1824), and of the Ethical Culture Society as represented, for example, by Felix Adler's *An Ethical Philosophy of Life.*

Auguste Comte (1798–1857), born in Montpellier, France, was the son of an orthodox Roman Catholic family. He is chiefly memorable as the so-called founder of the science of sociology. It was his ambition to reform society, hence a knowledge of social laws, a *science* of society, was for him a practical necessity; and he devoted his life to the development of such a science. His new conception of religion, the worship of Humanity, was one phase of his new science.

[2] For a short psychological discussion of this point see Coe, *The Psychology of Religion,* Chapter VI

the writings of the Old Testament. With the deepening of the moral insight of the Jewish people through the vision of their prophets, Yahweh or Jehovah grows from a tribal deity interested in wars and burnt offerings into a universal God who requires of his followers that they do justly and love mercy; and the changing conception of Jehovah reacts powerfully upon the moral beliefs and practices of the people. The challenge was ever before them: "If Baal be god, serve him; if Jehovah, then serve him." And this challenge was a powerful stimulus to moral advancement. It may be possible for an individual to give lip-service in religious matters, and belie his profession by his practice; but such is hardly possible for a race. In the long run the God a people believes in is one of the surest indices to the deeper drift of its life; broadly speaking, it remains true that one cannot serve both God and mammon. On one important side, the history of mankind is the history of mankind's deities.

(2) Different meanings of the idea. It is obvious on little reflection that the word 'God' conveys different meanings to different minds. This is evident from observation of one's immediate neighbors; no two would appear to have in mind precisely the same meaning when speaking of God. And when observation is extended to the great religions of the world and to the historical evolution of these religions, the variation in the meaning of the idea of God is seen to be very great. These differences in meaning cannot here be traced in detail; for our purpose it is sufficient to note certain fundamental views that have marked the course of mankind's religious development. These may be classified as those which concern the nature of God, and those which turn upon the relation between God and the world-order.

(a) *Different conceptions of the nature of God.* As regards the nature of God there are two main views, namely, polytheism and monotheism.

Polytheism is the belief that there are many gods, separate and distinct, and more or less in conflict with each other's interests and purposes. This view finds its clearest exemplification in the national religions of antiquity, which undoubtedly have a direct historical connection with the simpler polytheistic views of more primitive ancestors.[1] The religions of classic Greece and Rome, of Babylonia, Assyria, and Egypt of ancient days were polytheistic. The Jews had great difficulty in growing away from polytheism; they long held to the conviction that Jehovah was only one among many gods, and their loyalty was not infrequently divided.[2] There are many gods, an indefinite number, and all are in some degree worthy to be worshipped and served — this is the polytheistic conception.

Monotheism, on the other hand, is the view that there is one and only one God, besides whom there is no other. From this point of view the gods of polytheism are superstitions, idols, aberrations of the human mind; the God-idea is unified, there is only one reality to which it refers. Some of the Jewish prophets, particularly the second Isaiah,[3] seem to have attained this conception some three

1 Cf. Wright, *A Student's Philosophy of Religion,* Chapter VI, particularly pp. 59–64, and the references there given.

2 Note the numerous references to idolatry in the Old Testament. Manasseh, for example, one of the late Kings and typical of many of the others, "did that which was evil in the sight of Jehovah, after the abominations of the nations whom Jehovah cast out before the children of Israel. For he built again the high places which Hezekiah his father had destroyed; and he reared up altars for Baal, and made an Asherah, as did King Ahab of Israel, and worshiped all the host of heaven [sun, stars, etc.] and served them." (II Kings, 21.) This worshiping and serving of other gods was a common occurrence in those days.

3 "Thus saith Jehovah, the King of Israel, and his Redeemer, Jehovah of hosts: I am the first, and I am the last; and besides me there is no God." (*Isaiah,* 44, 6.)

or four centuries before the Christian era. It certainly was the view of Jesus and his disciples; St. Paul laid special emphasis upon it. Mohammed is never tired of emphasizing in the *Koran:* "There is only one God, and Mohammed is His Prophet." And the unity of all things in Nirvana is the burden of Buddha's message. In short, all the great religions teach the monotheistic conception of God. It is true that the religion of Zoroaster appears at first glance to be an exception to this statement; the *Zend Avesta* is constantly speaking of two deities, namely, Ahura Mazda (the God of Light) and Ahriman (the God of Darkness). But even Zoroastrianism is essentially monotheistic, since the victory of Mazda appears assured or, at least, very probable; Ahriman seems about on the level with the Christian Satan. There is one God who, though perhaps compelled to struggle, is alone truly divine — this is the monotheistic conception.

(b) *Different views of the relation between God and the world-order.* There are here three views to be distinguished: deism, pantheism, and theism. All three are monotheistic; their difference lies in the manner in which the relation between God and the time-space order of the world is conceived.

For *deism* the relation is a purely external, or, as it is sometimes technically expressed, *transcendent*, one. That is to say, God by the deist is conceived as a self-conscious being who exists outside of and independent of the ongoings of the things and events which constitute what we usually call 'the world.' God is the Creator of the world; but the world by means of its own laws runs of itself without either coöperation or interference on the Creator's part. Indeed, the Creator is powerless to interfere, since these laws were made by him immutable. God, then, is the self-conscious Creator of the universe to which he stands related as the inventor is related to his invention — such is the deistic view of God and the world.[1]

Pantheism is diametrically opposed to deism. So far from separating God from the world as the deist does, the pantheist identifies God with the world-process. Everything is in God, God is in everything; God is all, all is God. Hence the name, pantheism (from the Greek words, *pan* = all, and *theos* = God). The pantheist, thus, wholly denies transcendence; God for him is entirely *immanent* within the space-time order. The best example of pantheism, among the great religions, is Buddhism; though mystics generally, whether Hindu or Christian, are apt to hold the pantheistic conception of God. For the mystic, no more than the pantheist, can escape from the feeling that God is everywhere.

> They reckon ill who leave me out;
> When me they fly, I am the wings;
> I am the doubter and the doubt,
> And I the hymn the Brahmin sings.

God equals everything, everything equals God — this is pantheism.

Theism undertakes to formulate a view of God and the world which is between the extremes of deism and pantheism. The theist is not willing to go the whole way with

[1] The deistic conception is historically connected with a group of English and French thinkers of the late seventeenth and the early eighteenth centuries. The English group are known as Deists, and the French group as Encyclopaedists. Prominent among them were: Toland (*Christianity not Mysterious*, 1696), Matthew Tindal (*Christianity as old as Creation*, 1730), Voltaire (*Lettres sur les Anglais*, 1733), and Holbach (*Système de la nature*, 1770). For an interesting general account of the period see Hibben, *The Philosophy of the Enlightenment*. Influences of this movement were felt in early American thought (see Riley, *American Philosophy*, Book III).

either the pantheist or the deist. With the deist he denies that God can without remainder be identified with the space-time order; and with the pantheist he denies that God can be wholly external to that order. He agrees that the deist is right in his insistence that God is in some sense more than the world; and, on the other hand, he agrees that the pantheist is right in his insistence that God is found within the world-order or nowhere. In short, he holds that God is both immanent within the world and transcendent to it. Putting these convictions together into a constructive view, the theist conceives God as a self-conscious being whose nature is expressed within the structure and process of the universe. God's immanence lies in the fact that the ongoings of the world-order are expressions of His experiences; His transcendence lies in the directive and controlling influence exerted by Him within the process through which His nature is realized. Christianity, in certain interpretations of it at any rate, approximates this conception. God is a self-conscious directive Power within the world, and His nature is closely connected with, if not actually causally affected by, the events within which it manifests itself — this is the view of God and the world which the theist would have us entertain.

(3) Importance of these differences in meaning. It is clear that these differences in meaning have an important bearing upon the reasoned consideration of the belief in God. It makes all the difference in the world to the validity of arguments, pro and con, about God which of the views above outlined is in question. Arguments and objections alike may have weight with reference to one conception, and at the same time be wholly irrelevant with reference to other views. For instance, arguments for a pantheistic God may have little or no significance relative

to a deistic God; and objections raised against the deistic view may be simply irrelevant so far as the theist is concerned. Much of the confusion that has attached to the theistic controversy may, in fact, be attributed to failure on the part of the disputants to state clearly which conception of God is in debate; it is inevitable that men, holding different views about their fundamental terms, should widely vary in their conclusions. Under such conditions they are not really reasoning, they are vainly fighting with shadows.

On the other hand, the reader must not fall into the error of assuming that it is an easy matter to choose among the conceptions of God that men have entertained, to select one as valid and discard the others as fictitious. These views are not wholly arbitrary; men are not deists, or pantheists, or theists, for no reasons. On the contrary, much can be said in support of each of these views. If one is to believe in God at all, one must be either a deist or a pantheist or a theist; and there are important considerations in support of each position. So it happens that, while the possibilities of choice are rather sharply limited, choice among these possibilities is by no means easy. The truth is that precisely this choice constitutes one crucial step in the debate on the problem of God. This step we shall try to take in the next chapter.

§ 2. *Genesis of the problem of God*

Why, one may ask, raise any question concerning God? Is it not purely arbitrary to do so? We believe in God, that is, the majority of us do; and is that not sufficient? Why ferret out any problem here? Is it not better to say to our hearts: "Adore and be still!"? This is a natural feeling, and we may here pause to determine its justification before launching upon our further inquiry; there is no need to waste time discussing idle questions.

(1) BELIEF IN GOD PRIOR TO THE PROBLEM. The human mind entertained a belief in God ages before there was any problem about such a being. The mind of primitive man, upon whose horizon the problem never dawned, believed none the less. Indeed, his belief was so intense and basal within his experience that the problem was rendered impossible. For, strictly speaking, the *problem* of God is choked by the religious attitude. The devotee does not question the existence or the nature of the object of his worship, because he believes so intensely in it; and the more devout he is, the more intense is his belief and consequently the more impossible is it for the problem to arise in his mind. His attitude is rather that of St. Paul: "I know whom I have believed, and am persuaded that he is able to keep that which I have committed unto him against that day." And one who steadily maintains this attitude will hardly feel the push of the problem involved in it. Let one but begin to reflect on this belief, however, and the problem inevitably emerges; it grows directly out of the belief through reflection upon it. Thus man reasons about God, not in order that he may believe in Him, but precisely because he does believe in Him.

(2) GENESIS OF THE PROBLEM OF GOD. What, then, is the logical genesis of the problem? Once man begins to reflect upon his belief in God, why is he driven to question His nature and existence? One or two suggestions may here be offered in reply.

(*a*) In the first place, variations in the belief itself make the problem inevitable. If there were only one belief about God, if the religious consciousness were not equivocal in its pronouncement concerning the object of its faith, one potent reason for the problem of God would undoubtedly be removed. But the religious consciousness is decidedly equivocal in its pronouncement in this regard; here there is a veritable Babeldom. For some believers there are many gods with widely varying characteristics, for others there is only one God though conceived with an endless variety of qualities; some believe that God is the artificer of the world-process, others identify Him precisely with the world-process; at times He is conceived as a jealous God interested in a chosen few, then again He is supposed to be no respecter of persons; in the faith of some He is a self-conscious personality with a will to accomplish certain ends, while in other faiths He is an unconscious Power, Nirvana, or Heaven; and so the confusion runs on *ad infinitum*. Of course, even an inkling of reflection reveals that such confusion is logically intolerable; obviously, not all of these views can be true. What shall we say then? Shall we refrain from questioning, that faith may abound? That is impossible, and the religious consciousness of mankind itself will not tolerate it. Thus out of beliefs in God grows the problem of God; the very diversity of faiths makes the problem an inevitable one. And, be it noted in passing, the problem is for religion a tremendously practical one. If Baal really be God we must serve him; if Jehovah, then we must serve Him. It makes a vast difference which we serve, and before we can choose we must know which is God. So the problem of God is of great practical significance. For the religious consciousness, indeed, it is of all problems the most profoundly practical; for "What will a man give in exchange for his soul"?

(*b*) Again, the developing moral experience of the race tends to make the problem of God an acute one. Religious faith assumes that God exists as the guardian of moral values, and that the righteous are the special objects of His interest and care. But there are many facts that seem to make against this assumption. Not infrequently the wicked flourish despite their wickedness, even it sometimes seems because of their wickedness; while sorrows and disappointment dog the footsteps of the righteous, and death itself may at times be the reward of their righteousness. Certain it is, as the most causal observation shows, that success or failure in the life that now is has little apparent connection with the attainment of goodness. How can this be, if there is a Power in the world 'that makes for righteousness'? The problem is as ancient as the more reflective moral and religious experience of the human race. In the Old Testament it is frequently broached; and it finds there its classic expression in the tragedy of Job.

> It is all one; therefore I say,
> He destroyeth the perfect and the wicked.
> If the scourge slay suddenly,
> He will mock at the trial of the innocent.
> The earth is given into the hand of the wicked;
> He covereth the faces of the judges thereof:
> If it be not he, who then is it?"
>
> (*Job*, Chapter IX, verses 22–24)

Must a man, then, serve God for nought? Can it be that God is indifferent to the fortunes of the righteous? Furthermore, in the second place, there seems to be a marked indifference in the forces of nature to those moral values which man so highly prizes. Face to face with these forces moral values appear utterly impotent and of no avail. They seem, as it were, but a flickering candle which is soon ruthlessly extinguished by what Professor James picturesquely calls "the vast driftings of the cosmic weather."

In the maelstrom of the physical environment moral distinctions have little significance.

> Streams will not curb their pride
> The just man not to entomb,
> Nor lightnings go aside
> To give his virtues room:
> Nor is that wind less rough which blows a good man's barge.

Once again, how can such things be? Is God impotent within His world? Is His "arm shortened that he cannot save"? Or, perchance, is man's faith vain? And so, once more, the problem of God is inevitable; it springs directly from the facts of moral experience.

(*c*) Finally, the push of the problem of God is felt in the developing scientific experiences of mankind. When the great French scientist, Laplace, had finished his famous work on astronomy (*Mecanique céleste — Celestial Mechanics*) he is said to have presented a copy of the book to Napoleon. In looking over the book the emperor could find in it no mention of God. He called this fact to the attention of Laplace, so the story goes, and the scientist replied: "Sire, I had no need of that hypothesis." In an important sense this is true of science generally. It has more and more consistently explained phenomena by natural causes, and has progressively eliminated from the world supernatural agencies. Phenomena which formerly were attributed to divine intervention — the flash of lightning, the storm-tossed sea, the changing seasons, the rising and setting of the sun, earthquakes, famine, and countless others — have by science been gradually referred to causes that are as natural and non-mysterious as the phenomena themselves. The hypothesis of God has grown less and less a scientific necessity until at present it is never mentioned in the texts of the sciences. Does this mean that the notion of God is scientifically useless? And does this imply, further, that the basal belief of the religious consciousness lies in contradiction of rational reflection on the nature of the world? Surely the mind of man cannot be thus at war with itself; the apparent contradiction must in some way be resoluble. And so from this angle the problem of God once more forces itself upon us.

(3) CONCLUSION OF THE SECTION. The problem of God is an inevitable problem of the human mind. Given belief in God and reflection upon that belief, the problem at once arises. Possessed of this belief and confronted by the wide divergencies in view within the religious consciousness itself and by the hard facts of the moral and scientific experience of the race, man cannot but cry unto himself: "Where is now thy God?" Whether by searching he can find Him out, whether he must finally confess that the search demands powers of vision beyond those which he possesses, or, tragically enough, that it ends in negative results — in any event, for better or worse, he is committed to the search. The problem of God, therefore, is not an idle problem to be taken or left at pleasure; it is for reflection inescapable. Nor is it a trivial problem; it is, on the contrary, one of the most profound problems that it is the privilege of man's mind to formulate, and its solution touches upon the deepest depths as well as the farthest reaches of man's experience and the environment in which it runs. Some of the evidences which seem to justify the belief and some of the difficulties that lie in the way of its justification we shall consider in the following chapter.

CHAPTER XXV. QUESTIONS AND EXERCISES

1. Differentiate between polytheism and monotheism.
2. Define: deism, pantheism, and theism.
3. Give a brief summary of Tennyson's poem entitled "The Higher Pantheism." Is the point of view of the poem identical with pantheism as defined in the text? Discuss fully.
4. Trace the main points outlined in the text under the genesis of the problem of God.
5. Make a short study of the conception of God in any one of the following religions: Buddhism, Mohammedanism, Zoroastrianism. (In connection with this study the following references will prove helpful and will offer suggestions concerning other sources of information: Wright, *A Student's Philosophy of Religion,* Chapter VIII; Menzies, *History of Religions;* Moore, *History of Religions* (2 vols.). Translations of the sacred writings of these religions will be found in different volumes of the *Sacred Books of the East.*)
6. Read carefully Perry, *The Approach to Philosophy,* chapters III–IV. Make a list of those points suggested in these chapters that seem to you of special importance in connection with the nature of the religious consciousness and its implications for philosophy.

CHAPTER XXVI

ULTIMATE SIGNIFICANCE OF GOODNESS: BELIEF IN GOD (CONTINUED)

We turn now to the task of surveying the critical consideration to which the problem of God has been subjected in the course of man's theological speculation. Such a survey may, despite its difficulty, prove helpful; it will at least emphasize the tremendous sweep of the problem in debate and the consequent danger either of seeking a short and easy solution or of pushing the problem aside as of no importance. "Can a man by searching find out God?" Whether he can or not, the search is inescapably his, and the prize sought is above rubies.

§ 1. *Arguments for the belief in God*

There are two general fields from which evidence in support of the belief in God has been drawn, namely, the physical and biological environment on the one side and the social environment on the other — the order of nature, and the mind of man. Thus it happens that the arguments for the belief fall into two classes, and it will be convenient for us to follow this division in our attempt to summarize these arguments.

(1) ARGUMENTS BASED ON THE NATURAL ORDER. In Chapter IX above we had occasion to note the fact that causation is a fundamental assumption of the intellectual enterprise, and to consider some of the problems connected

with it. It happens that this assumption or postulate of reason has played an important part in some of the arguments advanced in favor of the existence of God, and so we must here return upon it from this angle; what was said in the previous discussion of causation is presupposed and should be reviewed by the reader. The causal arguments for the existence of God are chiefly two: (*a*) the argument leading to a First Cause, and (*b*) the argument from design or, as it is sometimes called, the teleological argument.

(a) *First Cause.* Every event in the world, whether past or present or future, is, so the assumption or postulate of reason goes, an element within a causal situation; every event, that is to say, is a caused event. Furthermore, every cause is in its turn an element within a causal situation that leads beyond it; that is, every cause is also an effect. There is thus a causal series running back indefinitely into the past, radiating on all sides into the present, and, in imagination at least, stretching into the apparently endless reaches of the future; and this (or *these,* if causal pluralism holds) causal series we call 'the world.' Now, so the argument runs, there must be a Cause of the series of causes, a First Cause of all causal situations, a Cause of 'the world'; and this Cause is God. There are two forms of this argument, according as the notion of a 'first' cause is understood in the temporal or teleological sense; and these should be distinguished. Interpreted in the temporal sense, the argument is that God is the *beginning* of the causal series; interpreted in the teleogical sense, it is that God is the *unifying principle or ground* of the world as "the far-off divine event towards which the whole creation moves."[1]

[1] The argument that God is the Creator of the world which He produced out of nothing as held, for example, by St. Augustine (see Thilly,

(b) *Design.* There are evidences of design in the natural order. To illustrate: the lungs of land animals are adapted to breathing air, while fishes have gills rather than lungs since they are compelled to breathe the air dissolved in water; the coloration of animals varies with their environment so as to afford protection from enemies; the bones of birds are light, and so lessen their weight for flying; weak animals are alert and fleet of foot, and they are thus, despite their weakness, enabled to survive; man's upright position and the peculiar structure of his hands are admirably adapted to the exigencies and excellencies of his life; and so on. These evidences of contrivance in the world necessitate the inference that there is a Contriver of the world-order, and this Contriver is God. Such is the drift of the argument from design.[1]

(2) ARGUMENTS BASED ON THE SOCIAL ORDER. Here, again, two main types of argument present themselves according as the purely theoretical and ideational, or the moral and religious side of man's nature is emphasized.

History of Philosophy, pp. 149–150), involves the temporal meaning of a 'first' cause. Aristotle first clearly formulated the argument in its teleological sense (see Thilly, *ibid.,* pp. 82–85). His statement of the argument is bound up with his doctrine of 'form' and 'matter,' see Chapter X, section 4, above); God is the 'first' cause in the sense that He is the 'Pure Form' of the world-process.

[1] This was a common argument in the eighteenth century, and was then supposed to have great weight. The famous analogy of the watchmaker developed by Paley in his *Natural Theology* is a classic formulation of it: one can conclude from the evidences of design in the structure of a watch that it was fashioned by an intelligent maker; God is the superhuman watchmaker who has fashioned the machine of the world, and this we know because He has left traces of His intelligence embedded in its structure.

William Paley was archdeacon of Carlisle and sometime fellow of Christ's College, Cambridge. The more important of his writings are: *The Principles of Moral and Political Philosophy* (1785); *A View of the Evidences of Christianity* (1794), long used as a text-book; and *Natural Theology, or Evidences of the Existence and Attributes of the Deity collected from the Appearances of Nature* (1802).

(a) *The theoretical arguments.* The mind of man is a knowing mind; it forms ideas about the world, and it tests the validity of those ideas distinguishing the true from the erroneous. Upon this aspect of human experience two arguments concerning God have been built, namely, the traditional *ontological* argument and a more recent argument based upon the *possibility of error.*

The *ontological* argument undertakes to deduce the existence of God from the idea of Him entertained by the human mind. Briefly stated it is as follows: Our idea of God is the conception of something than which nothing greater can be conceived, since it involves the notion of perfection; now, since a non-existent being is not as perfect as an existent being, the idea of God would not be the greatest idea thinkable if God did not exist; but this is contrary to hypothesis, and therefore God exists. Q.E.D. In short, the perfection involved in the idea of God implies His existence, since, if he did not exist, He would be imperfect.[1]

The argument based upon the *possibility of error* is highly technical and difficult to state in short compass without eliminating from it at least some of its essential elements. The following summary may be ventured, however, as presenting its high points. Error is a fact of human knowledge; but what is an error? It is a mistaken judgment; a judgment that fails to agree with its object

[1] The first formulation of this argument is commonly associated with the name of the mediaeval thinker, St. Anselm, (1033–1109), one of the leading representatives of thinkers known as the Schoolmen. His formulation of it appears in his *Proslogium,* and he seems to have been the originator of it. Later, Descartes restates the argument, and in so doing brings into it the idea of causation which is eliminated from the argument as conceived by St. Anselm. Kant criticized the argument and pointed out several points of weakness in it; and his criticism has generally been accepted as demolishing the argument in its traditional form. Hegel attempts to restate it in such a way as to escape the force of the Kantian critique, but his restatement changes the argument radically and makes it inclusive of practically all of the arguments mentioned in this section.

is an erroneous judgment, as we have already seen in our chapter on truth. However, a single judgment by itself alone could not possibly be known to be erroneous, since it would perforce supposedly agree with its object; only when it is included in a higher judgment whose object is the completed object of the erroneous judgment is its error disclosed. For instance: if a traveller on the desert judge that he sees on the horizon an oasis but dies before he can reach it, he will die in the conviction that the oasis is there even though what he sees be only a mirage; could he but know the larger truth he would also know his error, and his judgment is erroneous only because of the larger truth which lies beyond him. The existence of error, thus, implies the existence of truth. Now there is an infinity of possible errors even with reference to any object; error arises when the judgment misses its object, and the misses are infinite in variety. Therefore, since error implies truth, an infinity of errors implies an absolute truth, an infinite system of truth, as its counterpart. But truth must exist in a mind; and an absolute system of truth can exist only in an Absolute Mind. The existence of an all-inclusive system of truth as the logical counterpart of all possible errors, which are infinite, implies the existence of a Mind capable of comprehending the system. In short, the existence of an infinity of possible errors implies the existence of a Mind before which all truth is actually and eternally present as a harmonious and non-contradictory system. And such a Mind is what we call in religion God. God, the all-knower, is thus proved by the very fallibility of human reason and its sense of its fallibility.[1]

[1] This ingenious argument is presented in various writings by Professor Royce (1855–1916), though he should not be held responsible for the argument precisely as formulated in the text. If the reader is curious to get Professor Royce's own statement of it, he should consult *The Religious Aspect of Philosophy* (1885), Chapter XI. The argument is further

(b) *The moral argument.* The moral argument undertakes to show that the moral experience of the race implies the existence of God. And the main road along which it advances is this: Moral values are objective at least in the sense that they are essential qualities of human nature; they are therefore real parts of the world-order in so far as human nature is a real part of the world-order; now man cannot but hold, and as we shall see in the following chapter there are reasons why he may hold, that he and his values are real; the world-order must consequently be in some sense a moral order, in the sense, namely, that there is room in it for man and the ideal of goodness which is basal to his nature; and this could not be unless the world-order is directed by a conscious rational Being who wills the final triumph of goodness; God exists therefore as the necessary implication of the objectivity of moral values.[1]

§ 2. *Evaluation of the arguments*

A complete survey of the preceding arguments is here impossible, but a few critical remarks may be made as an aid to further reflection on the student's part.

---

elaborated with special reference to the problem of God and defended against specific criticisms in *The Conception of God* (1897). The meat of the argument as Professor Royce conceives it may be put in his own disjunction: "Either there is no such thing as error, which statement is a flat self-contradiction, or else there is an infinite unity of conscious thought to which is present all possible truth" (*Religious Aspect of Philosophy,* p. 424). See Rogers, *English and American Philosophy Since 1800,* pp. 284–286.

[1] This line of argument was emphasized by Kant as the only conclusive proof of God's existence which the human mind can of its own initiative frame, and so it is commonly associated with his name. The formulation which he gives of the argument, however, does not put it in its best light. His statement of the argument is to be found in the *Critique of Practical Reason,* Chapter II, section V (Abbott's *Kant's Theory of Ethics,* pp. 220–229). Sorley's *Moral Values and the Idea of God* (1919) is a more elaborate and more convincing statement of the argument.

(1) ARGUMENTS BASED ON THE NATURAL ORDER. The arguments based upon evidence drawn from the natural order, one can readily see, are not wholly convincing, if, indeed, they carry any conviction.

Taken first in its temporal sense, the argument from First Cause is particularly weak. For one thing, it assumes that the cause (God) existed in its completion while the effect (the space-time order of things and events) was actually non-existent; and this contradicts our whole analysis of causation, which revealed that cause and effect are, as science conceives them at any rate, merely two sides or aspects of one total situation; the argument therefore uses the conception of causation in a non-scientific manner, and must either justify the unusual meaning it attaches to the notion or surrender its claim to validity. Again, the argument reduces God to the status of one event or fact within the series of events, gives him causal significance only at one instant, and so makes his existence of little logical concern; if God is assumed to exist merely as a *first* cause of the causal series, then there is little need of such an hypothesis — let one simply assume that the series had no beginning (and such an assumption is apparently as readily conceivable as that it had), and the one reason advanced by this argument in support of God's existence is removed. If we interpret the argument from First Cause in the teleological sense, it is in a little better case; but, so understood, it derives its strength from the fact that it then is in essentials identical with the argument from design and the moral argument. Finally, it is to be noted that the argument from First Cause, in either interpretation, assumes without proof that causal monism rather than causal pluralism is the true view of the causal series, since it would be meaningless if pluralism were true; and, as we have already pointed out in our discussion of causation, this assumption is at least debatable and cannot therefore be taken without question as the basis of an argument.

The argument from design has some weight. At least it brings the hypothesis under consideration into direct touch with ascertainable facts. Two points of serious criticism, however, stand fairly clearly against it. In the first place, while there are indisputably evidences of design in the causal order of the world there are also, and equally indisputably, evidences of lack of design and maladaptations, and these must be taken into account in the final reckoning; for it is a well established principle of reasoning that no competent discussion of a theory can overlook what are technically known as 'negative instances' — instances of facts, that is, which seem to stand opposed to the theory in question. In the second place, recent discoveries in science tend to show that what design there is in the world can be accounted for in terms of discoverable natural causes, such as adaptation on the part of organisms necessitated by the struggle to exist. This is a simpler hypothesis in that it involves fewer assumptions than the other, and so, if provable, must be accepted, since it is a fundamental principle of rational procedure that of two hypotheses advanced in explanation of a given set of data the simpler is preferable. The argument from design, thus, is unsatisfactory; it was very much more weighty in the minds of eighteenth century thinkers than it is to-day.

The general conclusion concerning the arguments based upon the physical and biological environment is, then, that they are at best unconvincing. To many minds there seems to be no open road through nature to God. Are the other arguments in better case? Is there a road through the social environment to God?

(2) ARGUMENTS BASED ON THE SOCIAL ORDER. The ontological argument in its traditional form certainly carries little conviction to the modern mind. To St. Anselm and his contemporaries it had more significance, because of certain peculiar views then entertained about the origin and significance of ideas generally.[1] But now-a-days it seems obvious that the argument, strictly taken, proves (if it proves anything) only that the idea of perfection implies the idea of existence; it certainly does not prove that there necessarily exists a perfect Being corresponding to the idea.[2] Furthermore, there is a false assumption which

[1] These peculiar views of the Middle Ages came to a focus in the protracted debate in which the thinkers of this period indulged concerning the problem of 'universals' and 'particulars.' This problem was whether 'universals' (general concepts or notions) have any real existence in and for themselves outside of the mind which thinks them, or are mere names or symbols which man has invented for convenience in dealing with the 'particulars' of experience (objects of sense perception). In other words, put in the form of the question we have already considered (see Chapter XI above) the problem is: Which are 'appearances' and which 'reality,' the universals of thought or the particulars of sense perceptions? Two answers were given to this question during the Middle Ages. On the one hand were the Nominalists, who held that 'universals' are not real but are appearances only; they are 'names' or symbols which man uses to refer to different convenient groupings of the 'particulars' of sense-experience. On the other hand were the Realists, who maintained that 'universals' are not mere appearances but are realities having an existence as truly as do the 'particulars' or sense-experience. The Nominalist would say: All 'universals' are manufactured for practical ends by the mind of man, and exist in it alone. The Realist would say: All 'universals' exist independently of the mind of man and in the nature of the environment. For the Nominalist 'particulars' only are real; for the Realist 'universals' are as real as, if not more real than, 'particulars.'

St. Anselm was a Realist, and it is not difficult to see that his ontological argument for the existence of God is based upon the assumption of Realism. For further discussion and explanation of the mediaeval controversy the general histories of philosophy should be consulted; De Wulf, *History of Mediaeval Philosophy*, goes into greater detail.

[2] St. Anselm's argument has frequently been subjected to criticism. The first attack upon it was made anonymously by a contemporary of

underlies the argument, namely, that the idea of 'perfection' is the same in all minds. The truth of the matter is, of course, that there is wide diversity of views about the notion of perfection, and the real meaning of it will doubtless long continue to be a subject of controversy.

In connection with Professor Royce's ingenious argument founded on the possibility of error it would seem that three crucial points in the argument are: (*a*) that error is only "an incomplete fragment of truth"; (*b*) that truth exists, and can exist, only in an inclusive thought or mind which knows both the truth and the error which is an "incomplete fragment" of it; and (*c*) that there is only One Truth, one system of judgments all mutually involved and harmoniously related, and not many separate and distinct *truths*. The validity of the first thesis would seem to turn upon the answer to the question whether a judgment may ever be so hopelessly erroneous as not to be in any sense true — whether, in other words, a judgment may be sheer error; if so, then not every error is a partial truth. The second thesis is open to debate on the basis of the assumption that there is any intelligible meaning in the assertion that a judgment may be true or erroneous even though its truth or error be wholly unknown to any mind.[1]

St. Anselm's, Gaunilo by name, who suggested that the same reasoning might prove the existence of a perfect island should one choose to entertain the notion of a perfect island. St. Thomas Aquinas later submitted the argument to detailed analysis. The classic criticism of the argument, however, is given by Kant in the division of the *Critique of Pure Reason* entitled "Transcendental Dialectic," Book II, section IV.

[1] The point here, if pursued, would lead directly into the current controversy between the two groups of contemporary thinkers usually called the 'idealists' and the 'neo-realists' concerning the relation between the 'object known' and the 'knowing' of it (between the object of judgment and the act of judging) and the implications of that relation. Something of the nature of this controversy may be learned from Leighton, *The Field of Philosophy* (definitive edition), Chapter XX, and the references there cited.

The third of Professor Royce's theses raises again the problem of pluralism and monism, with special emphasis upon the puzzling question whether all relations are 'internal,' or some of them at least are 'external.'[1]

The moral argument is generally taken to be the strongest argument for the existence of God. And there seems no question (to the writer's mind at least) that it has great weight, if one thesis be granted, namely, that moral values are objective in the sense that they are real qualities of the order of the world. Indeed, if this assumption be granted, the argument seems all but conclusive. If man (however and whenever he may have appeared in the stream of time) and his values are 'realities' and not mere 'appearances'; if his intelligence is a genuine illumination emerging from the forces of nature and not a mere spark accidentally struck in the Stygian darkness soon to be blown out by the "vast driftings of the cosmic weather"; if his values, and, particularly, his moral values, are expressive of something that is of ultimate and eternal significance; if, in short, the world can in any genuine sense be called a moral order — then, apparently, it is decidedly more reasonable to believe than not to believe that there is a directing Mind in the ongoings of things, guaranteeing, or at least strenuously fighting for, the conservation and consummation of goodness. If moral values are genuinely objective, then they are predicable of the world; and it is not easily comprehensible how this could be unless the world were spiritual in its deeper drifts.

It appears from the preceding estimate of the moral argument that its weight turns upon the assumption that moral values are genuinely objective, that is, are qualities of the world. Is there reason for holding this view of

[1] See above, Chapter IX, section 3.

moral values? This would seem to be the crucial question to which we are finally driven in our attempt to estimate the significance of the argument.

A complete answer to this question could hardly be given short of a special volume devoted to it.[1] The general line along which an affirmative answer might run may roughly be outlined as follows: In his moral life man struggles to realize an ideal; this ideal does not attain its full realization within his experience since it always lies in a sense beyond him, but it has validity for him and with reference to it he approves and disapproves, praises and censures; it must therefore be accredited a reality independent of human experience, and so the order of reality is partly at least a moral order; goodness, thus, is genuinely objective and is a quality of the nature of things. Professor Sorley puts the argument here summarily outlined as follows: "Of moral values it clearly holds that it is in persons that they are realized, not in mere things, and that they belong to persons in as truly objective a sense as any other characteristics belong to them. But something more than this is true. It is not merely the value actually realized in some one's conscious life that must be held to belong to objective reality. In bringing value into existence the individual person is conscious of a standard or ideal which has validity as a guide for his personal endeavor, or of an obligation which rests upon him. The attainment of value is recognized as a value only because of its conformity with this standard or law of value, or because of its approximation to this ideal of value. It follows therefore that the value or goodness actually achieved in per-

[1] The volume by Professor Sorley, *Moral Values and the Idea of God,* is an interesting, though for the beginner somewhat involved, survey of the general problem. This survey, however, is about as direct as the complexities of the problem will permit.

sonal life implies as its ground or condition a standard or ideal of goodness. Accordingly, we are compelled to form the conception of an ideal good or of a moral order, which, as the condition of actualized goodness, must also be regarded as in some sense having objective reality."[1] And so goodness is supposedly shown to be, not only in the world, but a truly significant feature of it. It is, in short, genuinely objective.[2]

(3) CONCLUSION OF SECTION. It would thus appear that the moral argument, while not finally conclusive perhaps, is sufficient answer to the cautious hesitancy of the agnostic and the positive attacks of the atheist. It gives us the rational right to believe. Linked with the argument outlined by Professor Royce its value is greatly increased. The other arguments, in certain interpretations at least, are not without significance; but, to meet the criticisms of them, they would have to be revised in principle and reduced essentially to one of these two. The First Cause argument, to have value, must be read in terms of the argument from design; and this, in turn, must be translated so that 'design' means the ordered system of things taken in their scientifically or rationally determinable setting. The ontological argument is hopelessly out of date so long as it remains in its traditional form; if brought up to date it is, to all intents and purposes, identified with the moral argument. So the two main lines of argument (the moral and the epistemological — Professor Royce's) leading to the idea of God focus in man and

[1] *Moral Values and the Idea of God,* pp. 508–509.

[2] It should be noted by the student that the above argument rests upon the conception of goodness as an ideal towards which the moral agent strives and which for him has absolute authority. Is this the correct view of goodness? Here we are brought back to the considerations of our Chapter XXIII on goodness and into the field of ethics.

his values. Through human nature, moral and theoretical, lies an apparently open road to God.

§ 3. *The nature of God*

Thus far the discussion has been directed towards the problem of the existence of God. In conclusion let us briefly inquire into the problem of the nature of God. Granted that we have a rational right to believe, in what sort of God are we at liberty to believe? Whom may we serve, Jehovah or Baal or both? May we be polytheists or monotheists, pantheists, or theists, at will? or must we choose among these views? And how choose?

While it is true that our preceding discussion has not directly concerned itself with the problem of the nature of God, the problem has all along been implicit in the arguments we have studied and they, by implication, have had much to say concerning it. Let us now shortly draw out some of these implications.

(1) Polytheism and deism. So far as polytheism is concerned, it is clear that none of the arguments outlined above have anything to do with it. This conception of the nature of God is simply ignored in the debate. Nor can any of the arguments be said to favor deism, with the exception of the argument from First Cause (in the temporal sense) and the argument from design; and both of these arguments, we have seen, are peculiarly weak. The argument which tries to identify God with a temporally first cause gets us nowhere save through an apparently unjustifiable use of the word 'cause.' Furthermore, the God it provides us with is a logically useless conception so far as the actual ongoing of life and the world is concerned; the simple assumption that the world had no beginning in time, an assumption which is as justifiable as the one on which

the argument rests, is sufficient to overthrow it. And the argument from design is in no better case, it gets what strength it has by closing its eyes to the non-purposive mal-adaptations with which the natural order teems. And if one tries to strengthen it by defining 'design' in terms of the rational sequences and the ordered workings of nature, it leads forthwith away from deism towards either theism or pantheism.

And from this it would seem to follow that the implication of reason (assuming, of course, that the arguments above summarized are the main arguments) is that neither polytheism nor deism can be accepted as conceptions of the true nature of God. What reason has to say on the problem of God's nature seems to be against the claims of both these views. And here reason is in agreement with the deeper drift of mankind's religious experience. All of the great religions are in principle monotheistic, as we have intimated above and as history plainly shows; and the God of these greater religions is no mere Contriver sitting outside his machine watching it go and either unwilling or powerless (or both) to interfere in its movements, but He is rather embedded deep in the structure of the world and seriously active in its affairs and destiny. So both reason and the more or less unreflective religious consciousness concur in the exclusion of polytheism and deism. They therefore must be set aside as unsatisfactory.

(2) Theism and pantheism. The field is thus apparently left to theism and pantheism. What can be said of their relative merits? Here the religious consciousness of mankind does not speak unequivocally. One of the great religions, at least, is thoroughly pantheistic; and it numbers among its devotees a large part of the human race. But Buddhism stands practically alone in this regard; the

other great religions, particularly Christianity and Mohammedanism, are predominantly theistic in their view of God. So it would appear that from the standpoint of the religious consciousness the weight of authority lies in favor of theism rather than pantheism; and this is certainly the case if it can be shown (as many hold it can be) that modern Christianity expresses the profoundest insight that the religious consciousness of man has yet attained.

Like the religious consciousness reason, too, hesitates between pantheism and theism. But here also the weight of authority would seem to favor the claims of theism. The arguments above enumerated, especially the strongest ones (the epistemological and the moral arguments), lead more directly towards theism; indeed, it would be difficult to reconcile them with a thorough-going pantheistic view of the world. And in the historical development of philosophical thought the greatest thinkers have, on the whole, inclined towards theism rather than pantheism. One of the most serious charges that a critic can bring against a philosophical system is the accusation that in its theodicy it is pantheistic. For in a pantheistic universe moral values are in danger of being choked, since there seems little room in such a world for that freedom from which, as we have already seen, goodness springs.

Such facts as these seem to establish a presumption in favor of the theistic rather than the pantheistic conception of God. After all, however, the issue must be settled, not by authority, but by a reasoned consideration of the facts themselves. As an assistance to further reflection on the reader's part I would suggest that the issue ultimately turns upon those moral values because of whose existence the hypothesis of God seems rationally necessary. In which world can these values best thrive, a theistic or a pantheistic one? With which world is freedom most easily reconciled? Which makes room more readily for the creation of values, and provides most securely for their conservation? These are the type of questions that must be answered as the issue is settled; and they are the questions whose answers will lead, if I mistake not, towards theism and away from pantheism. For if it be true that

> We are no other than a moving row
> Of Magic Shadow-shapes that come and go
> Round this Sun-illumined Lantern held
> In Midnight by the Master of the Show;
>
> Impotent pieces of the Game He plays
> Upon this Checker-board of Nights and Days;

then moral values wither and fade away; they are as the grass of the field. Whether pantheism makes of life such a puppet-show may be questioned; but, strictly interpreted, it would seem to threaten precisely such a tragedy. Theism, on the other hand, gives a freer range to our moral wings and does not, at least need not, turn our moral values into a deception and illusion. But the reader must here be left to his own reflection for further pursuit of the problem.

(3) Two TYPES OF THEISM. If one accepts theism, however, one's perplexities are not at an end. For the troublesome question concerning the precise manner in which God is related to the world, particularly to finite conscious minds, presents itself. If God be a self-conscious Being working His will in the world, how can His relation to other wills, finite human wills, be conceived? I raise this question, in conclusion of this section, not to answer it, but to emphasize its importance for theism. Two views have been advanced, and I will briefly state each

and give references for the curious. Professor Royce argues that God must be conceived as an absolutely all-comprehensive mind or will in which exists everything that may be said to have existence; our wills, then, exist as a part of God's will and our thoughts are fragmentary parts of His all-inclusive thought. This looks very much like pantheism, but Professor Royce assures us it is not. But the argument by which he undertakes to justify his position the reader should learn in Professor Royce's own words.[1] Professor James, on the other hand, maintains that the only conceivable relation that a theist can hold exists between God and man is that of fellow-workers in a common cause, namely, the struggle against evil. But does this not make God, if not finite, then at least less than absolute by placing over against Him something (evil) which in some genuine sense lies beyond Him? Professor James answers in the affirmative; but he contends that this view of God is alone in the final analysis tenable, and that such is the God whom Christians worship and reverence. But Professor James also must be permitted to speak for himself.[2] The issue is a big one, and a little reflection will disclose the fact that it is of fundamental importance not only in connection with the problem of God but also in connection with the problem of freedom of will and other problems that at first glance seem to lie far afield.

[1] See the *Conception of God*, particularly the "Supplementary Essay."

[2] See *Pragmatism*, Lectures IV and VIII; and *Varieties of Religious Experience*, pp. 524–526. His general point of view is developed more elaborately in *A Pluralistic Universe*. In the passage in *Varieties of Religious Experience* Professor James speaks of his view as a sort of polytheism; but it is a polytheism in a sense very different from the meaning given to the term in the text above.

This view of a limited deity has entered into the literature of the day. See, for example, Wells: *God the Invisible King*, and *Mr. Britling Sees it Through*.

CHAPTER XXVI. QUESTIONS AND EXERCISES

1. Make a special study of one of the arguments for the existence of God mentioned in the text, and write a report on it.

2. Summarize the main points developed in Seth, *Ethical Principles*, Part III, Chapter II.

3. Write a short critical review of the argument advanced by Hudson in his *The Truths We Live By*, Chapter VIII.

4. Outline Coe's discussion of the genesis of the idea of God in *The Psychology of Religion*, Chapter VI. Does this have any bearing on the problem of the validity of the idea of God? Discuss briefly.

5. Outline the main points in the survey of religion and the meaning of God given by Hoernlé, *Matter, Life, Mind, and God*, Lecture V.

6. Compare and contrast the views of Royce and James with regard to the nature of God. (For references see the footnotes to the last paragraph above; Wright, *A Student's Philosophy of Religion*, pp. 376–387; and Leighton, *The Field of Philosophy*, Index.)

7. Outline the proof of God's existence offered by Locke in *An Essay Concerning Human Understanding*, Book IV, Chapter X.

CHAPTER XXVII

CONSERVATION OF GOODNESS: BELIEF IN IMMORTALITY

We turn now, in conclusion of our survey of the problems of philosophy, to a consideration of the second great venture of the religious consciousness, namely, belief in immortality. Like the belief in God, this is a widespread and apparently basal faith of most of the great religions of mankind. Is it a rational faith, or is it only the blind expression of a groundless will to believe? Let us undertake to see how the matter at present stands.

§ 1. *Belief in immortality*

It is by no means clear that all people believe in immortality, as is sometimes assumed. On the contrary, it is quite clear that such is not the case. There are many individuals who do not hold such a belief, as is abundantly shown in such a statistical study as that made by Professor Leuba in Part II of his *The Belief in God and Immortality*. It is also not to be forgotten that primitive peoples generally have no belief in immortality in the usual meaning of the term. To be sure they pretty generally believe in some sort of survival after death, but the 'ghosts' or 'spirits' which are by them supposed to survive enjoy no existence comparable to that which the modern man thinks of as immortality.[1] And it is to be remembered also that one of the great religions of the world, Buddhism, denies

[1] See Leuba, *The Belief in God and Immortality*, Chapters I–IV.

the desirability of immortality and seeks a way of escape from it.

On the other hand, there are many who yearn for and believe in continuance of personal existence in a happier state than this, where presumably gross inequalities and apparently undeserved misfortune shall be righted and "sorrow and sighing shall flee away." Such a belief is deeply embedded in most of the great religions, particularly Christianity and Mohammedanism; and even Buddhism is not without its conviction that a sort of immortality, however undesirable and dreaded it may be, is the lot of all who have not received complete and final illumination in the "eight-fold path" that shows the way of escape from its thralldom. Over against the many unbelievers stand, then, the host of those who believe, if not in the desirability of immortality, at least in its reality.

Thus humanity is divided into two groups with reference to the belief in personal survival of bodily death. It would perhaps be impossible to say into which group the majority fall, though the supposition generally accepted is that the believers outnumber the unbelievers. However that may be, these two groups exist; that is an indisputable psychological and historical fact.

§ 2. *The problem of immortality*

For those who venture to believe in personal survival of death, "the Arch Fear in a visible form" is a formidable monster. There is no escape from his power. All that breathe must die — this is the irresistible truth which common observation and scientific discovery alike force upon us. Death is a universal and, we now know, necessary biological phenomenon.

Out — out are the lights — out all!
And over each quivering form
The curtain, a funeral pall,
Comes down with the rush of a storm,
While the angels, all pallid and wan,
Uprising, unveiling, affirm
That the play is the tragedy "Man,"
And its hero the Conqueror Worm.
(Poe: "The Conqueror Worm.")

Translated into plain prose this allegory states a simple biological fact. And so between the believer in immortality and his paradise there flows the cold and sullen stream into which all must enter and egress from which is possible, if at all, only on the farther bank which is ever hid in apparently impenetrable mists. Where then is there justification for the belief in immortality? Face to face with the inevitable Catastrophe, can man still believe? Has the believer a rational right to his faith?

The history of the reasoned consideration of the problem of immortality is the story of the attempts that man has made to square the hypothesis of immortality with his intellectual conscience. Some have insisted that this can be done only through an out-and-out denial of the hypothesis; others have held that the hypothesis can be made consistent with a reasoned view of the world. Our purpose in the present brief study of the problem is to acquaint ourselves with the arguments that have been marshalled in support of this latter view. Only the main arguments fall here to be considered; and even among them we shall be compelled to leave on one side those which, because of their intimate connection with certain historical systems of philosophy, are unintelligible apart from those systems.[1]

[1] The reference here is to such arguments as those involved in the systems of Spinoza and Hegel — to mention two outstanding examples.

§ 3. *The agnosticism of Socrates*

Socrates was deeply interested in problems connected with human life. Though his primary concern was with the problems that have to do directly with the present life, he was not wholly indifferent to the mysteries of the future; and we may readily suppose that his interest in the problem of immortality was greatly increased during those last few days of his life between his condemnation and his tragic end. If we may accept the account given by Plato in the *Apology* as an approximately faithful exposition of Socrates's final views on immortality, we may say that this remarkable thinker got no farther with the problem than an optimistic agnosticism. He argues, in effect, that we do not certainly know whether there is anything like a personal life after death; but, whether there is or whether there is not, death, at least for those who in this life have lived well, is a gain. For if, on the one hand, death is the complete cessation of consciousness, all sensation ceases and with it all cares and sorrows; death is then but a restful, dreamless sleep from which there is no waking.[1] If,

[1] Compare the musical lines of Swinburne:

From too much love of living,
From hope and fear set free,
We thank with brief thanksgiving
Whatever gods may be
That no life lives forever;
That dead men rise up never;
That even the weariest river
Winds somewhere safe to sea.

Then star nor sun shall waken,
Nor any change of light;
Nor sound of waters shaken,
Nor any sound or sight;
Nor wintry leaves nor vernal,
Nor days nor things diurnal;
Only the sleep eternal
In an eternal night.

(*The Garden of Proserpina*)

on the other hand, death is not the end of all, then there is something beyond which, to the good man at least, offers untold possibilities of happiness and development. So in either event, whether death is the final act of the drama of life or is only the beginning of a new play, for the good man there is in it nothing but gain.

Plato's inimitable statement of this argument must here be set down in part; the student should read it entire and in its dramatic setting. It is the conclusion of Socrates's speech of defense before his judges, and is delivered after the sentence of death has been pronounced upon him. Having prophesied that soon after his death his judges will be called to account for his unjust execution and having expressed his conviction that death to him can be no evil since his accustomed 'sign'[1] has not warned him to the contrary, he continues: "And if we reflect in another way we shall see that we may well hope that death is a good. For the state of death is one of two things: either the dead man wholly ceases to be, and loses all sensation; or, according to the common belief, it is a change and a migration of the soul unto another place. And if death is the absence of all sensation, and like the sleep of one whose slumbers are unbroken by any dreams, it will be a wonderful gain. For if a man had to select that night in which he slept so soundly that he did not even see any dreams, and had to compare with it all the other nights and days of his life, and then had to say how many days and nights in his life he had spent better and more pleasantly than this night, I think that a private person, nay,

[1] Socrates often speaks of this 'sign' or 'inner voice' which frequently warned him when he was about to undertake that which, as he said, was not for his good. It seems that the 'sign' was negative merely, telling him what not to do. Socrates apparently regarded it with religious awe and reverence; Plato usually makes him speak of it as divine, "the sign of God."

even the great King [of Persia] himself, would find them easy to count, compared with the others. If that is the nature of death, I for one count it a gain. For then it appears that eternity is nothing more than a single night. But if death is a journey to another place, and the common belief be true, that there are all who have died, what good could be greater than this, my judges? Would a journey not be worth taking, at the end of which, in the other world, we should be released from the self-styled judges who are here, and should find the true judges, who are said to sit in judgment below, such as Minos, and Rhadamanthus, and Aeacus, and Triptolemus, and the other demi-gods who were just in their lives? . . . I am willing to die many times, if this be true. . . . And, above all, I could spend my time in examining those who are there, as I examine men here, and in finding out which of them is wise, and which of them thinks himself wise, when he is not wise. What would we not give, my judges, to be able to examine the leader of the great expedition against Troy, or Odysseus, or Sisyphus, or countless other men and women whom we could name? It would be an infinite happiness to converse with them, and to live with them, and to examine them. Assuredly there they do not put men to death for doing that. For besides the other ways in which they are happier than we are, they are immortal, at least if the common belief be true.

"And you, too, judges, must face death with a good courage, and believe this as a truth, that no evil can happen to a good man, either in life, or after death. . . .

"But now the time has come, and we must go hence; I to die, and you to live. Whether life or death is better is known to God, and to God only." [1]

[1] From Church's translation of the *Apology* in the volume, *The Trial and Death of Socrates* (Macmillan, "Golden Treasury Series," pp. 76–78).

§ 4. *Argument based on the 'simplicity' of the soul*

Plato was not himself content to accept the cheerful agnosticism of his master concerning immortality. He demanded a fuller inquiry into the problem. Such an inquiry he undertakes in his various dialogues, and he develops some ten arguments by which he thinks the immortality of the soul can be rationally established.[1] Among these there is one of great historical importance, namely, that which is based upon the supposed 'simplicity' of the soul. The soul — so the argument runs — is a simple entity in the sense that it is uncompounded; it is therefore indissoluble; hence by its very nature the soul cannot die, since death is nothing but dissolution.[2]

This argument was accepted in principle by many later thinkers. During the Middle Ages it was commonly regarded as one of the strongest arguments for immortality, though naturally it was colored by the theological bias of the thinkers of this period. And in modern thought, down at least to the time of Hume and Kant, the argument was by many supposed to have great weight. Berkeley, for instance, ends a discussion of the problem with the following conclusion: "We have shewn that the soul is indivisible, incorporeal, unextended; and it is consequently incorruptible. Nothing can be plainer than that the motions, changes, decays, and dissolutions which we hourly see befall natural bodies (and which is what we mean by the *course of nature*) cannot possibly affect an active, simple, uncompounded substance: such a being therefore is

[1] For a summary statement of these Platonic arguments for immortality see the article on "Immortality" by Hammond in the *Encyclopedia Americana*.

[2] See the *Phaedo*, 78, 79 (Church's translation in the *Trial and Death of Socrates*, pp. 143–147).

indissoluble by the force of nature; that is to say — *the soul of man is naturally immortal.*" [1]. The soul of man is 'simple,' that is, uncompounded; it is therefore by nature incapable of disruption, and hence by nature is immortal — such is one of the very ancient arguments for the immortality of the soul.

§ 5. *The moral argument*

Plato suggests another argument which has played an important rôle in the controversy about immortality. It is contained in the following passage from the *Phaedo:* "And shall we believe that the soul, which is invisible, and which goes hence to a place that is like herself, glorious, and pure, and invisible, to Hades, which is rightly called the unseen world, to dwell with the good and wise God, whither, if it be the will of God, my soul too must shortly go; — shall we believe that the soul, whose nature is so glorious, and pure, and invisible, is blown away by the winds and perishes as soon as she leaves the body, as the world says?" [2] The obvious answer implied in this ques-

[1] *Principles of Human Knowledge,* section 141 (*Berkeley's Complete Works,* edited by A. C. Fraser, Vol. I, p. 337). The same argument is found in Butler's *Analogy,* Part I, Chapter I. Descartes also accepts it in principle.

[2] *Phaedo,* 79; Church's translation, *op. cit.,* p. 148. Socrates is the speaker, addressing his friend on the day of his death; but the thought is probably the thought of Plato rather than of Socrates. Compare Tennyson's famous lines in *In Memoriam:*

> And he, shall he,
> Man, her last work, who seem'd so fair,
> Such splendid purpose in his eyes,
> Who roll'd the psalm to wintry skies,
> Who built him fanes of fruitless prayer,
>
> Who trusted God was love indeed
> And love Creation's final law —
> Tho' Nature, red in tooth and claw
> With ravine, shriek'd against his creed —

tion is, No! And the burden of its argument is that man's moral nature, the 'divine' element within him, demands immortality. This argument was emphasized among modern thinkers particularly by Kant,[1] and since Kant's day it has come to be generally regarded as one of the strongest arguments for immortality. It permeates the literature dealing with the problem. There are two sides of the argument which we may separate for purposes of emphasis.

The first is that justice demands immortality. In this life the virtuous soul is not always rewarded according to its deserts. This cannot be the final status of affairs if morality is of ultimate significance; virtue must be rewarded and vice punished, else the world is unmoral and unreasonable. But this requires a future life in which inequalities may be adjusted and wrongs righted. Plato himself lays great stress upon this side of the argument, both in the *Phaedo* and in the *Republic*.[2] And Kant, among the moderns, made it fundamental even to belief in the existence of God. "If we suppose, for the sake of illustration, that there exists a rational Being who has all power, it cannot be in accordance with the whole will of such a being, that his creatures should be unable to secure the happiness which their nature demands and of

---

Who loved, who suffer'd countless ills,
Who battled for the True, the Just,
Be blown about the desert dust,
Or seal'd within the iron hills?

(LVI)

[1] See the *Critique of Practical Reason*, Book II, Chapter II, section IV.

[2] "In the case of the just man, we must assume that, whether poverty be his lot, or sickness, or any other reputed evil, all will work for his final advantage, either in this life or in the next. For unquestionably, the gods can never neglect a man who determines to strive earnestly to become just, and by the practice of virtue to grow as much like God as man is permitted to do" (*Republic*, 613; translation by Davies and Vaughan, Macmillan's "Golden Treasury Series," p. 360).

which their obedience to the moral law makes them worthy. The highest good of a possible world must therefore consist in the union of virtue and happiness in the same person, that is, in happiness exactly proportioned to morality."[1] And this necessitates the assumption that the individual person continues to exist after this life, for in this life it is certain that happiness and morality are not "exactly proportioned."

The other side of the argument is that the moral life is a struggle to attain an ideal which can never in this life be attained, namely, the ideal of complete and perfect goodness. Therefore, either morality is a deception and a cheat or the moral agent survives death endlessly. Kant also places emphasis on this side of the argument. Moral endeavor, he points out, is progress from lower to higher levels of achievement, an endless approximation towards goodness. "Now, this infinite progress is possible only if we presuppose that the existence of a rational being is prolonged to infinity, and that he retains his personality for all time. This is what we mean by immortality of the soul. The highest good is therefore practically possible, only if we presuppose the immortality of the soul."[2]

According to the moral argument, then, immortality is a necessary presupposition of moral experience, a 'moral postulate' as Kant phrases it. Without this postulate justice is defeated and the moral struggle towards the ideal is meaningless. If moral values are objective, if, that is, we can speak of reality as in any intelligible sense moral, personality in which these values inhere must also be real; bodily death cannot be equivalent to spiritual or personal death. The 'soul' must live on. "In our present phase

[1] Watson, *Selections from Kant*, pp. 291–292.

[2] Watson, *Selections from Kant*, p. 295. Compare Tennyson's *In Memoriam*, sections XXXIV, LIV–LVI; and Browning's *Prospice*.

of existence the moral life cannot be lived out to its completion, it is not permitted to display its full fruitage of consequences for good and evil. Whenever Might triumphs over Right; whenever the evil doers succeed and the righteous perish; whenever goodness is trampled under foot and wickedness is exalted to high places; nay, whenever the moral development of character is cut short by death, — we are brought face to face with facts which constitute an indictment of cosmic justice, which are inconsistent with the conception of the world as a moral order. . . . How shall the ethical harmony be restored if not by the supposition of the prolongation and perfection of the moral life in the future? Only so can character be made of real significance in the scheme of things; only so it is something worth possessing, an investment more permanent and more decisive of our weal and woe than all the outward goods that men set their hearts upon. . . ."[1]

§ 6. *Empirical proof: psychical research*

During recent years a systematic effort has been made, through direct observation of alleged spirit activities, to bring the problem of immortality under something approximating experimental control and to solve it through scientific induction. To this end the Society for Psychical Research was founded in 1882. Many eminent men have belonged to the Society, such as Henry Sidgwick, Tennyson, Ruskin, Gladstone, Sir W. F. Barrett, Sir Oliver Lodge, A. J. Balfour, Sir W. Crookes, and William James — to mention only a few of the outstanding ones. The findings of the Society have been published in a series of volumes known as the *Proceedings of the Society for Psychical Re-*

[1] F. C. S. Schiller, *Humanism, Philosophical Essays,* 1903, pp. 252–253.

search. Some of the members of the Society, as Sir Oliver Lodge for example, are convinced that immortality has been definitely established by these findings; but others remain skeptical.[1]

The phenomena with which the Society deals fall mainly into two classes. First, there are the physical phenomena. These include the alleged movements of objects, responsive raps, levitation of human beings, noises and music, luminous appearances — all without known physical causes. The second class of phenomena are the psychical, which include thought-transference both in the normal and in the hypnotic state, phantasms of the living and dead, automatic writing or speaking of messages which lie beyond the medium's knowledge, and cross-correspondences. Concrete examples of each class of phenomena may be found in abundance in the *Proceedings* of the Society.[2]

Many of these phenomena, and perhaps most of them, are commonly regarded as having no relevancy concerning the problem of immortality. They can obviously be accounted for in terms of natural causes, and there is no need to search further for an explanation of them. There are other phenomena, however, particularly automatic messages and cross-correspondences, which are by some held to be inexplicable except upon the assumption that "there is some active intelligence at work behind, and apart from, the automatist, an intelligence which is more

[1] For a brief but fairly comprehensive survey of the history of the Society and its work up to 1911 see W. F. Barrett, *Psychical Research.* F. W. H. Myers, *Human Personality and its Survival of Bodily Death* (2 Vols.), gives an exhaustive account of many phenomena.

Sir Oliver Lodge remained for a long time skeptical, but in his recent book, *Raymond,* he accepts the hypothesis as established. An interesting critical survey will be found in Frank Podmore's *The Newer Spiritualism* (second impression, 1911).

[2] See Podmore, *op. cit.,* especially Book I, Chapters II–IV; and Book II, Chapters IV–VI.

like the deceased person it professes to be than that of any other we can imagine. And though the intelligence is provokingly irritating in the way it evades simple direct replies to questions, yet it is difficult to find any other solution to the problem of these scripts and cross-correspondences than that there is an attempt at intelligent co-operation between certain disembodied minds and our own."[1] Whether this could be called immortality is a debatable question; certainly it could hardly be called immortality in the ordinary meaning of the term. But if such an inference is logically necessary, whether it prove immortality or not, it certainly has an important bearing on the problem.

Psychical research, then, seems to some of its devotees to lead to this conclusion, namely, that the hypothesis of survival of bodily death is a scientifically necessary one. The argument by which the conclusion is reached is two fold. First, that there are indisputable facts that cannot be accounted for by reference to natural causes, in so far as these natural causes are known or are conceivable in terms of what is known. Second, that the hypothesis of the continued existence of spirits after death will explain these phenomena, and it is the simplest hypothesis which will explain them. If this be not proof of immortality, it at least opens the way to it by showing that the "Conqueror Worm" is not invincible. For some members of the Society even this would be an over-optimistic statement of the case, for others it would be entirely too conservative, while to others it would be acceptable as approximately correct.

[1] Barrett, *Psychical Research,* p. 245.

§ 7. *Critical review of arguments*

In attempting to estimate the logical value of the preceding arguments for belief in immortality, the following points should be borne in mind:

(1) The argument based upon the supposed 'simplicity' of the soul assumes that the traditional spiritual-substance theory of the soul is in principle correct. This theory, however, as we have already seen,[1] has been subjected to a vigorous criticism by both Hume and Kant, and that criticism has been generally accepted by later thinkers as valid. If this criticism is justified and the spiritual-substance theory is erroneous, then naturally the argument for immortality built upon it cannot stand.

(2) In connection with the argument drawn from the moral experience of mankind, two questions would seem to be crucial: (*a*) Are moral values objective in the sense that they express something fundamental to the world-order? and (*b*) If moral values are thus objective, does that fact warrant the conclusion that the affirmation of the continued existence of personality is more reasonable than its denial? The first of these questions has been discussed in the preceding chapter, and an affirmative answer to it has there been suggested and the argument for it briefly outlined. There seems reason to hold that moral values are genuinely objective.[2] Granted this objectivity of moral

[1] Chapter XV above.

[2] The reader must keep clearly in mind what is meant by this 'objectivity' of moral values. It means simply that moral valuations — moral judgments — tell us something about the nature of our environment as truly as do purely descriptive judgments. It does not mean that "I or any other human being is infallible in his judgments of value, any more than he is in his scientific or his historical judgments. It means rather that the concept of Oughtness, or Goodness, or Value is part of the real nature of things — that it is not a mere expression of my personal wishes or desires or idiosyncracies, or even of the mental and emo-

values, does personal immortality follow? To this question an affirmative answer seems to many logically necessary. For if moral values are expressive of the nature of things then personality must in some sense be permanent, since it is through personality that moral values are created and to personality that they attach themselves. Assuming that moral values are real, it therefore follows that personality is real and not a mere ephemeral appearance of no ultimate significance in the world-order. Personal immortality seems thus to be implied by the objectivity of moral values. The moral order demands immortality for the conservation of its values, as it demands freedom for the creation of them and God for the consummation of the ideal inherent in them. Thus the hypotheses of freedom, God, and immortality are intimately bound up with each other and enmeshed in the values of the moral order. In a reasoned consideration of the last two hypotheses the objectivity of the moral judgment is of fundamental importance.[1]

(3) So far as psychical research is concerned, one assertion can be made without limitation: it has not established the hypothesis of immortality in the sense in which we have been using the term throughout this discussion.

---

tional constitution of a particular species of two-legged animals which happens to have flourished during what Mr. Balfour has called a short and transitory episode . . . in the life of the meanest of planets. . . ." (H. Rashdall, lecture on "The Moral Argument for Personal Immortality," in the volume, *King's College Lectures on Immortality,* 1920, pp. 82–83). On this meaning of 'objectivity' clarity is essential to an estimate of the moral argument — whether for God or for immortality.

[1] There is danger that one may reason in a circle in connection with the moral arguments for God and immortality, as Professor Leuba has justly warned us: "One may start from the human moral constitution and its demands, and affirm that they imply the existence of a moral Creator. Then one may declare it impossible for such a God not to fulfill the expectations he has placed in man" (*The Belief in God and Immortality,* pp. 139–140). It is questionable whether Professor Leuba's criticism of the moral argument for immortality (pp. 137–146) does justice to its deeper significance.

The most generous estimate of psychical research could hardly say more than that it has established a presumption in favor of the continued existence of some vague sort of spiritual or mental activity. A more unsympathetic critic, however, might reasonably claim that even this presumption is wanting, since it has not been conclusively shown that some simpler hypothesis (such as 'telepathy') than the activity of disembodied spirits may yet be able to account for all of the important phenomena (such as automatic messages and cross-correspondences) still in serious debate. Certainly it is true that immortality has not yet been proved by scientific induction.[1]

(4) Summarizing the results of this section, we may say that the postulate of immortality finds its chief support in the argument based upon the data of moral experience. The results of ethical inquiry are therefore of basal significance in the controversy. Neither the argument from the 'simplicity' of the soul nor the results achieved by the Society for Psychical Research carry very much conviction; the first rests upon an exploded notion of the nature of the soul, while the other line of inquiry is still too much shrouded in confusion arising both from questionable data and questionable assumptions. The crux of the moral argument is the 'objectivity' of moral values and of the ideal implied by them.

§ 8. *Desirability of immortality*

A word in conclusion should be said concerning the diversity of views on the question whether immortality is desirable.

[1] For further details see Leuba, *The Belief in God and Immortality*, pp. 154–167; and Podmore, *The Newer Spiritualism*. For an interpretation more favorable to the positive significance of psychical research the writings of Sir Oliver Lodge should be consulted.

That there is a diversity of views on the subject there can be no doubt. There is indisputable evidence that many do not desire immortality, but, on the contrary, hold as a precious hope that " the ache and languor of existence " end with this life. There is equally indisputable evidence that others shudder at such a 'precious hope,' and look upon immortality as the most precious prize which falls within the vision of mortals. Some long for

> Only the sleep eternal
> In an eternal night.

Others believe that immortality alone can give to the life that now is a tolerable meaning; take immortality away and life becomes for them an utterly miserable affair. This difference in attitude is perhaps largely a matter of temperament, but it is also more. It appears to be indicative of a difference in conception of immortality itself.

Three conceptions of immortality are possible, and these differ widely in significance and, hence, in desirability. On the one hand, one may think of immortality as an endless continuance in unalloyed enjoyment of the same things from day to day, from aeon to aeon, of time. Again, one may think of immortality as an endless repetition of the foibles and failures of the life that we live here in this vale of sorrow and struggle. Finally, one may conceive of immortality as progressive expansion and development in spiritual (intellectual and moral) powers, as either the final attainment of perfection or uninterrupted progress in its realization. One holding the first view would naturally long for immortality — unless, perchance, it occurred to him to question whether such a state of existence could through aeons of time unimaginable be anything other than an unendurable monotony. The second is a dismal view of the future life, and could hardly be contemplated without a shudder; it is the view entertained by those who (like Schopenhauer, for example, or Buddha) most strenuously contend that utter annihilation of conscious personality is a consummation devoutly to be wished and striven for. The third view of immortality has its attraction for the one who, like Socrates, is deeply interested in the business of living and would like to continue the business under conditions more favorable to ultimate success than those that obtain here; and it is doubtless the view which many who profess a desire for immortality entertain concerning its nature.

Which of these views is intrinsically most valuable? Here the reader must be left to his own reflection. This suggestion may be offered as a stimulus: that conception of immortality which is intrinsically most valuable is the conception which can be rationally justified, and, if the moral argument is the one which most clearly implies the postulate of immortality, then that conception of immortality is intrinsically most valuable which has the deepest moral significance.

Chapter XXVII. Questions and Exercises

1. In connection with the discussion of the text read Chapters I and II of Galloway, *The Idea of Immortality*.

2. Summarize Chapter V of Galloway, *The Idea of Immortality,* with special reference to the consideration of the objections (pp. 170–192) raised against the moral argument for immortality.

3. Outline briefly the discussion by Professor James in his *Human Immortality*. To what extent does it seem to you that he has satisfactorily met the objections which he there considers?

4. For a brief description of " automatic writing " and " cross-

correspondences" see Barrett, *Psychical Research,* Chapters XV and XVI. To what extent would you agree with the general conclusions which the author seems to draw from his facts?

5. State summarily the main points in the argument by Professor Royce in *The Conception of Immortality.*

6. At the conclusion of his lecture on "Immortality in the Light of Modern Psychology" (*King's College Lectures on Immortality,* edited by W. R. Matthews, pp. 125–165) Dr. Brown states that "the verdict of modern psychology is in favour of the possibility of a future life." Show briefly how he attempts to justify this thesis in his lecture.

7. Give a summary of the lecture by Rashdall on "The Moral Argument for Personal Immortality" in the volume, *King's College Lectures on Immortality.*

INDEX